Sarah Orne Jewett

RADCLIFFE BIOGRAPHY SERIES

MARGARET FULLER
*From Transcendentalism
to Revolution*
Paula Blanchard
Foreword by
Carolyn G. Heilbrun

SARAH ORNE JEWETT
Her World and Her Work
Paula Blanchard

ALVA MYRDAL
A Daughter's Memoir
Sissela Bok

THE THIRD ROSE
Gertrude Stein and Her World
John Malcolm Brinnin
Foreword by John Ashbury

DOROTHY DAY
A Radical Devotion
Robert Coles

ANNA FREUD
The Dream of Psychoanalysis
Robert Coles

SIMONE WEIL
A Modern Pilgrimage
Robert Coles

WOMEN OF CRISIS
Lives of Struggle and Hope
Robert Coles and
Jane Hallowell Coles

WOMEN OF CRISIS II
Lives of Work and Dreams
Robert Coles and
Jane Hallowell Coles

CHARLOTTE MEW AND HER
FRIENDS
Penelope Fitzgerald

MARGARET BOURKE-WHITE
A Biography
Vicki Goldberg
Foreword by Phyllis Rose

MARY CASSATT
Nancy Hale
Foreword by
Eleanor Munro

RADCLIFFE BIOGRAPHY SERIES

RADCLIFFE BIOGRAPHY SERIES

On behalf of Radcliffe College, I am pleased to present this volume in the Radcliffe Biography Series.

The series is an expression of the value we see in documenting and understanding the varied lives of women. Exploring the choices and circumstances of these extraordinary women—both famous and unsung—is not merely of interest to the historian, but is central to anyone grappling with what it means to be a woman. The biographies of these women teach us not only about their lives and their worlds, but about ours as well. When women strive to forge their identities, as they do at many points throughout the lifespan, it is crucial to have models to look toward. These women provide such models. We are inspired through their example and are taught by their words.

Radcliffe College's sponsorship of the Radcliffe Biography Series was sparked by the publication in 1972 of *Notable American Women,* a scholarly encyclopedia sponsored by Radcliffe's Schlesinger Library. We became convinced of the importance of expanding the public's awareness of the many significant contributions made by women to America, continuing the commitment to educating people about the lives and work of women that is reflected in much of Radcliffe's work. In addition to commissioning new biographies, we decided to add reprints of distinguished books already published, with introductions written for this series.

It is with great pride and excitement that I present this latest volume.

Linda S. Wilson, President
Radcliffe College
Cambridge, Massachusetts

A MERLOYD LAWRENCE BOOK

ADDISON-WESLEY PUBLISHING COMPANY

Reading, Massachusetts   Menlo Park, California   New York
Don Mills, Ontario   Wokingham, England   Amsterdam   Bonn
Sydney   Singapore   Tokyo   Madrid   San Juan
Paris   Seoul   Milan   Mexico City   Taipei

RADCLIFFE BIOGRAPHY SERIES

Sarah Orne Jewett

HER WORLD AND HER WORK

Paula Blanchard

Many of the designations used by manufacturers and sellers to distinguish their products are claimed as trademarks. Where those designations appear in this book and Addison-Wesley was aware of a trademark claim, the designations have been printed in initial capital letters.

Library of Congress Cataloging-in-Publication Data

Blanchard, Paula.
    Sarah Orne Jewett : her world and her work / Paula Blanchard.
        p. cm.—(Radcliffe biography series)
    "A Merloyd Lawrence book."
    Includes bibliographical references and index.
    ISBN 0-201-51810-4
        1. Jewett, Sarah Orne, 1849–1909. 2. Women authors,
American—19th century—Biography. 3. Women and literature—Maine—
History—19th century. 4. Maine—In literature. I. Title.
II. Series.
PS2133.B58 1994
813'.4—dc20
[b]   94-7696
                                                                              CIP

Jacket design by Sara Eisenman
Jacket photo by Jack Ledbetter
Text design by Karen Savary
Set in 11-point Garamond 3 by DEKR Corporation

1 2 3 4 5 6 7 8 9 10-MA-9897969594
First printing, August 1994

SARAH de St. PRIX WYMAN WHITMAN
1842–1904

The motifs on the jacket, binding, and title page of this book were modeled on the work of Sarah Orne Jewett's friend Sarah Wyman Whitman. An artist and the leading book designer for Houghton Mifflin in the 1880s and 1890s, Whitman designed most of Jewett's books in their original editions, as well as those of many other prominent writers including James Russell Lowell, Oliver Wendell Holmes, and Lafcadio Hearn. Her work is seen today in the still-loved edition of Celia Thaxter's *An Island Garden* (1894), illustrated by Childe Hassam.

Contents

Acknowledgments

THE MAKING OF BIOGRAPHY INVOLVES
the help of dozens of people over a period of years. The biographer
never meets most of them, but nevertheless the book owes its
existence to their efforts. For sending photocopies, answering questions and granting access to their collections I would like to thank
the directors and staff of the following: Lawrence Lee Pelletier
Library, Allegheny College; American Antiquarian Society; Am-
herst College Library; Boston College Library; Mugar Memorial
Library, Boston University; Bowdoin College Library; Chicago Historical Society; Dinand Library, College of the Holy Cross; Columbia University Libraries; Robert W. Woodruff Library, Emory
University; Exeter Historical Society; Historical Society of Penn-
sylvania; Huntington Library; Isabella Stewart Gardner Museum;
Longfellow National Historic Site, U.S. Department of the Interior;
E. M. Cudahy Memorial Library, Loyola University; Maine Histori-
cal Society; Manchester-by-the-Sea Historical Society; Middlebury
College Library; Newark Public Library; Newberry Library; New
York Public Library; Princeton University Library; Smith College
Library; South Berwick Public Library; Library of the University
of California; Library of the University of Texas at Austin; Margaret
Clapp Library, Wellesley College; Beinecke Rare Book and Manu-
script Library, Yale University.

I am grateful to the following not only for granting me access
to their material but for permission to quote from manuscript

letters and diaries: Boston Public Library; Colby College Library, Special Collections; Connecticut Historical Society; Dartmouth College Library; William R. Perkins Library, Manuscript Department, Duke University; Houghton Library, Harvard University; Special Collections Library, Rutherford B. Hayes Presidential Center; Milton S. Eisenhower Library, Special Collections, Johns Hopkins University; Library of Congress; Massachusetts Historical Society; James Duncan Phillips Library, Peabody Essex Museum; Pierpont Morgan Library; Arthur and Elizabeth Schlesinger Library, Radcliffe College; Jewett Family Papers Collection, Society for the Preservation of New England Antiquities; Special Collections, University of New Hampshire Library; Doheny Library, University of Southern California; Special Collections Department, Clifton Waller Barrett Library, University of Virginia.

Finally, I would like to express warm personal thanks to my editor, Merloyd Lawrence, for helping me reach beyond myself time and time again; to my husband, Byron Blanchard, for electronic manuscript preparation and for patience sometimes approaching the heroic; to Marie Donahue of South Berwick and Patience-Anne Lenk of Colby College Library for assistance as friendly as it was valuable; to Sandra Armentrout and Ellie Reichlin, both formerly of the Society for the Preservation of New England Antiquities, and to Lorna Condon, the present Curator of Archives; and to friends and fellow biographers Megan Marshall and Phyllis Cole.

Introduction

IN 1915, WITH THE BOMBARDMENTS across the English Channel almost near enough to rattle the cups in his china cabinet, Henry James looked back on the last quarter of the nineteenth century in America as the time of "our ancient peace." When the Civil War ended he had just been entering his twenties, and he remembered thinking that so bloody and exhausting a conflict must be the final price America would have to pay for becoming the country she was meant to be. He now looked back at those "deep illusions and fallacies"—for so the horrors of 1915 made them appear—with "some soreness of confusion between envy and pity." The innocence of Americans' renewed faith in themselves had in it something of the pathetic, given how it had ended; yet the beauty of the ideal retained its hold on the present. Recalling that time, James said, "I see nothing but our excuses. I cherish at any rate the image of their bright plausibility." ("Mr. and Mrs. James T. Fields," *The Atlantic Monthly,* July 1915)

In the midst of this golden quarter century and representing it, James's memory placed Boston publisher James T. Fields, his wife, Annie, and—later, during Annie's widowhood—Sarah Orne Jewett. In the Fieldses' "long and narrow drawing-room" (it was really the library), *The Atlantic Monthly* had been born in 1857, and there the best-loved authors of the prewar generation, including Emerson, Hawthorne, Longfellow, Whittier, and Holmes, had met and thrived under the patronage of Fields, "that faithfully

xv

fathering man," before yielding their comfortable chairs to the youngsters who came to writing maturity in the 1860s and '70s. To this later group Henry James belonged, as did William Dean Howells. Sarah Orne Jewett both belonged to it and, as Annie's fellow hostess, helped preside over it. She was also one of those writers who, like James and Howells, expressed in her art and her life this generation's civility and its increasingly beleaguered idealism.

Born in 1849, Sarah Orne Jewett grew up in southern Maine. As an adult she spent roughly half her time in the literary hothouse of Boston and half in her home village of South Berwick. She was an urban woman, widely traveled and on friendly terms with most American and British authors of her time. Like her character Abby Martin of "The Queen's Twin" and like her world-ranging sea-captain grandfather, she was a citizen of the world. But she was also a village woman and a country doctor's daughter, and it is her village and its surrounding farmlands that gave her stories their unique life and character. A superb stylist, she puts the reader on intimate terms with a culture that since has been, if not entirely lost, at least radically changed. She lets us eavesdrop on the conversations around her exactly as she heard them. "I *hear* your people talk," Howells exclaimed over the Maine voices in *Deephaven*.

In recent years Jewett has become recognized by feminist scholars as an unsurpassed chronicler and interpreter of women's lives. This aspect of her work was totally ignored by the male critics and professors who had always ordained American literary taste. They paid Jewett their obligatory tribute of faint praise but set her aside as not being relevant to the real business of life. Jewett's women are not the self-effacing and compliant helpmates portrayed in the typical Victorian novel, but vigorous, independent country-women, mostly widows and spinsters, who support themselves and their children by farming, nursing, or whatever comes to hand. Warm, humorous, and practical, they are the mainstays of their families and communities, keeping alive not only the gardens that symbolize their vitality but also the ties of sympathy that hold any human society together and keep it from deteriorating into a surly and primitive individualism. In the characters of Mrs. Goodsoe of "The Courting of Sister Wisby," Mrs. Powder of "Law Lane," and Mrs. Todd and Mrs. Blackett of *The Country of the Pointed Firs*,

Jewett shows us women as mothers in the widest sense, who extend their nurturing and healing powers to everyone around them and who, in the face of economic hardship and the inevitable obstacle of human mean-spiritedness, "keep the balance true."

In her depiction of the independence and emotional strength of women, Jewett drew directly on neighbors and acquaintances she had known since childhood, but she also drew on her own experience as a self-supporting and successful woman whose strongest ties were not to spouse and children but to dozens of friends, most of them other women as independent and achieving as she. In a letter to one of them she once wrote of the "transfiguring effect of friendship," meaning the idealism by which we, trying to live up to the image our friends have of us, surpass ourselves and become better than we thought we could be. Jewett belonged to a large group of mothering women, each of whom strengthened and supported the others simply by means of her affection and confidence in them.

Among these women, as well as in a Maine village ethic that was still rooted in the vitally interdependent frontier settlements of the seventeenth century, Jewett found a working paradigm for the larger human community. And while her own village, like any other, was continually shaken by petty feuds and sometimes by violence, her community of friends was remarkably stable and free of ruptures. Jewett's vision of a human family based on sympathetic interdependence may seem unrealistic to us, whose social fabric sometimes seems weakened beyond repair. It would have seemed unrealistic even in her own time to people living in the mean streets of Boston, New York, or Chicago. But it corresponded to reality as she knew it. Sarah Orne Jewett's vision was as true as that of the period's darker prophets, like Henry Adams, Hamlin Garland, or Mary Wilkins Freeman. None of them was omniscient, any more than any one writer of a particular period. Jewett's realism was full of light, theirs of shadow; but the light she wrote about was the light she lived in.

Her gentle optimism perfectly expresses the mood of James's "ancient peace." It is a mood that is perhaps more familiar to us through the work of artists than through literature. Jewett's world is that of the Luminists, whose small, deceptively modest landscapes and seascapes are suffused with light and seem to emanate a silent tranquillity. New Englanders all, most of them living on the coast, the Luminists painted ordinary salt marshes and brooks slipping over granite ledges, each object exquisitely realistic yet expressing a quiet transcendence. They painted ships in calm harbors, floating on their own pure reflections, and harmless curled wavelets breaking on pebbled shores—all frozen like the figures on Keats's urn. Her world is also that of the era's figure painters—of John Singer Sargent's vibrant, speaking portraits or Mary Cassatt's mothers and women caught in the act of drinking tea. We can find her in Winslow Homer's paintings of cranberry pickers and Maine children playing snap-the-whip, or among his English fishermen's wives poised on rocks and waiting, like the women of Deephaven and Dunnet Landing, for their men to come home. She belongs with James Whistler's muted and serene Nocturnes and the quietly jubilant colors of Childe Hassam and the American Impressionists. Jewett herself acknowledged a debt to French Barbizon painter Jean-François Millet, whose paintings of ordinary peasants are infused, like the character of that "great soul" Mrs. Todd, with an aura of universal dignity and heroism. The confidence of the time is seen nowhere more clearly than in its paintings, which like Jewett's stories reflect not only the objects seen but the faith that each has its place in a larger and more permanent spiritual order.

Today Americans find themselves reexamining the late nineteenth century with a new appreciation and hunger for its faith and balance. That hunger is reflected in the resurgent interest in American art of the period; in a not-always-happy revisiting of its themes in architecture; in the chintz–and–china–dog decor that regularly greets our eyes in magazine articles on home design; and even in the election of Ronald Reagan as president. At the same time, one by one the cultural figures of that era are being reclaimed. Sarah Orne Jewett is one of those who best deserve that rediscovery.

Prologue

ONE MORNING TOWARD THE END OF THE last century, probably in January 1891, a woman and a man are driving into South Berwick, Maine. It is a picture-book winter day. The clean snow lies smoothly on the fields and frosts the boughs of oaks and hemlocks. The sunlight glances off its icy surface so brightly that it hurts the eyes, but the two in the sleigh have been looking all morning at scenes more brilliant still, where sea, sand, and snow along the coast at Wells play endless sparkling games with the sun in the few short hours it visits them. Everyone in the party is in a good mood. ("Everyone" includes the horse, for these people come from a household where the moods of horses are important.) Everyone is hungry, too, and the woman, who is driving, has to keep a firm hold on the reins in this last mile before they reach the barn.

The woman, while not precisely beautiful, has a face people admire and turn to look at. She has strong, regular features, with deep-set eyes, a humorous mouth, and what her contemporaries would term a notable brow. Sensibly dressed in dark woolens, she sits effortlessly upright, and she knows how to manage a horse. Her companion, who is both friend and stableman, is content to sit back and watch the scenery.

As they enter the village they meet a flock of boys, coasting on sleds from the top of Powderhouse Hill, a high ridge to their left. One after another the boys go racketing past, sliding to a stop

I

on the flats ahead. The horse, used to sharing the road with children, blows a little but does not shy. Presently they overtake a boy of about eleven, trudging back toward the hill and towing his sled behind him. "Stubby!" calls the woman. "Catch a ride!" So the boy, who is her nephew, ties his sled to the back of the sleigh and is pulled to the top of the hill. Suddenly the woman jumps out, hands the reins to the man, takes the sled from the delighted boy, seats herself on it, and goes hurtling down the slope. The wind stings her face and tugs at the edges of her hood. The sled, picking up momentum, bounces and skitters over the crusty snow. The children stare, then grin, then begin to shout. An hour later, glowing with borrowed triumph, Stubby reports to the kitchen that Aunt Sarah went down the hill *just like the rest of the boys!*[1] She is forty-one years old.

By 1891 Sarah Orne Jewett was one of America's best-loved and most admired authors. She had published ten adult books, two children's books, a history for young people, and many miscellaneous sketches and articles. A list of her close friends included most of the shining names of two generations of American literature: Holmes, Lowell, Howells, Emerson, Stowe, Longfellow, Whittier (some of them recently dead, most still glowing wanly above their respective horizons). People who wanted to meet her generally found their way to the Boston home of her friend Annie Fields, where Jewett received them with an easy grace and courtesy that, while it encouraged one to have an extra slice of cake, in no way betrayed the possibilities of Aunt Sarah and the sled. Her city setting became her well, and it is where the modern sensibility often prefers to place her. But, as she once said, she was made of Berwick dust. Although she sometimes chafed at its confinement, Berwick was always her primary home, the source not only of the subjects of her art but of the deeper emotional springs that fed its creation. Berwick gave her the right to be a child, a necessary sense of play, the freedom to go careening down a hill or write a story. It nourished her personal sense of time, which embraced not only her own childhood and adulthood, but the lives of parents, grandparents, great-grandparents, and elderly neighbors, reaching back through the Revolutionary War to embattled early settlers, and even to inhabitants of the Yorkshire Dales since William the

Conqueror. Berwick was the focus of her faith that each generation carries within it the cultural inheritance of all its ancestors, no matter how remote.

Nor did she limit that recognition to her own New England heritage. The French, the Irish, the Norwegians, the Italians—any distinctive people or place she came to know fascinated her primarily as the embodiment of a particular living tradition. She has been described as an antiquarian,[2] but that word implies a certain intellectual distance and perhaps a hint of dilettantism. Jewett did not celebrate old people because they were quaint, nor try to capture them on paper solely as representatives of a disappearing era. She saw them as irreplaceable links in the continuous, fragile structure of civilization, and her central concern was that the connection be maintained—whether it was between herself at nine and herself at forty-one or between a housemaid from Cork and an ancestor who had sustained and protected her children through the days of Cromwell's terror.

1
Beginnings

BERWICK WAS ONE OF A FAMILY OF SET-
tlements founded in the 1620s on the Piscataqua river system,
which forms part of the modern boundary between New Hampshire
and Maine. It is an old community: the Piscataqua towns are
scarcely younger than the more famous ones in Massachusetts and
Virginia. In fact, the first English settlement in Maine dates from
1607, though it was abandoned the following year. Coastal Maine
had been inhabited, if not permanently settled, by French and
English fishermen since the mid-1500s.

The Piscataqua is a tidal river, flowing southeast and emptying
into the sea at Portsmouth, New Hampshire. A few miles above
the coast it divides and subdivides into many small rivers and bays,
the whole area forming a complex watery network that offered
many promising sites for fisheries, sawmills, and small ports. From
1623 on, beginning at Portsmouth, the rivers, bays, and adjoining
coast were settled under a series of royal grants, chiefly that of the
Laconia Company, an offshoot of the Plymouth Company headed
by Sir Ferdinando Gorges and Capt. John Mason. The first arrivals
from England bartered with the natives for settlement rights, and
within a few years a series of tiny hamlets had sprung up, among
them the beginnings of what are now Berwick, Kittery, York, and
Wells, Maine; and Exeter and Dover, New Hampshire. Berwick
was founded between two fine waterfalls, one on the Salmon Falls
River (the main branch of the Piscataqua) and one where that

4

stream meets the busy little Great Works River. At this latter site, where the Great Works plunged thirty feet on its way to the sea, the Laconia Company built the first sawmill in America.

From the first, the Piscataqua settlers more resembled those of Virginia than they did those of Massachusetts Bay and Plymouth. They were mostly well-to-do, royalist, middle to upper class, Episcopal or secular, fond of good living, and more interested in promoting prosperity than in founding the New Jerusalem. Although there must have been religious nonconformists among them, and although they were soon joined by Puritans from Massachusetts and England, they were remarkably lacking in zeal and self-righteousness, and the tolerant atmosphere they created was never effaced. The variety of their religious persuasions speaks for itself. Exeter, New Hampshire, was founded in 1638 by the Rev. John Wheelwright and his flock, followers of Anne Hutchinson who had been banished from Massachusetts. (A few years later, when New Hampshire came under Massachusetts rule, Wheelwright crossed the river to Maine and settled in the village of Wells.) York, Maine, was founded by Episcopalians and was a haven for royalists exiled during the English civil war. Some of these drifted into the "parish of Unity" in Kittery, which later became the village of Berwick.* In Berwick, too, Quakers were left in peace and allowed to build their first Maine meetinghouse; later the town welcomed the Baptists as well. A few miles downriver at Portsmouth, royalist sentiment persisted right up to the early days of the Revolution, when the town was the seat of the defiant Tory governor John Wentworth.

These early Piscataquans resented any interference with their freedom of religion, whether from the Crown or from the theocratic government in Massachusetts Bay. They belonged in spirit with the Maine settlers described with some distaste by a visiting sea captain in 1671: "They have a custom of taking tobacco, sleeping at noon, sitting long at meals, sometimes four times a day, and

---

* Sarah Orne Jewett thought that some might have come from Berwick-on-Elmet in Yorkshire, and that the Yorkshire accent would account for the peculiar spelling of "Barvik" in early parish records. If they had come from Berwick-upon-Tweed, farther north, she thought they would have said "Berrik." See SOJ, "The Old Town of Berwick," p. 590.

now and then drinking a dram."[1] Looking at the same phenomenon from another point of view, Sarah Orne Jewett wrote proudly of the early residents of Berwick, "They lived well, and in fact seem to have cared a good deal more for feasting than fasting, and to have had a sense of propriety in household affairs and great hospitality; and all these traits have come down to their descendants."[2] She might as well have been describing her own family, and perhaps in her own mind she was.

Although the Jewetts were, as Sarah put it, "comparatively late comers" to Berwick,[3] they fit comfortably into the town's tradition of social and religious civility. The Jewetts came to Boston from Bradford, Yorkshire, in 1638 and soon founded the town of Rowley, Massachusetts. Religious nonconformists fleeing persecution under Charles I, they came from a family of wealthy clothiers, and their ancestors had held various honorable appointments from the Crown. Heraldic records suggest descent from an eleventh-century French knight of the Crusades. The first Jewetts on the Piscataqua, Sarah's great-grandfather and his mother, were living in Portsmouth just after the Revolution.

Her mother's family, the Gilmans of Exeter, had a similar history. They too were nonconformists of comfortable means, possibly tracing back to yet another French knight, though family tradition takes them back to ninth-century Wales. They came from Hingham, in Norfolk, and like the Jewetts emigrated in 1638, a year of particular severity for Puritans in England. They settled in Exeter about nine years later.

Less is known about the Ornes. Sarah's great-grandfather, James Orne, was descended from the Ornes of Dover, New Hampshire, who were among the original settlers of that city. His wife had a French grandmother, and it pleased Sarah to think that through Sally Orne she had some claim to what she called "that peculiarly French trait, called *gaieté de coeur.*"[4] In fact, as we have seen, she could have claimed that much-diluted drop of French blood through either the Jewetts or the Gilmans. On such tenuous ground many staid New Englanders carry around their moiety of *gaieté de coeur,* though few have made as good use of it as she did.

While a gentler style of life was one difference between the Piscataqua settlements and those farther south, another was that

during the French and Indian Wars the villages of the Piscataqua
and the Maine coast, like those on the Connecticut River, were on
the vulnerable frontier. Attacks on the Piscataqua settlements
lasted from 1675 to 1724, and were so persistent and destructive
that it is hard to understand how the English found the courage
to rebuild. Berwick, Casco (later Portland), Dover, Exeter, Wells,
and York were repeatedly attacked, their buildings burned to the
ground and their inhabitants killed or captured. Berwick's fate was
typical: it was leveled three times in fifty years. In the terrible
attack of 1690 an ancestor of one of the Jewetts' neighbors saw her
baby murdered before her eyes and was marched to Canada, where
she was taken into the house of a military widow, probably as a
servant, and converted to Catholicism. (She later returned to her
husband in Berwick, and they had six more children.) One of the
Dover Ornes was killed in a devastating Indian raid on Dover in
1689, and an Orne woman was snatched away and sent to Canada
in 1707. A treaty in 1725 brought calm, at least to southern Maine;
but fifty years later, infuriated by heavy taxes, impressment of
Maine sailors, and the expropriation of lumber by the Crown,
Mainers threw themselves into the Revolution and once again
became vulnerable to attack, this time by the British from the sea.
The distant authorities in Boston never cared much about the
defense of Maine, and the people there learned bitterly that they
had to rely on themselves and not look to any government to
help them.

These historical circumstances—religious toleration, and the
fact that for 250 years Maine was a battleground—explain much
about the hardiness and quirky independence of the Maine character, as reflected in the country people Jewett knew and the fictional
people she drew from them. She was proud of the Mainer's ability
to endure just about anything, and the maverick streak that says
he will be beholden to no one. At the same time, proud of her own
family's roots in Yorkshire and Norfolk, she was conscious of strong
cultural and historical ties to England. In Exeter, where most of
Jewett's Gilman ancestors were conspicuous patriots during the
Revolution, one of the family had remained Loyalist throughout
the war, and such was the town's respect for the family that he was
not obliged to flee. On the Jewett side, too, there were apparently

some "honest but mistaken Tories."* Jewett's acknowledgment of the complexities of political allegiance coexisted easily with her pride in the family revolutionaries. Raised a Congregationalist, she converted to the Episcopal Church in 1871 and eventually worked out some of her dual sympathies in her novel *The Tory Lover.*

Both sides of the family were active in the Revolution. Sarah's great-grandfather, Dearborn Jewett, was a nephew of Henry Dearborn, a well-known revolutionary soldier who later became Jefferson's secretary of war. Enlisting in the army while still only a child, great-grandfather Jewett wintered at Valley Forge at the age of twelve. He married Mary Furber, an ensign's daughter, and late in life they moved to a farm near South Berwick, where she died in 1837.

Their son, grandfather Theodore Furber Jewett, ran away to sea as a boy and shipped on a whaler. In due time, following a pattern familiar to Maine seamen, he became a captain. In the early years of the century he sailed the lucrative route between Portsmouth and the West Indies, carrying New England lumber and produce to the islands in return for molasses and rum. He ran Jefferson's Embargo with the blessing of the government, and later on he defied the British blockade. Captured in 1813, he was briefly interned on the infamous Dartmoor prison ship at Bristol, England. His wife, the first Sarah Orne Jewett, was a Portsmouth sea captain's daughter who was married at eighteen and died at twenty-five. Her granddaughter and namesake, imagining a small drama of innocent dalliance, would cherish a watercolor given to "charming Sally" before her marriage by a French prisoner of war.[5]†

After his wife died, Theodore Jewett, left with three little boys, retired from the sea and went courting. In 1821 he married Olive Walker, another Portsmouth captain's daughter. They moved to South Berwick, where Captain Jewett's father already lived, and after a short period bought a chastely grand Georgian house in the

---

* Sarah Orne Jewett refers to them as "my father's ancestors," but both her great-grandfather Jewett and his maternal uncle fought in the Revolution. ("Looking Back," p. 5.)

† In the years before the War of 1812 both French and British vessels preyed on American shipping, and sailors of both nationalities were interned.

center of town. Theodore Jewett's brothers, Thomas and Elisha, had also moved to South Berwick, and Theodore and Thomas established a shipyard at Pipe Stave Landing on the Salmon Falls River, sending their own ships to the Caribbean and indeed all over the world. The goods they imported were traded with Maine farmers and lumbermen for goods they exported, very little money changing hands in the process. The Jewett brothers' brick store became a gathering place for lonely country people whose rare trips to Berwick were major social occasions. Two generations of Jewetts—Sarah's father, his brothers and cousins, and their children—spent many childhood hours perched on barrels in that store, sucking molasses candy and listening to Maine talk.

In Captain Jewett's beautiful house across the street they heard another, no-less-vibrant kind of Maine talk. There gathered a more or less constant assembly of retired sea captains and their wives, along with an assortment of physicians, lawyers, judges, editors, and politicians, most of them distantly related to their host or one another through the close intermarriage of Piscataqua families. Each came from that generation of two wars, and each carried around enough personal history to fill a novel. The wives were no less interesting than the husbands, since they shared their husbands' voyaging. The objects that surrounded that garrulous company spoke of its history: not only the conch shells and bric-a-brac scattered about, but the very wallpaper on the walls and the china on the table had been brought from Europe or Asia by Grandfather Jewett's ships. He himself told of dodging British men-of-war, of following the whales, and of being left on a remote island with three shipmates for a year. Great-uncle Commodore John Long, a frequent visitor from Exeter, had been a midshipman on the U.S.S. *Constitution* when she captured the *Java* in 1812. Added to their memories, presumably, were those of great-grandfather Dearborn Jewett, survivor of Valley Forge, who lived until Sarah was four and her sister Mary was six.

Theodore Jewett prospered. He became a bank director and a town leader: when the Marquis and Marquise de Lafayette visited Berwick in 1825, he was on the committee of arrangement. A Thomas Jewett, presumably Theodore's brother, had become the wealthiest man in Berwick by 1860. And as the Jewetts throve, so did Berwick.* The War of 1812 and Jefferson's Embargo hit the Piscataqua economy hard, and some of the towns took until mid-century to recover. Berwick was not spared, but with the river and the sea before it and the forests and farms behind it, the town was able to adapt relatively quickly to the new economic climate. Transatlantic shipping died, but produce and lumber continued to be shipped down the coast, while the Jewett shipyard built ships through the 1840s and the larger yards in Portsmouth built clipper ships, schooners, and steamships throughout the century. A cotton mill was built at Salmon Falls in 1832, and in 1855 the Jewetts' neighbor John Burleigh, another retired sea captain, founded a woolen mill on the Great Works. Both created jobs for young people from the farms and attracted growing numbers of newcomers, chiefly from Ireland and Quebec. The faces and names on the street became more diverse, new shops and businesses opened, and blocks of houses and tenements sprang up around the mills. But there was no major social upheaval, and the town managed to retain its serene character.

Throughout the transition from shipping to manufacturing, farming remained Berwick's economic mainstay, although some of the poorer hill farmers were seeing their sons and daughters quietly pack up and head west. Piscataqua sheep provided wool for New England mills, and Piscataqua apples and hay stocked Boston's kitchens and barns. Produce was shipped down the river to Portsmouth in gundalows, those peculiar lateen-sailed craft found only on this river and designed by a sea captain after his memory of boats on the Nile. The region's two cities, Portsmouth and Portland, still were active ports, and Portland became an important rail terminus as well. Both enjoyed a social life that, at least as far as their own citizens were concerned, yielded nothing in vivacity or elegance to Boston and New York.

Only one untoward circumstance seems to have marred the course of Grandfather Jewett's long and comfortable retirement: in an age when many men buried one or two wives, Theodore Furber Jewett buried three and married four. His second wife bore him

---

* South Berwick, North Berwick, and Berwick became separate towns in 1814; but Sarah Orne Jewett always referred to them all simply as Berwick, and I follow her example except when a distinction must be made.

two more sons and died at thirty-two. The third, Mary Rice Jewett, survived twenty-five years of married life before dying in 1854. Sarah remembered her chiefly as a stern old lady who, when small Sarah plucked the only rosebud from a prized bush and presented it as a gift, received it with scolding. After her death the indefatigable captain married Eliza Sleeper Jewett, the widow of his brother Nathan. She outlived him by a decade, surviving to become Sarah's confidante and occasional source of stories. Each marriage brought a flock of new relations—Walkers, Rices, and Sleepers (the latter being next-door neighbors to the Exeter grandparents), forming a wide New England constellation of cousins to visit.

All the captain's wives belonged to the literate, well-traveled ranks of the new upper-middle class. Family records say as little about them as such records generally say about women, but one of them—probably Sarah's great-grandmother Mary Furber—left an unsigned diary that the Jewett sisters discovered in the old house when they were well into middle age. Set in Exeter in 1782, it shows us a young woman much like one of Jane Austen's Bennet sisters (the younger, flighty ones), engaged in a ceaseless and rather cold-blooded appraisal of the marriage market. Young men are ruthlessly sorted into two categories, "Somebodies" and "Nobodies." The writer's life is a constant round of calls, parties, and flirtations with officers married and unmarried. Through it flit, in phrases of tantalizing opacity and brevity, images of the near-great. The famous Gen. John Sullivan, whose parents would later find a prominent place in *The Tory Lover,* is a "Sweet man," who makes "a Droll Scene in his Chamber—but he is a Party Concerned So it Shall be a Secret. . . ." We glimpse various members of Sarah Orne Jewett's grandmother's family, the illustrious Exeter Gilmans, and a "Coll Dearbon" (*sic*) who is almost certainly Sarah's great-great-great-uncle Henry. There is a "Mrs. Jewett," presumably Mary Dearborn Jewett, at whose home the writer passes a "fine merry afternoon." And there is a young "Mr. Jewett" who in spite of the fact that he is "pretty" and "very Bold," is mercilessly dismissed: "He is . . . Awkward I think the Gentlemen that are anybodys Never appear So Much to advantage as when he is by or Somebody like him. . . ." If the two principals in this little scene are indeed Mary Furber and Dearborn Jewett, then she was twenty-one and he, a seasoned war veteran, was sixteen.[6]

Interesting as the Jewetts were, the Gilmans were absolutely stellar. Great-great-grandfather Col. Nicholas Gilman was New Hampshire state treasurer, continental loan officer, chief member of the Committee of Safety, state councillor, and New Hampshire receiver general. He was rumored to be the force behind the Revolution in New Hampshire, outweighing the powerful Tory governor. His son John Taylor Gilman had an even more remarkable career than his father's, was thrice elected governor, and donated the ground on which Phillips Exeter Academy now stands. Another son, Nicholas Gilman, was delegate to the second constitutional convention and a member of Washington's staff, and served in both the U.S. House of Representatives and the Senate.

Sarah's great-grandfather, Col. Nathaniel Gilman, might be termed the family underachiever: he was a member of the New Hampshire state senate and house of representatives, and a state treasurer. Twice married, he had four daughters and seven sons, and his second wife—a genial woman who survived into Sarah's tenth year—presided over a home celebrated for its hospitality. Thither came, in 1814, William Perry, the twenty-six-year-old new doctor in town. Four years later he married Abigail, the Gilmans' second daughter. They had five children, one of whom was Caroline Frances, Sarah Orne Jewett's mother.

Grandfather Perry did not come from a grand, seagoing family. A farm boy from Rehoboth, Massachusetts, he suffered a small panic when he was bidden to his first Exeter party, wondering if he had to wear gloves and, if so, where he was going to find some. (The families of Exeter were not so easily to be balked of their chance to meet the new doctor: gloves were sent by a friendly matron with a few encouraging words, and the doctor went to meet his fate.) Nor were his first years in Exeter easy: he arrived penniless, in the middle of the War of 1812, and had to make his way against the opposition of three established doctors. He did so brilliantly, becoming one of the leading physicians in northern New England, an expert surgeon who was often called in to consult on difficult cases or testify in court. He took up the cause of the insane, who in those days were often chained to walls and bedsteads, and was chiefly responsible for the building of the state mental hospital. Offered a professorship at Bowdoin Medical School, he declined, preferring the attractions of Exeter and his own practice. When his children began to grow up and bills began to mount, he went into business on the side, developing a potato starch that found a ready market in the New England textile mills. He might have made a fortune if he had not been too busy to patent the process, and unluckily the formula was stolen by someone in upstate New York. After that, in his early sixties and temporarily slowed down by overwork, he decided to resign most of his practice to his son, the second Dr. William Perry. This semi-retirement ended when he found he couldn't stand the peace and quiet, and he returned to share the practice for many more years. The "old doctor" lived to the age of ninety-eight, performing three operations when well into his eighties and one at ninety-two. He was so loved in Exeter that in the last two presidential elections of his life (Chester Arthur and Warren D. Harding), his fellow townspeople waited to vote until they were sure the doctor had cast his ballot.

His wife, Abigail Gilman Perry, died in 1860 when Sarah was ten. She was one of several Exeter women whose "serene dignity, grace and intelligent conversation . . . were often held up as a model to granddaughters."[7] Sarah Orne Jewett, her sisters, and cousins remembered her with tenderness, and undoubtedly she influenced the consistently high social tone of two generations of Gilman and Jewett women: their impeccable manners, public kindness, social ease, and community involvement, and much of their family loyalty and strict courtesy to one another, even in dislike. Sarah's mother, aunts, and great-aunts were cast in the same mold and served to reinforce her grandmother's example throughout her life.

As for Grandfather Perry, his vivid personality shines out through the sometimes saccharine recollections of Sarah and her cousin Frances. When he was not tending his old patients, some of whom would see no other doctor, he could be seen spinning around town in his light gig behind a fast chestnut mare. He had a great weakness for good horseflesh, which he passed on to his grandchildren. He shrugged off spills like a boy, and once when tossed from the gig in his eighties came home mud-spattered but triumphant because the mare "didn't run away, she waited for me!"[8]

He loved to travel, within the confines of Exeter or beyond it, and he enjoyed taking along a grandchild or two. He and Sarah often went on excursions to New York or Boston together, and it was he who escorted her to and from Cincinnati when she spent a winter there in 1868–69. Sarah adored and feared him as a child, and her later affection for him was more and more tinged with a kind of teasing, maternal pride as he marched on through his nineties with undiminished vigor: "Grandpa departed [for Exeter] yesterday afternoon in high feather," she writes in 1882. "I never did see such a chipper old lark!"[9]

Grandfather Perry always wore the soft collar and black stock of Napoleon's day, along with a top hat—traditional badge of the learned professions—made a little too big so as not to blow off. (In this he resembled the thrifty ladies of Exeter, who were always well behind the times in matters of dress. One fashionable friend of the family claimed she could always recognize an Exeter woman by her bonnet.) He could remember the death of Washington and even of Marie Antoinette, but unlike most old men he was not given to reminiscing. Busy with the present, he embodied the past rather than talked about it.

He came from Scottish Covenanter stock and in his youth had been permanently fired by the Second Great Awakening. A deacon at the First Parish Church (Congregational) for sixty years, he stood out among the easygoing Gilmans and Jewetts as the only passionately religious member of the family. On Sundays he could be found seated facing the congregation, the better to watch the door in case he was wanted. From there his dark eyes under bushy brows could easily note every tardy entrance and premature exit. Despite his benevolence he was a fierce-looking old man, and he would lash out sharply against any kind of "vanity, frippery, a love of cheap and tawdry things and people, a *lack of seriousness* in short." He was ambitious for his grandchildren and impatient of shilly-shallying. "*Act—act!*" he would say to Sarah. "Go and *do it* if you think you are right. Make the best of yourself!" The son of a strong, sympathetic mother to whom he largely owed his education, he made no distinctions in his expectations of granddaughters and grandsons. Sarah wrote that of all the Exeter relations, "It was he . . . who was proudest and most sympathetic at any flicker of success."[10]

2
Early Years

DR. PERRY HAD COME TO EXETER straight from medical school, set up a practice, and married a Gilman woman. In 1842 he saw his own history repeated when his eldest child, Caroline Frances, married a young doctor who had come to study under him. Theodore Herman Jewett was twenty-seven, a graduate of Berwick Academy (in those days the best prep school in the region except Phillips Exeter), Bowdoin College, and the Jefferson Medical College in Philadelphia. His gentleness and humor promised well for the marriage, and Perry was impressed by his formidable intelligence and the depth of his learning, both medical and general. He once remarked that Jewett had been the only student he was ever afraid of.[1]

The young doctor was ambitious. He wanted to practice near a large urban center, where he would have access to well-equipped hospitals and libraries and stimulating colleagues. But he had had a brief bout with tuberculosis, and the year he married, his younger brother Henry died of the same disease. His grieving father asked him to settle in Berwick, at least for a while, offering the young couple room in his spacious house. They agreed, and no doubt Berwick made its native-son doctor welcome. In 1846 Captain Jewett lost another son, Samuel, who was shipwrecked off the Cape of Good Hope while commanding one of his father's ships. Now there were only two Jewett sons left, young Theodore and his brother, William. The pleas to remain in Berwick must have be-

15

come irresistible, for the young man quietly resigned himself to becoming a country doctor. In 1847 his wife bore their first child, a daughter they named after Mary Rice Jewett. She was born in Grandfather Perry's house in Exeter. The second child, Theodora Sarah Orne Jewett, was born September 3, 1849, in Grandfather Jewett's house.

The Jewett house, today restored and maintained by the Society for the Preservation of New England Antiquities, seems so apt a visual expression of the voice we hear in the stories that our imaginations insist on placing the author in the house once we have seen it. We will have her growing up in the square, sunny rooms, measuring her height against the richly carved moldings, and sliding down the banister of the wide central staircase. William Dean Howells, visiting her there toward the end of her life, felt the same rare coincidence of spirit: "Your house," he wrote, "will always remain a surprise to me, not because it was not the fittest possible setting for such literature as yours, but just because it was: literature does so often have such alien settings."[2]

The facts are more complicated. When Sarah was very young, probably two or three years old, Captain Jewett decided that his son's growing family needed a house of their own, so he built one for them next door. It was a modest Greek Revival house; one can find any number of houses like it in New England villages—tidy and economical, presenting their narrow gable ends to the street like thrifty New England matrons not wanting to take up too much room. The front hall was big enough to hang one's hat in; the parlor opening to the left was long, narrow, and probably rather dim on cloudy days. A large, sunny room to the rear, probably the dining room, overlooked the garden and was the finest room in the house. Besides these, there were a kitchen and pantry, with bedrooms upstairs and a maid's attic. The doctor's office occupied a small ell off the parlor and had its own entrance. Clearly this was not a home for the "New England aristocracy" (the term has become a cliché in discussions of Sarah Orne Jewett) but the ordinary house of a village doctor and his family, less grand than the houses of many of his patients.

Of course the children were constantly in and out of their grandparents' house next door. It was the expression of the entire family's tradition and standing in town, and of the standards they set for themselves. Still, it was not their parents' own space, nor theirs until they inherited it more than three decades later. Sarah Orne Jewett believed that a house shapes the personality of the people who live in it:

> One often hears of the influence of climate upon character;
> there is a strong influence of place; and the inanimate
> things which surround us indoors and out make us follow
> out in our lives their own silent characteristics. We uncon-
> sciously catch the tone of every house in which we live,
> and of every view of the outward, material world which
> grows familiar to us, and we are influenced by surroundings
> nearer and closer still than the climate of the country which
> we inhabit.[3]

Her own character was influenced by two quite different surroundings, merged so closely that the line between them was blurred under common grass and trees. One boldly commanded attention at the main intersection, as nearly aristocratic as New England democracy allowed; the other was comfortable and non-descript, a purely functional house of no pretensions whatever.

Sarah Orne Jewett used her baptismal name of Theodora in signatures, but only through adolescence. She seems always to have been known to family and friends simply as Sarah. Her sister Mary Rice, two years older, was named after her father's stepmother. Caroline Augusta (Carrie), named for her mother and her aunt Augusta, was born in 1855. More than six years younger than Sarah, she eventually was closer to Mary, who was partly a mother to her. To some extent the two older girls shared friends, reading, and the outdoors, while for several years Carrie was left behind. But in spite of Sarah's closeness in age to Mary, she later persistently described her childhood as having been largely solitary. Partly this was because Mary would have entered school at least two years ahead of Sarah, and those years —roughly from age three to age five or six—are years on which many of her childhood memories were centered. Even after Sarah began school, however, she was often alone, for she was not a healthy child and often stayed home. Add to this her temperamental, lifelong love of solitude and nature, and one begins to understand why, even though she and Mary were good company together, they often went their separate ways. Alone, Sarah would sneak into her grandparents' formal front garden to play under the huge lilac bushes beside the walk or sit on the fence and watch the people go in and out of the "quaint-roofed village shops" across the road.[4] Alone and unreproved she spent long hours roaming the woods and fields, building twig dams along the brooks or coaxing small animals and birds to eat from her hand. When the winter convoys of ox-drawn lumber sleds arrived, each laden with logs to be sent down the river, she would run to meet the leaders and ride the entire length of the town perched on the load. And when she became old enough to be trusted alone with a boat, she would row out on the millpond or one of the two rivers, gathering cardinal flowers and water lilies and sneaking up on morning herons. So the three girls grew more or less separately, until the age difference became less important and all three were known collectively as "the doctor's girls."

As they grew they found Berwick rich in amusements. There were skating parties on the millpond in winter, which might end in a general thawing out of numbed fingers and toes in somebody's kitchen and the consumption of hot cider and doughnuts. With their schoolmates at Berwick Academy the sisters joined in sleighing parties, taffy pulls, concerts, and occasional dances. When the circus came to Dover or Berwick the whole family would go, with Grandfather Perry leading the way, and in summer there was the Rochester Fair, with agricultural exhibits, horse-pulling contests, and races. In November, when all the trees but the oaks had shed their leaves and the landscape opened up, someone would propose "rising Agamenticus," and the family would pile into the buggy and drive up a rough, half-overgrown track to the top of the local mountain (height 691 feet), which despite its modest size offered a panoramic view for twenty miles: straight ahead out to sea, southwest past the Isles of Shoals to the coastal hills of Massachusetts, northeast to Portland, and west to the distant outlines of New Hampshire's White Mountains.

These pleasures notwithstanding, the Jewetts were not immune to the natural shocks that flesh is heir to. Setting aside the death of great-grandfather Dearborn Jewett, which was only the quiet ending of a long and fruitful life, they experienced a rapid succession of changes and emotional realignments beginning in

1854, when grandmother Mary Rice Jewett died. The third of Captain Jewett's wives, she had ruled his household many years, and she orchestrated the ceremony of her own dying as she had everything else. The younger Jewetts were summoned from next door for a formal leave-taking, and everyone went except five-year-old Sarah, who had feared her grandmother living and now, despite "an intense curiosity to see what dying might be like," feared to be anywhere near her as she left this world. Terrified to stay alone in the empty house, she huddled alone on the stone step in the December cold, watching the lighted windows next door, until her parents finally returned and took her indoors to comfort and warm her.[5]

Two months later Uncle William married a young relation of his late stepmother. Augusta Maria Willard Rice was a year younger than Sarah's mother, and she must have dramatically changed the climate of the big house and made it a welcoming place for small girls. In December of that year Carrie was born, and in February 1856, a year after Uncle William's wedding, Grandfather Jewett took to wife his brother Nathan's widow, Eliza Sleeper Jewett. She too loved the children, and she brought a bit of home and Exeter to Sarah's mother, whose neighbor she had once been. In the space of two years the two households, with the loss of the stern matriarch and the arrival of a baby and two warm-hearted women, both previously connected to the family, had gained an atmosphere of ease and increased domestic bustle.

It did not last. In April 1857 they lost Aunt Augusta, who died at the age of thirty-seven. The next three years saw three more family deaths: great-grandmother Dorothy Gilman in 1859, and Grandmother Perry and Grandfather Jewett both in 1860. The series of losses was not unusual in a nineteenth-century family, and in Sarah's adulthood, almost as if in compensation, her beloved grandfather, aunts, and great-aunts lived so long as to make the natural progress of time seem miraculously retarded. But the list of family deaths in her childhood, and the unusual fluctuation from mourning to joy and back again, reminds us of the continual disruptions and realignments children and families experienced in the last century (one thinks too of the Emersons, the Dickinsons, and the Brontës) and the need to develop a more solid defensive armor than we have today. Without being in the least dour or rigid—that is, without being in the least the stereotypical Yankee family—the Jewetts all possessed a truly impressive degree of sangfroid. Like most traditional New England families they minimized and denied grief; but they seem to have carried their denial to the point of actual defiance. The death of a loved one often would be followed by a celebration of some kind—a wedding or a trip abroad. Funerals, so important in Jewett's fiction as community rites and solemn festivals, were central events in her own childhood. The funeral of a Jewett or a Gilman was a wholehearted affair, and the funeral of Grandmother Jewett, unlike her death, held no terrors for small Sarah. On the contrary, it gave her "vast entertainment" and was "the first grand public occasion in which [she] had taken any share."[6] The whole town attended, and there were eulogies followed by genteel feasting, and afterwards dozens of condoling letters to answer. The expression of grief was all packed into that event, and within days the ordinary discourse of life was briskly resumed and outward grieving was discouraged except for the wearing of mourning and the use of black-bordered stationery. The beginnings of Sarah Orne Jewett's emotional calm, including that aversion to ordinary evil and squalor for which she is often criticized, can be seen early in the habitual family attitude toward grief and loss.

In 1853 Miss Olive Raynes, who taught at Berwick Academy, opened a dame school a few doors from the Jewetts. There Sarah presently joined her sister Mary for what seems to have been a relatively painless introduction to formal schooling. "Aunt Olive's" school was a beloved institution in town, and like many other things in Berwick it was long-lived: when Miss Raynes finally retired, well after the turn of the century, she had taught three generations of Berwick children.

In 1861 Sarah enrolled at Berwick Academy, the pride of the town and the center of its intellectual life. Founded in 1791, it was a solid preparatory school where her father and his brothers had studied and where a number of prominent nineteenth-century scholars, including a dean of Harvard and presidents of Bowdoin, Bates, Colby, and the University of Maine, prepared for college. Here Sarah may have entertained thoughts of a medical career, but they cannot have been very serious. For one thing, she strongly disliked systematic study. Although she would always speak highly of Miss Raynes and of Berwick Academy, and although she won one of the academy's prize books for scholarship, she was thoroughly bored by classroom learning and would often accuse herself of "laziness" as her besetting sin.

Another strong disincentive was illness. Beginning in childhood and through most of her life, Sarah suffered from what was then called simply rheumatism and is now known as rheumatoid arthritis. Her joints, particularly knees and shoulders, would ache and swell to many times their size; sometimes she could not see her own feet. Attacks were related to season and weather and were always worst in the alternating freezes and thaws of early spring. Midwinter was also trying, especially just before a snowstorm. The family ruefully came to know Sarah's pain as a kind of barometer.

She was often absent (a school record for 1864 shows her missing twelve days out of forty-eight, not the worst record in the class), but she graduated with her friends in 1865, having gleaned enough education between school and home to launch herself into a literary career at eighteen. In an autobiographical article, she says she was "given to long, childish illnesses, and it must be honestly confessed, to instant drooping if ever I were shut up in school. I had apparently not the slightest desire for learning, but my father was always ready to let me be his companion in long drives about the country."[7] Here she implies that her "instant drooping" was caused by her illness; but the following sentence is nearer the mark. She really disliked studying, and her illness gave an indulgent father an excuse to liberate her from the stuffy classroom. Normally the school year ran right through the summer at Berwick Academy, with only a short vacation break; and it was probably mostly during the hot days of the summer term that father and daughter, in a tacit conspiracy at truancy, would join in what they both liked to do best: drive the back roads, heal the sick, and be together.

They called on all kinds of patients, from the wealthiest jurist to isolated farmers whose parched hill farms would support nothing but a few sheep. Often Sarah was left in the dooryard to shoo flies off the horse, but sometimes she was asked inside and given an apple to eat while the grown-ups, distracted by worry over the invalid, forgot her presence and talked as if she did not exist. There were advantages to being small. As an adult she would often wish she could be a fly on the wall when she knew some particularly tasty talk was going on. As a child, only one of the doctor's girls, she almost was.

Sarah Orne Jewett has described her adoration of her father, both in reminiscences and in *A Country Doctor,* as resembling that of a "little dog."[8] The suggestion of abject slavishness is disquieting, but in this context it is harmless enough, if only because her father's respect for everyone's individuality prevented any attempt to exploit his daughter's devotion for his own ends. Like Dr. Leslie in the novel, Theodore Jewett seems to have been so far from smothering his child with possessive love that he was even a little distant: not unaffectionate, but reserved, humorous, a bit abstracted, alternately absorbed in ideas and in moment-to-moment experience. To his daughters he was a teacher, an intellectual comrade whose mind ranged effortlessly over medicine, philosophy, science, and the humanities. He taught Sarah the central principle of her art, to "write about things *just as they are,*"[9] and he taught it as much by example as by precept. The observant eye that helped make him a superior doctor missed nothing in his natural surroundings, and his daughter's extensive knowledge of herbs was learned through his interest in traditional healing. The picture in *A Country Doctor* of Nan Prince and Dr. Leslie each scanning the roadside for interesting fruits and flowers rings true. So too does Leslie's detachment from Nan's vocational choice, even after she decides to follow him into medicine. The metaphor of the natural growth of an untrammeled plant—a fitting one in the context of the botanizing Jewett family—is used repeatedly in the novel. If Sarah's spaniel-like dependency never seriously weakened her ability to stand on her own feet, it was at least partly because her father simply would not permit her to follow him too closely.

3

Father and Mother

THEODORE HERMAN JEWETT WAS BORN
in 1815, the second of Theodore Furber Jewett's five sons. After
attending Berwick Academy he enrolled at Bowdoin College, where
he decided to study medicine. Graduating in 1834, he taught
school for a year or two and then undertook an informal medical
training typical of the time: lectures at Dartmouth and in Boston,
work at Boston military and charitable hospitals, study under two
prominent physicians, and a winter's course at Jefferson Medical
College in Philadelphia, where he got his degree. One of the
doctors he studied with, William Perry of Exeter, marked him as
a youngster of extraordinary promise, a man of "wonderful powers
of mind and singularly close habits of study and observation."[1]

After casting his lot in Berwick, Jewett never looked back. He
focused his considerable talent on his own community and was a
superb doctor, known throughout the region as his father-in-law
was. He became professor of obstetrics and diseases of women and
children at the Medical School of Maine, and consulting surgeon
at Maine General Hospital in Portland; he was also a lecturer at
the Bowdoin Medical School, an honorary member of several professional societies, and president of the Maine Medical Society.

Physically he was slender and dark-haired, with large gray eyes
deeply set below the distinctively long, downward-slanting brows
that he would pass on to his daughters. They lent his face a pensive
cast in repose, but since he was a man of warm wit and sympathies

his face was almost always lit with an intelligence and readiness to smile that drew people to him as soon as he entered a room. Perhaps, though, that slight suggestion of sadness, overlaid as it was with a mild, open manner, invited reticent New Englanders to trust him with their private griefs. As a doctor he was remarkably unassertive, having a kind of diffidence that, because of its rare lack of self-involvement, suggested a willingness to listen and understand. He took as his model the seventeenth-century physician Thomas Sydenham, another notably modest man whose contributions to medicine included the development of a method of close, case-by-case observation and conclusions, emphasizing the treatment of the individual patient in accordance with the physician's intelligence and experience rather than by rigid, universally unquestioned medical dogma.

A Bowdoin classmate remembered Theodore Jewett as never imposing himself on anyone, while at the same time preserving his own distinct and marked individuality. "His modesty," this old friend recalled, "amounted almost to bashfulness oftentimes."[2] Professor Altheus Spring Packard of Bowdoin,* an early mentor and lifelong friend, also remembered him as "a most lovable young fellow, somewhat quiet and diffident but very winning in his manner and a very great favorite. . . ."[3] A friend who knew him in middle life, Dr. J. E. Tyler of the McLean Hospital in Massachusetts, called him "a type of the courteous, cultivated, Christian gentleman and physician" and "the best physician of my acquaintance." Praising Jewett's medical knowledge, intellectual depth, humor, and kindliness, he mentioned especially his "tact in managing a case" and his qualities as "an *understander* of men."[4]

His influence on Sarah cannot be overstated. He was father, teacher, comrade, and model. Its most obvious effect was her (probable) brief flirtation with the idea of following him into medicine. It was, after all, a family tradition. Not only her father and grandfather, but her uncle William Perry and her great-uncle John Taylor Gilman were doctors. (On the Jewett side, reaching far back, there was Gen. Henry Dearborn (1751–1829), who was a country doctor before the Revolution.) If she had seriously wanted

---

* Packard, Collins Professor of Natural and Revealed Religion, was also the college librarian from 1869 to 1881.

to pursue medicine, her family certainly would have supported her. But medicine was still largely closed to women, and the struggle to gain a degree and establish herself would have been enormously difficult.* She would have needed perfect health to withstand the pressure, and in any case, as has been said, the father's aptitude for disciplined study was a trait the daughter, who loved to roam at will through the fields of literature, conspicuously lacked.

Instead, her identification with her father expressed itself in other ways. She absorbed his love of reading and his wide-ranging intellectual curiosity, following his explorations of literature, science, history, and religion. She shared as well his interest in herbs and plants, and from reading his botanical journals and medical textbooks and watching him dispense medicines she gained a basic pharmacological knowledge that, for better or worse, she used all her life to prescribe for herself and her friends. From her father she gained her emotional poise, the sensitive balance of compassion and humor with which she viewed the human scene around her. The physician's stance of disinterestedly sympathetic observer became the writer's, and like him she learned to imaginatively participate in the intimate griefs of others without either retreating or being overwhelmed. Without herself becoming a doctor, she gained some of the artistic advantage enjoyed by physician-writers like Oliver Wendell Holmes and William Carlos Williams, becoming privy to aspects of human experience from which most girls her age were rigorously shielded.

Like her father she became retiring and courteous to the point of diffidence, while at the same time maintaining underneath a sturdy respect for her own abilities. Sarah Orne Jewett's modesty was well adapted to the social expectations of literary women, which of course reinforced it, but she had an early example to follow. Father and daughter both tended to hide their light under a bushel. Both knew they were remarkably gifted in their separate

---

* The first American woman doctor, Elizabeth Blackwell, gained her M.D. the year Sarah Orne Jewett was born, but only because the school where she studied, Geneva College in New York, had accepted her application as a joke. The medical school at Bowdoin, Dr. Jewett's alma mater, was one of many that refused her application. Not until 1868 did Blackwell establish the first medical school to accept women on equal terms, and by then Sarah had written her second published story.

ways, and both were able to fully respect other people's egos and talents while quietly sustaining their own.

Finally, she and her sisters learned that practical common sense without which no country doctor of the day could survive, confronted as he was daily by afflictions that would not begin to be recognized for another half-century or more. It was a trait Drs. Jewett and Perry shared not only with the famous Sydenham but with the women of their own family, and ultimately both daughters and doctors probably absorbed it from mothers, aunts, and grandmothers. In the course of caring for their own children and visiting the sick and poor, talking the senile or demented into doing what was good for them, soothing the dying, and humoring the balky child, all the women constantly had to improvise and reinvent their human responses on the spot. Sarah's father and grandfather developed a therapeutic approach that was almost domestic in its pragmatism and humor. Confronted with a patient suffering from acute nervous strain, Dr. Perry advised him to buy a cord of wood and chop it all up: he did, and felt much better. When Dr. Jewett visited a particular ailing old sea captain, he did not take him a dose of bitters but a bottle of wine and a box of cigars.

In his personality and tastes Dr. Leslie of *A Country Doctor* closely resembles Dr. Jewett, on whom he was consciously modeled. He shares his love of books and solitude, his modesty, his Christian humanism ("I have long believed that the powers of Christ were but the higher powers of our common humanity"),[5] and above all his flexibility and tolerance. He does lack one trait that Sarah attributed to her father: he is not an eager host. He welcomes the visit of his old friend Dr. Ferris, but one would not praise him, as Sarah praised her own father, as "the hospitable generous master of his own house," nor as "the delightful guest."[6] Dr. Jewett seems to have enjoyed his role as master of a hospitable household. At the same time, his practice and other commitments kept him away from home much of the time, and there must have been many hours when, like Dr. Leslie, he liked best to sit by the fire with a substantial medical tome. Generally it was the Jewett women who sought and entertained company.

Although their small house had limited room for guests, the Jewetts received a steady flow of visitors yearly throughout the summer and fall, with scattered visits continuing through the winter. (Possibly some were put up in the house next door, where Uncle William and Grandmother Jewett had space to spare.) Like all Gilmans, Caroline Jewett and her daughters thrived on entertaining in the style of country towns: not by giving musicales and elaborate "at-homes," but by having people for a long, comfortable stay and sharing the family table and fireside, afternoon drives, neighborhood calls, and occasionally the great treat of a passing circus or a church fair. The Gilman and Perry women especially loved to entertain each other. The greater number of Jewett guests were relations, and of those the majority were women. In this custom Caroline Jewett was typical not only of her family but of her class, and like her mother before her she set her daughters an enduring example of openhandedness, along with a frank, unflappable simplicity of manner that could support them through any domestic disaster, no matter how embarrassing.

Mrs. Jewett apparently hated to write letters. As her daughters grew up this became something of a family joke, and her daughter Mary would tease her for letters in the up-country dialect they sometimes used among themselves: "Why dont Ma write to me. Tell her she might spare time for a few particulars once in a while, being a clever Ma."[7] The aunts, siblings, and cousins were almost all proficient and copious letter writers, but Caroline Jewett kept mum, and except for a few stiff little missives that only confirm her dislike of the pen, we are left with no voice to know her by.

We do know that, like her father with his top hat (and her grandfather for that matter, who wore a queue all his days), she was old-fashioned. To Sarah in adulthood this was always a quality to be cherished, and she mourned its disappearance as the older generation of friends dropped away one by one. A woman she meets late in life is "mother's kind of *lady before everything else* and *so dear!*"[8] A biography of Catharine Maria Sedgwick (1789–1867) delights Sarah because it re-creates for her the New England of her mother's girlhood. Caroline Jewett's family name, "Ma" (or sometimes, with a Maine accent, "Mar"), seems to have been a tenderly ironic reference to precisely what she was not: a sturdy countrywoman out of Sarah's own sketches, able to weather long winters in a lonely hill farm, keen of eye and prolix of tongue, equally capable of making a miraculously light sponge cake or mucking out a barn. Caroline Jewett belongs rather to the other tradition in Sarah's stories, that of the gentle and rather ceremonious aunt, the doer of good works and preserver of domestic civility. She was not at all intimidating; in fact she was rather frail, and began in middle life to show symptoms of the unidentified disease that eventually would kill her. For all her beautiful manners and distinguished ancestry she seems to have been a village woman at heart, with all the lively interest in her neighbors that the term implies. A good talk about "the particulars" of other people's lives was what she liked best, and when Mary wrote from Europe in 1889, she would apologize for having so few "particulars" to tell, knowing that descriptions of castles and cathedrals were a poor substitute. The pet name "Ma" suggests the contrast between the family's status and the deliberate simplicity of the woman called upon to publicly represent it, as well as mockery of other people's upper-class pretentions, and a link of humor and common sense between this mother and all the sturdy countrywomen who were, as a matter of course, called "Ma."

Like her husband, she liked to read and guided her daughters' tastes. But while Dr. Jewett directed Sarah toward Fielding, Smollett, Sterne, and Cervantes—authors she found understandably daunting as a child—her mother led her to Jane Austen, George Eliot, and Margaret Oliphant. Unfortunately, the list did not stop there, and Sarah's indiscriminate taste for popular novelists like the cloyingly sentimental Ouida was probably derived from her mother and aunts. For the rest, Sarah's feeling toward her mother after childhood was protective and tended to center on her illness. She is rarely mentioned in the letters, and then only in passing. She did not continue to be her daughter's comrade as her husband did, and inevitably as the gifted daughter surged ahead the mother was left, figuratively speaking, by the fireside. In a provocative study of the Persephone myth in Jewett's work, Sarah Way Sherman has suggested a continuing intensity of feeling between mother and daughter and even a degree of "maternal overidentification" that, to my way of thinking, the biographical evidence does not support.[9] But that does not undermine Sherman's basic thesis that the myth of mother and daughter was a powerful influence in the novels and stories. The basis of the myth is the universal experience of perfect union found in infancy and afterwards lost; the reunion of Demeter and Persephone, while not similarly universal in real life, still finds powerful resonance in the lifelong need of adult daughters and mothers to be reconciled in their common woman-hood despite their separation as individuals. The themes of love between mother and daughter, the daughter's fear of separation from the mother, and the need to emulate the mother and therefore be symbolically reunited with her are indeed pervasive throughout Jewett's work. Whatever her later shortcomings as comrade or companion, Caroline Jewett gave her children generous amounts of love in infancy and childhood. She also gave them a sense of their place in the world as women and as members of family and community. How much more she gave them we must infer, not least from their lifelong pleasure in the company of other women and their frank enjoyment of children, food, clothes, furniture and decorating, entertaining, and, especially, "the particulars."

4

Girlhood

THE ILLNESS THAT SENT SARAH OUT
into the woods and fields was also, as illness often was in that
century of sickly geniuses, a strong incentive for bookishness. Long
days of enforced rest were spent exploring the contents of the family
library. The choice was rich: Sarah Orne Jewett was not one of those
nineteenth-century writers whose childhood hunger for books was
fed on the dry crusts of *Pilgrim's Progress* and the graveyard poets.
The Jewett household literally overflowed with books. All the
bookshelves were full, and hundreds more were stored in closets
and the attic. Tidy stacks of books were removed from chairs so
that visitors could sit on them. Sarah had available to her not only
the standard eighteenth- and nineteenth-century poets and novelists but books on history, philosophy, theology, and the sciences.
There were journals on horticulture, medicine, and religion as well
as *The Atlantic Monthly, Littell's Living Age* (a selection of material
from European papers), *Punch,* and probably at least one of the
English quarterlies. Nor was the choice confined to her parents'
library, since her father's scholarly friends could lend her books and
journals. At Berwick Academy, where Sarah enrolled in 1861, a
magazine circle shared seventeen magazine subscriptions among
about thirty members, and the academy's library was available to
townspeople. Word from the American West came via the *Cincinnati Gazette,* edited by her uncle John Taylor Gilman, and from
Boston via *The Boston Transcript.*

All the Jewetts were addicted to the pleasant custom of reading aloud in the evenings, and Sarah had a special literary friendship with her grandmother Jewett, whose poor eyesight prevented her from thoroughly indulging her appetite for books. Sarah visited her grandmother daily and spent many hours reading and rereading new books aloud; by the time she was ten she knew many of them almost by heart. One favorite was George Eliot's *Adam Bede* (1859), whose picture of English rural life in many ways resembled the manners and customs of Berwickers.

A southern Maine winter in the days before central heating could be torment to anyone with rheumatoid arthritis, and as soon as Sarah grew old enough the family either took her on trips in the winter or sent her visiting, usually to friends in Boston. In summer she would spend two or three weeks at the nearby seashore, where her aunt Mary Bell and her family had established a kind of Gilman compound at Rye, New Hampshire, a few miles south of Portsmouth. Visits to Exeter were frequent; when she was eight she spent an entire summer with her Perry grandparents and attended the local school for a term. There were trips to see cousins in Portland and Brunswick and in Concord, New Hampshire, and in her teens she began to visit friends in Newport. In the fall she felt particularly well and stayed home, and November was always her favorite month.

Not surprisingly, the Jewetts took a philosophic view of Sarah's illness, neither denying and belittling it nor allowing it to tyrannize over her life. They were sympathetic, but there was always the expectation that as soon as the pain subsided there were duties and diversions waiting, most of them outdoors. Her father believed that exercise was as important as rest in keeping the disease at bay, and she became amazingly active and sturdy, considering her handicap. A strong cross-country walker, she liked best to strike out across the fields, taking a book along, hunting out rare flowers and herbs and visiting favorite trees as if they were old friends. She was an expert horsewoman and rower, and she enjoyed skating, swimming, and coasting. At the shore she clambered easily over the treacherous coastal rocks and spent many hours fishing for cunners.

She once described her childhood self as "wild and shy,"[1] as if she had been a kind of wood nymph like Sylvia of "A White Heron" or Nan Leslie. It is unlikely she was ever socially timid, like Sylvia,

or aloof from other children, like Nan. The term *shy* seems rather
to refer to her decided preference for nature over society—her
pleasure, for example, in sitting for hours in the woods with a book,
her back propped against a tree, enjoying the small bustle of
animals and birds about her and savoring the lack of human
intrusion. She liked to capture and tame small wild creatures, and
she built up her own small collection of insects impaled on pins.
Her fearlessness in the woods, her curiosity, and her love of solitude
were less usual for girls than for boys, but no one ever reproached
her for being unfeminine, and nothing she wanted to do was
discouraged for reasons of health or sex. Not only her sisters but
her father and grandfathers were her comrades, and Stubby's remark
that his aunt in middle age could coast "just like the other boys"
neatly reflects her conscious androgyny. Her nickname in letters to
one of her teenage friends was "Dear Boy," and all her life she was
proud that she could row and drive as well as a man.

Probably because she was never reproved for it, her tomboy-
ishness, unlike that of Louisa May Alcott or Willa Cather, did not
imply rebellion against the restraints of being a girl. The "wild
and shy" side of her nature, the side that loved the freedom and
physical vigor of the male world, was balanced by a social, domestic
side that was comfortable within the circle of village and hearth.
All three daughters resembled their mother in this, and their
mother accepted her own role without complaint and was, as far
as her strength would allow, a thorough homebody. As an adult
Sarah would refuse confinement to the woman's sphere by rejecting
marriage and her own sexuality; but in childhood, before there was
any pressure to make such a choice, she moved freely between the
two worlds. There is one interesting difference: in letters and
autobiographical essays Jewett almost always wrote about the active, outdoor part of her life and her friendship with her father. To
find evidence of the quieter female world we have to turn to her
children's stories.

Most of the young heroines in *Play Days* (1878) are securely
anchored in the domestic sphere, though they belong to the natural
world as well. Their preferred playthings are dolls, but if they are
poor and have no dolls they play with natural objects like shells,
"sea-eggs" (the egg cases of skates), acorns, pine cones, and stones.
Generally speaking, boys are seen as a separate species, sometimes

enviable and sometimes tiresome. They can be enlisted as playmates if there are no other girls around, but it is understood that boys and girls have entirely different tastes and tasks. In "The Ship-wrecked Buttons," Jack "would have preferred a boy to play with, and Kitty a girl, but they only had each other." (p. 153) In "My Friend the Housekeeper" and "Marigold House," Jewett has imagined a playhouse so elaborate that it may once have been the object of a wistful childhood fantasy of her own. In "Woodchucks," brother and sister like to do the same things, but Nelly accepts the prospect that "by and by" her work will be "nearly all indoors and Joe's nearly all out-of-doors." This does not occasion tears; on the contrary, she concludes she is "glad" she is a girl. (pp. 118, 130)

These stories were originally published when Jewett was in her twenties. The "wild and shy" child does not appear in them, but she is alive and well in "Jake's Holiday" (1874),[2] where she is a frankly androgynous heroine with a boy's name. Jake Brant does not spurn dolls, but she likes best to play with the boys up the road (based on the sons of the freewheeling, eccentric Doe family, friends of the Jewetts), who have "carts, and wheelbarrows, and a tent, and garden tools, and iron spoons to dig the sand with, and nobody to scold at you, and two tame calves, and a goat, and three good-natured dogs." (p. 14) When an itinerant organ-grinder passes by, Jake runs away and follows him. She is not angry or rebellious, but neither does it occur to her that her parents will worry; she has the thoughtless, fearless impulse to explore that was traditionally thought of as male. Eventually her older brother tracks her down and brings her home. She is not punished. The point of the story is her naughtiness in running away, but it is not made conditional on her sex.

Jewett herself ran away at least once as a child, for in an undated letter written sometime in the 1880s she describes seeing a little girl on the trolley at Salem, who

had reached the age of some six years and sat up so prim
and neat—but when the conductor came along she wasn't
prepared with her fare, and looked *so* pleasant and told the
passengers she was going to Beverly Cove to a picnic. The
conductor laughed and we all did and she was *so* pleasant

all the time looking round and bobbing her head like a
bird and being ascertained to live in Derby Street was set
off there with best wishes from the crowd, she stepped off
as prim and little! . . . She really made me think of myself
running away at her age: deep sense of enjoyment and all![3]

Like Jake, and like Barbara in "Beyond the Toll-Gate," this little
girl who reminded Sarah of her childhood self was not running
away *from* anything or anyone, but just mildly exploring the world
around her. The inevitable return to the nest is taken for granted.

In sum, two strains in her childhood personality which in our
culture we find contradictory, the "wild and shy" child of nature
and superfeminine miniature housekeeper with her dolls and patty-
pans, coexisted without apparent conflict. The heavy tilt toward
the latter in the children's stories may not reflect a corresponding
imbalance in life, for the nature of the market demanded that a
woman writer produce appropriately feminine role models for little
girls. Yet there is no doubt that the stories about traditional girls,
cramped and sticky sweet though they seem today, were genuinely
felt. She turned them out for a decade, and indeed continued later
on, as *Betty Leicester* demonstrates. It is worth remembering that
during the 1870s she was being unwillingly forced out of a prolonged adolescence into an adult world in which she had to find
her own place as woman and artist. It may be that the *Play Days*
stories and others like them were a kind of valediction to a role
she enjoyed as long as it did not impinge on her freedom, and
which she continued to respect and idealize in her adult fiction.

Sarah's childhood relationship with her mother is largely un-
documented and therefore difficult to trace, but there is some
significant indirect evidence. Sometime in Sarah's childhood or
adolescence her mother began to show symptoms of a disease that
her husband, skillful diagnostician that he was, privately recognized would be fatal. As it happened, Mrs. Jewett outlived her
husband by thirteen years, perhaps in part because of the tender
care lavished on her by the family. By the time her daughters
reached adulthood it was understood that their mother was not to
be left alone overnight in the house, even though servants were
within call. Vacations were sometimes canceled or postponed on
this account, and the girls rarely enjoyed the luxury of traveling

together. We do not know how early this pattern became established, but we can infer a continuing family willingness to put the mother's safety and comfort first.

Despite her illness, Mrs. Jewett emphatically was not a sighing, neurasthenic invalid. The brisk family attitude toward illness included mother as well as daughter and could be found in families throughout New England. (This despite the equally common opposite tendency to encourage debility and dependency, often leading to lifelong invalidism.) The Maine tradition of hardihood and independence demanded that every family member shoulder a full share of responsibility. If someone was ill, a courtesy born of historic necessity demanded that she or he make as little of it as possible so as not to burden others. Added to this was the Jewett-Gilman enjoyment of whatever small pleasures life dished up. Besides running her home and entertaining frequent guests, Caroline Jewett participated in church and town affairs. She drove out in fine weather and paid extended visits to relations in Exeter, Portland, and Brunswick; once she even ventured as far as Quebec with her husband and Sarah. When the currant bushes or grapevines in the garden grew heavy with summer fruit, she joined her daughters and the cook in picking it and in the subsequent jam making. Between Thanksgiving and Christmas they all made gifts for family and friends and for sale at the annual church fair, Mrs. Jewett tutoring her daughters in fancywork (which, truth to tell, Sarah always disliked) and encouraging their better efforts. She probably was an enthusiastic gardener, even if she was limited mostly to planning and directing, for the Exeter Gilman women had a strong gardening tradition (Great-aunts Mary Bell and Mary Long both established locally famous gardens), and both Sarah and Mary developed a lifelong enthusiasm for gardens and flowers.

Although Mrs. Jewett had to forgo many of the family excursions—it is doubtful, for instance, that she braved the heat and dust to go to the circus or the summer fairs—she could join their gentler forays into the countryside. The boating picnic in chapter sixteen of *Betty Leicester* is undoubtedly based on a real family outing, with father, daughters, and friends rowing down the river in convoy and Mrs. Jewett driving to meet them later. Pushing off from the landing on an ebb tide, the boating party would glide past stretches of dark pine woods, slabbed granite ledges fringed with blueberries, and shabby farms where children, dogs, and chickens mingled in the dooryard and cows peered nearsightedly from the bank. The river traffic, though declining in volume by the 1860s, was still busy enough to keep an oarsman alert, while above them the air was full of seagulls' voices, and song sparrows, vireos, towhees, and redwings sang from the woods and marshes. If it was summer, the little crooked, shaded coves on either side were bright with white or yellow water lilies and fringed with luxuriant, overhanging ferns. If it was spring and the sun was bright, the drifting logs and downed trees along the shore were heaped with basking turtles, and the girls would compete to see how many each could count.

At some point between the landing and the city, under a grove of pines, they would all climb out and tie up the boats, and Dr. Jewett and other male members of the party would build a fireplace of stones and kindle a fire, while the women and girls spread blankets and unpacked baskets. Presently they would hear hoofbeats, and the Jewett carriage would appear, driven by the family stableman and carrying Mrs. Jewett and perhaps an aunt or two, along with a shaded basket of pies, custards, and other perishable treats. There would be a leisurely feast enlivened by stories and banter, and afterwards people would sing, while others would take the boats out for fishing. The children and their mother might drive into the city, past tall, three-storied mansions topped with widow's walks, and call on their cousin Maria or their friends the Havens. In the afternoon they would row back with the returning tide, arriving in time for a sumptuous tea, and everyone would fall into bed by nine.

The meal would have been prepared by Kate Drinan, the Jewetts' "help." The Jewett family always included one or two women who did most of the cooking and housework. They might be girls who came in daily from somewhere in the village or from outlying farms, but increasingly after midcentury they came from Ireland and lived in. (In 1870, when the population of South Berwick was about 2,500, there were fifty-one live-in servants in town, or roughly one for every fifty inhabitants.) In earlier days these women might have stayed with one family all their lives— not, as in England, because they were forbidden to marry, but simply because the supply of men in small New England villages did not offer a wide choice of mates. Hannah Driscoll lived in the big house next door for at least twenty years, continuing to take care of Uncle William after Grandmother Jewett died in 1870. In Exeter, Grandmother Perry had been partly raised by one such woman: Molly Hatch had stayed on to care for the four children of Nathaniel Gilman after their mother's death, and when Nathaniel remarried and fathered seven more children, Molly Hatch was still there as second mother to the whole brood. She stayed to direct the running of the household into old age and presumably until she died. Both Marilla in *A Country Doctor* and Serena in *Betty Leicester* are based on village housekeepers like these. Their opinions carry considerable weight in the family, and their practical knowledge and emotional strength make them important maternal figures to the two heroines. Marilla is a comic character, a fiercely conservative countrywoman whose tyranny Nan and the doctor quietly subvert; but Serena is a sensible, mild soul who helps the motherless Betty through a difficult adolescent problem.

By the 1860s most hired helpers stayed in one household only a relatively short time: the Jewetts seem to have kept their help, on average, two to five years. As soon as they could, they would take their accumulated savings and move to the city, or return to Ireland to help their families. There was a good deal of play and shared work between the Jewett women and the women in the kitchen, and the girls grew up on Irish folktales and idealized memories of the Irish countryside, until it was more familiar to their imaginations than most of their own country. All the same, the sisters were called "Miss Mary" and so on, and the maid could not go to a church sociable without formal permission from the mistress.

With the help, the girls shared in the annual cider making and pig killing, and from them they learned whatever of cooking and sewing their mother did not teach them, as well as useful extras like how to catch a swarm of bees. John Tucker, who came to the Jewetts ten years after the Civil War and whose painful wound was a perpetual reminder of its cost, had charge of the stable as well as all the heavy work and decisions pertaining thereto. He ordered and hauled wood and hay, tended to household repairs, and advised the doctor and Mary on which horse should be on grass and which on grain. It was a family ritual every fall for John to announce just when the apples were ready for cider, drive them to the press, and stay all day to supervise the process and pronounce on the results. Stored in basement barrels, cider had been the staple refreshment of northern New England since settlement, and on its quality depended some small but vital part of a family's reputation.

Like cider making, the winter pig killing was a custom brought from rural England. Every town of any size had its pig butcher. Sarah's uncle William Perry must often have told the children about "Doctor" Flood, Exeter's self-appointed veterinary herb doctor and pig killer in the 1830s. In his healing capacity Flood "kept all sorts of herbs, and different kinds of animal oils," which he administered to ailing creatures with generally dubious results. As pig killer he was a familiar sight in winter, "a bustling little man coming down the street with his wheelbarrow, a half hogshead upon it, and his rope and knife."[4] The family pig was slaughtered in January or February and its meat consumed, cured, or packed in barrels of snow. Extra roasts were sent to neighbors who had not yet killed their own pig and who were expected to return the favor. In the kitchen a full team of mistress, daughters, and help threw themselves into the competitive sport of sausage making. The Jewetts continued some form of this annual rite as late as 1899, when Sarah teased Mary about going "pigging" with a raw-boned horse so as to "ensure a much more 'near bargain.'"[5]

Still another seasonal ritual was the coming of the dressmaker. Once or twice a year Mrs. Jewett would request a visit from this indispensable person, who traveled from household to household and whose schedule, like that of a modern medical specialist, dictated that of everyone dependent on her. The Jewett women would arrange their calendars accordingly, and when she arrived all female attention in the household was centered on the making and altering of the gowns (or more commonly "waists" and skirts) each woman required. Normally the dressmaker came from some distance away and was installed in a guest room; but the Jewetts' dressmaker, at least when the girls were young adults and probably earlier, was Olive Grant, who lived in South Berwick and supported herself and her illegitimate daughter. "Olly" Grant's discretion was as valuable as her needle, for she knew the intimate secrets of a great many families. No doubt she let slip enough innocent gossip

to keep her hostesses entertained. Sarah described her in later life
as a "lively friendly quaint busy creature" who "made a great part
in the rustic side of my life and so in the town side." The stories
were "full of her here and there."[6]

From childhood on, Sarah accumulated a little circle of elderly
friends on whom she would pay a ceremonious call once or twice
a year. Most of them were patients of her father's, and most were
still middle-aged when she was little, and their friendship belonged
more properly to her parents than to her. But there were some who,
even when she was small, had a special friendship with her alone.
One of these was Elizabeth Cushing, a descendant of that Wallingford family whose name and house Jewett would borrow for *The
Tory Lover.** Madam Cushing had been a child when Lafayette
visited Berwick and could remember the day he had walked up
their box-bordered walk to pay a call on his old friend, her mother.
At the age of seven or eight, dressed for the occasion in shawl,
bonnet, and white gloves, Sarah would walk up the same path and
be received gravely by the slender, reclusive, blue-eyed woman.
Seated on a parlor ottoman so tall her feet could not reach the floor,
she would make conversation for the customary twenty minutes or
so and be offered cake and wine, which she would eat very carefully
without removing her gloves. Years later the incident in Madam
Cushing's childhood, blended with a fantasy about a small chair
that had belonged to Sarah's grandmother or great-grandmother,
would produce the story called "Peg's Little Chair" (1891), in
which a child offers her own chair so that the aged Marquis can
dismount from his horse.

Another elderly friend was Anne Rice, "Aunt Anne" to the
Jewett children, a maiden lady who was related to both their
step-grandmother and their aunt Augusta Rice Jewett. She owned
a Newfoundland dog of which even dog-loving Sarah was afraid,
but she also possessed a wonderful house in Portsmouth, inherited
from her sea-captain father. The garden ran right down to the
harbor's edge and gave Sarah her first acquaintance with the tide

* Her father's family, Jewett would explain to Annie Fields, "were Boston
Cushings originally, and were for a long time *newcomers*! having moved to Berwick
in [']95! when Berwick, though small, was as proper a place to live in as Boston,
'at least so thinks Madam Cushing!' " (SOJ to AF [Monday morning], HL)

and the river; the scent of its roses and box always mingled in her memory with the smell of the sea. The house was large and rambling, "filled with quaint old furniture, and just like some English housekeeping of a very old fashion indeed."[7] It was one of many houses that evoked a cast of characters for Jewett's imagination by virtue of the almost palpable presence of everyone who had helped to wear its old doorsills smooth. The story belonging to Anne Rice's house is "Lady Ferry," written years after Aunt Anne herself had died. One of Jewett's several ventures into the realm of dreams and the supernatural, the tale was very long and William Dean Howells rejected it for *The Atlantic.* The character of poor deluded Lady Ferry is not at all based on the apparently quite sane Anne Rice. But the way the story formed itself around a particular house, in this case a house known from early childhood, is common to many Jewett stories; and it shows us how three aspects of her personality—the consciously preserved child, the traditional domestic woman with her sensitivity to objects around her, and the shaping artist—collaborated to re-create a particular setting and people it with the characters it seemed to need.

The characters were composites modeled on actual people, but Jewett was wary of offending her community, and her fictional people were never borrowed whole from life as her houses were. Small Sarah's acquaintance with human material was wider than that of most adults. Like Miss Grant, Dr. Jewett knew everyone's business; and so, of course, did the two Dr. Perrys in Exeter and Dr. Gilman of Portland. None of them would divulge the personal secrets of a patient, but they all took a lively interest in the families they visited, and it was a favorite family occupation to discuss the affairs of the neighbors. "Gossip" was forbidden, but there was a fine line between gossip and what was considered harmless comment. Uncle William Perry could recount the history and idiosyncrasies of the occupants of almost every house in Exeter, and at family gatherings would tell of early characters like Dr. Flood; or Miss Betsy Clifford, who ran a millinery shop with her sister and often carried her green parasol aloft in church out of sheer absent-mindedness; or the four industrious but "very peculiar" Gilman sisters (no relation) who supported a retired sea-captain brother; or the meticulous great-aunt who "always stopped her fires on a

certain day in the spring and began them again on a particular day
. . . in the fall," regardless of weather.[8] Constantly in and out
of their relations' houses, Sarah and her sisters grew up on a satisfying diet of not-quite-gossip derived from at least three different
communities.

5

"Neither Marrying Nor Giving in Marriage"

SARAH'S YEARS AT BERWICK ACADEMY, 1861 to 1865, exactly span the Civil War. The town sent 192 volunteers to the conflict, and many were maimed or killed. Graduating at fifteen, Sarah was too young to lose any of her own classmates, but families she knew were hurt or changed, as women struggled to raise families alone or children were introduced to new stepfathers. Black gowns and veils became common among her mother's and aunts' friends, and on the outlying farms she visited with her father, widows and newly bereft, middle-aged mothers were wondering whether they could hang on if they sold the woodlot, or if they would finally have to go and live with the grudging daughter-in-law in the city. Maine agriculture as a whole did not permanently suffer from the war, but many Maine farm women did.

The Jewett family was lucky. They lost none of their men, and their fortunes were undamaged. Dr. Jewett's practice gave him more than enough to do, while Uncle William continued to operate the West Indian Store until 1870, when it was closed and he retired in comfort. Nine years later he became president of both the town's banks.

Although the war did not affect Sarah's material well-being,

42

it would subtly influence her life in other ways. The sleepy square outside her front door was gradually transformed into a regional shopping center as a block of new stores and services sprang up over the next twenty years. The West Indian Store, which had served as a kind of central emporium, was replaced by a general store and a cluster of small shops. Law and insurance offices, a tailor, a shoemaker, and a milliner made their appearance. Several small manufacturing firms joined the two big mills, which between them employed 375 workers by 1880. South Berwick gained rail service when two rival companies, each offering service between Portland and Boston, converged at the Salmon Falls depot. It now was possible to travel to towns along the New England coast, or for that matter to reach almost any American or Canadian city, practically from the Jewetts' door. From Dover, four miles away, trains ran to the new resort communities of the White Mountains and New Hampshire lake country. Letters mailed in Boston in the morning arrived in Berwick by afternoon, and a regular steamer ran from Portsmouth to New York. In short, although Berwick's ships no longer sailed the Atlantic, the town was more closely linked to the rest of New England and America than it ever had been before.

At the same time, the handsome, slow-paced community of Sarah's childhood was disappearing. The pace of development had accelerated, and the new buildings often sorted oddly with the spacious old houses of the Piscataqua's golden age. Gardens were whittled away, fine old elms and oaks were hacked down, and pastureland receded to the edge of town. Commercial traffic on the river declined and then died altogether, and the wharves rotted. City people discovered the Maine coast and began to dot the landscape with summer cottages. As Sarah grew older she would watch the transformation with growing alarm. "Berwick . . . is growing and flourishing in a way that breaks my heart," she wrote in 1877, the year *Deephaven* was published.[1]

One effect of the war was that the number of young men a few years older than Mary and Sarah, which had never been very large, had been depleted. To many of the remaining Berwick men the Jewett sisters—handsome, highborn, and wealthy—must have seemed encircled by an invisible ring of fire, and potential Siegfrieds are not born every day. Even setting family rank aside, from the point of view of Sarah's fresh and original mind, the choice of serious mates must have seemed rather thin, had she thought about it at all. There is no evidence that she, or Mary, ever did.

In Sarah's case, I believe the reasons are complex. For one thing, the family was sufficient unto itself. To a remarkable degree, it reflects the contained, contented female society described in Carroll Smith-Rosenberg's classic 1975 essay "The Female World of Love and Ritual,"[2] except that in this family the resident males, especially Theodore Jewett and the Old Doctor but also the genial, urbane uncles and great-uncles, were not alien beings but simply provided an elevated level of male society that few brash young outsiders could hope to rival. The result was a charmed circle, with the women at the center. Although they all had friends outside the family, the Jewett-Gilman-Perry women could have been entirely happy limited to each other's company. Sarah and Mary were not only sisters, they were good friends. They looked alike (though Sarah was handsomer), and they had the same puckish sense of humor and the same distinctive kind of wise innocence. With their mother and Carrie they formed a complete little universe in themselves; and added to it were two aunts and three great-aunts—all lively, literate women—plus Grandmother Jewett, plus some distant Jewett cousins in Berwick and Exeter, plus cousin Fanny in Exeter, cousin Abby in Concord, cousin Alice in Brunswick, cousin Nelly in Portland, and so on.

The family idyll, along with the privilege of being her beloved father's companion and pupil, would be threatened by maturity. Young women married and left their families—under what compulsion Sarah did not know, having never felt it, but evidently it struck swiftly and no adolescent girl seemed entirely safe from it. A new allegiance swept family and friends ruthlessly aside, and the ties of childhood were never the same afterwards. The only way to defend oneself against this threat and stay within the loving circle of the family was to emulate, or anticipate, Peter Pan and never grow up.

Moreover, the extension of childhood was essential to the preservation of the writer she would become. The sense of seeing everyone and everything with a fresh eye, the playfulness, the absolute honesty and lack of pretense that we associate with the characteristic Jewett style, all belong to her childhood self and are typical of the voice heard in the earliest available letters and diaries. Simplicity is the very essence of the Jewett persona; and while she matured intellectually and deepened emotionally in the normal course of events, her ability always to remain surprised by the world around her was inseparable from her ability to re-create it. Of course she would not have presented the choice to herself in just these terms. But as she began to write sometime in adolescence, on some level the need to protect the integrity of her vision may have helped her postpone the inevitable blurring that came with adult responsibilities.

Then, too, the extension of childhood helped her avoid the practical question of who she was and how she meant to live her life. It was plain that she had to do something, but she had no interest in the conventional alternatives of marriage and teaching, and even after she began to write she had no clear sense of vocation apart from the retreating fantasy of medicine. The problems of sexuality and identity were intertwined and had to be worked through together. Because she so successfully remained her child-hood self, the process took a long time, lasting until she was well into her twenties and ultimately precipitating a long and painful emotional crisis.

But reading the diaries she kept intermittently from 1867 through 1869, one is struck by how serene and free of conflict she seems to be. The evident zest with which she extracted pleasure from the simplest daily experience is one of her most endearing, and enduring, characteristics. A walk in the woods with her dog, Joe, a feast of deviled ham and biscuit, an evening of reading aloud and good talk with her grandmother, or a visit from a city friend are all cause for private celebration. Despite the fact that a few years later she would complain of loneliness in Berwick, her friend-ships there seem to content her, and the names of neighbors Annie Barker and Sarah Lord, of Youngs and Nealleys and Hayses flit through the pages as comfortably as she and these friends—some of them distant cousins—flitted in and out of one another's houses. Nor were Berwick friendships necessarily mundane or provincial: Edith Haven Doe, a particular friend, was the wife of Charles Doe of Salmon Falls (now Rollinsford), New Hampshire, just across the

river from South Berwick. Doe was a brilliant judge and a spec-
tacularly eccentric man: a chief justice who refused to sit at trials
because they bored him; a fresh-air fanatic who ordered all the
windows in his house removed (though he replaced half of them
in winter); a hypochondriac who relied heavily on the medical
advice of his friend Theodore Jewett to pull him through his
various ailments—none of which, for some reason, seems to have
been pneumonia. His wife, much younger than he, was only eight
years older than Sarah and they often rode or walked together.
Edith Doe had a lively mind and shared her husband's iconoclastic
tastes. The Jewetts often dined in the Does' draughty Salmon Falls
house, and Edith Doe, at least, often dined at the Jewetts'. The
dinner-table atmosphere, even apart from the bracing air, was never
soporific.

Throughout Sarah's diaries small excursions evoke superlatives.
Of a drive with her father, her sister, and a friend to Bald Head
Cliff in nearby Ogunquit, she says, "I never enjoyed anything of
the kind so much except Niagara."[3] When she drives to York with
her father to see a patient, and afterwards they lunch on cheese and
biscuit and drive along the beach road, it is "one of the most
delightful days I ever spent." (November 30, 1869) A visit from a
girlfriend is the occasion of "real rioting at night!" (September 12)
The diary seldom mentions Sarah's mother, but it makes clear that
her father is still her good friend and comrade, the butt of teasing
when he has his hair cut too short, or when, seeing that a tiresome
guest preacher is going to deliver the Sunday sermon, he ducks out
of church before the service and streaks for home. In late October
Sarah goes to stay with friends in Boston, where she visits a Turkish
bath, sees Albert Bierstadt's new painting "The Sierras," drives
with her friends through the city's beautiful rural suburbs, hears a
concert, and attends three different churches. When she returns in
November she gets a note from Horace Scudder of *The Riverside
Magazine* accepting her children's story "The Shipwrecked Buttons"—"which," she puns to her diary, "I consider as being in a
safe harbor!" (November 1)

Here she is a few days past her eighteenth birthday, writing
a diary to an imaginary girl named Phebe, who will read it a
hundred years hence. She has been cleaning her room and has

Sarah Orne Jewett as a young girl
(*University of New Hampshire*)

Dr. Theodore Herman Jewett
(University of New Hampshire)

Sarah Orne Jewett's childhood home, now the South Berwick Public Library
*(Halliday Historic Photograph Company; courtesy Society for the Preservation
of New England Antiquities)*

Sarah Orne Jewett
(Colby College)

Mary Rice Jewett
(University of New Hampshire)

Upper Hall, Jewett house, Sarah's writing desk at right
(Houghton Library, Harvard University)

The Jewett House, South Berwick
(Arthur Haskell; courtesy Society for the Preservation of New England Antiquities)

"'triumphed gloriously' over the rubbish though I will confess to tucking divers and sundry trash away where I ought not to." She has had a wonderfully satisfactory birthday, highlighted by a day trip to the resort hotel on Star Island in the Isles of Shoals with her father, sisters, and some friends. Her Sunday is a happy mélange of unrepentant girlish trivia:

> I havent been improving Sunday at all today This morning
> I and Mary ("I" being first for *reasons*) eat nearly a box of
> sardines and I read Harpers and Mary wrote and after
> mother came from church we had dinner since then I have
> cleaned my watchchain explored mothers jewelry drawer in
> search of her coral charms, eaten apples, and Carrie brushed
> my hair.

She warns Phebe that she, Sarah, is not an improving example:

> Let me tell you first that I am a very *"sinfle"* bad girl, and
> it is very much for your interest that you live in the time
> you do instead of the age in which you might have come
> across me. And I will add for your instruction the Maxim
> "Be virtuous and you will be happy." . . . Phebe! do "Keep
> Sunday" in a moral manner![4]

Knowing her own chronic laziness, she foresees that keeping this diary is going to be uphill work: "I hope this wont share the fate of some half dozen [diaries] that I have commenced, and forgotten in two days." Inevitably it does. She writes four entries, followed by a gap of over a year, followed by a blank.

All this—the laziness, the habit of taking life easily, the refusal to take herself or the rules of behavior too seriously, and even the little gustatory binge of sardines—is the mature Sarah Orne Jewett, traits that will not significantly change. And yet there are small indications even in this short journal, and in others from around this time, of submerged difficulties that will rise to plague her.

On the inside cover of this diary, and of an 1866 extract book, Sarah drew a curious monogram: her own initials, S.O.J., the *S* and the *J* both drawn as serpents threatening the *O*. In one of them the

O is actually a fleeing stick figure with the serpents in pursuit, and underneath she has written, "my monogram with 'O' in trouble."[5] Of course there is always the strong possibility that a doodle is nothing but a doodle, but this one was repeated, which raises questions. From a Freudian perspective we might see an expression of fear, if not of men at least of sexuality. If we distance ourselves a bit from Freud, we might infer a mild anxiety about who this S.O.J. was, and whether she would survive in an Eden so peaceful and comfortable that its dangers would never show themselves except in the guise of some aspect of her own self.

On the inside cover of the 1866 extract book she has played with various versions of her own name, evidently at different times: Sarah Orne Jewett (1866); Fimmer Jewett (1867); Theodora Sarah Jewett; Theodora; Th. S. O. Jewett (this last with many flourishes).[6] "Fimmer" was one of her many family nicknames; others were "Piffy," "Seddie," "Sally," and "The Queen of Sheby." The choice begins to seem excessive, maybe even bewildering. At sixteen, adrift on a sea of aimless domesticity that stretched pleasantly and formlessly into the future, she had to choose which person she was going to be.

Over the next two or three years, following the custom of the time, she would copy lines that had particular resonance for her, among them poems about love and tragic death, religious poems, and several war poems, for the war was still fresh in everyone's mind. There are passages from Elizabeth Barrett Browning's "Romaunt of the Page," Wordsworth's "Tintern Abbey," Whittier's "The Pipes at Lucknow," and Christina Rossetti's "Somewhere or Other," and poems by Thomas Bailey Aldrich, Owen Meredith, Thomas Hood, Alice Carey, Julia Ward Howe, and the now-forgotten British poet Dinah M. Mulock. A chapter heading from George Eliot's *Felix Holt* shows she read that book soon after it was published. Several of the love poems are about hopeless love from a woman's point of view: Aldrich's "Maggie of Nantucket" dies of grief over her lost lover; the persona of Rossetti's "Somewhere or Other" yearns for a fantasy lover never met, perhaps dead; one of the two girls in the anonymous "After the Ball" will be a bride in a year, the other dead. Meredith's "Madame la Marquise" is rather startling among all these, a discreetly titillating male reverie of desire; but most of the love poems are directed at no immediate object and simply express vague romantic yearnings. Among them all was a verse admonition by Charles Kingsley to

Be good sweet maid and let who will be clever
Do noble things not dream them all day long.*[7]

At about the same time, she read Adeline Train Whitney's *A Summer in Leslie Goldthwaite's Life* (1866), a book she took much to heart, writing to thank the author, who replied kindly and at some length. In later years Jewett often recommended the book to young girls, saying it had done her a world of good when she was growing up. *Leslie Goldthwaite* is an interesting period piece that had, as we shall see, some bearing on the writing of *Deephaven*. As a guide for young women it had all the limitations of its time. Female life, Whitney clearly means to say, is meant to be useful, not interesting. Keep a low profile. Do the duty nearest at hand. Be good, and let who will be clever.

It was not, after all, a difficult assignment, when life at home was so very, very pleasant. It blended well with that native diffidence Sarah shared with her father, who had forgone a flashy city practice to become a simple country doctor. The message was all the more powerful coming from both society and the loved parent. It conformed to model womanhood as well as her own temperamental bent. Yet there was also her grandfather's advice to *"Act, Act,"* to be up and doing.

In the winter of 1868–69, visiting her uncle John and aunt Sarah Gilman in Cincinnati, she took painting lessons once a week, and in the diary she wrote that winter, there is one startlingly vehement entry: "Got mad and stayed up in my room an hour or two after I came home, bit my lip and my hand guess I was crazy!"[8] She had just returned from an art lesson, and she may have painted

---

* The Rev. Charles Kingsley (1819–75), passionate social liberal and moral conservative, was one of the founders of the Christian Socialist movement in England. A friend of James and Annie Fields and one of the many British writers published by Fields in America, he was the author of the sentimental historical novel *Westward Ho!* and the Victorian children's classic *Water Babies,* both great favorites of Sarah's.

badly. She was writing stories and poems as well, and had even
seen some of her work published,* but it would be some time
before she began to think of writing as a serious vocation. Except
for the art lesson, the context of the entry gives no clue to the
cause of this sudden, untypical fit of rage. Whatever the cause, the
entry allows us a rare glimpse into an emotional life more complicated than one would suppose from the otherwise placid tone of
the diaries.

While anger was too dangerous to be expressed, in one's diary
or anywhere else, love, especially love of one's friends or family, was
always to be pondered and savored. The diaries show that by her
late teens Sarah had developed a pattern of intense, though often
temporary, attachments to other women. Beginning with a series
of adolescent crushes, these attachments became more powerful and
enduring as she grew older, culminating in her lifelong attachment
to Annie Fields.

The 1867 diary, apart from its playful admonitions to Phebe
and its recitations of Sunday pleasures, tells us something about
her attitude toward that assumed goal of all young ladies' existence,
marriage. Sarah had just turned eighteen, and though she was still
maintaining the illusion of childhood, her own womanhood, advancing inexorably from birthday to birthday, could not be put off
much longer. It may be significant that she felt impelled to begin
this diary just now, between her birthday and the impending
wedding of a favorite cousin.

The cousin is Nelly Gilman of Portland, and the sisters are
deep in preparations. Sarah will attend the wedding with her
mother, but Mary must stay behind, evidently to look after their
father and sister. Mary has just bought Sarah a blue silk dress with
"a regular train," an unmistakable mark of adulthood. "Oh dear,"
Sarah writes, "I cannot believe I am grown up. It doesnt seem as
if I was at all[.] I do believe that if any one should ask me how
old I am and I didnt think I should say, ten."9 The wedding is less
than two weeks away, and "dear darling cousin Nelley" has just

* A story and some verses were printed in a local paper when she was about
fourteen. "Jenny Garrow's Lovers" appeared in the weekly *Flag of our Union,*
January 18, 1868, and the poem "The Baby-House Famine" in *Our Young Folks,*
September 1868. Both the later pieces, and presumably the earlier ones as well,
were published under pseudonyms.

paid them a flying prenuptial visit. Eagerly anticipating the wedding, Sarah is nevertheless already mourning her cousin's loss: "I hate to have her married for which I can give no definite reason." (September 21) On the night before the wedding, staying in her aunt's house, she is so agitated that she walks in her sleep and has actually begun dressing when her mother wakes her up.

The wedding guests mentioned are all relations; the others, of whom there must have been many of both sexes, simply escape her notice. Men, except for male relations and neighbors, are simply ignored in her diaries except for one 1868 entry when, visiting Exeter (where she has been royally entertained by Aunt Perry and Great-aunts Long and Bell), she attends a masquerade party dressed as Highland Mary. "It is so easy to get up anything of the kind in Exeter," she says dismissively, "on account of the [Phillips Exeter] Academy students." (November 1, 1868)

The Exeter students were all younger than she was, which might account for her lack of interest, if every other letter and journal, of this period and later, did not show the same sexual indifference. There is no sign that she was ever strongly moved by the friendship of a man, or that she ever languished for the sight of a male friend or tormented herself with fear of his defection. She was so moved, and she did languish and torment herself over a succession of girls and women.

The earliest documented of these friendships was a crush on Cecily Burt, a girl Sarah met in Cincinnati in 1868–69. During that winter Sarah attended church often, and it was there she met Cecily. They see one another two or three times a week, and soon Sarah has grown to "love [Cecily] dearly," but Cecily seems quite casual in her response. At one point Sarah is reduced to trying to catch a glimpse of her in church, and she spends an entire day at home vainly hoping her friend will call. Finally they meet at a prayer meeting and walk together: "I do love her best of anyone here in the whole city. 'Happy Day.'" (February 14, 1869) There is a little crescendo of entries about Cecily, highlighted by their attending a "calico party"—a dance to which the girls wore dresses they had made themselves. Sarah "danced every dance" (it is not clear if there were any men present) and was "happy because I was with C.B." (February 16) A month later Grandfather Perry arrives to escort her home, and on April 4 she says good-bye to Cecily, who gives her a gold ring: "I had rather have it than anything for I shall always have it with me."[10]

Home in Berwick she falls back into the old pleasant round and her feelings cool a bit, but the friends correspond faithfully and Sarah pins her hopes on Cecily's promise to visit Boston in the spring. But in May she receives a letter saying Cecily is engaged to be married, "and what nearly broke my heart, . . . she's not coming to Boston." (May 27) A few days later she has another letter: "[Cecily] is altogether too spooney and it seems so funny!" (June 4) She is rapidly relinquishing the friendship and turning to other, older friends. She goes to Portland with her father and then to visit her friend Grace Gordon in Boston.* On June 26 she mentions a "dear letter" from Cecily, but she is mostly thinking about a promised visit from Grace: "I do love her with all my heart." Grace arrives, and they go to an exhibition at the academy and spend a day pleasuring in Portsmouth. Sarah says she hasn't enjoyed herself so much for a long time.

Other friends and cousins visit over the next few months, sometimes sharing a bed with Sarah and talking far into the night. In November she guiltily writes Cecily a long letter to make up for "past neglect." In December Cecily is married; Sarah expects a letter immediately afterwards and is "awfully mad" when none arrives for almost two weeks. Meanwhile she has heard from another friend, "my dearie and my chickie and my darling Ella [Walworth]." (December 17)† Cecily gradually disappears from the diary, though they corresponded now and then after her marriage. "So ends 1869," Sarah wrote on December 31, "the happiest year I think I ever had because my friends are dearer than ever. . . . E. W. [Ella Walworth] is my best friend. I hope I can say these same things next year."

In two respects this episode is totally unremarkable: the friendship is a typically fragile adolescent crush, such as countless

---

* Grace Gordon, whose parents' home at 1 Walnut Street was a regular winter refuge for Mary and Sarah, was the daughter of Katharine Gordon, a family friend who was probably related to Grandmother Eliza and Aunt Augusta Rice Jewett. The girls had been friends since childhood.

† Ella Walworth, later Ella Walworth Little, was one of her Boston friends. This friendship endured a few years after Ella's marriage, probably because her husband allowed her a good deal of freedom in seeing her own friends.

girls have experienced before and since; and girlhood friendships, including hardier ones than this, have historically been disrupted by marriage. What makes it worth our notice is its intensity, which anticipates some forty-odd years of others like it, and Sarah's wholly negative reaction to her friend's engagement. There is no vicarious rejoicing, no girlish exchange of confidences about the groom or teasing speculations about the eligibility of his friends; only disappointment and the rapid disengagement of Sarah's affections. The prospect of marriage, whether of herself or her friends, seems to have been an unmitigated nuisance from the start.

This early pattern never wavered, until by the time she reached her late twenties Sarah was confirmed in a fixed aversion to marriage—no longer for others, but for herself. By then, of course, she had established herself as a writer and was secure in a vocation that not only was a joy in itself but also fulfilled that primary injunction to nineteenth-century womanhood, Be useful. And unlike other women writers who perforce put their families before their writing (Harriet Beecher Stowe with her infants tugging at her skirts comes immediately to mind), Sarah Orne Jewett came to feel that her literary talent was a gift worthy of her primary attention, and that some women have not only the right but the obligation not to marry.

Dr. Leslie in *A Country Doctor* stoutly defends his ward's independence, and incidentally links it to her apparent asexuality:

> "I see plainly that Nan is not the sort of girl who will be likely to marry. When a man or woman has that sort of self-dependence and unnatural self-reliance, it shows itself very early. I believe that it is a mistake for such a woman to marry. Nan's feeling toward her boy-playmates is exactly the same as toward the girls she knows. You have only to look at the rest of the children together to see the difference; and if I make sure by and by, the law of her nature is that she must live alone and work alone, I shall help her to keep it instead of break it, by providing something else than the business of housekeeping and what is called a woman's natural work, for her activity and capacity to spend itself upon."[11]

We do not know if Sarah's own father expressed similar views; obviously, if he did she had substantial early support for the life she chose. Certainly the description of Nan's relationships with males exactly fits Sarah's, and Nan's choice of a vocation instead of marriage was Sarah's own, although she only slowly achieved full dedication to it.

So she solved the problems of vocation and nonconforming sexuality together. Her vocation gave her a rationale for living as she wanted to live, and her celibacy gave her the freedom to pursue her vocation. At the end of the 1867 diary, among several miscellaneous passages, is what may be a fragment copied from a book (the quotation marks suggest as much) or possibly a draft dialogue of her own:

> "'There' said he 'is a house wherein live [six?] old maid sisters. . . . Isnt it funny? And the youngest is nearly fifty—' 'Little foretaste of heaven' said I 'neither marrying or [sic] giving in marriage.'"[12]

There could be no more fitting comment on this whole episode, or on the future pattern of her life and work.

The fact that Sarah Orne Jewett's deepest affections were always centered on women has naturally led to the question of whether she was lesbian. I believe she was not, in the strictest sense of the term. To quote Smith-Rosenberg's discussion of romantic love between nineteenth-century women, "The twentieth-century tendency to view human love and sexuality within a dichotomized universe of deviance and normality, genitality and platonic love, is alien to the emotions and attitudes of the nineteenth century and fundamentally distorts the nature of these women's emotional interaction."[13] Sarah Orne Jewett's love for other women was as passionate and absorbing as any heterosexual man's, but from all available evidence it never led to direct sexual expression. It belongs in a category hardly imaginable to the modern sensibility, that of romantic friendship. There are two references in the 1869 diary to sharing a bed with a loved friend, but in both cases the attraction is clearly conversational, not sexual. In all the subsequent letters and journals there is no evidence to suggest sex between women, although there are many references to hugging and kissing, many love poems, and many passages in letters that can only be read as expressions of romantic love.[14] Sarah Orne Jewett fell in love many times, both before and after she met her dearest friend, Annie Fields. But that love always remained idealized, and perhaps because of that very quality her friendships with women, as stable as they were intense, became the emotional center of her life.

Sarah's hostility to marriage may have been unusual in Berwick, but the fact that she did not actually marry was not. Of the three sisters only Caroline married, and their friends in Berwick included many unmarried women of their mother's generation or their own: Elizabeth Cushing, Aunt Anne Rice, Mary and Elizabeth Barrell of York, their close friends Rebecca Young, Susan and Hetta Hayes Ward, Hattie Denny, and Anna Johnson.* They daily encountered single working women like teachers Olive and Mary Raynes, Lizzie and Annie Goodwin, dressmaker Olive Grant, Miss Polly Marsh of "An Autumn Holiday," and the many farmers, nurses, housekeepers, milliners, and shopkeepers who lent their piquant individuality to the spinster characters of Sarah Orne Jewett's sketches. Spinsterhood did not carry a social stigma in Maine, although the unmarried women in Jewett's stories often have a lower social standing than wives and widows simply because they have "less to do with." ("The Guests of Mrs. Timms" and "Miss Tempy's Watchers" are both exquisitely nuanced stories that show us just such shadings of social status.) Obviously the upper-class Jewetts, Barrells, and Wards did not have to endure any snubs on account of their unmarried state, and in general women who made useful lives for themselves were respected, regardless of the number and degree of their male relations. In her book *A Maine*

---

* Mary and Elizabeth Barrell, elderly descendants of an old family, lived in a fine ancestral house in York that still exists and is open to the public. Rebecca Young, a classmate from Miss Raynes's school and Berwick Academy, was treasurer of the South Berwick Savings Bank and lived a few doors from the Jewetts. Susan Hayes Ward was literary editor of *The Independent* and became the first editor to publish Robert Frost in America; her brother William was general editor, and Hetta was their sister. All three were graduates of Berwick Academy. Mary Harriet Denny, a nurse and the daughter of a Boston medical colleague of Dr. Jewett, was one of the friends who toured Europe with Mary in 1889. Anna Johnson, another member of that party, was headmistress of Bradford Academy in Bradford, Massachusetts.

Hamlet, Lura Beam has described the standing of the unmarried working women of the 1890s in a Maine village. Although "marriage was supposed to be the way things are, . . . single women were admired for their work. As wage-earners, they appeared more positive personalities, usually of better education and dress than the average housewife."[15] Although Beam's village is in northern Maine and has quite a different economic base from Berwick's, this is one of many cultural traits they share.

In short, the Jewett sisters' spinsterhood was part of a common, accepted phenomenon within their own region and generation. A generation earlier, Margaret Fuller had pled for understanding and acceptance of single women. A generation later, as urbanization and industrialization increased, fewer families inherited wealth, and there were fewer opportunities for work in rural areas, women would again become more dependent on male economic support. In the Jewetts' own time, in poorer, inland New England villages like those in the stories of Mary Wilkins Freeman, there were stronger pressures on women to conform to the marital norm. But on the Piscataqua from the 1870s to the 1890s, it was possible for a woman to stand on her own.

6

Finding Her Way

N O   O N E   K N O W S   E X A C T L Y   W H E N   S A R A H
Orne Jewett first began to write stories. As a child she wrote verses
far more easily than prose and agonized over school compositions;
it was only gradually that prose began to come easily to her. Some
verses and a story were published locally when she was fourteen;
her first published story, "Jenny Garrow's Lovers," appeared when
she was eighteen but may have been written much earlier. She
thought so little of this story she always silently ignored it afterwards, implying that her fiction career began with "Mr. Bruce" in
the December 1869 *Atlantic.* Following that her poems and stories
for children appeared in other publications, but it is in the first
Deephaven sketch, "The Shore House" in the September 1873 *Atlantic,* that we begin to hear the mature Jewett voice and meet the
native Maine characters who distinguish her works from all others.
In "Jenny Garrow's Lovers" and "Mr. Bruce" she had tried to write
conventional romantic fiction, forcing herself into a narrative mode
for which she had neither inclination nor experience. "The Shore
House" is the first adult work written out of her own life, but it
did not mark a definite launching on the waters of adult fiction.
She continued to cling to childhood in her work as in her life, and
although some other adult works, including the second and third
Deephaven sketches, appeared over the next few years, it was not
until she was entering her thirties that she published more for
adults than for children.

The children's stories charm for the same reason her other works do: they have the same meticulously observed settings and the same humorous insight into character, except in smaller amounts proportional to the whole. When Prissy in "The Water Dolly" putters along the beach with her father, picking up stones and skates' eggs, or when a farm dog confronts its archenemy in "Woodchucks," the descriptions have an unmistakable ring of authentic New England experience. Yet the stories are hopelessly dated now, of interest only to Jewett scholars combing them for clues to the adult work and life. The child characters speak stilted British English (as do the adults in the earliest stories), and despite the spontaneous realism of detail, each story is focused on the inevitable lesson at the end. Lacking the ambiguity of her grown-up works, these stories necessarily also lack human breadth. They were meant to Teach the Young and tend to be—as Jewett herself said of one—"severely moral."

Before she achieved the regular succession of published works in the 1870s, she had to serve a long and mostly silent apprentice-ship, marked by repeated rejections and editorial comments from James T. Fields and William Dean Howells, editor and assistant editor respectively of *The Atlantic Monthly.* Sarah sent at least two stories to *The Atlantic* before "Mr. Bruce" was accepted and at least two in the months following, a pattern that implies she sent others that left no trace. Each rejection was accompanied by an encour-aging note. "Uncle Peter's Legacy," evidently written around male characters, was turned down in June 1868 by "the Editors" (prob-ably Fields) with the suggestion that she not try to write from a man's point of view—advice that she herself would hand on to Willa Cather forty years later. Undeterred, she sent them another story in less than two months. This one was about a girl, but it was not (one of them explained) told "in a way to interest older folk," and it was marred by an improbable plot. He clearly wished he could have taken it: "We hope you will understand us aright, when we say that you are one of our most difficult cases. If your story were only a little better, or a great deal worse!"[1]

Almost exactly a year later they accepted "Mr. Bruce," but soon afterwards they turned down two more. Then, her confidence apparently beginning to wane, she wrote and asked them frankly if they thought she should give up writing. Their reply was delayed—probably by Fields's retirement—and it was Howells, now editor, who finally wrote to say that they thought it "eminently worth while" for her to keep on and making it clear they preferred her prose to her poetry.[2] Almost immediately she sent him an early version of "The Shore House," set in a Maine fishing village. Intended for a conventionally plotted story, it was strong in description and weak in narrative, and Howells wrote asking her to strengthen the plot. She replied that she felt more confident of making the piece into a sketch, and he encouraged her to go ahead, agreeing that she needed to develop the characters more fully and "give ample amounts of the old house, the sea-faring and light-house people, as you propose."[3] Jewett had it back in his hands the following month. With what rejoicing at his own editorial finesse Howells accepted it we can only guess; he and Fields had patiently cultivated this young talent, and the long harvest now would be his. Even so, possibly because of a backlog left by Fields, he made her wait a year and a half until publication.

Sarah met Howells soon after he accepted "The Shore House," and from then on she was an occasional guest at the Howellses' successive homes in Cambridge and Belmont. Both personally and professionally, the Howells friendship was a giant step into the adult world. In their similar stances of optimistic realism, their sympathetic, forgiving views of human nature, and their understanding of rural people, Jewett and Howells had a natural affinity as writers. The most perceptive editor of his day, Howells held Jewett to her best mark, consistently returning anything he thought fell short of it. His praise generally steered her toward her own strengths. After she had evidently revised "Deephaven Cronies" in 1875 according to his suggestions, he wrote,

> Your paper is perfectly charming. You've worked in the old
> material skillfully and the new is good. You've got an un-
> common feeling for *talk*—I *hear* your people. And I have
> had a better laugh than I've enjoyed for many days at the
> lecture on True Manhood.[4]

Twelve years older than Jewett, Howells had been Fields's assistant at *The Atlantic* five years before succeeding him as editor in 1871. Under his guidance the magazine began to broaden its

scope and shed its patrician Boston image. Howells's small-town
Ohio boyhood had left him always slightly on the defensive against
the literary establishment, and his sense of being the perpetual
outsider made him editorially hospitable to women, westerners,
and southerners. But personally Howells lived at the very heart of
the New England literary scene: the families of Charles Eliot
Norton and Henry Wadsworth Longfellow lived within walking
distance of Howells in Cambridge, and a half-mile beyond Longfellow was James Russell Lowell's "Elmwood," housing not only
Lowell himself but (during intervals when he lived abroad) Thomas
and Lilian Aldrich and the Norwegian violinist Ole Bull and his
American wife, Sarah. Charles Dudley Warner was a frequent
visitor at the Howellses, and Warner's Hartford neighbor Mark
Twain roared through now and then, leaving ructions and hilarity
in his wake. All these people except Twain later were close friends
of Sarah Orne Jewett. How many of them she met through Howells
is an open question; but at the very least, to visit the Howellses
was to domesticate the names of all the others and give them
friendly reference. Besides, Sarah's own "dear darling cousin
Nelley," now Mrs. John Nichols, lived on Brattle Street not far
from Longfellow.

Another near neighbor of Howells, at least in mid-decade, was
Horace Elisha Scudder. As editor of *The Riverside Magazine,* Scudder
had published several of Jewett's early children's works and, like
Howells, had established himself as literary advisor and confidant.
After he left the magazine in 1871, she continued to look to him
for criticism.* His kindly but unimaginative remarks prodded her
toward thinking out a rationale for her style and beginning to
define herself as a writer before she was twenty-one. In 1870 he
made a comment that would become a familiar refrain: "There seem
to be good characters for a story and good scenery but no incident,
no story. In other words . . . here is a sketch and not a picture."[5]
Since he was referring to a piece he himself had published

---

* As a close associate and sometime partner of Henry O. Houghton of the
Riverside Press, whose firm later merged with Sarah's publisher Osgood to evolve
into Houghton Mifflin, Scudder had a long working relationship with Jewett.
Although he left publishing in 1874 to write independently, in 1885 Scudder
became editor-in-chief of Houghton Mifflin; he also was unofficial assistant editor
of *The Atlantic* 1885–90, and edited the magazine 1890–98.

("The Girl with the Cannon Dresses"), the complaint was mild enough; but it was the first of a long succession of similar criticisms, culminating in the widely held view that *The Country of the Pointed Firs* was somehow not quite successful because it was not quite a novel.

The question of orthodox structure puzzled and discouraged Jewett herself for some time, particularly since Howells later echoed it in his comments on "The Shore House":

> I believe the only thing [Howells] found fault with was that I did not make more of it. "The characters were good enough for me to say a great deal more of them". But I don't believe I could write a long story as he suggested, and you advise me in this last letter. In the first place I have no dramatic talent. The story would have no plot. I should have to fill it out with descriptions of character and meditations. It seems to me I can furnish the theatre, and show you the actors, and the scenery, and the audience, but there never is any play! I could write you entertaining letters perhaps, from some desirable house where I was in most charming company but I couldn't make a story about it. I seem to get very much bewildered when I try to make these come in for secondary parts. And what shall be done with such a girl? For I wish to keep on writing, and to do the very best I can.

Yet Howells himself had faulted at least one early story for its improbable plot, and Jewett knew that when she reached too far after plot she marred her work. Her explanation to Scudder, though couched in typically self-deprecating terms, shows that even this early she understood where her strength lay and would not be deflected from it:

> I am certain I could not write one of the usual magazine stories. If the editors will take the sketchy kind and people like to read them, is not it as well to do that and do it successfully as to make hopeless efforts to achieve something in another line which runs much higher?[6]

It was an appeal to him to let her go her own way, and apparently
he did, for by the time he wrote to congratulate her on "Deephaven
Cronies" (1875) the word *sketch* had become a comfortable term
between them, as indeed it had with Howells, and she had settled
into the genre at which she excelled and which she perfected for
American literature. But she always would feel that hers was
somehow a lesser art, not on a level with "higher" fiction; and she
took for herself, as both artist and person, the image of the daisy—a
flower too ordinary to be in any way remarkable but nevertheless
having its own perfection and, above all, its own integrity.

Her early use of a pseudonym might at first glance seem to
be related to her chronic modesty. Several early works were published under the name of "Alice Eliot" or "A.C. Eliot." (One story,
accepted by an unfamiliar editor, appeared in February 1871 under
the name "Sarah O. Sweet." Since Scudder had already printed a
story under her own name in July 1870, it seems likely that
someone simply misread her signature.) Women writers often used
pseudonyms to protect their delicate sensibilities from the common
gaze, but this does not seem to have been Sarah's motivation, for
she relinquished that "protection" very early and afterwards mostly
enjoyed her literary fame. In part, no doubt, she wanted a cover in
case her work was badly received. But she also wanted to savor the
pure joy and pride of having created something that was hers alone,
which of course was a feeling generally disparaged among women
as selfishness. She told nobody but Mary about "Mr. Bruce" until
it was accepted by *The Atlantic,* and after Mary persuaded her to
tell her parents, she wrote in her diary, "I wish with all my heart
I had never told any body; it seems as if it no longer belonged *all
to me.*"[7]

"Mr. Bruce," which is about the daughter of a wealthy family
who masquerades as a maid, seems totally unlike Jewett and in fact
was based on an anecdote told by her grandmother. Sarah rushed
right home after hearing the tale one evening and wrote it down,
finishing it the next day. The rapid pace is typical of the way she
worked at first. A story would present itself to her mind, taking
form around a house or a person, and she simply wrote it down,
rewriting once to make a fair copy. Later she took more time, but
she always distrusted heavy reworking, afraid to spoil the freshness

of the original impulse, and she remained a rapid writer, sometimes allowing herself digressions or authorial comments that second thoughts might have deleted. Her manuscripts show a keen awareness of the shading and rhythm of words from the beginning, and she was adept at tidying a word here and a phrase there; but she seldom moved or deleted whole passages. Exceptions to the rule were the *Deephaven* sketches, which she apparently revised in their original form before revising them again for the book. The last revision took several months and left her exhausted and prostrated with rheumatism, for of course all the copying had to be done by hand. Not until the writing of *The Story of the Normans* in 1886 would she again work so intensively for so long.

For a few years writing was no more than a pleasant game, and she wrote now and then, whenever she could fit it in. By 1873, when "The Shore House" came out, she was taking her work more seriously. She spent her twenty-fourth birthday "hard at work at my writing all day." She took great satisfaction in the symbolic way she spent the day, and in "being tired from real hard work—and not from laziness!"[8]

She still maintained a deferential, girlish tone toward her chosen mentors, but she could be surprisingly brisk and professional when corresponding with strange editors. Deferential and girlish she might be, but she never allowed an editor to intimidate her, and she stuck to her guns when she knew she was right. Moreover, her authorial ego was remarkably tough. She took rejections easily, both when she was young and uncertain and later on, when she might well have thought her work deserved automatic acceptance. "I think about my sketches very much as I do about other people's," she once wrote, and it was the literal truth.[9]

She solicited honest criticism from everyone she knew who had any pretense to literary experience, including Mellen Chamberlain, a Boston municipal judge and amateur historian who became director of the Boston Public Library from 1878 to 1890; Theophilus Parsons, a retired professor at Harvard's Dane Law School whose friendship will be discussed in a later chapter; and Harriet Waters Preston, an author and translator whose work frequently appeared in *The Atlantic*. All of them sent advice, most of it now lost, and she was always grateful. Thanking Scudder for his 1873 comments, she voiced a complaint that must have been common among women writers whose friends and families unwittingly trivialized their work with mindless praise:

> I am more than glad to have you criticise me. I know I
> must need it very much and I realize the disadvantage of
> never hearing anything about my stories except from my
> friends, who do not write themselves, and are not unexceptionable authorities upon any strictly literary question. I do
> know several literary people quite well, but whenever they
> read anything of mine I know that they look down from
> their pinnacles in a benignant way and think it very well
> done "for her" as the country people say.[10]

While her writing was not, as she put it, a "bread and butter affair,"[11] she did eventually earn enough from it to be financially independent. The fact that many of her stories were published by *The Atlantic,* and later by periodicals of equal stature like *Harper's* and *Century,* was a stroke of luck not shared by many other writers, mostly female and mostly poor, who scribbled for small journals and had to produce enormous quantities of work to get by. *The Atlantic* paid writers fairly, and her first effort there brought her $50, while Scudder paid her $34 for "Cannon Dresses." Other early standbys, *The Independent* and *St. Nicholas,* paid only $5 a page; but she soon gained enough stature to pick and choose, and if she sold her work short it was because she had a strong personal reason for wanting it to appear in a particular publication. By the 1880s *The Atlantic* paid her upwards of $200 for a story, and presumably others followed suit; and since in a typical year she might publish five or six stories plus a poem or two, she was soon financially her own person, especially after she began receiving book royalties. The fact that she had a safety net of family income beneath her should not disguise the fact that her independence was due solely to her own effort and the quality of her writing, and would have come about even if she had not been the daughter of Dr. Jewett of Berwick. She was capable in financial dealings, bargaining firmly with publishers and managing her own investments with occasional advice from male relations.

As she gained in professionalism she set herself goals of so many stories per year and so many hours of writing per day. Always a night owl and late riser—partly because her aching joints made her sluggish in the morning—she resolved to rise early and work regularly. But that was easier said than done, for not only was illness a serious hindrance, she really was not free to set her own hours as long as she lived at home. To say the problem was simply one of willpower, while partly true, is to oversimplify the delicate balance of duties as a woman saw them. A daughter's primary duty was always to cater to her parents' real or perceived needs, and of course the vocation of any woman, whether married or unmarried, was to be of service to others. In the absence of the traditional, more substantial tasks of their grandmothers, upper-middle-class women defined as more or less sacred duties not only consulting with the cook, arranging flowers, and inspecting the linen closet, but paying calls, writing letters, and giving dinner parties. However irrelevant these functions may seem, they had by default become important to many women, who saw themselves as maintaining social order and upholding a small pillar of western civilization. Even respected scholar-administrators like Anna Eliot Ticknor and Elizabeth Cary Agassiz (founder of the Society to Encourage Studies at Home and first president of Radcliffe College) put their domestic and social duties before anything else. A few resolute (and poor) nonconformists like Lydia Maria Child and Lucy Larcom threw socializing ruthlessly to the winds; but generally speaking, the higher a woman's social position, the more she expected of herself in the way of social obligations, and a woman who had spent a whole afternoon driving around leaving cards could sleep the sleep of the just.

Sarah's list of obligations did not, at least while she lived in Berwick, include leaving cards. But there were Berwick friends in and out of the house all day and there was a frail mother to be lovingly tended. Nor would Sarah ever turn down one of her father's increasingly rare invitations to drive. The aunts and great-aunts regularly coaxed and pleaded with the sisters to come to Exeter or Portland, and affection as well as duty urged acceptance. The dressmaker, church fairs, and regional religious conferences were all allowed to preempt everything else. Visitors were constant in the summer (thirty or more were not unusual), while Sarah maintained a list of at least that many correspondents, to whom she dashed off

letters before she settled down to regular writing. In winter and
spring she was laid up with rheumatism or sent off on a round of
visits, making any work but proofreading impossible.

Fall remained; fall was her window of opportunity, not only
for work but for riding and walking and rowing and simply
enjoying the free movement of her own limbs. Although she
worked in any season, it was in autumn that she produced most of
her self-imposed yearly quota, working in her own room or at a
desk in Uncle William's spacious upper hall overlooking the square.
She worked sometimes in the morning, sometimes in the afternoon,
aiming at five hours of work a day. She hardly ever achieved them,
although on one memorable day she wrote eighty-five pages (including letters). She constantly reproached herself for laziness, and
in fact her easygoing, pleasure-loving nature was ill suited to the
solitude and confinement of writing. Above all, she was tormented
by doubts about what her "work" really was. Certainly writing
stories was work, but she did not know whether writing letters,
running errands, visiting the aunts, and so on was not equally her
"work" as a woman. Trying to do everything, she accomplished
very little, and in an 1874 letter she compared herself to an
unpruned apple tree,

> a wilderness of "suckers" and unprofitable little scraggly
> branches. . . . It's hard for me to know what to do: I don't
> like to shut myself up half of every day and say nobody
> must interfere with me, when there are dozens of things
> that I might do. I have nothing to do with the housekeep-
> ing or anything of that kind, but there are bits of work
> waiting all the time that use up my days. I hate not to
> do them and I'm afraid of being selfish, and shirking—
> and yet—Well, I'll not talk any more about that, but
> let it wait.[12]

Nevertheless, except for 1877, when she worked herself to
exhaustion on *Deephaven* and consequently produced nothing else
(although even then she worked at proofreading and publishing
chores), she was an increasingly prolific writer, somehow meeting
the goals she set herself and finding ways to work productively
within the limits of a complicated life. It was never easy, and she

often felt frazzled and irritable, occasioning more self-reproach. Encountering Louisa May Alcott on the Isles of Shoals one day in 1880, she commiserated with her on the trials of female authorship and later quoted her feelingly to a friend: "It is *not writing:* it is trying to write and do everything else beside!"[13]

7

"Be Good Sweet Maid"

IN THE SEVENTIES SARAH ORNE JEWETT regarded herself primarily as the bearer of a moral message. In this respect she was thoroughly mainstream American: Harriet Beecher Stowe and Elizabeth Stuart Phelps were really ministers manqué, while William Dean Howells, Louisa May Alcott, and Mark Twain in his fierce way were all committed in some degree to the betterment of human behavior. Henry James, of course, was an exception, and when *The American* was serialized in *The Atlantic* in 1876, Sarah, writing to her friend Anna Dawes, noted with displeasure its studiously amoral tone:

> I dont like Mr. James's characters—that is I shouldn't like
> real people who acted and thought after his fashion, but I
> think he writes cleverly about them and makes them more
> or less interesting. And I think as you do that the moral of
> the thing is not good.[1]

Three months later she came down hard on George Eliot, whose *Adam Bede* had ranked high among her adolescent favorites:

> There is always something lacking in George Eliot's books
> because, however high her standards of morality and how-
> ever grand her ideas of life one misses the least suggestion
> of our having a true and real friendship with God, and that

[*sic*] our success must depend upon this after all. Perhaps
you say this is inferred—many people do—but it does not
seem to me so—and I have the same feeling in reading
Middlemarch that I do in reading—Antigone perhaps; or
any of those tragedies of Sophocles—it is fate, it is hopeless-
ness, we are working helplessly against resistless and unchangeable forces, or if we are lucky enough to hit upon
some line of action which leads us to apparent success, then
we are none the wiser and none the surer.

She goes on to cite approvingly an essay in *Studies in Poetry and
Philosophy* by John Campbell Shairp:*

[Shairp] shows plainly at the end that nothing but our own
Christian religion gives the help or is the "motive power"
toward a perfect life. . . . I am sure this belief must under-
lie every thing—we are in the world for our spiritual education and every thing is planned for that isn't it?—and
success is not a thing of chance but a thing of choice
with us.[2]

These comments were made apropos of *Daniel Deronda:* not that
she had read it, but she was excusing her reluctance to do so, having
decided from glancing through it that it was "almost a heathen
book after all."

At least the second and perhaps both of these letters were
written while she was revising the *Deephaven* sketches, and she
herself regarded *Deephaven* as an improving book. That it is not so
regarded by its affectionate readers and rereaders is due partly to
Jewett's literary gift, which far outshot her intention, and partly
to her own dislike of preachy writers. Even her contemporary stories
for children teach more by example than by precept, although there
is inevitably—as in most of her early adult stories—a didactic
paragraph or two to hammer the message home.

We have seen how cheerfully disrespectful of religion she could
be at eighteen, admonishing the imaginary Phebe of the future to

---

* John Campbell Shairp, poet and essayist, was principal of St. Andrew's,
Edinburgh.

"'Keep Sunday' in a moral manner!" But a year or two later she entered a period of painful religious searching, when she was assailed by religious doubts and by a sense of aimlessness and isolation. In November 1871 she left the Congregational faith in which she had been raised and was confirmed in the faith of her ancestors at St. John's Episcopal Church in Portsmouth. Mary Jewett was her sister's companion in this as in many things, but the depth of Mary's commitment is not known, since almost none of her letters from these years have survived. Sarah's, however, was intense, involving a great deal of anxious self-examination along with earnest efforts to guide the faltering steps of others. Continuing to attend the Congregational church in South Berwick (the nearest Episcopal church was a tiny one in the neighboring village of Salmon Falls), she became more active in its affairs, cataloguing and updating the Sunday school library and at least once taking on her share of parish calls. She taught a Sunday school class of women a few years younger than herself and undertook a sort of moral-tutorial correspondence with Lillian Munger, the teenage daughter of a Methodist minister who had lived briefly in Berwick. Perhaps exorcising her younger self, she took in hand a young local girl who, like Nan in *A Country Doctor,* lived a rather lonely life and was "a wild, out-doors sort of girl very fond of horses and all that sort of thing."[3] Soon she could report to Dawes that the girl was "growing stronger and happier in every way . . . and isn't it a great thing to be used in helping somebody, and to have people associate you with their pleasures and blessings?"[4]

She often compared her own slothful ways with the industry of more virtuous friends and relations, as in this passage from her 1872 diary:

> [Aunt Helen's] life is more Christlike and more filled with
> faith, and love to her neighbor and kind thoughtfulness,
> trust in God and brave earnestness and unselfishness than
> any life I know. . . . It is the life that tells, and my life is
> just nothing but a selfish one I am good-natured when I
> am amused and interested—but when I am left to myself
> and ought to be at work—Horrors! I cannot write about
> it!—The sweetness and goodness of her face haunts me, and
> having been with her and seeing how entirely unselfish and

true her life is, makes myself seem unbearably selfish and wicked.[5]

She remarks on how improving the company of this or that friend is, as if their main function in her life is to reform her evil ways. Thus Harriet Seeger, who visits several summers in a row, does her "ever so much good" in 1873, and in 1874 leaves her "a wiser and a better girl, and more ready to put down self and work manfully than ever I had been before."[6] In her despair at her own unregenerate character she once refers to some passively suicidal feelings:

> I believe I am not like other people in anything and it
> never will amount to anything, all this trouble and perplex-
> ity and sorrow I have gone through with. . . . I have all
> that old feeling back again which used to come so often
> when I first knew Kate {Birckhead}, when I used to wish
> with all my heart I could die and end it all. I would not
> live a day longer if it were not for my friends being
> troubled.[7]

Like the earlier reference to biting her hand in rage, this passage is a startling flash of something dark and fierce in her mind, but there is no hint of the cause of the "trouble and perplexity and sorrow" to which she refers. Perhaps the death of her beloved Grandmother Jewett in February 1870 triggered the onset of a long misery that seems to have been rooted in a feeling that she had no clear purpose in life and no will of her own—that she was, in terms she herself often used, a "lazy, good-for-nothing girl." The misery was not expressed to everyone at large. It is doubtful she said much about it to her family, for example, and in this diary it is instantly pushed aside, and she writes about how much she enjoys visiting Aunt Helen and how the sea air always makes her "contented and happy." She fled from her own despair, as she fled from the impli-cation of "resistless and unchangeable forces" in *Daniel Deronda;* but there is ample evidence in letters of this decade that the despair itself was deep and real.

Her depression can be roughly divided into two phases. The first, lasting about two years, culminated in her 1871 confirmation.

The second, lasting about six years longer, gently lightened and disappeared after the publication of *Deephaven*. Throughout these troubled years she had a few close friends in whom she could freely confide. The first of these was Kate de C. Birckhead of Newport, mentioned in the diary entry quoted above.

Sarah's feelings toward "my dear dear darling Kate"[8] flared into something close to veneration in 1871–72, resembling the earlier meteoric love for Cecily Burt and the later one for Harriet Preston. "If I found myself disappointed in [Kate]," Sarah wrote with characteristic hyperbole,

> it would have been one of the bitterest things in all my
> life, for to lose Kate would be losing a powerful influence
> for good, and an influence which enters not merely into
> great things but into my little every-day interests. . . . I
> think she cares more for me than she used, and she tells me
> she enjoyed my visit, and that a letter of mine helped her,
> and all this makes me so happy.[9]

In the difficult year of 1870, Kate was Sarah's spiritual confidante and mentor, urging her toward a formal avowal of faith that, despite its Episcopal setting, resembled a born-again evangelical conversion. "My dear little girl," she wrote Sarah on Easter Sunday,

> I have just been asking our Heavenly Father, to bless you
> and watch over you, and I feel that even my weak plead-
> ings will be listened to, and that He will. He sees and
> knows all you are passing through, and if you only con-
> tinue to ask for His help He will give it.[10]

Although Kate's personal ascendency waned after a year or two, the storm of religious feeling continued to be shared by a group of friends to which both Sarah and Kate belonged, all of whom experienced the same phase of strenuous piety and rigorous self-improvement. These young women, all of them Boston residents or frequent visitors, had been drawn into the orbit of the charismatic Episcopal minister Phillips Brooks.

Born and raised in Boston, Brooks was ordained in the South and served for several years as rector of Holy Trinity in Philadelphia, where he quickly earned a reputation as one of the most exciting young preachers in America. He returned to Boston in 1869 to assume the pulpit at Trinity Church, where he continued to draw large crowds of worshipers for over three decades. Like Henry Ward Beecher, Brooks was a media event, a clerical superstar. A giant of a man whose thin voice and rapid delivery contrasted oddly with his physical presence, he drew people by the generosity of his views and the beautiful clarity of his sermons. Passionately liberal on social issues, Broad Church in theology, he emphasized the moral and ethical teachings of Christ in his sermons and avoided controversial dogma. Many non-Episcopalians, including his friend Oliver Wendell Holmes, went to hear him regularly just to experience the sweetness of his mind and his prose.

When Sarah was in Boston she and her friends attended Brooks's sermons twice on Sundays and acted as one another's moral boosters, each trying to help the others to heaven through praise and example. Being Episcopalians, they were not given to fasting and mortifying the flesh, but they were extemely earnest about their faith. Kate Birckhead was probably the first of the group to direct Sarah toward the church, but Georgina Halliburton of Portsmouth, Anna Dawes of Washington and Pittsfield (Mass.), and Ellen Mason, Ella Walworth Little, Cora Clark, and Grace Gordon all belonged to what might be termed the Episcopal Cluster, and Grace married the rector of St. Paul's Cathedral in Boston. They were intelligent, well-to-do young women, to whom religion was not only pleasantly elevating but an escape from anxieties, for God would make everything all right always. At the same time, like Sarah's writing it was something entirely their own. In an age when there were few ways for a young woman to separate herself from her family, the church offered her a way to leave the parental nest without actually leaving it; as it had in medieval times, it offered an ambition of sorts, even if it was only the ambition of a blameless life. Into that unforbidden goal a girl could throw all the pent-up energy that a man could throw into sexual pursuit and vocational choice.

Moreover, in Jewett's case as in that of Stowe, Phelps, and Adeline Whitney, among others, religion did not conflict with literary ambition, but rather provided a convenient justification for it. The impulse to create a story for the fun of seeing it unfurl inside one's own mind, and for the secondary fun of reaping praise in the telling of it, was suspect. It entailed guilt even in women who were well removed from the Puritan tradition. But if one's writing could be made to serve religion—if "Be good sweet maid and let who will be clever" could be transposed to "You may be clever, maid, because you are so good"—then it became a vocation in both senses of the word. Writing was "no longer an amusement but *my work*."[11] This validation of her talent and ambition was strongly fortified when, in the early seventies, she formed a friendship with Harvard law professor and Swedenborgian writer Theophilus Parsons.

During these years Sarah's reading, though still ranging widely if desultorily over many subjects, began to include more works by and about various exemplary Christians. She steeped herself in the essays of the liberal seventeenth-century Catholic educator Fénelon,* and there are several references in her letters to her old favorite Charles Kingsley, whose biography she read at the suggestion of Harriet Preston. She placed high on her list of favorite books Thomas Hughes's anonymous novel of schoolboy muscular Christianity, *Tom Brown's Days at Rugby* (which she attributed to Matthew Arnold). But the religious works that moved her most profoundly and that she returned to most often were those written by Parsons.

A writer of considerable persuasive power, Parsons sought in his books to make the basic tenets of the "New Church" clear and accessible to all. Minimizing or ignoring whatever seemed strange or bizarre in Swedenborg's own writings (his claim to have conversed with angels, for example), he made the faith seem so attractive to Sarah that she did not see how any rational person could resist it and began to find traces of it everywhere—rejoicing, for example, when she thought she detected Swedenborg's influence in the preaching of South Berwick's new minister. The fact that several of her Episcopal friends were drawn independently to Swedenborgian views confirmed her belief that it was a rapidly growing movement that soon would be accepted by almost all thinking Christians.

---

* François de Salignac de La Mothe-Fénelon (1651–1715) was archbishop of Cambrai and, for a while, tutor of the grandson of Louis XIV.

Jewett met Parsons at Wells Beach in the summer of 1872 when, coming up to her on the piazza of the hotel where they were both staying, he lent her a spyglass so that she could watch a passing yacht. Afterwards she found the gesture prophetic, for she came to feel he had dramatically extended her spiritual vision. On that summer afternoon they fell into a conversation on religion, and he offered to lend or give her some of his books. She began to write to him, on the understanding that he was not obliged to reply, and thereafter she wrote him several long letters a year, reporting on her moral progress or lack of it and soliciting his opinions on everything from her friendships to her work to interpretations of biblical passages.

Parsons's influence was both spiritual and psychological. Spiritually he encouraged her actively to shape her own life, rather than wait passively for God to reveal His plans to her. Swedenborgian teaching emphasized individual responsibility: the degree to which one discovered and acted on God's purpose in this life determined one's state of being in the life to come. Each person, Parsons told Sarah, was presented daily with opportunities to choose well or badly, according to God's will or against it, and one had to decide what God's will was and act accordingly, using Scripture as a guide. He encouraged her to set herself specific goals and finish whatever she began; to stop repining at her loneliness in Berwick and become involved in her community; and to work steadily at her writing, since it was a way of exerting beneficial influence on others. All these injunctions she took conscientiously to heart, and the determination with which she followed them was not unlike the determination with which a modern young woman might approach a college curriculum. Her Sunday school class and her friendship with the troubled Lillian Munger are two enterprises that she reported proudly to Parsons and that can be attributed more or less directly to his advice. "It is such a comfort," she told him, "to know that things dont come by chance and however puzzled we may be at first—everything is really right, unless we make it wrong ourselves."[12]

Most important was the encouragement he gave her to keep on writing. "The best we can do is the thing we ought to do," he told her, and it was clear that writing was by far the best she could do.[13] From a literary point of view his influence was unfortunate,

since it was all in the direction of explicit moralizing. Commenting
on the children's story "The Kitten's Ghost" (*The Independent,* May
8, 1873), he criticized its lack of moral muscle:

> What I mean is, that your stories lack—what it would *now*
> be impossible, perhaps, for you to put into them; and that
> is, positiveness, substance. You learn easily, think quickly,
> and write excellently. The time will come when you will
> never write without knowing that you are going to say
> something which will make your readers wiser and better,—
> unless they reject it, which is not your affair. And that
> thought or truth you will do your best to give access to the
> minds of your readers. Then you will rejoice when you feel
> that you have succeeded in clothing a valuable truth with a
> beauty that is at once attractive and transparent;—that
> wins reception for the truth and does not obscure or dis-
> guise it.[14]

But the harm Parsons did in literary terms was minor, especially
if one remembers that almost all the stories written before
Deephaven were for children. It was far outweighed by the beneficial
effects of helping Jewett achieve discipline and motivation as a
writer.

At times the responsibility of her moral influence, either
through her writings or through her assumed guidance of younger
women, actually frightened her. Her pleasure in the success of
Deephaven was dampened by its implications, and she comforted
herself with the faith that God had given her a talent to use for
the greater good, and that in its use she was guided by a Higher
Power:

> It has not been wholly pleasure, this success which I seem
> to have—though there is so much pleasure—It is very hard
> for me to "take it in" that all the praise is meant for me—
> indeed I believe I am somehow hindered from taking it
> in—Except in the very vaguest way—Sometimes I have
> been sorry because I do not feel more *pleased* and *"set up."*
> . . . But dear, isn't it a tremendous thing to be put into
> ones hands and can a girl help feeling that she is living a

more conspicuous sort of life, and that it is frightful to
think what a little bad influence will do.—Ah well! does
not one grow more and more thankful that there is a
Strength that never fails and a Wisdom that never is found
wanting and a Love that is always ours.[15]

The ultimate responsibility, she thought, was not hers at all.
In these years she gave religious expression to the belief, common
to artists in all ages, that some force beyond herself created her art.
By the mid-eighties she still held that belief, though she no longer
named the power: *"Who does it,"* she wrote Annie Fields, "for I grow
more and more sure that I don't!"[16] In her twenties this sense of
detachment from her own work became part and parcel of her
religious creed, and words like *tool* and *servant* cropped up frequently in her letters. Parsons encouraged this; replying to an
admission that she was "growing ambitious" about her writing, he
absolved her from guilt, reassuring her that "God does good always,
be the instrument of God."[17]

The conviction that she was but a humble instrument is
reminiscent of one of her father's favorite biblical sayings, "He who
would be chief among you, let him be your servant."[18] Here we
come back to the daisy symbol: parental example, religious faith,
and the tradition of womanly self-effacement all combined early to
reinforce a habitual dislike of seeming in any way extraordinary.
The self-defined role of "minor writer," to which Louis A. Renza
called attention in his 1984 study of Jewett, may have been the
extension of a deeply ingrained, familial, cultural, and personal
attitude concerning her place in the world.[19]

Parsons's philosophic influence was lifelong, but there is also
a strong suggestion in the letters that he briefly fulfilled a kind of
quasi-psychiatric function, helping her achieve a necessary distance
from her father. For a while Sarah metaphorically followed Parsons
"like a little dog," as she had once followed her father, distancing
herself slightly from Dr. Jewett and temporarily focusing on Parsons an adoring, childish dependence. Certainly Parsons's doctri-
naire, sharply defined views and specific advice provided an
authoritarian structure that was altogether missing from her relationship with the easygoing Theodore Jewett.

Now and then she subtly compared the two in her letters,

usually to her father's disadvantage. Writing of how Swedenborgian ideas "have spread and crept into people's minds," she remarked with the barest detectable assumption of superiority that her father "amuses me particularly for as far as I can tell he 'believes' almost exactly as I do, and yet he declared one day with great solemnity that there was a great mysticism to him in Swedenborgian ideas."[20] In an early letter she appealed to Parsons for advice on how to refute a friend (and fellow skeptic) of her father's, who "knows a great deal and could easily upset my arguments," as of course her father could as well. "It was not what he said," she explained, "but what he suggested that I could not answer."[21] One suspects that she had to deal with similar suggestions, in the form of mild teasing, from the relentlessly rational doctor. When she was looking for a publisher for *Deephaven,* it was to Parsons and Howells she turned for advice, such things being "not much in [Father's] line at any rate!"[22] In short, by becoming a kind of temporary alternate father, Parsons may have helped her to intellectually challenge her real father and begin a new relationship with him on an adult footing. Certainly that change was coming about by September 1874, when she wrote that

> I have had some delightful drives lately with Father who
> has been very busy, and we have had some nice talks. It has
> always been one of my grand ambitions to be able to "talk
> with Father" and it [is] so pleasant now that he talks with
> me as he does to his own friends besides it teaching me so
> much. We go from medicine, and theology, and law,
> down—and sometimes talk nonsense and tell each other
> "yarns" all the way![23]

Roughly speaking, the height of the Parsons friendship lasted from 1872 until after the publication of *Deephaven* in 1877. Sarah's first letter after the book was published is addressed "My dear Prof. Parsons" instead of the usual, simpler "Dear Prof. Parsons." The small change suggests a new recognition of her own status as an adult and a newly celebrated author. They continued to correspond often during that year, mostly about his moral criticism of *Deephaven* (a subject we will return to), but the childish, worshipful tone of Sarah's letters was gone, and presently she wrote less and less often. The letters seem to have ceased altogether in June 1881, a few months before Sarah spent her first winter with Annie Fields. It seems clear that the new relationship with Annie, which would overshadow all others for the rest of her life, dealt the final blow to the waning friendship with Parsons. With his help she had achieved a fully adult identity and—inseparable from it— success as a writer; in the natural course of events the friendship had outlived its usefulness, and it was quietly allowed to lapse.

But the effect of Parsons' Swedenborgian teachings can hardly be overstated, and we must take at face value Jewett's statement that she kept "a sense of it under everything else."[24] Without becoming a professing Swedenborgian or understanding the creed as a whole, without indeed referring to Swedenborg more than once or twice more in her letters, she had absorbed what she needed from Parsons and made it her own. She came to rest on the plane she had reached during these few difficult years, assuming the calm, cosmic view of life for which she has been both praised and blamed. As much as is humanly possible she had lost the fear of death, as well as the fear of losing to death those she loved. And she had become committed to developing a divinely sanctioned talent and to a sense of responsibility, if not active service, toward other people. Stated that way, her faith might seem to resemble the most banal and sentimental of Victorian platitudes, an embroidered plaque hung on the wall. But because she was who she was, it simply confirmed the strength she already possessed, fostering her native capacities for sympathy and language and freeing her to express them fully through friendship and work.

Deephaven

DEEPHAVEN WAS A LONG TIME EVOLV-
ing. Sarah Orne Jewett wrote the first of the original three sketches,
"The Shore House," when she was twenty or twenty-one, and
Howells published it in *The Atlantic* in 1873. "Deephaven Cronies"
followed in 1875, "Deephaven Excursions" in 1876. The revised
sketches, with additions, were published in book form when she
was nearly twenty-eight, and much of the work already shows the
authority and craftsmanship of the fully mature writer, along with
a clearheaded, unsentimental vision that places her squarely among
the first American realists.

There is no plot as such, but a series of character sketches and
episodes centers around a pair of young women from well-to-do
city families, Kate Lancaster and Helen Denis, who spend a summer together in the fishing village of Deephaven. Kate's grand-
aunt, Katharine Brandon, has died and left the "family estates in
Deephaven," including her "charming old house" (p. 11) to Kate's
mother; and Kate and Helen are allowed to spend the summer
there while Kate's parents travel abroad. In the course of their stay
they come to know some of the villagers well, among them the
widow Patton, who "did for" Miss Brandon; the retired sea captains
Captain Sands and Captain Lant; the fisherman Danny; and the first
of Jewett's memorably strong, warm, downright earth mothers,
Mrs. Kew. They explore the old Brandon house from kitchen to
attic, visit Mrs. Kew at her lighthouse home, go cunner-fishing

with Captain Sands, and gradually become friends with many of the village people. Each person they meet has a distinct place in the community, and all of them, through the stories they tell, expand the imaginative experience of the two green city girls. By the end of the summer the girls have not only come to love the village but have incorporated into their own lives and memories those of people much older and very different from themselves. The book ends with a quietly elegiac anticipation of the passing of these older friends and their way of life.

When she began writing the sketches, Jewett probably had no idea that there would be enough of them for a book. But as early as 1873 she was thinking of eventually publishing *some* kind of collection.[1] So when Howells suggested that the *Deephaven* sketches might make up a book, she quickly took up the idea and began asking for advice about publishers. Parsons suggested Roberts Brothers and Howells suggested James R. Osgood. She decided to be safe by sending her manuscript to both. Howells must have been as amused as he was nonplussed:

> You have been *too* successful with your book. If Osgood said he would take it—or thought he would—you ought (oughtn't you?) to have had his decision before going to [Roberts Brothers]. Suppose they should both accept the book?[2]

In fact they both did accept it, but Jewett somehow smoothed away the awkwardness and Osgood published it.* It was a pretty volume, taupe and black with Kate Lancaster's cat-o'-nine-tails, drawn by Sarah Orne Jewett herself, stamped in gilt on the cover and spine. Jewett participated actively in all phases of production, and there were frequent trips to Boston to consult with Osgood in his office.

* James Ripley Osgood had previously been a partner of James T. Fields in Fields, Osgood, the successor firm of Ticknor & Fields. Fields left in 1871, and when *Deephaven* was published in 1877 the firm was in difficulties. In 1878 Henry Oscar Houghton of the Riverside Press became a partner, and the firm became Houghton & Osgood. By 1881, when Jewett published her fourth book, George Mifflin had joined, Osgood had left, and the firm had assumed its permanent identity as Houghton Mifflin.

In a preface written for the illustrated 1894 edition, Jewett recalled how distressed she had been in the seventies by the growing tension between the country people she knew and the fast-increasing hordes of summer visitors. She said she might have had the "unconscious desire" to write the sketches in order to explain one group to the other, to keep "timid ladies" from the city from mistaking a selectman for a tramp simply because he was in his shirtsleeves, and to keep country people from suspecting that the kindness of these same timid ladies came from condescension and *noblesse oblige*. She remembered, too, her alarm at how rapidly the summer people had transformed the coastal villages, as if

> tradition and time-honored custom were to be swept away together by the irresistible current. Character and architecture seemed to lose individuality and distinction. The new riches of the country were seldom very well spent in those days; the money that the tourist or summer citizen left behind him was apt to be used to sweep away the quaint houses, the roadside thicket, the shady woodland, that had lured him first. . . . It will remain for later generations to make amends for the sad use of riches after the war, for our injury of what we inherited, for the irreparable loss of certain ancient buildings which would have been twice as interesting in the next century as we are just beginning to be wise enough to think them in this.

By the time she wrote this late preface some of those youthful fears had disappeared. She thought the character of the people, at least, had withstood the assault and that "the individuality and the quaint personal characteristics of New England . . . are better nourished and shine brighter by contrast than in former years." Old houses, too, were no longer being demolished in great numbers, thanks to a new spirit of historic preservation. Only the natural landscape still seemed threatened, as it would increasingly throughout her life. "Sometimes," she wrote in 1892, "I get such a hunted feeling like the last wild thing that is left in the fields."[3]

Although Jewett in her preface told the truth as she remembered it, she failed to mention a motivation that was at least as important as these to her youthful self, that of the moral instruction of her readers. Always shy of preachiness herself, she may have thought that an open admission of moral purpose might cast her as a preachy writer. By her mid-forties she had long outgrown the constant churchgoing and self-conscious pieties of her *Deephaven* years, and her moral convictions, while still profoundly felt, were simply a part of who she was, as comfortable as old clothes. Nevertheless the young woman who wrote *Deephaven* took very seriously her role as moral instructor. Her conscious purpose was expressed in a letter to Parsons, where she says,

> I dont know that my chief thought in Deephaven is very
> evident, but I think I tried most, to show the truth of what
> "Kate" says on page 244*—that success and happiness are
> not things of chance but of choice, and they might so easily
> have had a dull summer. It was certainly not at all the kind
> of place that most young ladies would enjoy for their sum-
> mer's campaign—but *didn't* they have a good time! And
> there is another thing—I wished to show how interested
> they became in the town's people, and how interesting
> these people were. I am so sorry for girls who are shut up
> in their own set in society—I should be so glad if anybody
> had a better time in the country this summer because she
> had read Deephaven!"[4]

It was only recently that Jewett had changed her attitude toward her own village and begun to see it as something more than a place of tiresome exile. Under Parsons's tutelage she had come to believe that God meant her to be responsible to everyone around her. The reconciliation of country people to city people was only one aspect of her new, larger conviction that each person is respon-sible for leading an engaged life, no matter how unpromising her surroundings are.

That conviction had not changed when she wrote her criticism of Flaubert's *Madame Bovary* in 1891:

* Kate remarks that "success and happiness are not things of chance with us, but of choice. I can see how we might so easily have had a dull summer here. Of course it is our own fault if the events of our lives are hindrances; it is we who make them bad or good."

> The very great pathos of the book to me, is not the sins
> of her but the thought all the time if she *could* have had a
> little brightness and prettiness of taste in the dull doctor—
> if she could have taken *what there was* in that dull little
> village!—She is such a lesson to dwellers in country towns
> who drift out of relation to their surroundings not only
> social, but the very companionship of nature unknown
> to them.[5]

Flaubert was one of Jewett's highest literary models, and she habitually kept two maxims gleaned from his writings pinned before her when she wrote: "Écrire la vie ordinaire comme on écrit l'histoire" ("Write about daily life as you would write history") and "Ce n'est pas de faire rire, ni de faire pleurer, ni de vous mettre à fureur, mais d'agir à la façon de la nature, c'est à dire de faire rêver" ("It is not to provoke laughter, nor tears, nor rage, but to act as nature does, that is, to provoke dreaming").[6] The first underlines the precept she had learned from her father, "Write about things *just as they are.*" The second is related, as Josephine Donovan suggests, to Jewett's evocation of "a transcendent realm by means of images drawn from earthly, everyday reality": in other words, to Jewett's tendency toward symbolism, or the aura of larger meaning that surrounds things "just as they are" when they are brought into relationship by the artist.[7] Thus Flaubert exerted a double pull on Jewett as a writer: the pull of the meticulously observant observer of fact, and the pull of the poet who invests everyday reality with a new and magical significance. But his habitual stance of emotional disengagement was utterly at variance with Jewett's personal and literary temperament.

The revision of the original *Deephaven* sketches took many months of rewriting and rearranging, a kind of exhausting work to which Jewett was not at all accustomed. A comparison of the final sketches with the originals shows evidence not only of a high artistic intelligence but of a great deal of hard slogging. The original three rambling, anecdotal pieces have been rearranged and compressed to form several shorter chapters, each having its own rough thematic unity and centering on one or two characters. Names mentioned in passing in the originals have been eliminated, so as to sharpen the focus on a few people central to the narrative.

The chapters "The Circus at Denby," "Cunner-Fishing," and "Last Days at Deephaven," as well as the passage on Mrs. Patton in "Deephaven Society," are among the material added. The two friends age, from "nearly twenty-two" (p. 336) in the early sketches to "twenty-four" in *Deephaven* (p. 42).

Stylistically the work is uneven, showing its disparate origins and the author's relative mastery or clumsiness with various parts of her material. Biographically it is an interesting assemblage, showing traces of Jewett's personal and artistic development that would be more fully integrated and harder to identify later on. Sources for people and places are relatively easy to identify. For example, although she was careful to deny it publicly, the community of Deephaven is loosely based on the towns of York and Wells as Jewett knew them in the 1860s and early '70s. "If I had never known York and Wells," she later wrote, "I never could have imagined Deephaven, and so perhaps I never could have begun to write at all!"[8] It is specifically not based on South Berwick, though some of the characters and incidents may originate there. Deephaven is twelve miles from the railroad, while South Berwick was right on the line. Deephaven is fixed in the past and gently decaying, while South Berwick was economically viable and was accommodating itself, albeit with some inevitable strain, to new influences and new people. Deephaven, in the person of Miss Honora Carew, is thankful "that there had never been any manufacturing element introduced. She could not feel too grateful, herself, that there was no disagreeable foreign population" (p. 71); Kate represents enlightened South Berwick opinion when she answers, "But, wouldn't you like to have some pleasant new people brought into town?" (p. 72)

The friendship between Kate Lancaster and Helen Denis, in which one girl is the secure leader and one the worshipful follower, closely resembles several in Jewett's own life at that time—especially, as Josephine Donovan suggests, that with Kate Birckhead, but also aspects of those with Ellen Mason, Hattie Seeger, and Georgina Halliburton.[9] The source for the circus at Denby is the annual circus at Dover, a treat she continued to enjoy occasionally well into middle age. Mrs. Bonny's mountain closely resembles Mount Agamenticus, and the chapter "In Shadow" is taken from a personal experience. At least one of the male characters, Danny the fisherman, is based on a person she knew,[10] and it seems likely that Captain Sands and Captain Lant are liberally drawn either from people at York and Wells or from a composite of her grandfather's cronies. The *Pactolus* (pp. 90 and 155) was the name of one of her grandfather's ships, and the account of Captain Sands's father being left on an island as a boy is taken from her grandfather's life. The queues worn lifelong by Sands's father and Mr. Joshua Dorsey may have come from the similar hairstyle of Great-grandfather Gilman. The accounts in "Captain Sands" of the various ways sailors and captains outwit the law, and the comments on using salt for ballast in "Cunner-Fishing," are undoubtedly lifted straight from dinner-table conversation in Sarah's childhood. One wonders—on no evidence, alas—if Captain Sands himself does not owe something to Grandfather Jewett, and whether the "women-folk" from whom he takes refuge in the old warehouse are not indebted to the formidable Grandmother Mary Rice Jewett.

The sources for women characters were rich and various even this early in the writer's life, and one doubts very much if there was a single living person dominant in the character of Mrs. Kew or Mrs. Bonny. Mrs. Patton must be one of the many characters in Jewett's work partly based on Olive Grant, for she "knew everybody's secrets, but she told them judiciously if at all. She chattered all day to you as a sparrow twitters, and you did not tire of her." (p. 56) Jewett herself said that the character of Miss Chauncey was based on an encounter that happened more or less as it is described in the book;[11] the original was Miss Sally Cutts of Kittery. (It is interesting, by the way, in view of recent critical focus on Jewett as a writer for and about women whose interest in men was secondary, to note that she told Parsons in January 1877 that she had added the passage about Mrs. Patton because "I thought there ought to be one old woman gossip—as I have so many old sailors and 'longshore men.'")[12]

The references to the books that the girls read during their holiday were added during revision. Several are allusions to significant influences on Jewett's thinking and on *Deephaven* itself. One well-known influence, mentioned not in the text itself but in the preface, is Harriet Beecher Stowe's *Pearl of Orr's Island,* a chronicle of Maine country people set in a place Jewett knew well. From letters and journals we know that Stowe's books (especially *Pearl,* but also *Oldtown Folks*) meant a great deal to Jewett in the 1870s. No other writer had so accurately caught the rhythms of Maine speech and the spare emotional style of Maine people as Stowe had in *Pearl,* which Jewett read soon after it was published. Orr's Island was not far from Brunswick, where her father lectured at Bowdoin and where her cousins Charles and Alice Gilman lived. She visited it at least once while she was growing up, and an 1878 letter shows that she probably returned to it during or just after the writing of *Deephaven.*[13]

Another strong influence is "Fenelon" (*sic*), which Helen and Kate have brought along because they never go anywhere without it. The reference is almost certainly to the vastly popular *Selections from the Writings of Fénelon,* translated and edited by Eliza Cabot Follen in 1829 and reprinted many times. Introduced to the *Selections* by Ellen Mason, Jewett was drawn to the example of the archbishop's extraordinary tolerance and mildness of spirit. An advocate of liberal education for women and an opponent of the coerced conversion of the Huguenots, he was banished for suspected heresy to a remote parish, where he lived among the peasants as their priest, earning the admiration and affection of everyone who encountered him, including various invading armies. His involvement and sympathy with his small parish in spite of his high birth and high office became an example to the young, dissatisfied Jewett, and as late as the 1890s she would speak of "Fenelon" as "*the* religious book of my life."[14]

A particularly interesting antecedent to *Deephaven,* mentioned on page 74, is Elizabeth Gaskell's *Cranford,* which Jewett reread in September 1874. The chapter "Deephaven Society," with its tone of half-loving, half-mocking nostalgia and its elderly aristocrats fussing over social protocol and wearing their ancient bonnets to church, is clearly a homage to Gaskell's 1853 work, and like Gaskell, Jewett gently spoofs the gentry while cherishing their innocence and integrity. Deephaven is described as "more or less out of repair," (p. 71) and more English than American; and Miss Carew and Mrs. Dent, like the ladies of Cranford, are "contented to stay in their own house, with their books and letters and knitting," (p. 72) reading the literary journals and sending quiet thanks to heaven that their village remains unnoticed by the world. Like *Deephaven, Cranford* was originally written for serial publication. It too is anecdotal and rather static, such movement as it has centering on the moral progression of the narrator rather than on any pretense at plot. As in *Deephaven,* the care people take of one another in a small, largely female community is an important theme, though in *Cranford* it is by no means the most important.

The differences between Gaskell's book and Jewett's are as instructive as their similarities. Ineluctably British, *Cranford* is largely concerned with minute class distinctions, which loom especially large in this isolated hamlet. Gently but persistently Gaskell mocks the Cranford ladies' anxious maneuverings around the matter of precedence by birth. She spoofs, too, their practical and economic helplessness, their intellectual vacuity, and the limitations of their amusements. The few men in the village are all hearty, sensible types who, as a matter of course, are seen as potential rescuers and husbands. In keeping with literary fashion, Gaskell ties up her work with a tidy series of marital knots. Moreover, the narrator's nostalgia sweetens the hard truth that the women of Cranford are totally unable to look after themselves. The establishment of Miss Matty Jenkyns's little shop, patronized by her friends with the tacit blessing of her male competitor, only underlines that fact. The main characters all belong to the gentry; except for Matty's loyal servant, Martha, members of other classes are simply invisible.

To step from *Cranford* into the brisk sea air of Deephaven is to experience an American Revolution in miniature. The fact that the American girls are wealthy and genteel seems minor when one considers that their rank is not immutably fixed at birth, and that their parents or grandparents may have been born in just such a sleepy Maine village as this. Everyone in the village is seen as a fully developed human being. There is no parallel in the English book to the vitality of Mrs. Kew or the economic resourcefulness of Mrs. Patton and Mrs. Bonny. Where Gaskell emphasizes the helplessness of her women, Jewett emphasizes the strength of hers.

The American gentry of "Deephaven Society," a little flock of aged Anglophiles who are, "like the conies of Scripture, a feeble folk," (p. 70) are clearly no threat to the republic. Nevertheless, the author's attitude toward class in *Deephaven* has often, in this age of the politically correct, offended American readers. Gaskell and Jewett share a double view of the upper middle class, seeing its members both as preservers of traditional civility and as entrenched, often absurd upholders of an obsolete hierarchy. But whereas Gaskell—solidly middle class herself and having no pride of birth—creates a firmly middle-class protagonist who is distanced from Cranford's upper crust, Jewett's protagonists are, like the author, themselves part of the upper crust. As the daughter of Katharine Brandon's heir, Kate Lancaster inherits her status and privilege, while Helen Denis assumes for herself a social rank equal to her friend's. Both are guilty of making remarks that are ludicrously patronizing by American standards, such as Kate's about "simple country people" or Helen's about clothes: "We did not always dress as befitted our position in town. Fish-scales and blackberry-briars so soon disfigure one's clothes." (p. 251) The voice Jewett gives them is what I call her transatlantic voice: prim, anglicized, but stripped of all vigor British or American, so that it seems a kind of precious relic of the schoolroom, a memorial to childhood efforts not to fall into slovenly colonial idiom. It is the voice of one who would rather die than split an infinitive, and whose utmost expression of joyful anticipation can go no further than Kate's "We shall have such jolly housekeeping!" (p. 14) And it is very close to the voice of Jewett's own letters to Anna Dawes and Lillian Munger.

The questioning of Jewett's class consciousness is not misplaced. She held some opinions about the genetic superiority of early Scandinavians, for example, that today we would find as objectionable as they are absurd. Genetics was in its infancy in Jewett's day, and like many of her contemporaries she had some confused notions about nature versus nurture. She valued gentility in its radical form, as deriving from the quality of being gentle; it is safe to say that she valued it above any other human trait. She knew it best in the elderly in her own life, among them her great-aunts, Anne Rice and Elizabeth Cushing. Chaucer's "gentilesse" seemed an immutable, perhaps biological quality in those who possessed it.

In *Deephaven* Kate Lancaster has inherited her aunt's status in the community as an unquestioned right, and in the chapter "Miss Chauncey," Helen pronounces Kate and Miss Chauncey to be of the same "stamp and rank" in what seems to be a genetic allusion. But gentility is also an instinct of the heart, and ladies can be made as well as born. The nuns who heal Danny are "real ladies" by inclination (p. 109); and in a passage about Miss Brandon, Jewett talks of gentility as a matter of choice, the conscious preservation of behavioral standards:

> It seems to me that it is a great privilege to have an elderly
> person in one's neighborhood, in town or country, who is
> proud, and conservative, and who lives in stately fashion;
> who is intolerant of sham and of useless novelties, and
> clings to the old ways of living and behaving as if it were
> part of her religion. (p. 44)

Both Miss Chauncey and Miss Brandon come of "good stock" (although Miss Chauncey's is lamentably burdened by a curse). But it is not Miss Brandon's pedigree that is important, it is her integrity and her way of living. As for Miss Chauncey, we are left to decide whether her beautiful manners are as biologically fixed as breathing. Sarah Orne Jewett's cousin Frances liked to tell the story of calling on an old gentleman in Exeter, a retired headmaster of Phillips Academy. The old man's wits were completely gone, and he mistook Frances for her long-dead aunt and presently forgot she was there at all. But when she rose to leave he said with exquisite courtesy, "Will you not stay and drink tea with us? You will always find a place at our table."[15] Like Miss Chauncey's, his beautiful manners seemed an indelible part of his being, surviving long after reason itself had departed.

The upper-class airs of Helen and Kate are softened in two ways. One is their conscious adherence to childhood. Like Jewett herself, they distrust adulthood; they come to Deephaven to play house together and be free of the bothersome carping of grown-ups. Like Jewett's, their choice can be seen as an irresponsible flouting of privilege or a fearful regression.* But the narrator clearly distinguishes between "childish" and "childlike," (p. 42) and in their playfulness the girls gain what Jewett herself gained: a freshness

---

* Ann Romines, for example, argues that Helen and Kate retreat into childhood to avoid confronting adult experience. ("In *Deephaven*," Nagel, pp. 44–45)

and enthusiasm that allows them to enjoy a circus or a fishing expedition with all the zest of a ten-year-old, while subverting the class divisions that would separate them from Deephaveners. To the villagers their naiveté makes them seem approachable and nonthreatening. Older people like Mrs. Kew, Mrs. Patton, and Captain Sands take an indulgent, slightly protective attitude toward them, while the shy fisherman Danny lets down his guard and Miss Chauncey invites them to invisible tea. Everyone sees them as they see themselves, and the book becomes possible. In Jewett's own life, the same openness and lifelong ability to be delighted and surprised disarmed the people she met and kept her perpetually engaged, at once the wondering child and the observant, inquisitive writer.

Even more important, in terms of the book's theme, is Kate's "unusual power of winning people's confidence." (pp. 42–43) Whatever upper-class pretensions she has are canceled out by her impulsive sympathy. It is Kate who tames the local pirate by nursing his injured hand, and who helps Danny out of his embarrassment at having told too much about himself to strangers. It is Kate who reacts most strongly to the hardhearted aunt in "In Shadow"; and it is Kate who, belying her own snobbery, answers Miss Carew's comment about the "foreign element" with the question about bringing "pleasant new people" into town. Specifically because she *is* upper class, she has a responsibility to demonstrate the irrelevance of class in human relationships.

When Mrs. Patton meets the girls, her initial confusion briefly reflects the social ambiguity of their relationship. She half curtsies to Helen when she mistakes her for Kate, but then shakes Kate's hand like a democrat and calls her "dear" like a mother. She has taken care of the house out of pure neighborly goodwill, but she is half-apologetic about it, as if she had been hired. She *has* been hired, in the past, to help Miss Brandon from time to time, and Kate's mother has in fact sent her "a handsome present o' money." (p. 52) But we know she would have looked after the house whether or not she was paid, just as Miss Brandon looked after her thirty or forty years earlier when she was sick and destitute. She is both friend and servant, the very embodiment of New England "help," a personage unthinkable in the world of *Cranford.* She mourns for Miss Brandon "as if it was my own sister." (p. 50) Miss Brandon was a "proud woman," but far more important, she was a "good Christian woman." (pp. 49–50)

Closely related to class in both *Deephaven* and *Cranford* is the role of ritual. In Cranford, as in any English village of its time, ritual serves to reaffirm the fixed place of each character in the class system. Gaskell has some fun with this, but nevertheless it is an immutable given. In *Deephaven* and in Jewett's work generally, ritual serves to bring people together: through the small daily ceremonies of tea-drinking and calls and the larger ones of funerals and town celebrations, people acknowledge and strengthen their responsibility to one another. Miss Carew's adherence to old, endangered forms of civility is a tie both to the gentle dead and to the people around her. Miss Chauncey's manners demonstrate the strength of her sense of responsibility to other people, which outlasts her memory of who they are; and her piety demonstrates the strength of her responsibility to God. Tradition, in this sense, is an expression of community.

But of course Miss Carew is absurd, and Miss Chauncey is mad, and neither one has or ever has had any social conscience to speak of. Tradition has its limits and must be supplemented by living experience. It can be outworn and empty, and then it becomes comic, as in the chapter "The Circus at Denby," when Helen and Kate invite Mrs. Kew to go to the circus with them. Mrs. Kew regards this as a formal invitation and is a little flustered at consorting with the gentry. She sets out decked out in her Sunday best and bowing stiffly to all her acquaintances. But her honesty and vitality cannot sustain this performance, and it all collapses when she makes one of her pungent remarks and all three women break up laughing. The proprieties always get short shrift from Mrs. Kew, as in the scene where she first meets the girls and they offer her a sour orange. "Lemons with oranges' clothes on, aren't they?" she says, (p. 17) and the girls throw theirs out the window. Mrs. Kew has just been effusively grateful because Helen has changed seats with her, but she won't be polite over a sour orange. Her great strength is that she is "straightforward and kindly"; and she and Miss Carew share an abhorrence of sham. Tradition and ceremony are valuable only when they are nourished by human experience; when they lose that vivifying influence, they become a barrier to be overcome.

Another direct influence on *Deephaven,* again mentioned directly in the text, is *A Summer in Leslie Goldthwaite's Life,* by Adeline Dutton Train Whitney. Jewett's delight in discovering this book in her mid-teens had led her to write an admiring letter to the author, and she was still singing its praises to her friends a decade later. "I think no book ever did me more good than that blessed 'Leslie Goldthwaite,'" she wrote Anna Dawes in 1876. "The older I grow the more I find in it."[16]

The resemblances to *Deephaven* are not hard to find. In *Leslie Goldthwaite* an upper-middle-class girl from the city spends a summer at a resort in the White Mountains with some friends, encountering a variety of people from whom she learns lessons of compassion, usefulness, and tolerance. The social environment is mostly, though not entirely, female, and although the book is largely focused on the city people, there are character vignettes of country people as well. The natural world is both setting and moral touchstone for the social scene, and the moral sensitivity of the characters is directly related to their sensitivity to nature. The underlying message is both Christian and Emersonian: one of Leslie's moral tutors is Marmaduke Wharne, an eccentric English clergyman whose kindly temper is severely tried by the noisy invasion of summer tourists in God's wilderness. "'Who shall ascend into the hill of the Lord?'" he booms at Leslie, sensing a kindred spirit and slightly misquoting the 121st Psalm. "'And who shall stand in his holy place? He that hath clean hands and a pure heart; who hath not lifted up his soul unto vanity.'" (p. 56) Even more important to Leslie's moral education is a vigorous elderly spinster, Miss Craydocke, who fills her room with ferns, flowers, and curious rocks and her days with unobtrusive good deeds. "God had given her, the lonely woman, the larger motherhood," says the narrator. (p. 166) Together they point the girl toward the Emersonian ideal of an integrated universe in which the social order and the natural order both reflect and express an all-pervasive divine will. And Whitney's concept of "the larger motherhood," along with influences in Jewett's own life, must have contributed to the creation of a long succession of motherly women characters, from

Mrs. Kew to Mrs. Todd, who draw on the power of the natural order to heal and minister to their neighbors.

It is not surprising to find that Kate and Helen in *Deephaven* have tucked Emerson's essays into their luggage and look forward to reading them "together, out of doors." (p. 250) Jewett had been familiar with the essays since childhood, and she knew the Emerson family through her old friend Annie French Bartlett in Concord. Dr. Jewett himself was an Emersonian man, relying more on individual sympathy, reason, and experience than on formal medical lore for his skill in medicine. His love of nature, too, went beyond love of the picturesque and suggests a naturalist's fascination with the unifying principles, whether material or spiritual, underlying the natural world.

The need for tradition to be refreshed and revised by experience is one clearly Emersonian theme in *Deephaven*. Another is the moral influence of nature. The natural world is an active and benevolent presence, enfolding the characters and subtly influencing and reflecting their feelings and behavior. Thus Katharine Brandon's house is set among flourishing poplars, elms, roses, and boxwoods, and the girls spend their days roaming woods and beaches and, like Whitney's Miss Craydocke, fill their sitting room with wildflowers and ferns. Mrs. Bonny, the first of Jewett's mediators between nature and humanity, lives in a clearing in a cathedral-like forest, where the young beech leaves color the light like stained-glass windows, and the hemlock branches bear bright tips of new growth like candles. Often Jewett's nature passages serve as interludes between episodes or chapters, framing the action in the calm and beauty of nature: in the sunset passage at the end of "The Brandon House and the Lighthouse" (pp. 39–40)—a passage added in revision—the hint of a world beyond and an immanent divine intelligence becomes an open simile, with the image of a small boat drifting into an infinity made visible by light.

A less obvious Emersonian theme is kindness and mutual responsibility. Too individualistic to value community in the usual sense, Emerson nevertheless measured the height of a person's spiritual attunement in terms of moral responsibility. "So much benevolence as a man hath," he said in the "Divinity School Address," "so much life hath he." For our own purpose, we might gloss this sentence with another from "The American Scholar":

"The only thing in the world, of value, is the active soul." The active soul is one that is alive to the resonances of larger life in all beings, and one way to read *Deephaven* is as a picture of a community of active souls. Mrs. Whitney in *Leslie Goldthwaite* clearly distinguishes between active and passive souls, with the Rev. Mr. Wharne as her Emersonian model. In the course of revision, Jewett varied this by showing us *only* active souls; that is, she eliminated extraneous characters so that we are introduced only to a select few of the inhabitants of Deephaven. We know they are not all as generous-spirited as these, for the village contains people like the late, unlamented Jim Patton, who once threw an ironstone bottle at his wife that left a permanent dent in her forehead. But Jewett concentrates on the miniature community within the larger one, the people who serve as mentors to the two girls and whose spiritual health is the best hope of the rest. These are the characters who show the girls how the human spirit, enclosed in its own fears, needs, lethargy, and obsolete customs, can break free to connect with others.

A final powerful influence on *Deephaven,* not mentioned in the book but vitally important to Jewett herself when she wrote it, is the Swedenborgian belief of Theophilus Parsons. This is not to say that Jewett was familiar with Swedenborgianism itself, with its complex supernatural hierarchies and its demons and angels. She only knew the New Church through the medium of Parsons, who emphasized the Christian and ethical aspects of Swedenborg's teachings and explained the core beliefs in an innocuous and accessible form. In Parsons' writings Jewett found a universe where barriers between spirit and matter become negligible, pain becomes but a temporary test of the eternal soul, evil is a necessary and explainable accompaniment to free will, the afterlife is certain and will be comfortably familiar, and everything is infused with the divine spirit. No person is excluded from the hope of eternal life, and love and compassion for our fellow human beings is our single most important task on earth.

Presented thus in simple terms, Parsons's teachings reinforced Jewett's readings of Emerson and the Christian precepts of loving interdependence she had absorbed from a number of sources since childhood. There is one thematic thread in *Deephaven* that we can probably trace directly to Swedenborg, and that is the belief in the transmigration of consciousness. As Parsons explained it, "The soul while in the material body makes that body live, and through it perceives the things of this material world." In death, "we, in our spiritual body, rise from the material body." But the spiritual world to which we pass is only a purged replica of the one we have left. In such a universe, it does not seem unlikely that spirits might communicate not only between worlds but within the material world.[17] In a century of unsettling religious and scientific flux, when none of the old dogmas was immune to question, many intellectually respectable and even brilliant people, including William James, Elizabeth Barrett Browning, and Sir Arthur Conan Doyle, accepted the possibility of some kind of extra-body communication while rejecting the obvious flummery of table-rappings and "ectoplasmic" phenomena. Parsons belongs in this company, and it seems certain that, as Elizabeth Ammons suggests, Jewett's enduring interest in spiritualism and ESP began during her friendship with him.[18]

In *Deephaven* instances of extrasensory phenomena are common and are evidence of the power of the unconfined spirit. Both Captain Lant and Captain Sands believe in ESP and tell stories about it. Captain Lant's story about Ben Dighton's uncle (in "The Captains") is a rattling good tale, told within a double frame so that both the narrator and the author are well distanced from it. (Jewett often used such frames for stories of the supernatural, presumably to avoid any tiresome questions about her own beliefs.) Captain Sands, for his part, has arrived at his tentative belief in ESP through observation ("One time I waked a man up out of sound sleep looking at him, and it set me to thinking" [p. 173]) and through the experiences of three members of his family. When he and the girls narrowly beat a storm to shore, he believes his wife has warned him by a thought-message, as he thinks she has before. Captain Sands's tales about his relations and ESP were added in 1877, suggesting the growing importance of Parsons to Jewett over the intervening years.

Accepting the possible fluidity of human consciousness, Sands possesses an imagination that will not acknowledge any limitations on the human spirit. In keeping with this generosity of soul, he is surrounded in his warehouse retreat by objects that each carry a bit of living human history. We have seen that objects and houses had a keenly evocative quality for Sarah Orne Jewett. They were a means of restoring lost connections with people whose lives, long past, continued to shape the lives of those who came after them. As Helen says at the end of the book, "something of [the dead] still lingers where their lives were spent":

> We are often reminded of our friends who have died; why are we not reminded as surely of strangers in such a house as this,—finding some trace of the lives which were lived among the sights we see and the things we handle?
> (p. 246)

The contents of the Italian sailor's chest, like Aunt Katharine's old letters and like the circus recalling the past to Kate and Mrs. Kew, are a means of healing the ruptures in communal consciousness caused by time and death. Captain Sands does not, of course, summon up the dead; but his sympathies reach back and imaginatively reknit their lives to the present, just as his wife's sympathy has reached across space to warn him of danger.

The narratives involving the Deephaven men—Captain Lant, Captain Sands, and Danny—are roughly grouped together, so that their related tales of imaginative communication, whether with the past, or between living persons, or between persons of different (Christian) faiths, or even (in Danny's case) between members of different species, are interwoven as different threads of the same theme: the extension of human affection across barriers of matter, time, or prejudice. In *Deephaven* terms, these chapters give us the male version of the theme of community, based largely on the community they know best, that of sailors and fishermen. The role of the men is largely anecdotal and their characters necessarily more cobbled-together than those of the women, but nevertheless we see in the men the same human concerns and the same elevation of spirit over letter as in the women. As kindly in his way as Mrs. Patton or Mrs. Kew, Captain Sands is proud that he managed to convince the captain of the *Polly and Susan* to insure his life, saving his widow from destitution. His moral education, like that of all the main characters, has been slowly and painfully gained by experience: "I've tried to be honest, and to do just about as nigh right as I could, and you know there's an old sayin' that a cripple in the right road will beat a racer in the wrong." (p. 123)

But it is through the characters of the older women, members of "the larger motherhood," that the power of sympathy is most fully expressed. The power of womanly community and the maternal relationships between older and younger women in Jewett's works have become a focus of feminist criticism in recent years, particularly in relation to *The Country of the Pointed Firs.* Women as mothers, women as healers, women as upholders of enduring human values—these are the most distinctive and appealing characters in Jewett's work, culminating after twenty years in the imperturbable and unforgettable Almira Todd.[19] In *Deephaven* we meet the first of Jewett's long succession of motherly mentors and wise countrywomen. Mrs. Kew and Mrs. Patton establish their maternal relation to the girls at once by addressing them as "dear." Mrs. Bonny is more distant, as befits her wilder, less conventional way of life, but Jewett establishes her motherliness immediately by means of an injured horse in the yard and an invalid hen behind the kitchen stove. Mrs. Bonny is a healer, a brewer of herbal remedies, the first of many intermediaries between the natural and human worlds. Mrs. Patton is a nurse and accommodator, bringing to households disrupted by sickness or loss a comfort that is the more valuable because of the suffering she herself has endured. Mrs. Kew's main function is candor; she tells the truth. But she comes to love the girls more than they realize, and tells them as they leave that she loves them as if they belonged to her. All these women are middle-aged or older, and all are mothers in the larger sense. They have learned what they know simply by living long and conscious lives. Or, to come back to Emerson, "So much only of life as I know by experience, so much of the wilderness have I vanquished and planted, or so far have I extended my being, my dominion." ("The American Scholar")

In one crucial respect *Deephaven* turns away from Emerson. The natural world is a hostile as well as a benevolent environment. In its Emersonian aspect, nature is seen not only as a divine manifestation but as a practical source of food. No one starves in Deephaven, and when the girls have forgotten to buy fish for dinner they can simply catch some. But we are never far from the darker side of nature, the side Emerson never acknowledged but that this captain's granddaughter, whose uncle had been lost at sea, knew very well. The wives in these stories—Mrs. Kew, Mrs. Lant, and Mrs. Sands—dislike the sea and know it first of all as dangerous. Its power to kill and maim flickers along under the surface of the sketches, showing itself in the gravestones, in the maiming of Danny and the death of the Italian, in the wrecks along the coast, and in Captain Sands's sudden alarm at the sight of storm clouds. The lighthouse itself testifies to the destructiveness of the sea.

Life beyond the village is not necessarily miserable, and we cannot set up a rigid schema in which safety lies entirely within the embrace of community and danger lurks outside. Helen says there are prosperous farms to the west, although the author does not show them to us. It is clear, however, that the farther one goes from the watchful eyes of the active souls of Deephaven, the more chancy life becomes. Outside the village and its protective network of human affection, isolation and natural calamity can set up their own cycle of suffering. The first hint of this is seen in "The Circus at Denby," when the girls meet the consumptive Mr. Craper and his ragged children some distance outside of town. Later they visit East Parish, where Miss Chauncey lives. Hardly more than a dilapidated hamlet, it is still barely within the limits of the town, and Miss Chauncey is not allowed to starve.

The chapter "In Shadow," based on an experience of Jewett's that she never described except in *Deephaven,* shows us both faces of nature. The girls choose a tourist-perfect July day for their drive up the coast with Mr. Dockum, but the land is so poor that "even the trees looked hungry," and they wonder what it would look like "when there was a storm and the great waves come thundering in?" (p. 205) Even so, the place is by no means desolate, and wildflowers and thin grass blades manage to survive. The family they meet is as spunky as the wildflowers, but spunk is not feeding them. The man's trade has failed, his land is too poor to feed his family, and their only means of support is a son working in a Boston factory. The girls overpay the farmer for watching their horses and afterwards send "some things" to his family, but they put off going back until October.

The second excursion also is undertaken on a delightful day, but the mood darkens almost imperceptibly. Leander Dockum laughs at the tale of the mad old man watching for his lost fisherman son, and is puzzled when the girls don't join in. Leander is only a boy—a kind of savage in the smaller community of caring adults—and his role as guide on this expedition, like his father's on the earlier one, is in keeping with its general tone. Appropriately too, the roadside plants and animals subtly change in a description Jewett added in revision. Fragrant bayberries give way to faded ferns and frostbitten asters, while the barberry fruit, which any attentive Maine housewife would have gathered, hangs neglected. Jewett is never bitter toward nature and never portrays it as melodramatically hostile, and so the friends see squirrels gathering acorns, a sleepy owl, a rabbit, flocks of migrating birds. But there is a faint sense of oncoming threat, as well as of life providing for itself and hunkering down.

They find the family broken. The parents are dead of disease and drink, and the orphaned children are about to be divided up between a whining, tightfisted aunt (somewhat redeemed by a gentle husband) and some anonymous "folks over to the cove." (p. 212) The girls leave a basket for the children and helplessly watch as the dead father's funeral procession walks down the road. The air turns cold and bleak, and the gulls high above them fight the wind and give "now and then a wild, far-off ringing cry." (p. 200)

Here Jewett has written herself into the social reality for which, as has been often observed, she had no adequate answer. This far from the safe "haven" of the town, community fails; the girls themselves fail, although they could easily have helped these children. They are baffled, presumably, not only by this one suffering family but by all the others it represents. Baffled herself, Jewett falls back on Swedenborg. Helen and Kate are suddenly conscious of "the mystery and inevitableness of death; it was not fear, thank God! but a thought of how certain it was that some day it would be a mystery to us no longer." They think of "how close this familiar, every-day world might be to the other." (pp. 221–22) Cold comfort to us, this represented to Jewett herself a solid belief to which she held all her life. Wrongs would be righted, suffering expunged: it was not a vague hope but a certainty.

Incidentally, there was an amusing editorial sleight of hand connected with this passage. Apparently William Dean Howells, editing the funeral description for the *Atlantic* sketch "Deephaven Excursions," silently deleted the above passage and several other similar paragraphs. The resulting narrative is short, lean, and movingly understated. Parsons, reading it in the magazine without being aware it had been changed, criticized the sketch in general and this passage in particular for lack of explicit moral content. In her reply, Jewett lamented her lost paragraphs:

> I know you would have felt better satisfied with the funeral sketch if the authorities (Howells!) had not left out a few paragraphs which I wrote carefully and which held for me the meaning of that pathetic break-up of a pitiful family. I don't remember it very accurately now, but I know I said something about our lives having two sides and although we might be apparent failures in this world there was still a chance that life had been a grand success. And I said how few in this world poor or rich touched satisfaction, and how this man's hopes and wishes might all have been realized in a decent sort of farm and a thousand or two dollars in the bank. And I said that when his wife died his world had come to an end, as it were, and he was bewildered and discouraged and could not fight so hard and so useless a battle as life seemed to him.—There was something, too, (which followed the man's saying that he had "gone"—when the funeral had left the house—) about the invisible world's being so near—but I can't remember that at all.[20]

Jewett was too shy to ask Howells for her original manuscript, but when she revised the sketches as a book she rewrote as much of the excised material as she could remember. Some of it appears in a stilted dialogue between Kate and Helen on pages 216–17.

Like the themes of women's community or female bonding, various aspects of Jewett's transcendentalism have been examined in the scholarly literature. Again, most of these discussions have centered on later works, with particular emphasis on *The Country of the Pointed Firs.* As early as 1973, Michael Vella published a discussion of *Pointed Firs* linking it to themes of Emerson and Thoreau. Gayle L. Smith has said of Jewett's 1884 story "A White Heron" that "it is clear that [the close connection between man and nature] is but part of a larger, truly transcendental vision unifying man not only with green nature but with animal life as well, the past with the present, and one human sensibility with another." Marcia McClintock Folsom has noted the power of empathy in *Pointed Firs* not only to unite the living inhabitants of Dunnet Landing but to bind people across time, the living and the dead.[21]

In *Deephaven* we see the earliest expression of the transcendentalism that became the spiritual underpinning of Jewett's work. Clearly owing much to Emerson and Parsons, it is limited by neither and assumes a pervasive, divinely infused continuum embracing all forms of life and reaching across barriers of time and death. Warmer and more human-centered than Emerson's transcendentalism, it is domesticated and particularized, based less on mystical experience than on the breathing reality of daily life. It envisions no cold Oversoul but a highly personal and attentive Deity, whose love for humanity is expressed not only through nature and the workings of Providence but through human affection and moral responsibility.

To say this is not to insist that Jewett in her early twenties intended to sit down and write a transcendentalist book. She has said that her purpose in writing *Deephaven* was (at the time) to morally educate her readers, and (retrospectively) to mediate between country and city people and to draw attention to an eroding cultural heritage. Both these stated purposes are clearly evident in the book. But emerging from the finished work, beyond all these, is a picture of spiritual community that reflects, possibly more than she realized, the pattern of values she herself was beginning to hold dear. The *Deephaven* sketches show us the young Jewett trying, like anyone that age, to fit her own experience into some kind of ethical framework, drawing now on Swedenborg, now on Emerson, now on the Christian ethos of Fénelon and the church. That the framework is not, in the end, quite large enough is not surprising. What is surprising is the amount of human experience she quietly tucks into it, including death, severe injury, insanity, suicide, loneliness, poverty, public humiliation, alcoholism, disease, wife abuse, and the torture of animals. Somehow, all this can be seen as a bearable part of the whole. Misery and cruelty are seen in a context in which most people, most of the time, can still cope. The unspoken but constant assumption is that they cannot cope if the living currents of sympathy and memory between people and between generations fail. Physically excluded from the spiritual network maintained by a few active souls within Deephaven, the Crapers, the orphaned children, and some other sufferers in the book will face continued pain. Jewett in the 1870s, and indeed all her life, was not able to write them out of that pain. She did persistently depict (and who can argue with her?) compassion and the recognition of human interconnectedness as the only defense against the darker forces outside the village bounds.

9

Beyond the Village

CONTRIBUTING TO SARAH'S UNHAPPI-
ness in the early seventies was her sense that, although she was on
good terms with many young women in Berwick, she had no
"crony" there to confide in. In her twenties she found herself
suddenly alone, without intellectual peers, left behind by casual
childhood companions who had married or moved away, grieving
for the grandmother who had been her friend, suddenly critical of
the confinement and pettiness of small-town life. Her sisters were
still there, to be sure, and Mary at least seems to have qualified as
a "crony": "I can scarcely wait until Saturday to see Mary," Sarah
wrote to Aunt Lucretia Perry in 1872. "I 'want to see her' in the
same fashion that I do Kate or Grace—only more so. . . ."[1] But
since the pattern of the sisters' lives decreed that they never were
away from home at the same time, Mary was absent for weeks at
a time during those winter months when Sarah was ill and needed
companionship. Winters were hard to bear, both because of her
illness and because she did not feel she could in fairness invite her
city friends to Berwick when it was so "cold and forlorn."[2] "Berwick
has grown quite uninteresting to me for once in its life," she
complained to Howells, "and everybody is distressingly grown up
and I have 'nobody to play with.'"[3]

Considering the actual amount of time she spent away from
home, her discontent is surprising. For example: In the fall of
1872–73 she undertook a marathon round of visiting that took her

to the West, New York, and Philadelphia; she was away from home at least five months. In the fall of 1873 she traveled to Canada with her parents. Most of the following winter was spent in Philadelphia with her Orne and McHenry cousins. In 1876 she went to the Philadelphia Centennial twice, once with her sisters and once with her father. Early in 1877 she was away seven weeks, visiting in Concord, Massachusetts, Boston, and Exeter. From January through April 1878 she amused herself in Washington, D.C., Philadelphia, New York City, Springfield, Massachusetts, and Boston. The winter of 1878–79 found her spending several weeks in Cambridge, Newport, and Boston. All this, plus many shorter excursions and several weeks at the coast every summer, meant that she was hardly ever at home for more than two or three months without a break. Clearly her loneliness had more to do with her general depression in the seventies and her intellectual distance from her Berwick neighbors than with any physical isolation.

In part the problem began to solve itself when, with Parsons's help, she began to interest herself in village affairs and feel that her life and work were meant to evolve in relationship to that particular place. But she was also reaching out beyond Berwick, as she began to meet people who took her well outside her customary sphere. She met them in various ways: some of them came to her through her new literary associations, especially Howells, and some through her own family or old friends. Soon they began to form the nucleus of the wide circle of friendships that would always secure her to the larger world, no matter how much time she actually spent in Berwick.

One tantalizing question for the Jewett scholar is how many of the intimate friends of the eighties and nineties, whose collective minds and experiences would have extended a young writer's vision very rapidly indeed, were established friends before Sarah became the companion of Annie Fields. In default of hard evidence, it is easy to suppose that the escalation of the Fields friendship in 1881 brought about a sudden debut into the cosmopolitan world the Fieldses inhabited, and that except for her correspondence and occasional meetings with her editors, Sarah was very much a country mouse until then. But we have seen how the very act of visiting her editor brought her close to several people who would later become dear to her. The Boston-Cambridge literary fellowship being what it was, Howells's house was only one of several where such meetings could occur. Although the question of precisely when she met each friend cannot be answered, when one counts up the people she definitely knew in the 1870s and considers the overlapping circles they moved in, one begins to see that she was rapidly expanding her horizons as early as mid-decade. The comfortably involuted social pattern of the city's writers, publishers, and literary fellow-travelers in some ways resembled the Gilman-Perry-Jewett clan, with its intricate network of double in-laws and double cousins. To be friendly with two or three key people in the group was to run into most of the others at one time or another, especially if one were young, gregarious, and socially interesting. When the physical venue widened, as it did in Jewett's case, to include New York and Washington, the chances of encountering the same people in several different houses multiplied. Even though we cannot know (to use the familiar modern phrase) exactly Whom She Knew and When She Knew Them, we can make some fairly educated guesses.

To begin with the obvious, some of these friendships dated from childhood, for the family's distinguished connections were not limited to politics. Aunt Helen's close friends in Portland, for example, included the sister of Henry Wadsworth Longfellow. Among Sarah's childhood playmates in Exeter were the sculptor Daniel Chester French and his sister Annie, now Annie French Bartlett of Concord, Massachusetts. Sarah visited Annie at least twice in the seventies, and through her came to know the entire Emerson family—especially the sprightly Ellen—and other Concord literati. Through Aunt Mary Bell and her husband, Charles,*

---

* Charles Henry Bell (1823–93) was yet another of Sarah's distinguished relations, although related only by marriage. A lawyer, judge, and historian, he was president of the board of trustees of Phillips Exeter Academy, helped found the Robinson Female Academy in Exeter, edited *The Exeter News-Letter*, and was governor of New Hampshire in 1880–82. A local obituary described him as representative of those qualities in the older generation Sarah Orne Jewett most revered: "He was among the last of those 'gentlemen of the old school,' who are passing away so rapidly under the adverse influences of this age of hurry . . . [who are] courteous to women, even to the extent of a little formality; who do not slight etiquette through fear of becoming bound by it, and who, when most off duty, are never off guard."

she met Judge Mellen Chamberlain in 1874, one of several mentors in her early writing years. Among the others was Eben Norton Horsford of Cambridge, a professor of applied science at Harvard whose theories on early Norse settlement in New England may have stimulated Sarah's own later interest in Germanic peoples.

Sometime in the early seventies she met the family of Charles Eliot Norton. Sarah often formed friendships with children, and during one of her Philadelphia visits she met young Sara Norton (born 1864), her sisters, and their mother. She rapidly grew fond of them, but the family spent much time in Europe, where Sara's mother died in 1872. After mid-decade the Nortons traveled less, living at their Cambridge estate, Shady Hill. An affectionate letter to Sara Norton in April 1875 suggests Sarah saw them as often as possible when her Cambridge and Boston visits coincided with their residence there. (In a refreshing reversal of the humility she expressed to those she perceived as her elders and betters, she boasted jubilantly to Sara, "I think by the time you come home (if you give me time enough!) I shall be a *great* author!"[4])

When she grew older, Sara Norton became an accomplished cellist, one of several gifted Boston-area women musicians whose talents were necessarily confined to private musicales; and all the Norton women, especially Sara's Aunt Grace, were remarkably well educated and well traveled, their experience as citizens of the world equaling that of their Cambridge neighbors the Jameses. Charles Eliot Norton, former editor with Lowell of *The North American Review,* was just beginning his legendary career as professor of fine arts at Harvard, during which he singlehandedly established the study of art history within the college curriculum. The family belonged to a transatlantic network of literary friendships that included Henry James, Jr., Emerson, Dickens, Ruskin, Carlyle, Lowell, and Elizabeth Gaskell, for whom Norton's daughter Lily was named. They were related to the Darwins and James Russell Lowell by marriage and to many of the Boston intelligentsia by blood.

An encyclopedically learned man, Norton was also a lugubrious and prescient critic of American mores and culture. The saintly Episcopal minister Phillips Brooks, who spent his days trying to change the society Norton despaired of, once remarked in exasperation, "Norton says that art is dead, patriotism is dead, religion is dead. What are you going to do with a man like that?"⁵ In spite of this he became a sympathetic critic of Jewett's work, one who as she put it late in life "in the old days . . . always saw and knew what I tried to do in my stories." With a serenity greatly at variance with Norton's own bitterness, Jewett's sketches express that veneration of the best of the past which for Norton was the very heart of his thought and work. "You teach me," she wrote him, ". . . to hold fast to the best things and not forget them for the sake of the second best."⁶ Probably the friendship did not mature for several years after they met, but the seeds for this relationship, also, were sown in the seventies.

Friends she met toward the end of the decade included Elizabeth (Lily) and Charles Fairchild of Boston and Newport. The very type of cultivated, literate, wealthy Bostonians, the Fairchilds were patrons of John Singer Sargent and Robert Louis Stevenson, whom they welcomed to America when he arrived with his family in 1887 in search of a cure for his lung ailment. Another was Harriet Waters Preston, whom Sarah met in 1877 through the Bartletts and with whom she spent two weeks or more at York that summer. Preston was the first older woman author she knew well, and for a time she regarded her with all the childlike awe she felt toward Howells or Parsons, overlaid with that adoration she felt only toward other women. At age twenty-seven she pleaded for guidance from Preston, whom she had in fact already far outdistanced as a writer:

> I hope you will tell me the faults of [*Deephaven*]—I think it
> is beautiful to be praised and it helps one of course. I know
> you said in your first letter to me that perhaps your belief
> in me would help me, and you do not know how wonder-
> fully true that has been, dear Miss Preston. But honest criti-
> cism helps one so very much, and do not ever be afraid to
> scold at me or to say anything you please. I love you so
> much and I cant get over that dear feeling that I belong to
> you, and wont you talk to me and teach me and tell me
> where I am wrong?—I am finding out as I grow older, that
> I am very young about many things—and in spite of this I
> am used to taking care of myself and all that sort of

thing—and putting those two things together sometimes
brings an unhappy result.[7]

Sometime within the next two or three years the friendship suddenly and unaccountably went sour; Preston, offended at something
Sarah said or did, withdrew into the distance, leaving Sarah—who
never offended anyone, except on those rare occasions when she
meant to—puzzled and vexed. They met accidentally some years
later and were polite, but the friendship was never renewed.

Within the Episcopal Cluster, Ellen Frances Mason was already
beginning one of those quietly useful careers that, because of their
informality, their variety, their unsalaried status, and the fact that
the women who undertook them deliberately avoided attention, are
generally lumped under the term *philanthropy.* Like several of
Sarah's later friends, including Annie Fields, she was a conservative
woman who worked conscientiously for various social causes within
the existing system. She also published a translation of Plato, was
one of the founders of Radcliffe College, and helped found a
precursor to Radcliffe, the Society to Encourage Studies at Home.
In 1873, led by Norton's cousin Anna Eliot Ticknor, a group of
Boston-area women, including Mason and her sister, Ida, Elizabeth
Cary Agassiz, and Katharine P. Loring, set up a correspondence
course for women on the college level with the modest aim of
preparing them for motherhood or teaching, establishing sound
study habits, and breaking their addiction to romantic novels.
Mason took charge of the French department, which meant enlisting faculty, setting up a curriculum, and individually tutoring a
number of students through correspondence. (Loring, head of the
history department, enlisted her friend Alice James as an instructor.) Soon the program took on a life of its own. Word of it spread
across the country, helped along by some plumping by Howells in
The Atlantic, and women hungry for instruction flooded Ticknor's
desk with applications and pleas for advice. The society, which its
founders had thought would only be a local affair, lasted over two
decades and filled an important need before it was gradually eased
out by women's colleges. Sarah Orne Jewett did not participate in
the program but sympathized strongly and through Mason must
have met at least some of the faculty members. In 1875 she asked
Ellen to send the society's circular to her Washington friend, Anna

Dawes, and when Ellen forgot to do so, Sarah addressed the envelope herself and sent it to Ellen to forward.

Eben Horsford's daughter, Lilian, was an active member of a similar organization, the Women's Education Association, which for several years lobbied Harvard's stubbornly resistant president, Charles Eliot (another Norton cousin), in order to gain admission for women undergraduates. Helped by some prominent male liberals, the women eventually won their case, and the "Harvard Annex," later Radcliffe College, was opened in 1879. Several of Sarah's close friends in the 1880s and 1890s—among them Annie Fields, Sarah Wyman Whitman, Elizabeth Cary Agassiz, and Agnes Irwin—were among the supporters or founders of Radcliffe, Agassiz becoming its first president and Irwin its first dean. In the 1870s she was at least acquainted with some of the early activists, who besides those just mentioned included Alice Longfellow and Stella Scott Gilman, the niece of Sarah's publisher, Henry Oscar Houghton, and a close friend of the Jewetts' friend Annie Johnson of Bradford Academy. Among the WEA's supporters in the press were Jewett's good friends William Hayes Ward and his sister Susan of *The Independent*.

Another influential friend she met sometime in the decade was Julia Ward Howe. In 1879 Jewett was invited to read from her works at the Saturday Morning Club, a group organized by Howe some years earlier for the purpose of broadening the education of her daughters and their friends. In the fifteen years since "The Battle Hymn of the Republic," Howe had freed herself from her husband's jealous restraint and become a respected author and lecturer, founder of the New England Women's Club and (with Lucy Stone) the New England Woman Suffrage Association and the American Woman Suffrage Association. Twenty years hence she would be the grand old lady of Boston, the last of the line of beloved elders that included Emerson, Whittier, Longfellow, and Holmes before her. Sarah Orne Jewett would particularly cherish her as "*dear* Mrs. Howe" and sneak forbidden sweets to her while her daughters pretended not to see. Now, in Sarah's younger days, we can say only that Sarah knew Howe and with Mason sometimes may have attended the meetings of the club, whose speakers in the seventies and eighties included Howe herself, Lucy Stone, Louis D. Brandeis, James and Annie Fields, Henry James, and Mark Twain.

Yet another circle of acquaintances revolved around Mary Bucklin Davenport Claflin, her husband, William, and their family. A former governor of Massachusetts, William Claflin served in the U.S. Congress during the Hayes administration (1877–81) at the same time as Anna Dawes's father. When they were not in Washington the Claflins lived in Boston and attended Trinity Church, and it may have been there that Sarah met them. Early in 1878 Mary Claflin invited Sarah to D.C. for an extended visit. She stayed there several weeks, flanking her visit with visits to friends and relations in Philadelphia, Brooklyn, Springfield (Mass.), and Boston; altogether she was gone about three months. A bit daunted at first by the thought of the hectic Washington social scene, she quickly recovered her spirits after she arrived and maintained an astonishing pace, considering the fact that she had been a semi-invalid most of the preceding year. Several people she knew were in the city, among them Dawes and the Horsfords, and her days were spent in a whirl of calls, dinner parties, and sightseeing. *Deephaven* had come out a few months before, and no doubt she was agreeably lionized. In a letter to Emma Claflin Ellis she described a typical day, prefiguring the impressive social stamina of later years and confirming that, despite lingering religiosity, the cheerful hedon of the sixties was alive and well:

Addie and I went to the market on a lark in the morning and when I got back after a call on the way . . . [Mrs. Claflin went out and] Mary and Miss Cushing and I felt very grand—you see it was Tuesday and we had to receive and we had ninety calls and entertained the nobility and gentry and behaved just as well as we could. Then we scurried off, when there was a pause just after five, and went to a grand reception at the Lincolns, and spent an hour there and met ever so many people we knew—Then we came home to dinner, and Gov. Claflin had somebody to dine— then we rigged for the President's reception and had *such* a good time there.* I wouldn't have missed it for anything—

* President Rutherford B. Hayes, whose election following the scandalous Grant administration had caused great rejoicing among liberals, was incidentally a cousin of Elinor Mead Howells, William Dean Howells's wife. Howells had written a campaign biography for the election, dashing it off in twenty-two days.

and we came home in the watches of the night—*and* wasn't that a day![8]

Among the Claflins' friends were Harriet Beecher Stowe, whom Sarah met at their house in 1878, and John Greenleaf Whittier, whom she encountered briefly there in 1877. She already had met Whittier in Osgood's office two months earlier, but their mutual fondness for the Claflins was another bond, and their meeting is one more reminder of how closely knit New England's literary family was. At sixty-nine America's best-loved poet, Whittier was the shyest of public figures, fleeing before his eager fans like a stag in the mist. When Sarah saw him at the Claflins' he was, typically, about to disappear upstairs. Nevertheless, afterwards he did not forget her. No man in American letters was more generous to women writers, and after *Deephaven* was published he wrote to Sarah:

> Dear friend,
>
> I must thank thee for thy admirable book "Deephaven." I have given several copies to friends, all of whom appreciate it highly, and I have just been reading it over for the *third* time. I know of nothing better in our literature of the kind though it recalls Miss Mitford's "Our Village" and the Church of Carlingford.*
>
> I heartily congratulate thee on thy complete success and am very truly thy frd,
>
> John Greenleaf Whittier[9]

Sarah replied with an invitation to come to Berwick (which, as was his custom, he tactfully evaded), and thereafter they met and corresponded with growing affection and frequency. Whittier never offered constructive comments on her works, only indiscriminate support. It did not matter; she had criticism enough from others. In a few years she would call herself his "honorary daughter," but he was more like a doting grandfather, all sugarplums and no

---

* Mary Russell Mitford, *Our Village* (1856–57); Margaret Oliphant, *Chronicles of Carlingford* (1863–69).

discipline. No one's praise meant more, for she had absorbed his poetry and learned from its rural American themes since childhood.

It was sometime in the *Deephaven* period, or possibly earlier, that Sarah met Annie Adams Fields, who would become her companion and dearest friend: the first surviving letter dates from 1877. In spite of scores of mutual friends in Boston, they seem to have met through James Fields's connections in Portsmouth, where he had grown up; possibly they met through their mutual friendship with Portsmouth Unitarian minister James de Normandie.[10] However it began, the friendship was slow to ripen. Both were caught up in a frenetic social schedule, and their chances of meeting were few; then, too, in the beginning the disparity between Sarah and Annie must have seemed wide to both of them. Sarah had not yet published her first book and was still the diffident ingenue, far younger than her years in demeanor; while Annie Fields, in her early forties, was not only an internationally acclaimed hostess and the wife of a distinguished editor, but a poet in her own right and a well-known social reformer. Her marriage to Fields was singularly happy, and as has been said, she devoted herself primarily to being her husband's consort, fitting in her own work around the edges as best she could. The amount she was able to accomplish on these terms testifies to the abundant energy and organizational skill she brought to everything she did. In 1877 she would have flashed now and then on Sarah's horizon, but she does not seem to have focused her attention on the younger woman, who in any case was too ill that year to spend much time in Annie's line of sight. And so things remained for a few years.

Even as the new friendships of the seventies were formed, several that had seemed deathless a few years earlier were quietly fading away. The correspondence with Anna Dawes, Hattie Seeger, Ella Walworth Little, and Lillian Munger dwindled to occasional notes, while that with Howells, Scudder, and Whittier, though still occasional, gained in importance. *Deephaven* marked a social as well as literary watershed, the emergence of the little-known children's writer as an adult author whose fresh new voice was immediately recognized in the literary world. The book was not widely heralded in the press, but the notices it did receive were welcoming, with only *The New York Times* giving it a pan review. According to Sarah,

the serial "Deephaven Excursions" received a "stunning compli-
ment" in "one of the big English reviews," though no Jewett
scholar has yet succeeded in identifying it.[11] The book was followed
in 1878 by *Play Days,* a collection of children's stories, and in 1879
by *Old Friends and New,* a collection of sketches for adults. By 1880
any lingering questions about whether the girlish young woman
from Berwick could sustain the achievement of *Deephaven* had been
put to rest.

In December 1879 *The Atlantic* gave Holmes a breakfast party
in honor of his seventieth birthday. Bowing to public protest that
the Whittier seventieth birthday dinner the year before had excluded women, the editors made this a mixed affair, inviting
prominent women writers as well as the wives of editors and
socialites. Seated at the head table with Holmes and several male
notables were Adeline Train Whitney, Helen Hunt Jackson, Harriet Beecher Stowe, Sarah Butler Wister, and Annie Fields; women
at the foot table included Elizabeth Stuart Phelps, Julia Ward
Howe, and Rose Terry Cooke. Sarah Orne Jewett, apparently not
yet considered worthy of inclusion in these ranks, was seated at one
of the middle tables with Osgood, her new friend, Lily Fairchild,
and a group of prominent Bostonians. She was not within conversational reach of Annie Fields, but Annie encountered her at some
point and afterwards wrote to Ellen Mason how particularly she
had enjoyed seeing Miss Jewett. Actually, Ellen reported that Annie
had been "delighted . . . to make your acquaintance,"[12] which of
course could not have been true. Nevertheless the spirit of the
report was probably true enough: Annie Fields had finally focused
her attention. No one in Boston was more adept at gathering in
her chosen friends, and despite some obstacles in her way she would
succeed in gathering this one in before the new year was out and
the new decade fairly begun.

10

Keeping Her Balance

WHEN SARAH ATTENDED THE HOLMES breakfast, she had entered her thirty-first year. Since mid-decade, and especially since the writing of *Deephaven,* the spiritual angst of adolescence had gradually subsided, and religion, while still important, was no longer a thorn in her side. Having discovered a sense of purpose both in work and in daily life, she had achieved an uncommon and characteristic serenity that would never again be seriously shaken. Her Boston friendships sustained her from a distance, and though she still suffered from loneliness in Berwick, she no longer chafed to leave her native village. She was, she said, "getting to have a very old-maidenly liking for being quiet—I suppose my writing makes me dislike a 'racket' more and more."[1] Berwick had become the place where she felt she belonged and where she could write in peace, a place to be continually savored and rediscovered, an inexhaustible source for her art. "I think Berwick is new to me every year," she wrote in 1876,[2] and that sense of being an explorer in her own territory would, if anything, increase over the years.

In two letters written just before and after *Deephaven* was published, she included brief, lively descriptions of encounters with local people, and we can see how she thriftily tucked away on the shelves of her imagination bits and pieces of daily experience. One day an elderly woman from a neighboring village, long a patient of her father's, stopped to call:

Such toggery as she wore! I regret to say that she is too
stingy to buy herself a "front"* and she had a grass green
veil around her head under a cap which was brave with
bright purple ribbons—She prides herself on having
'means' and being beholden to nobody—and I just wish
you could have heard her edifying conversation—The first
thing she said after we sat down this morning was Have
there been many deaths [in] the place lately—and then she
gave full particulars of her being in Portsmouth and she always likes to go early to the depot because sometimes the
cars come along before you expect them—and she met a
Second Advent woman—she had never seen one before but
she appeared as well as anyone ever see! We had a great conversation on the subject of herb teas—which diverted Carrie beyond measure. At dinner-time she was asking Mother
about our matrimonial prospects and you would have been
pleased when you heard me solemnly say I thought it was a
great risk—and she responded that *she* thought so too—[3]

In another letter she tells how she and Mary had gone to York
to see the elderly spinsters Elizabeth and Mary Barrell, whom the
Jewett sisters called "The Barr'll Girls," probably for much the
same reason they called their mother "Mar."

Mary sat and laughed as much as she dared. The *old* cat is
dead—it was very sad, but she had a long and peaceful life
and her last moments were described most touchingly. It
was so pleasant and sunny in the old parlor and nothing
ever went straighter to my heart than the look they gave
me and the way they told me of so many of their home
affairs.

On the way home that day they stopped to see Miss Lizzie Goodwin, one of two unmarried sisters who lived with a large family in
what would someday be known as Hamilton House, but was then
only the farmhouse on the Goodwin place. Miss Lizzie, looking

* A "front" was a fringe of false hair over the forehead, worn with a cap
or bonnet. The plot of one of Jewett's best-loved stories, "The Dulham Ladies,"
turns on the decision of whether or not to wear one.

even more thin and anxious than she usually did, came out to say that her uncle was dying and to ask the visitors not to make any noise. Sarah asked the boy who took care of their horse about the sick man,

> but he only knew that "He seemed to get discouraged" and then he said "He's been sick goin' on two years. Well, he got discouraged."—I wonder what it was that discouraged him—and I think one could tell the same story of a good many people. Somehow I know almost as well as if I had been there what it was for Lizzie to "watch" with that dying man all through the summer night with the dawn coming so early and the sea shining in such a dismal glitter as the sun went higher and higher.[4]

Apart from her renewed enjoyment of her own village, there was another, more mundane reason for being content; she was frankly enjoying the novelty of making money. From 1877 on, her income from writing brought her increasing control over her own life. Both before and after she received a share of the family inheritance, she spoke of her writing income as if it were her sole resource. (From the 1880s on, she mentions investments, but even those must have come wholly or in part from her writing returns.) She took pride in managing her own affairs and in pacing her expenditures so as not to overshoot her means; at the same time, Jewett-like, she enjoyed spending money and never stinted if she could help it.

Financial freedom led to greater physical freedom, which in turn helped ease any lingering discontent with Berwick. Horses and the outdoors had always been of central importance to her, and the chance to ride "too fast for good manners" was a crucial safety valve.[5] The Jewett horses were loved and fussed over as distinct personalities, each a favorite of some particular member of the family. If one sister was away, the others would report on whether Princess had thrown a shoe or Dicky had shied in harness. They were as important as the dogs, which is saying a good deal. (Cats, on the other hand, though always present, were anonymous, utilitarian animals, often reduced to a generic "kitty" or "puss.") Until *Deephaven* was published, Sarah had to wait her turn with the horses and could seldom treat herself to a ride or drive just because the weather was fine and she had done a good stint at her desk. That changed when her royalties began to come in and she bought herself a handsome Thoroughbred mare, dark chestnut with a star, whom she called Sheila after the heroine of William Black's *A Princess of Thule* (1874).* Broken to saddle and harness, Sheila was both companion and liberator. She was gentle enough to follow her mistress around the stable yard begging for sugar, but to ride her over the fields at a canter was to be more fleet and powerful than any merely human animal. Moreover, like any good horse worthy of its breeding, she maintained strong opinions on various subjects and was never totally amenable to authority. It was not long before her name was pronounced "Shy-la" in accordance with her unpredictable footwork on the road.

Unhappily, even the possession of her own horse could not give Sarah complete freedom of movement. In the middle to late seventies her illness worsened, and she was incapacitated for weeks and months at a time. Overwork on her book in 1876–77 brought on a winter attack that lingered through spring and summer. The inflammation, settling in chest, shoulder, and right arm, curtailed hopes of bringing out a Christmas collection of children's stories and brought all new writing to a halt. It was to escape more of the same the following winter that she went to Washington to visit the Claflins, and there were shorter sieges of illness in 1878 and 1879. In 1880 she was laid up from January through May and again had to put all work aside; she was not able to ride at all, though she drove in cool weather. That summer, plagued by pains in her head and back as well as limbs, she was examined by some Boston doctors, who diagnosed weakness of the nerves and prescribed rest and change, which of course is what she had been treated with for years. Fortunately she was not entirely forbidden

---

* The Princess of Thule is one of those interesting proto-feminist heroines in nineteenth-century fiction who, like Charlotte Brontë's Shirley or Henry James's Isabel Archer, grew too independent for their creators and had to be tamed in the end. A spirited Scottish girl and child of nature, Sheila eventually is married off to a visiting Englishman and is destined to become a docile keeper of the hearth. Sarah identified strongly with the girl as she is before this fate overtakes her. Among her talents is the ability to row and sail as well as any of her fishermen neighbors.

to work, and she did so whenever she was able. Work was an incentive to get well; she gauged her condition by whether she could push a pen, and she was always impatient. In spite of everything she published twenty sketches and poems in the period 1878–80, some of which were included in the two collections mentioned earlier.

Reviewing this sorry history of pain and restrictions, one is struck by her resilience, and especially by her consistent image of herself as physically strong. However long her spells of illness were, she thought of them as aberrations from a normal state of glowing health. Whenever she was free of pain in winter, she made the most of it, driving over the snow-covered roads or skating on the river when the ice was clear and the weather fine. In September 1877, in spite of having been crippled since the previous winter, she totally ignored her illness in a daydream of how she would go rowing with Anna Dawes if Anna were there:

> We would stay out doors all the time and spend all our af-
> ternoons down river, for the tide is high of an afternoon
> just now and I should like to pull you down two miles and
> then stop in the shade and read and gossip until it is time
> to come home to supper.[6]

Clearly the thought that she might have to ask Anna to take the oars never crossed her mind. But nowhere does her confidence in her basic health and strength come through more clearly than in reference to her horse. "You dont know how much I enjoy 'Sheila,'" she wrote Anna in May 1878. "I began to think she had gone back to colthood and must be disciplined and broken anew. But I am luckily very strong and Sheila knows I mean to be captain."[7]

Her attitude toward work, though still tinged with missionary zeal, has become more positive and complex. Work is a necessary part of health. She hates her illness as much because it interrupts her work as because it interrupts her life. Work is an antidote to the "Berwick blues" and to the depression that used to settle over her whenever she returned from a visit to city friends: "My writing has had a great influence over that naughtiness. I can always throw myself heart and soul into that."[8]

Another factor in her sense of well-being may have been the

maturing of her sister Carrie. As Carrie neared womanhood, the gap that had separated her from Mary and Sarah narrowed, then disappeared. The sisters were all women together. In 1876, in a rare treat, all three went off together to the Philadelphia Centennial, escorted by a Mrs. Furber, who was probably a distant relation. In the spring of the following year, when Sarah fell ill while working on *Deephaven,* Carrie caught diphtheria and nearly died. Sarah's anxiety over her sister and the subsequent experience of convalescing together inevitably brought them closer, and that summer they went to the coast and the Isles of Shoals together while Mary stayed home.

Always the least literary of the three sisters, Carrie was also the least genteel. In delicate health like her sister and mother (although for different reasons), she did not absent herself often from Berwick as her sisters did, but stayed home and relished the passing scene around her. She had a keen sense of the ridiculous, and there was little that escaped her eye; she must have delivered treasures of anecdote to Sarah. In 1875, at nineteen, she became engaged to young Edwin Calvin Eastman, South Berwick's only apothecary, called "Dr. Eastman" by courtesy. Probably her parents asked the couple to put off their wedding until she was older, for it did not take place for another three years. There is no record of Sarah's reaction, but she seems not to have resented Ned Eastman. He was a familiar of the household long before the marriage, and she was fond of him. The couple planned to live in South Berwick, so there was no danger of Carrie's disappearing from her life as so many of her friends had done.

Throughout these years ran one dark thread of anxiety that could not be entirely ignored: their father's failing health. Even though Dr. Jewett had had tuberculosis as a young man and was never particularly robust-looking, the family had always assumed he would outlive his ailing wife. But in 1873 he was severely ill and nearly died, and five years later he had a heart attack that thoroughly alarmed his family. For several weeks he was pale and weak, tiring at the least exertion. The standard remedies of rest, change, and mountain air were decided upon, and with his wife, elder daughter, and brother he set off by rail for the White Mountains. There, at Crawford Notch on September 20, 1878, he died. He was sixty-three years old.

The shock of the telegram left Sarah numbly competent, mechanically helping to arrange for the funeral, receiving her father's body, ministering to her distraught mother, accepting the awkward sympathy of dozens of callers, enduring the service and burial that took place only two days after his death. The clan gathered, and both houses were filled with aunts and uncles, Aunt Helen Gilman being a particularly stalwart support. Some months afterwards Sarah described experiencing an epiphany of sorts when she first saw her father's peaceful, faintly smiling face. She felt an overwhelming reaffirmation of the sentiments she had expressed in *Deephaven* that the boundaries between life and death were fluid: "It is all one life that we are living together—I am here and Father is there—the two worlds are one world after all." Convinced that her father was still present in her life, taking an active interest in everything she did, she implicitly denied any anger that he had been taken away, reaffirming her faith in God as "my own dear loving Best Friend."[9]

As usual the Jewetts responded to death with an élan that surpassed the name of fortitude. Mrs. Jewett did not picturesquely collapse as her illness gave her every excuse to do, and exactly one month and a day after Dr. Jewett's death, in a characteristic gesture that must have startled many of their more traditional friends, the family saw Carrie and Ned married in a quiet ceremony at home. They moved into a house a few doors away, opposite the Misses Raynes', and very soon afterwards Carrie became pregnant. Inevitably the baby boy, born August 4, 1879, was named Theodore.

For Sarah the initial numbness inevitably gave way to real grieving, as each day brought its small cluster of painful reminders:

> I know that the later loneliness is harder to bear than the
> despair that comes at first. It clings to one so, and lies so
> heavily on ones heart and such a sorrow is the thing that
> says good morning and good night and follows one all
> day long.

But she did not lose that initial feeling of beatific acceptance, and she continued to believe that "[Father and I] love each other better and know each other better than we used and it makes up for my having to do without him in the old way because I have something better."[10]

Practically speaking, Sarah's life seems to have changed surprisingly little. It was Mary who became head of the house and who, together with their invaluable factotum, John Tucker, saw to it that the furnace was kept clean and the roof mended. Sarah continued to be granted the wide latitude she had always enjoyed as younger sister, semi-invalid, and *artiste,* and when she needed to travel for her health Mary simply stayed home. Her work went on as before. She busied herself with preparing *Play Days* for the press, the proofs having been sent to her for the second time just before her father's death. Not surprisingly, she published almost nothing new for a few months, but soon she resumed her usual pace, writing two stories that were published in summer 1879 and later appeared in *Old Friends and New.** As she had earlier with religion, she turned her grief into a spur for work, believing she was now accountable not only to God but to her father.

Emotionally the death of her father can be said to mark the first real break with girlhood. She herself, believing in presentiments, recalled thinking she had left her girlhood behind when she left Washington the preceding spring. She still cherished the child in herself, but she had learned to distinguish between that child and the self that must live in the world. The last tendencies toward morbid self-analysis, indeed toward self-analysis of any kind, seem to have been swept away by the shock of her father's death. She abandoned her old diary. Looking it over soon after the Holmes breakfast, she wished she had been more frank about her feelings, even at the risk of later embarrassing an older and wiser self.

Just before she left off altogether she wrote a curious entry regretting the loss of her father as literary collaborator:

> It seems very strange to me now that Father should have
> been taken away. I think if we had worked together, I with
> my writing and he with his insight and great thoughts
> which I could express for him sometimes better than he

---

* "A Sorrowful Guest," *Sunday Afternoon,* July 1879; "A Bit of Shore Life," *The Atlantic,* August 1879.

could for himself, we might have done a great deal of good
and helped a great many people.[11]

Confirming the contribution Dr. Jewett made to his daughter's
stories, the entry also hints at Sarah's possible willingness to subvert
her own talent for the sake of expressing his "insight and great
thoughts." Perhaps it is no more than the passing fancy of a
grieving daughter; but bearing in mind the role of women in
similar collaborations—Dorothy Wordsworth, Harriet Taylor Mill,
and for that matter, Annie Adams Fields—it does seem that even
Sarah Orne Jewett, secure as she was in her career, might have been
willing had her father demanded it to sacrifice independent
achievement and retire gracefully into the shade.

Surprisingly, Sarah seems to have escaped serious illness in the
winter following her father's death. Leaving the generous Mary at
home, she visited for several weeks in Boston, Cambridge, Exeter,
and Newport. December 1879 found her in Boston again, where
she attended the Holmes breakfast, but then her luck ran out and
she was crippled by a wicked siege of rheumatism lasting several
months. Annie Fields, acting in the afterglow of their meeting,
invited her to stay at Charles Street for a week in February, but
Sarah had to refuse. In July she went to the shore, visiting her
Aunt and Uncle Bell at Rye and, with Cora Clark Rice, traveling
by boat to Star Island in the Isles of Shoals, twelve miles off the
Portsmouth coast. There she stayed at the Oceanic Hotel, one of
two large, fashionable resorts on the islands, finding "a great many
Boston people there whom I knew," among them Annie and James
Fields.[12] With Annie and Cora she explored the rocky coves of the
island and the old village of Gosport with its deserted church,
whose bell Sarah could not resist ringing just for the fun of it. The
long- delayed friendship with Annie finally sprang to life.

In August Sarah joined the Fieldses for a few days at their
summer house in Manchester-by-the-Sea, on Massachusetts's North
Shore. Three months later Annie sent Sarah a copy of her newly
published book of poems, *Under the Olive*. Sarah, knowing how
many older friends would feel entitled to this gesture, understood
it as a mark of the significance of this new friendship: "I take it,
as I know you will let me, as a sign of something that is between
us, and since we have hold of each others hands we will not let

them go."[13] Annie also invited Sarah to spend January with them, but Sarah, fighting another attack, replied that she would probably go on a cruise to Bermuda in early spring, but that she hoped to spend a few days with them before she left. By February she was still postponing both cruise and visit, and finally she did not go at all. Instead, while Mary took a holiday in Boston, Sarah stayed home and tried some electrical devices recommended by Osgood, a fellow rheumatism sufferer. The young leaves were budding in Berwick and on Boston Common when James Fields, looking out his library window one day, turned to say something to his wife, suddenly collapsed, and soon afterwards died in her arms.

11

Annie

TO MANY PEOPLE OF HER OWN TIME AND for some years afterwards, Annie Fields was known primarily as a famous hostess, a woman of surpassing charm and tact, a flower nurtured in Boston's highest and best days lingering on to perfume the air of its twilight. She still does inspire such language, the extravagance of which is not very far from the fact. She was, moreover, a flower around whom the best literary minds of two continents hovered like so many hummingbirds. Their names become a blur of brilliance—Dickens, Hawthorne, Emerson, Stowe, Holmes, Lowell, Longfellow, and so on and so on—until inevitably they have tended to obscure the identity of the person at the center. The image was epitomized in the title of M. A. deWolfe Howe's eulogistic 1922 biography, *Memories of a Hostess.* It was enhanced in equally affectionate vignettes by Henry James, Willa Cather, and Harriet Prescott Spofford.[1] All of them picture Annie in the Fieldses' famous library, serene and attentive, surrounded by legendary faces, dispensing balm and wit in equal proportions to all.

It is only in recent years that scholars have begun to uncover a clearer, more complex picture of Annie Fields than her contemporaries—all writers themselves and therefore most interested in Annie's relationships with writers—were able to give us. We can now see that the passive flower image, while not exactly false, is partial and distorts the essentially active and activist nature of the woman. Sitting still in her own library was only one of the things

Annie Fields *did*; and almost all the others required energy, initiative, decisiveness, and organizational skill. Annie Fields was an efficient manager, and she managed her hostessing as well as she did everything else in her life. At the same time, the dominant quality in her personality, the power behind the activism, and the trait she conspicuously shared with Sarah Orne Jewett, was a lively sympathetic engagement with other people.

Ann Adams West Fields was born in Boston in 1834, the daughter of Zabdiel Boylston Adams and Sarah May Holland Adams. Like Sarah Jewett she came of distinguished families on both sides, her father being related to the presidential Adamses and her mother to the abolitionist, social-reforming Mays. Her father was a physician, as was her older brother, Zabdiel (and like Sarah's nephew, Theodore, Annie's nephew would carry the medical tradition into the next generation). The family was Unitarian, attending the Federal Street Church under the Rev. Ezra Stiles Gannett, who interestingly enough had been the pastor of Margaret Fuller's family twenty years earlier. Like the Fullers, the Adamses held progressive views on social issues, and like Timothy Fuller Dr. Adams believed in a sound education for girls. He sent Annie to the George B. Emerson School for Young Ladies, where she studied a curriculum strong in the classics and literature, but with an added heavy emphasis on the particular obligation of Christian women toward the poor.

She grew into a striking young woman, with auburn hair and brown eyes. Her features were just irregular enough to escape conventional prettiness, and she had a pleasant speaking voice that she used to advantage in the popular pastime of reading aloud. As she reached adulthood she attracted the attention of a family friend, publisher James T. Fields, who previously had been engaged to one of Annie's cousins and married to another, both of whom had died of galloping consumption. In 1854 he and Annie were married. He was thirty-seven and she was twenty.

Born in Portsmouth in 1817, Fields was the son of a shipmaster who had died early, leaving his wife with two sons to bring up alone. James had finished high school at thirteen and come to Boston to work for a bookstore. By the time he married Annie, the bookstore had evolved into the firm of Ticknor & Fields, and Fields himself was America's leading publisher, a man who assembled under his imprint virtually all the best writers of Boston's golden age. The list included many British names as well, for Fields was the first American publisher to pay royalties to foreign writers rather than simply helping himself to their works according to prevailing custom. With her husband, Annie traveled twice to Europe, where she was enthusiastically "taken up" and where she and James made something of a literary royal progress from dinner party to dinner party. When she was home a procession of English visitors, including Anthony Trollope, William Makepeace Thackeray, Charles Kingsley, Charles Reade, and Charles Dickens, made their way to the Fieldses' door at 148 Charles Street. There they would find the local authors already ensconced: Holmes, who lived next door until he moved a few blocks away; Aldrich, who for a time lived across the street; Longfellow, Lowell, and Howells from Cambridge; Emerson and the whole Hawthorne family from Concord; Harriet Beecher Stowe and Charles Dudley Warner from Hartford; Celia Thaxter from wherever she was nesting at the moment. Even Whittier, who shunned staying under any roof but his own, consented to shelter with the Fieldses now and then and have his migraines ministered to by Fields's angelic wife.

It is as difficult to define the quality of Annie Fields's charm as it is Sarah Orne Jewett's, but they were similar. Both women had honed tact and modesty to a fine art, and both wore their learning as carelessly as a fine old cashmere shawl, to be used as the weather dictated but never to be flourished about. Like Sarah, Annie had an extraordinary ability to project herself into another's experience, except she limited its application to living people and could not extend it to fictional creations of her own mind. Empathic understanding was a trait Sarah valued highly in her friends, as the emphasis she gave it in fictional characters amply suggests. In both Sarah and Annie, as in two living Jamesian heroines, it was daily expressed through the fine nuances of relationships, so that the only people who felt ill at ease in their presence were those who felt diminished or imposed upon by an excess of grace, or those who felt it had to be a sham, or those luckless few who had offended and were being deliberately punished. The discomfiture of the latter was managed with exquisite skill. Carrie Jewett Eastman refers in one of her letters to Sarah meeting a Berwick woman she disliked and snubbing her "as only Seddie can do these things," with such exquisite finesse that the poor woman hardly knew that, like Prufrock, she had just had her head served to her upon a platter.[2] Annie, who was tough-minded enough to refuse alms to the "undeserving poor," could freeze the undeserving rich with a word.

Like Sarah, Annie was by nature conservative, honoring and emulating eighteenth-century manners and furnishing her Manchester house with antiques. Impatient for women to gain the vote (in part so that they could exert a civilizing influence on the ruffianly male electorate), and working for them to gain access to higher education, she had no patience with the most radical feminists, whom she criticized for alienating the better sort of people from the cause. On the other hand, she welcomed any innovation, whether political, social, or aesthetic, unless she perceived in it a threat to cherished values. She encouraged her husband to publish that most conservative and radical of innovators, Henry James, and late in life greeted the first telephones and automobiles with unmixed delight. She would remark to Willa Cather that she was "not to escape anything, not even free verse or the Cubists!"[3]

Another trait she shared with Sarah was her sense of humor, which ran along quietly under her conversation and flashes out now and then in her diaries. Like Sarah's, her humor could be pointed and personal but was never cruel. "I had seldom heard so young, so merry, so musical a laugh," says Cather,[4] while Henry James remarked that "all her implications were gay," though "no state of amusement . . . [was] perhaps ever so merciful."[5] She liked to tell funny stories but was often too broken up in laughter to do justice to the punchline. Like Sarah, too, she had free access to the child in herself (some portion of the days they spent together at the Isles of Shoals in 1880 was spent in making dolls out of handkerchiefs) and in intimate company would let that child out to play without fearing any threat to womanly dignity. The ability to be children together would be an enduring bond between the friends, and their uninhibited use of childish language would cause their friend M. A. deWolfe Howe some embarrassment when he came to help Annie edit Sarah's letters.

Annie differed most from Sarah, as has been said, in that her sympathies and intelligence were best employed outside of literature. It took her many years to accept this, if indeed she ever did.

Both the Fieldses were authors, and both tried to soar to poetic heights. James tried only halfheartedly, publishing a volume of verses in 1849 and another thirty-one years later. In the interim his editorial duties commanded almost all his attention, although he edited several anthologies and wrote articles, lectures, and a book of reminiscences. Annie's poetic ambition persisted unabated for years. She published three long poems plus a collection of shorter poems before 1881, another collection in 1895, and "Orpheus: A Mask" in 1900. Rita Gollin aptly describes her poems as "well-crafted and high-minded";[6] that is the best that can be said for them, and a good deal more than can be said for her early anonymous novel, *Asphodel.* Her husband respected her enough not to encourage her efforts with flattery, and her press notices were subdued. Like James, she eventually turned to prose writing, publishing a number of articles and biographies and one pamphlet on social welfare, *How to Help the Poor* (1883), which sold 22,000 copies in two years. But she never thought much of herself as a prose writer, and in fact these works are valuable more for their historical content than for any distinction of style. Annie wanted a laurel crown, and because she never achieved one she undervalued her other accomplishments and was dogged for years by a pervasive sense of failure.

While her husband lived she was first of all a devoted wife, throwing herself into providing for the comfort of her "Jamie" and furthering his career. Since furthering his career meant a constant round of entertaining, her wifely role was very demanding and drained off energy she might have used for writing. Biographer Judith Roman regrets this, seeing Annie Fields as a failed poet who "[sublimated] her ambition in a half-hearted commitment to the doctrine of 'true womanhood.'"[7] But it is unlikely that Annie's poems would have been any better had she had all the time in the world to put into them. It was in a third vocational role, as pioneer social worker and community organizer, that she made a real contribution to her time. The fact that she never received adequate recognition for this may have contributed to her tendency to self-disparagement. In her own eyes and those of others she was simply one of many lady volunteers, doing what George B. Emerson, feminine tradition, and Unitarian values had taught her to do. On one level she must have suspected she was one of the leaders in American social welfare reform. But to acknowledge as much to herself would have seemed immodest. All middle-class women were expected to do good works, and if she did more than most she was only gaining points in heaven.

Her achievement came fairly late in life. For the first fifteen or sixteen years of her marriage, Annie apparently did little outside the home. Around 1870, under the pressures of ill health and overwork, her husband retired from publishing and turned to lecturing and writing. At about the same time, Annie experienced a period of intense religious searching apparently similar to Sarah Orne Jewett's. Both of these circumstances may have impelled her toward charity work, James's retirement creating a temporary lull in professional entertaining while religion supplied a moral motivation. Added to these was her friendship with Charles Dickens, who came to America in 1867–68 at Fields's instigation and who won the adoration—the word is not too strong—of both husband and wife. Roman believes it was Dickens's powerful social conscience, along with grief over his death in 1870, that finally woke Annie's sleeping May blood. Soon after he died, enlisting the help of friends, she had begun to establish coffeehouses in the Boston slums, where the poor could buy a cup of coffee for five cents as an alternative to drinking in bars. Within a year she had founded five (though not all survived), as well as a lodging house for working women. In 1872, after a fire in Boston's manufacturing district threw hundreds out of work, she was a leader in practical relief efforts, setting up workrooms where unemployed women could work as seamstresses and occasionally helping them set up businesses of their own.

As the decade advanced, it became clear that Boston's social problems were dwarfing these and any other efforts to ameliorate them. Charitable agencies offering outright alms had existed for years, but as immigration and urban displacement increased, the sheer numbers of the poor overwhelmed available resources, creating organizational chaos and severe suffering. Annie saw that what was needed was, first, a central bureau to coordinate the efforts of the several agencies and eliminate duplication and, second, an employment agency and some type of vocational training to help the able-bodied poor become self-sufficient. She perceived this, to be sure, from the vantage point of her own class prejudice. She assumed for her organization the right to distinguish between the redeemable and the irredeemable poor, and she advocated denying alms to hopeless "paupers"—those, for example, who refused to give up drinking or accept the work offered them. She believed, too, that the children of these people, or of abusive parents, should be placed in foster homes, essentially as domestic slaves, and she assumed as a matter of course that they could aspire to no other vocations than those of servants or farmers. Nevertheless, she genuinely sympathized with the poor and labored to help them break free of the cycle of despair. Her mixture of condescension and compassion is typical of women of her class and time and is reminiscent of Kate Lancaster of *Deephaven,* who was based on one or several of Sarah's earlier friends.

The idea of a central agency employing visitors was not original with Annie: similar programs had been tried with varying degrees of success in Germany, England, and Scotland, and had been advocated in America by Unitarians Joseph B. Tuckerman and William Henry Channing. But Annie and her friend Mary Greenwood Lodge were the first to implement it in America. In 1875 they set up an agency they called The Cooperative Society of Visitors, naming it after its central feature of a corps of volunteer visitors, each of whom regularly called on several individuals or families and tried to identify their needs and find whatever help was available—employment, medical care, housing, and so on. Above all, the visitor was expected to become personally involved and to work with the clients rather than dispense aid from some distant and impersonal height.

Needing more participation and money, Annie appealed to a number of prominent Bostonians for help, and the following year saw the founding of a larger, more comprehensive organization called the Associated Charities of Boston. Annie Fields and Mary Lodge both became directors and volunteer visitors, since all who served as officers were expected to do their share of visiting as well. Like its predecessors, the Associated Charities did not succeed in stemming the tide of poverty in Boston, but it did reach hundreds, if not thousands, of people and made a permanent difference to many. It became a model for similar programs in other cities and eventually evolved into the Family Service Bureau of Boston.

It would be misleading to imply that Annie devoted all or

even most of her time to the Associated Charities. She was no Jane Addams; she continued her writing and remained a typical upper-middle-class wife, busying herself with agreeable domestic and social pursuits. But except in summer she seems to have given at least one full day a week and half of most other days to visiting the poor, helping to manage the organization's affairs, and attending its weekly conferences. After her husband, it became the single most important focus in her life, shouldering aside her poetic aspirations.

In fact, Annie did find ways to contribute to literary history, if not to literature itself. In the 1860s and '70s, and intermittently thereafter, she kept diaries in which she recorded encounters with friends both ordinary and extraordinary, as well as occasional opinions. Like the later biographies, parts of which are based on them, the diaries are stylistically unremarkable. But their observation of human detail, as well as their warmth and humor, have made them valuable sources for later biographers and social historians. James Fields silently appropriated portions of his wife's diaries for articles on Dickens and Hawthorne, published in *The Atlantic* and in his *Yesterdays with Authors.* In Annie's diary we see Harriet Beecher Stowe in a state of inspired untidiness, sitting at dinner after a reading, scattering bread crumbs on the tablecloth and spilling food down the front of her dress: "Her obliviousness to all cares of this sort," says Annie, "are wonderful and terrible."[8] We see Ralph Waldo Emerson at a lecture by the French historian Ernest Renan, not understanding the French and sneaking glances at Lowell to see how he reacts. We see Henry James scouring the shops of Hastings, England, looking for a muzzle for his dog. And we see suffragist Mary Livermore as a girl with her sisters and cousins, braving Harvard's President Quincy in his den to plead for admission to the college, only to be reduced to tears by his patronizing refusal. (The girls, six in all, had been educated with their brothers and were equally well prepared for college. Quincy listened to the summary of subjects and books they had mastered, and then interrupted with, "Very smart girls; unusually capable girls. But can you cook?" "Oh yes, sir," they said. "We have kept house for some time." "Highly important," he remarked, and let them go on pleading for the better part of an hour before remarking that

Harvard would never, under any circumstances, allow girls to enroll and that "the place for girls is at home.")[9]

Annie also served as unofficial editorial advisor to her husband, encouraging him to publish not only Henry James but Harriet Beecher Stowe, Elizabeth Stuart Phelps, and Rebecca Harding Davis. Not surprisingly she was partial to women writers, who appealed to her to intercede for them or to read, criticize, and occasionally correct their manuscripts. She published a number of essays on achieving women and established two clubs for women writers, one in 1874 and another in 1878, where they could read their new work to one another. She was a mother confessor to many troubled friends but especially to Celia Thaxter, whose financial and marital troubles and difficulties with her emotionally disturbed son could be safely confided to Annie.

She supported a number of causes besides the Associated Charities, including higher education for blacks and various working-women's organizations. But she gave highest priority to suffrage and higher education for women, even though she had little time to give to them. In 1870 she wrote exultantly to a friend abroad about the "surging condition of women" in America,[10] noting that the Women's Club and *The Woman's Journal* in Boston had their own building, that the city's working-class women were forming their own society, and that suffrage was gaining momentum in the individual states. In 1871 she joined the first group formed to lobby for coeducation at Harvard, the precursor of the Women's Education Association. In the same year she persuaded her husband to arrange a series of free Saturday lectures for women, featuring Ralph Waldo Emerson, Phillips Brooks, and Fields himself among other speakers and intended, in Annie's words, to "forerun a university we hope for *women* in this city."[11] After the Boston fire in 1872, she no longer had time to actively campaign for women's rights, but she continued to informally exercise her considerable powers of persuasion and she kept abreast of events through activist friends like Mary Livermore, Elizabeth Cary Agassiz, and James Freeman Clarke.

In the 1870s the pace of the Fieldses' life became increasingly hectic. James Fields became immensely popular as a lecturer, and what had been intended as a pleasant avocation became a demanding career, involving a good deal of exhausting travel. Annie went with him sometimes, but she too was heavily involved in her own work. Their summer house in Manchester, built in 1875 as an idyllic retreat, was immediately besieged by summer visitors, and the Fieldses found less and less time to be quiet together or alone. James's health worsened; his symptoms now included chest pains in addition to older complaints of migraines, rheumatism, and what Annie called "ague." He cut back on his lecturing, but in 1879, 1880, and January 1881 he suffered serious cardiovascular crises. He seemed to recover each time, but he finally could not withstand the attack of April 1881.

Annie was devastated. She had nothing of the Jewett-Gilman insouciance toward death: her life seemed suddenly robbed of meaning. With Holmes's help she set about writing a memoir of her husband, but she refused to speak of him or allow her friends to speak of him, and like Queen Victoria she retreated within herself and privately nursed her grief. After several months Celia Thaxter, who was as close to Annie as anyone and who had been in the room when James died, wrote pleading with her not to continue to shut out her work and her friends:

> Of all things, on earth don't shut yourself away, throw
> bridges over your moat and let love come to you or you
> will die a thousand deaths of silence, and sorrow and de-
> spair—*The darkest hour comes just before the day*—Do not give
> up your work—what will become of you without it?[12]

Sometime before his death, James Fields had mentioned Sarah Orne Jewett to his wife as the friend he would choose for her above all others; but perhaps because of Annie's withdrawal, or because Sarah's visiting schedule was unusually full that summer, it was autumn before the two met again. In November, soon after Celia wrote her letter and perhaps as a result of it, Sarah came to stay at Charles Street and the two began the companionship that would last the rest of her life. Initially, no doubt, the visit was intended to last the customary one to four weeks; but these two strong women found great satisfaction in taking care of one another. To Sarah, Annie in her new widowhood seemed pitiable, especially in the long nights when she had closed the door on the last solicitous friend. She seemed pathetically glad of company, and once there it was unthinkable to abandon her. Annie, for her part, saw that Sarah was in pain much of the time (1880–81 was that especially difficult year when she resorted to consulting Boston specialists), and she forgot some of her own grief in order to become the maternal comforter she by nature was. So they went on together, amusing and taking care of one another, until mid-February, when Sarah finally returned to Berwick and gave her sister a turn at Boston visiting. By then the friends had decided that they would go abroad together in May, Annie to seek the traditional distraction after loss and Sarah to seek the traditional invalid's rest and change.

12
Europe

THE TRIP TO EUROPE WAS SET FOR LATE
May. Sarah spent most of the intervening time at home, sick and
impatient at first, later sewing with Olive Grant and writing.
Although she would be away almost half the year, she completed
her usual quota of writing in 1882, and "The Mate of the Daylight"
(*The Atlantic Monthly,* July 1882) as well as a contribution to *The
Atlantic*'s "Contributors' Club"* were two pieces she wrote in early
spring. She fretted at being away from Annie and wrote of flying
back to Charles Street in imagination, "as if I could really put my
head in your lap and tease you as you sit at your desk—It is just
like being with you still—I believe everything of me but my boats
and clothes, and the five little stones and the rest of the things in
my pocket, and the hairpin—all goes back to Charles St. and stays
with you half a day at a time."[1] "Are you sure you know how much
I love you?" she wrote a few weeks later. "If you dont I cant tell
you!"[2] They signed their letters with pet names they used only
with each other: Annie was "T.L." (the significance of which I have
not discovered) or "Fuff" or "Fuffatee," Sarah likening her friend

---

* The "Contributors' Club" was a potpourri of anonymous, untitled short
essays by regular contributors to the magazine. Sarah contributed often, but her
pieces have not yet been fully identified, though Richard Cary tracked down
several of them. (See Cary, "Some Bibliographic Ghosts.") The remarks on the
color cure in the March 1882 issue are hers, as is the piece on literary characters
as friends in January.

to a small, fluffy mouse. Sarah was "Pinny" or "Pinny Lawson"—the first a family name, perhaps from adolescence when she was tall and thin and "her head no bigger than a pin's,"[3] the second after the feckless, lovable Sam Lawson in Harriet Beecher Stowe's *Oldtown Folks.* * Sarah's philosophic acceptance of Berwick in all weathers temporarily failed, and February in Maine had never seemed so damp and dreary nor the walls of home so implacably confining and lonely. Mary was away, Carrie was sick and had to stay indoors, and their mother, feeling rather better than usual, took herself off to Exeter to see her father. Even though Cora Clark Rice came with her baby to ease Sarah's ennui for a few days, she felt the separation from Annie keenly. She missed too the invigorating atmosphere of Annie's house: the procession of amusing visitors, the concerts, theatre, museum and shops, the drives out to see friends in the suburbs and the muted, but always audible, sound of the city's possibilities beyond her window.

From now on she would divide her time between Boston or Manchester and Berwick, spending about half her time at home and half with Annie. The alternation came to be an enriching and even a necessary pattern of living. Access to Annie's more systematic literary education and her rich variety of friends extended Sarah's intellectual reach, and she was already beginning to work her way through the Fields library. But life with Annie proceeded at a fast clip, with the faces around her whirling past and Sarah herself constantly responding and receiving, dancing the social dance with one foot on the ground and the other perpetually extended for the next step. She was not only Annie's darling, she was everybody's darling: in Boston as well as Berwick she was "our dear Sarah." It was exhilarating, and despite her earlier claims to be a quiet country body she rarely seems to have tired of it. But it did not nourish and in fact must have depleted her as a writer. She needed to go back to Berwick often to revisit kitchen, garden,

---

* Although these particular nicknames were used only between Sarah and Annie, the use of affectionate diminutives was common not only among the Jewetts but among their friends. Celia Thaxter was "Sandpiper," Thomas Bailey Aldrich "the Linnet" or "the Duke of Ponkapog," his wife, Lilian, "the Duchess of Ponkapog," Mary Lodge "Marigold," Annie's sister Louisa Beal "Tudy," and Whittier—after his own signature—"thy Friend." Sarah was "Owl" or "Owlet" to Celia Thaxter and "Sadie Martinot" to the Aldriches.

and stable, listen to her mother and sisters recount the local gossip, and drive alone up half-deserted wood roads to small gray houses where a single woman, or an old couple, kept the encroaching junipers and sumacs at bay. And although she managed to make time for work in Boston, it was in Berwick, away from the city's distractions and seated by the window in Uncle William's upper hallway, that she did her most productive writing. Nor, dearly as she loved her friend, did she now emotionally abstract herself from her family or think of her time in Berwick solely as duty visits. She retained her affection for them all and may have grown even closer to Mary. She wrote to someone at home, generally Mary, every day from Boston as she wrote to Annie every day from Berwick, and although there are sometimes hints of underground rivalries between the family and Annie, on Sarah's part the feeling is as lively in one set of letters as in the other.

Annie went to Berwick once that spring, principally to meet Sarah's mother. She did not stay more than a day or two, and in general her visits to Berwick would be few and short. It was up to Sarah to shuttle back and forth; Annie was anchored and would not be tempted away, however much Sarah pleaded. Her letters, too, were shorter than Sarah's and sometimes almost perfunctory. Yet it would be too simple to conclude that therefore Sarah was the more dependent of the two. Sarah lived her life at a normal speed, while Annie tended to be constantly in motion. Sarah's work was more or less portable, while Annie's was fixed. The pattern developed accordingly.

On May 24, 1882, escorted to the pier by Henry Mills Alden of *Harper's Magazine,* the two friends sailed from New York on the *Scythia.* Among their fellow passengers were Matilda Burleigh, widow of the Hon. John Burleigh of Berwick and family friend of the Jewetts, and that doughty champion of Boston liberalism, James Freeman Clarke, with his wife, Anna. The voyage was smooth, and Sarah, who sometimes got seasick on local harbor sails, defied her mother's predictions and stayed well in spite of increasingly unappetizing meals that toward the end "tasted as if they had been kept in bureau drawers."[4] On the morning of June 3 she rose at dawn and went on deck to see the fields of Ireland ahead, as improbably green as she had been led to believe through years of listening to wistful exiles. By early afternoon she and Annie were comfortably settled at the Imperial Hotel in Cork.

They stayed a week in Ireland, for the most part seeing that beautiful and tormented country with the tunnel vision of the middle-aged, middle-class literary ladies they were. Sarah had been primed beforehand by the cook, Ann Rogers, with "every desirable particular about the little people,"[5] and it was in that spirit that she found poetry in the very dandelions that grew by the road. Of evictions and the continuing plague of the potato blight she knew nothing, save what she gathered from "three young Irish ladies" on the train to Enniskillen, who complained of threats from surly and ungrateful tenant farmers.[6] Charles Stewart Parnell, at the height of his career, had been released from jail a month earlier, on the same day that the new liberal chief secretary for Ireland had been murdered by Fenians in Dublin's Phoenix Park. But Sarah, aside from a momentary *frisson* while passing near the park, saw what she wanted to see: only a land of ruined castles (not inquiring too closely about how they came to be ruined) and "donkeys that would make John [Tucker] choke himself laughing—about as big as dogs in *large* ramshackle carts" and whitewashed cottages that, she observed, were "as pretty to look at and picturesque as some kind of a bird's nest always provided you arent too near!"[7] She and Annie were charmed by Mrs. Casey, an old woman they met on the road who fell on her knees among the daisies and blessed them when Annie gave her some money. As for politics, they learned from their ladies that (as Sarah put it with grim unconscious irony) "lots of people have had their incomes cut off." She conceded that "of course, as in all such questions there is wrong on both sides—but the Irish mob is a crazy headed one—we all know *that*!"[8]

Yet before they left they had a chance, thanks to Annie's maid, Liza, to see beneath the surface and perhaps beyond their own prejudices. In the course of their tour they spent a day at the village of Blacklion with Liza's family, who welcomed them with ceremonious warmth and plied them with "milk, oatcake, little roasted chickens about the size of partridges, cakes and 'something to take!'" Finding out that Sarah had a special predilection for all creatures equine, they offered her a chance to ride their donkey, a feat that enlivened everyone's day except perhaps the donkey's and that took some skill, since the donkey was "only a middlesized donkey, and it was a good deal like riding a dog!"[9] These were not poor people—Liza's uncle was the parish schoolmaster—but they were country people, and Sarah was instantly at home with them as she was with country people anywhere. Living in their landscape for a few hours and eating the food they grew must have strengthened the affection she already felt for the Irish, although for the time being it did not alter her political conservatism.

From Ireland they proceeded to England, which was almost like a second home to Annie, though mined with painful memories at every step. To Sarah, as to most educated Americans, London was strangely familiar, and as she trailed Annie through Westminster Abbey, the National Gallery, Temple Court, and Piccadilly she felt like a character come alive from a beloved old book. Her capacity for wonder, here as in the familiar woods of Berwick, was nearly inexhaustible, and every day was marked off in superlatives as she wrote her nightly missives home. Her pleasure is expressed in the private, childhood language she and Mary used with one another, which is very like the language she and Annie habitually used. "Sister is [*sic*] no sense at all she is having that beautiful of a time," she exulted on her first day there, having been to Covent Garden and come back loaded down with apricots, strawberries, cherries, and flowers.[10] Literally overwhelmed by the Abbey, she had to leave after a short time, finding that its long vistas and "great stained glass windows and the carvings and the great bells ringing over head are all so wonderful and beautiful that it fairly upsets you."[11] Attending the theatre, where they saw Henry Irving and Ellen Terry in *Romeo and Juliet,* she is the quintessential unspoiled, provincial American girl, as if Henry James had drawn Daisy Miller from her on the spot: "Did I tell you you have to go to the concerts and theatres here in evening dress as if it were a party? Without a bonnet for they wont let you in with one *on!*"[12] Nothing disappointed her, from tea cakes to Tower, and if the damp English climate stirred up her rheumatism she gave no sign of it: "We have nice open fires (at one and sixpence) and sister is that contented she is ashamed of herself—and tuppance will buy her raspberry tarts that make her forget all troubles of mind and body."[13] She happily adopted the custom of drinking only wine and no water at meals, and declared she felt better than she had in a long time.

It is hardly likely that in 1882 they escaped such discomforts of travel as wet feet, damp and muddy skirts, primitive plumbing, chilly public buildings, and the inevitable consequences of unchlorinated water, but at no time did Sarah outwardly acknowledge their existence. One would suppose from her letters that the inconvenience of having to stay indoors a day or two with a traveler's cold was the worst she ever had to endure. And no doubt—since there were no crowds to speak of and everything was accessible, and since she and Annie traveled with a maid who saw to laundry and small errands, and since they usually had a suite of rooms and took their meals privately, and Europe was well supplied with porters, and they traveled by rail and carriage with willing attendants always handy—no doubt in some ways they were less uncomfortable than travelers of similar means are today. But some notion of what they may have dealt with silently lies in Sarah's cheerful aside that "the fleas eats [sister] *shameful*—and let A.F. alone except once or twice when they have lost their way to me."[14]

Annie's English friends made them abundantly welcome, especially Dickens's children and sister-in-law and Mr. and Mrs. Francis Bennoch, old friends of the Fieldses and of Hawthorne. (Bennoch's benign figure can be glimpsed from time to time in Hawthorne's *English Notebooks.*) Some friends were absent, but several favorite authors were there to take Sarah's hand: Christina Rossetti; Dinah Mulock Craik, whose poems the sixteen-year-old Sarah had copied into her commonplace book; Anne Proctor, mother of the English poet and feminist Adelaide Proctor and widow of the poet "Barry Cornwall"; Scottish novelist and poet George MacDonald; and Shakespearean scholar Mary Cowden-Clarke, sprightly at eighty-one, visiting England from her home in Italy. Annie's work was not entirely neglected, for they toured Bartholomew's Hospital, attended a charity meeting, and met Octavia Hill, a feminist and pioneer community organizer whose work in London had been a primary model for the Associated Charities.

In mid-June they went to the Isle of Wight and called without prior notice on the Tennysons, who hardly ever received anybody.

Tennyson's friendship with Annie dated from Ticknor & Fields's publication of his poems many years earlier, and the aging laureate and his invalid wife welcomed the two women warmly and invited them to stay longer or visit them later in Surrey. Tennyson was impeccably courteous and, though frail, still moved in a kind of leonine splendor that thoroughly captivated Sarah. She would always accord to his poetry the same uncritical admiration she felt for the man.

From the Isle of Wight they went to Devonshire, where they stayed at the tiny fishing village of Clovelly, boyhood home of Charles Kingsley (another of Fields's English flock) and setting of parts of his novel *Westward Ho!* Arriving on the high road above the village, Sarah and Annie found themselves perched four hundred feet above the pier, at the top of a main street far too steep for their vehicle to descend. A passerby hallooed until he attracted a boy, who toiled up the hill with a donkey to fetch their luggage. The next day, hiring another boy with a small carriage and a miniature, very lazy mule, they made their slow way to the neighboring village of Morwenstow, named after the ancient Welsh martyr St. Morwenna.

This part of the Devonshire coast was exceedingly wild and rough. Its hedges were stunted and bent by the winds, and its best crops were gorse, briar roses, honeysuckle, wild fuchsia, and foxglove, which Sarah gathered in profusion. Beyond the cliffs the seabed was studded with rocks and ledges; for lack of a better livelihood smuggling and scavenging from wrecks (some of them deliberately caused) had been popular trades until well into the nineteenth century. In 1834 there arrived at Morwenstow a young vicar, Robert Stephen Hawker, who for the next forty-one years made his parish and home a refuge for shipwrecked sailors, while with great effort infusing a modicum of civility and religion into the surly and suspicious villagers. A large, mischievous, hot-tempered, stubborn, untidy priest with more than a little of the berserker in him, he dispensed blankets from his own bed and whiskey (which he claimed warded off cold) from his own cabinet to the luckless souls tossed onto the rocks below the village. He died in 1875; his biography, published in 1880, had drawn Sarah and Annie to see for themselves the place where this heroic, eccentric man spent his life. They visited the rectory with its fantastic chimneys (built by Hawker, each chimney copied from one he had seen and fancied) and saw the tiny Norman church that Hawker had restored from a state of semi-ruination. Nearby they found the graves of dead sailors he had buried, each marked with a bit of ship's wreckage. Because of the slowness of the mule, the little expedition took all day, and on the way back, perishing from hunger, they stopped at a farmhouse to ask for supper. They were invited into the big kitchen, with its flagstoned floor and beamed ceiling, and refreshed with bread, butter, and milk while their hostess showed them some catechism questions written by Hawker that the family had reverently preserved. They arrived at their inn by the afterglow of a lingering sunset, well pleased with a day that proved to be one of the highlights of their trip.

The rest of their time in England was spent mostly in London, with side trips to various stately homes, to Oxford, and to Stratford-on-Avon, where Sarah took Annie rowing on the river. In London they were joined by Sarah Chapman Bull, a friend from home, the American-born widow of the Norwegian violinist Ole Bull. She was on her way to visit in-laws in Norway and had invited them to go with her. On July 15 they all arrived at the island of Lysö, not far from Bergen, where they stayed in a Norwegian farmhouse that had been many generations in the same family, and visited the neighbors by boat, admiring the traditional dress worn by some of the men and many of the women. The sense of a vigorous, unbroken rural tradition was powerful here as it had been in Devonshire, and here too they visited a tiny church many centuries old. Sarah felt at home among these seagoing farmers, who were humorous, hospitable, downright, and ceremonious, much like Maine people. She was bemused at being invited to visit the family crypt on a neighboring estate and finding there, instead of the expected stone wall with neat little plaques, an open room filled with "long rows of huge oak coffins with here and there a little one, all stowed away." She and Annie walked obediently up and down the rows, peering at the dates and admiring the iron decorations. "I almost laughed out loud there was something so funny about the ship's company after all. Nobody seemed affected among the live ones and you were not reminded of the next world particularly—It seemed as if the departed Formans and Nicolaisons felt a good deal of pride in their excellent coffins, and some rivalry about who had the best one!"[15]

The first few days of August found them back in Britain, where Sarah made an overnight excursion to Edinburgh alone with Liza, the maid, just because she could not bear to miss having a glimpse of Scotland. Two days later, after a rough channel crossing, they arrived in Antwerp; from there they went to Amsterdam, and thence up the Rhine through Germany to Switzerland, where they stopped at Interlaken. Annie's elder sister, Sarah Adams, joined them and, worn out by their strenuous sightseeing, they stayed two weeks, spending much of their time indoors while Annie taught Sarah the rudiments of Italian. Outdoors it rained much of the time, but in clearing intervals they could see from their window the clouds blowing about the peaks of the Jungfrau and her attendants, and a drive through flower-spangled fields would bring them to a waterfall 1,000 feet high, its distant silvery thread half-veiled by gauzy mists of spray.

On August 30, well rested, they left for Italy, reaching Venice the day after Sarah's thirty-third birthday. Venice was the climax of their trip and they gave it a full week, always ending their days at sunset on the Grand Canal, watching the lights wink on and listening to the banter of the gondoliers, which Sarah already partly understood. She fell thoroughly in love with the mellow light and sensuous appeal of the city, which met her romantic expectations as no other place on earth, not even England, could.

After such fulfillment, the more academic delights of Florence could not help but disappoint, and that city's fabled resemblance to Boston did nothing to make up for its stern façades and the damp, dark hotel in which she and Annie unfortunately found themselves. Here Sarah was as close to expressing discontent as she was anywhere during the trip, although she conscientiously made the rounds, seeing "ever so many" (and probably far too many) pictures and churches, and dutifully contemplating the Baptistry doors until a shower sent her scurrying for cover. Thinking that Rome would be an improvement in all respects, they left for that city with relief; but Rome was as hot and stuffy as Florence was damp and chilly, and they left that in turn after five days.

By now Sarah was homesick and finally beginning to run out

of superlatives. In Paris, where the October air was fresh and cool, and where she and Annie had pretty rooms in a hotel on the rue Caumartin, her spirits revived a little. A visit to the country house of an American expatriate friend cheered her even more, and in the sun-drenched city the sheer beauty of the streets and shops relieved her of the remembered weight of Roman monuments. She visited the Louvre in conscientious installments, spent a day at Versailles, and squandered a little store of money Annie had made her save on three sumptuous new dresses and a fur-trimmed cloak. Sarah enjoyed clothes, although she seldom allowed herself to spend so much on them at one time: not for nothing was she currently known at home as "The Queen of Sheby."

Their tour had come to an end, and after a few more days in England, they sailed from Liverpool on the *Parthia.* How much the trip meant to Sarah intellectually is difficult to say. Most of her friends had had a "grand tour" in their early twenties, and it was mostly due to her health that she had not had the experience years earlier. At the very least it made her more at home in the world, particularly the transatlantic world she would now inhabit with her friend. In a more personal sense it further satisfied her curiosity about old, homogeneous cultures—particularly rural ones—and deepened her sense of history as a living, nourishing force. The day spent with Liza's family, the visit to Lysö, and the excursion to Hawker's parsonage had extended her imaginative experience of country people whose way of life was naturally rooted in their landscape. Again she had touched the past and found it not only alive but full of resonances of the familiar.

The most immediate result was the final confirmation of her friendship with Annie Fields. Five rigorous months of sharing close quarters and living out of trunks together had not shaken Sarah's affection for Annie in the least. At the very end of her trip she was still exclaiming to Mary how "lovely and kind dear Mrs. Fields is. . . . I always mean to do everything I can for her and to be with her all the time I can spare and that I dont owe to my other friends."[16] Sarah's good humor and enthusiasm had helped ease Annie's pain at revisiting places she had thought she could never see again without James. For her part, Annie, having always leaned on her husband to smooth the way, had found in taking care of her less experienced friend that she could deal very efficiently, in several languages, with timetables, landlords, customs officials, ticket agents, and waiters. Practically speaking, they had found beyond doubt that they functioned well together as a unit, that they were good for one another. Marriages, Boston or otherwise, can do with no less.

13

Sarah and Annie

CHARLES STREET IN BOSTON, WHICH
abuts the Boston Common, Beacon Hill, the Back Bay district, and
the Charles River, was moderately fashionable in the 1880s, its
cachet somewhat deleted by a huddle of saloons at its east end and
a row of shops near the Common. Annie Fields lived a stone's throw
from the saloons, which were strategically placed at the head of the
only bridge to teetotaling Cambridge; but except for an occasional
walk along the river or drive across the bridge, she and Sarah never
had to see them, since all their usual destinations lay the other way.

The neighborhood was rife with old money, new money, and
literature. Old money lived in chaste Georgian brick on the Hill;
new money lived in brocaded brownstone in Back Bay, on land
newly reclaimed from the river. There William Dean Howells, who
was very new money indeed, built a house in the early eighties and
found in that experience the germ of *The Rise of Silas Lapham.*
Several of Sarah's literary cronies lived within easy walking distance
of Charles Street, popping in and out of one another's houses much
as the Cambridge literary set did across the river. Thomas and
Lilian Aldrich, who had been Howells's Cambridge neighbors when
Sarah met him in the seventies, were now his neighbors and
Annie's. So was Oliver Wendell Holmes, now dancing into his
seventies and known privately at Charles Street as "the little doc-
tor." Both Celia Thaxter and John Greenleaf Whittier lived in
Boston in the winters of 1881 and 1882, and Sarah's girlhood friend

Ellen Mason still lived on the Hill. In short, if the houses of all Sarah's and Annie's friends within a half-mile radius were lit up on a map with little colored lights, the map would glow like a Christmas tree. Cambridge friends like Alice Longfellow (whose father died in 1882) and the Nortons could easily be reached by horsecar. On Saturday afternoons Annie would throw open her doors and be "at home" to fifteen or twenty friends, a ritual in which Sarah enthusiastically joined.

One hundred forty-eight Charles, which has now disappeared, was a narrow row house four stories high, with windows at the front and rear. On the ground floor were a formal reception room that was hardly ever used, furnished in blue and gray, and behind it a pretty dining room that overlooked the garden and the river through windows framed in ivy. Upstairs one flight was the heart of the house, the room Henry James called the Fieldses' "waterside museum,"[1] a long library extending the full depth of the house and crammed with bookshelves, pictures hung frame to frame, plaster and marble busts, a piano, and the miscellaneous memorabilia of thirty years of personal literary history. No horizontal surface was unburdened, and glass cases held treasured autographs and small mementos. The general busy-ness of the walls was broken only by the further busy-ness of two fireplaces and a central arched doorway. The woodwork and walls were dark, the floor was carpeted in moss green, and the windows at either end, swathed in more of the same, were embellished with stained-glass panes designed by Boston artist Sarah Wyman Whitman. To modern eyes the effect would be one of oppressive dimness and clutter, brightened hardly at all by several bowls of fresh flowers. But Victorians saw in the dimness the subdued light and color of a forest glade, and in the clutter abundant evidence of lives rich in experience.

Pride of place over one mantel was given to an oil likeness of Dickens, symbolic plume in hand. Among the other pictures was a portrait of Keats by Severn, while nearby was displayed a lock of the poet's hair. The Fieldses had not known Keats but they had known Severn, and nearly every object in the room carried some like association, while the shelves were crammed with signed editions of the works of friends living and departed—mostly departed. What saved the room from ossifying into a kind of chapel dedicated to beloved ghosts (including the ghost of Fields himself, who had died there) was the unexpected vitality of the resident curator. Exquisitely dressed in gray, white, or some pale, muted widow's color and surrounded by the stiffening effects of the dead, Annie managed to embody the past while emphatically living in the present. Young people liked to prod her into reminiscing about Pen Browning's pony or the sprightly vagaries of Leigh Hunt, and she remembered Harriet Martineau at Ambleside, Wordsworth at Rydal Mount, the full beauty of the young Hawthorne, and the magnetic spell cast by Emerson in his prime. The older she grew, the more her visitors would coax her to produce such trophies of memory. Yet, like Sarah's irrepressible Grandfather Perry, she carried the weight of the past lightly even while expressing it in her slightly archaic manners and high-minded expectations of the world in general. Brisk and decisive in everything, "she kept her whole connection modern," as Henry James observed; but when she consented to recount the past, "the very sound of the consent was as the voice of a time . . . much less strident" than the one in which she found herself.[2]

On the third floor of the house were Annie's and Sarah's rooms and two or three frequently occupied guest rooms. Further up was the attic, to which the servants climbed four weary flights of backstairs each night from the basement kitchen. The house was centrally heated, and presumably the forward-looking Fieldses had had running water "laid on" while James was alive.

Behind the house a long, walled garden ran down to the river's edge. At the end of it a bench under a trellised vine was still known as "Dickens's bower," and across a wide expanse of tidal river the sun sank daily behind the scattered buildings of Cambridge and the wooded hills beyond. Looking out from house or garden across the shimmering water, watching the slow barges creep along behind their tugs or the comfortable points of light appear along the shore at dusk, it was easy to believe in the essential survival of New England's rural past. The modern city barked and snarled at one's back, but the river never changed and has barely changed to this day.

In June every year all this was left behind. Boxes and trunks were packed, furniture was sheeted, and there was great domestic upheaval while Annie rushed from room to room, giving orders like a military strategist and personally wrapping selected small treasures in newspaper. A waiting horse-van from one of the local movers was loaded up and the annual trek to Manchester began, with Annie following by train. If she was not still occupied in Berwick, Sarah participated in this ritual, her main role being to keep Annie from utterly wearing herself out. "A.F.," she confided to Mary,

> gets in such afflictions and funny despairs and forgets
> where the lampshades are and says "no matter they can
> wait!" and next thing I go upstairs and there she is catch-
> ing up a yellow one with a fall of lace in anxious haste.
> The blood of all the reforming Adamses and Mays is
> brought to bear in these days, but it is enjoyed as you
> know, only she *will* get too tired.[3]

All over Beacon Hill, Back Bay, and Cambridge some form of this process was repeated, as the whole upper middle class shifted itself and many of its considerable possessions northward, some as far as Maine or New Hampshire but most to the resort villages of the North Shore, about thirty miles from Boston. Every summer Manchester, Beverly, and Nahant received their wandering city children like comfortable grandmothers, and when all the trunks were unpacked, the summer's books uncrated and lined up on shelves, the kitchen and pantry stocked, and the cat restored to its favorite piazza chair, everyone put on bonnets and hats and called on the same people they had called on all winter. Thus Annie's and Sarah's Manchester neighbors included the Longfellows from Cambridge (who came to visit their Dana in-laws), the Fieldses' long-time pastor, Cyrus Bartol, the Henry Lee Higginsons, and the James Freeman Clarkes.* In Beverly, a short jaunt away by train or carriage, were Dr. Holmes, Mary Lodge, Katharine Loring, and a whole compound of Loring relations, as well as two other women who would soon become Sarah's particular friends: Sarah Wyman Whitman and Susan Burley Cabot. In Nahant, a little farther

---

* Dr. Cyrus Bartol, early transcendentalist and pastor of the West Church from 1837 to 1889, was originally from Maine and was a Bowdoin classmate of Sarah's father. Henry Lee Higginson, a cousin of Thomas Wentworth Higginson, was a major benefactor of the city and the founder of the Boston Symphony Orchestra; his wife, Ida, was a daughter of Louis and Elizabeth Agassiz.

distant, were Anna Eliot Ticknor, Elizabeth Cary Agassiz, and Annie's sister, Louisa Beal, and her family.

At the beginning of the century Manchester had been a thriving fishing village, not much different from York or Wells. But the fishing never recovered from the War of 1812, and around mid-century the beautiful miniature harbor and fine sandy beach began to attract summer people from Boston. The poet Richard Henry Dana came first, like a pioneer braving the wilderness, and presently Dr. Bartol, displaying a wholly unlikely talent for real estate speculation, began buying up large chunks of choice property and reselling them to his friends and parishioners. The Fieldses did not buy their land from Bartol, but they probably followed his lead. The five acres they bought in 1873 were known locally as Thunderbolt Hill, from their unenviable position as the highest, barest point in the village. There, on a rocky knoll overlooking the harbor and close to the village center, James and Annie built Gambrel Cottage. Modest compared with most of the neighboring "cottages," it was two stories high plus an attic in front, and gained another floor in back where the land fell away sharply. A sheltered piazza wrapped the front of the house and provided dry walking in rainy weather, and another looked out over the tops of trees to the village and fields to the rear. The site was fully exposed both to sea breezes and the baking summer sun, but Annie and her factotum, Patrick Lynch, worked yearly to establish a garden, planting young trees, shrubs, and perennials. A path was laid out along the cliff behind the house, and a tea bower set up among the trees at its foot. Sarah liked to clamber down there and sit, as she did in Maine, "watching the birds and feeling the little birch I 'made a back of' move when the wind wagged its head."[4] Her companion, in the woods or on the beach and whether or not Annie joined her, was her Irish setter, Roger, a dog of perspicacity and humor who endeared himself to the Manchester and Boston households and who, when Sarah went home to Berwick, often remained behind as a kind of surrogate for his mistress and hostage for her return.

Sarah had always been sent to the shore for some part of the summer, but always before she had been a boarder or visitor. Now, as co-mistress of the house, she could stay all season. Her family could not help but approve. All the same, there must have been

some tension at home over Annie's virtual adoption of Sarah, not
only because she was missed but because her absence shifted more
onto Mary's shoulders. Mary was the responsible daughter, the one
people turned to in trouble. Being the mainstay of family and
community had become her vocation, and she did it well. Sarah,
on the other hand, was the pampered younger sister (Carrie having
forfeited that position by reason of marriage and motherhood), and
while the family was proud of her success there was sometimes a
whiff, in a letter from one of the aunts, of resentment or jealousy
on Mary's behalf. "Where is dear Sarah now?" one of them would
sweetly query Mary. "I do hope *wherever* she is she is well and
happy."

Between Mary and her mother on the one hand, and Annie
on the other, flowed a constant stream of compliments and little
gifts, with the balance on the Berwick side. Mary and her mother
sent cut flowers, plants for the garden, eggs, apples, and other rural
bounty. Annie, having less to draw on, returned exclamations of
delight and surprise, with now and then a box of figs, candy, or
some other urban delicacy. There is no reason to suppose the gifts
from Berwick were not sent with real generosity, but they also
served to smooth over whatever nascent rivalry there might be and
to placate the power who had spirited away the chief light of the
Berwick household. Sarah, shuttling back and forth between family
and friend, treated them with scrupulous equality. Sometimes,
especially in the early years, she was torn by conflicting allegiances.
Staying at home in the spring of 1882 while Mary was on vacation,
before she and Annie went abroad, she allowed herself to betray
her impatience in a letter:

> I came so near seeing you today darling that I miss you all
> the more because I gave it up—This morning I said to my-
> self why shouldn't I go to you and spend Sunday and come
> down Monday . . . and it was the loveliest thing in the
> world to think about, so pretty soon I tumbled out of bed
> and felt very eager and happy. . . . Oh darling I cant bear
> to give up this lovely long evening I might have had with
> you! But you must see that when I came down stairs I
> found that Mother looked even more pale and tired than
> when she came home last night and she told me that she

was not feeling quite well by every thing she did much
plainer than if she had talked a great deal about it—And a
little later John (who rarely takes a holiday) said that he
hoped to go to Portsmouth. . . . Mother brightened up
amazingly after it was too late to go! and I suppose I really
might have been away as well as not but it did not look
like it and I did what was right then—I felt as if I were ty-
ing myself to the rigging this time![5]

The provocation had to be great for Sarah to permit herself
even so mild an implication of complaint about her mother; and
if she tied herself to the rigging once, we can safely assume she
did it again. Often, rather than fretting to go to Boston, she would
try to coax Annie into visiting Berwick; but Annie, as has been
mentioned, would usually plead the pressure of work and wait for
Sarah to come to her. Sarah's attempts to lure Mary south (apparently she did not try to bring her mother, even when her mother
was feeling well) were a bit more successful. Mary did visit once
or twice a year, but it was difficult to get her to stay more than a
few days, even after her mother died in 1891. Annie, for her part,
had early hopes of bringing both Mary and her mother permanently
to Boston, away from what she termed the "narrow round" of
village life;[6] but it appeared there was more than one Jewett made
of Berwick dust, and Mary seemed insensible of her plight. So it
was Sarah who traveled to each in turn, fine-tuning her schedule
according to her perceived responsibility to three other people
besides herself. Regardless of any underlying tensions, she maintained her triple residency with calm efficiency, broken only when
she forgot a manuscript in one house or another—which, considering the complexity of the arrangement, happened surprisingly
seldom.

The friendship between Sarah and Annie has often been called
a classic, or perhaps *the* classic, "Boston marriage." Certainly it was
like a marriage of the best kind, as a permanent and loving
partnership offering mutual support. But, as Judith Roman has
pointed out, it was entirely free from any of the assumptions of
power common in traditional male-female marriages: "The secret
of the success of this relationship for both their personal and their
professional lives lay in its complete reciprocity and in their ability

to create for themselves a form of marriage in which all roles were interchangeable and neither partner was limited by the relationship."[7] Equal comrades and colleagues, both women also had uninhibited access to the maternal and the dependent in themselves, each expressing one or the other as needed. Sarah's impatience when she was away from Annie, for example, was based not only on her love for her friend, but on her understanding that depression was likely to descend whenever Annie was alone to brood upon her widowhood. Even (or particularly) after the successful tour of Europe, Annie was often overwhelmed by the sense of James's absence from familiar places, and when she had to open the Manchester house in the spring of 1883, Sarah made sure to go with her. "It was a hard day for poor T.L.," Sarah wrote Whittier,

> but we made the best of it, and had a great many pleasures after all. The frogs had thawed out—they were talking in their sleep at any rate,—and the barberry-bushes were covered with dry fruit on top, where the improvident people had not thought it worth while to harvest. The sun shone through the berries with marvellous effect. . . . We were in an excellent buggy with its top put back and the sun kept us very warm, and we gathered some pussy willows almost grown into cats—if one judged by their fur—The sea was as blue as it could be and further more we had had a picnic at the back of the house on the hilltop where we were sheltered from the wind.[8]

Sarah's talent for appreciating the meager charms of a Massachusetts April, with its frogs still half-drugged with cold, its shriveled barberries and gone-by pussy willows, made her an ideal companion in grief—the essential New Englander who, to borrow a phrase from Robert Frost, knows what to make of a diminished thing. It is also one of her most enduring qualities as a writer; one that makes her, for example, able to portray a group of old pauper women in "The Flight of Betsey Lane" exactly as they might be, not at all full of Dickensian lamentation but shelling peas in the shed chamber of the poor farm, gossiping and blinking in the sunlight, and somehow setting up (to quote another northeastern poet) "a shrill piping of plenty."*

Sarah early recognized Annie's tendency to ward off grief by frantic immersion in work and play, to the point of exhaustion. "I think," she wrote to Whittier in 1882, "in [Annie's] wish to drive away her sadness, she has tried to carry too much care and work, and she feels the burden of it beside the weight of the sorrow itself."[9] A year later, staying alone at Manchester, Annie seems no better:

> It seems to be a great sorrow to our dear friend to stay at Manchester, and neither can she bear to be away— . . . I stay with her every minute that I can get, but of course at this time of the year I often ought to be here—She is better contented while I am staying with her, but every letter almost, makes my heart ache with the story of her miserable loneliness whether she tells it or I only "read between the lines." I am dreadfully troubled sometimes for in spite of everything it seems as if it were harder and harder for her just to be alive—And there are still so many things to please her and comfort her—The only thing is to keep as close to her as we can and love her all we can—I do truly love her—but I pity her as I would pity a little child that has been run over and hurt, and yet has to get up and keep on its way.[10]

Sarah Orne Jewett's protective tenderness toward her older friend, in spite of her appearing to be the ingenue as well as the junior partner in their relationship, reminds us that as creator of some of the most memorably maternal characters in American literature, she could draw on her own experience of "the larger motherhood," as well as on Annie's or that of a number of women friends, many single or childless but all involved in some absorbing cause, be it social action, education, or philanthropy. Mrs. Kew, Mrs. Goodsoe, and Mrs. Todd could claim as part of their complicated lineage not only Sarah's own mother, grandmother, and aunts, and the scores of countrywomen Sarah knew; not only literary

---

* William Carlos Williams, "To Waken an Old Lady."

precedents as varied as Anne Whitney's Miss Craydocke, Dickens's Esther Summerson, and Harriet Beecher Stowe's Aunt Roxy and Aunt Ruey; but also Sarah's own protective solicitude toward Annie, toward the perpetually ailing Whittier, or for that matter toward her own mother, whom she nursed tenderly in her final illness. Her maternal characters were not so much a construct of outward observation as an expression of a personal quality that, as the date of *Deephaven* indicates, was fully mature even while Sarah herself was consciously rejecting adult womanhood.

Annie, for her part, had no objection to the teasing admonitions that arrived from Berwick and allowed Sarah to coax her out of what might have become truly self-destructive behavior. Strictly maintaining her air of competent independence, she rarely mentioned her weariness or loneliness, but signaled them indirectly in ways that Sarah (as Annie must have known) could read as easily as words. In answer to Sarah's daily missives full of family and Berwick doings, Annie sent hastily scribbled notes of a few lines, betraying fatigue in the brevity of their contents and the illegibility of their lines. Sometimes she would write in pencil by the fading light of a window, being (as she explained) too tired to find a pen or light a lamp; and Sarah would duly express concern and sympathy the next day. She never made a major decision without consulting Sarah (nor did Sarah without consulting Annie), and she looked to her friend for reassurance and confirmation on a number of fronts. She was, for example, apparently hesitant at first to go into society alone as a new widow, in spite of being one of America's most celebrated hostesses. "Oh my darling Fuff," Sarah wrote, "you *mustn't* feel so about going to places where every body welcomes you and feels so loving and proud at seeing you: this is only because your tiredness makes you timid for the moment."[11] Annie looked to Sarah for support as a writer, and Sarah obliged with extravagant enthusiasm, as when Aldrich ("the Linnet") accepted one of Annie's poems for *The Atlantic.*

> [Of] course the linnet loved [your poem. I] *knew* he would.
> . . . I was more delighted than *you* were when I got your
> letter and his—the *dear* linnet. . . . Didn't I always say you
> *would* have more lovely things to say?[12]

Her defense of Annie's writing turned fierce in 1884, when Horace Scudder, who filled in as *Atlantic* editor during Aldrich's frequent absences, apparently offered Annie less for an article than she was accustomed to receiving from *The Atlantic;* in fact, he offered her exactly the same rate as the *Century* paid her. This kind of slight, coming especially from a magazine her husband had helped found and once edited, and from one that paid her companion (Sarah) premium prices for *her* work, stung Annie a good deal; and to Sarah it implied a literary rivalry with Annie she was at great pains to avoid. "I can imagine Scudder sneaking and asking some Century person how much they paid you," she fumed, and she advised Annie in future to firmly state her price when she submitted a manuscript, as Sarah always did.[13] (This was evidently the beginning of Sarah's temporary coldness toward her old editor, which was exacerbated by a long rivalry between Scudder and Aldrich. After Scudder replaced Aldrich at *The Atlantic* in 1890 amid bad feelings on both sides, Sarah refrained from sending any full-length sketches or articles to the magazine for about eighteen months. But even then she stayed on friendly social terms with Scudder, who was also editor-in-chief at Houghton Mifflin and a summer neighbor of her Gilman relations in Rye. Eventually the rift was healed, and when she heard that he was planning to write a biography of Lowell, she remarked that, though he was a "tame sort of person" to write that life, he was after all "so good, Mary, and so industrious and faithful."[14])

Annie's easy acceptance of Sarah's protectiveness and advice in no way diminished either her own or others' consciousness of her essential strength and vitality. For her own part, she often assumed the role of senior, mothering figure in the friendship, beginning many of her letters with "Dearest child" and assuming in her turn the right to protect and nurse her friend through periodic spells of illness. The memory that James Fields had, in a sense, specifically bequeathed Sarah to her as a friend received a kind of sanctification when, encouraged by Celia Thaxter (who became intensely interested in spiritualism in the early 1880s), Annie and Sarah separately visited a Boston medium in March 1882 and received assurances that their friendship, and indeed their trip, were being actively encouraged and even engineered by James Fields and Theodore

Jewett from the other side. During their months away Celia often
sent Annie messages purportedly confided to her by Fields, who
assured her he had "continually spoken to [Annie] through Sarah"
and that it was "the greatest pleasure to [him] that [he was] able
to do it."[15] Although they later became skeptical of spiritualism,
both Sarah and Annie were susceptible to its claims while their
losses were recent, Sarah having been long predisposed to belief in
a spirit world through her interest in Swedenborgianism. The
medium's statements seemed to confirm their own intuition that
their friendship was no accident, but had been divinely sent as a
comfort and compensation for the deaths of husband and father.
"What an unusual experience mine is," Annie wrote to Whittier,

> to have this dear sweet child brought as it were directly
> into my arms! I think nothing indeed I know that in no
> possible way could I feel so assured day by day of the di-
> vine love and the nearness of the unseen.[16]

In any discussion of this mutual protectiveness there is one
other habitual trait of Sarah's that deserves attention, and that is
the satisfaction she took in prescribing medicines and tonics, not
only for Annie but for anyone she knew who was ailing. Here,
obviously, she was exercising her prerogative as doctor's daughter
and granddaughter; yet the precedent was also her mother's and
grandmothers', for if male doctors prescribed medicines, it was the
women who served them up in spoons and cups and stood by until
the dose was more or less reluctantly swallowed. Sarah's early
leanings toward medicine are difficult to document, and such later
casual comments as "Sometimes I think I should like to give up
the world the f—— and the d—— and be a doctor"[17] suggest they
were fleeting. But she retained all her life the medical knowledge
she had absorbed as a girl, and her letters are peppered with
pharmacological advice. In a modern context they would appear
fussy and overanxious, yet in the context of the abysmal state of
medical knowledge and the high rate of death and disability from
common ailments, Sarah's concern over the illness of her friends
and her pride in her expertise are understandable. Apart from the
long illness of Sarah's own mother, consider that Alice James, Mary
Greenwood Lodge, and (probably) William Dean Howells's daugh-

ter Winifred all died prematurely of cancer; James Fields's fiancée and first wife died young of tuberculosis, as did Lowell's daughter Mabel Burnett and the Aldriches' son Charles. Sarah's beloved cousin Minnie (Mary Fiske), a year younger than Sarah, died early of some unspecified disease, and Emerson's son Waldo died at six of scarlet fever. Phillips Brooks died of a cold that, complicated by exhaustion and overwork, escalated into pneumonia—a fate Sarah constantly feared for Annie. Especially alarming was the death rate among children and young adults in the Boston slums, where Annie worked daily, and where measles, diphtheria, and the like took a high toll in an underfed and overcrowded population.

As might be expected, Sarah's medical "practice" was largely focused on Annie, who was prone to colds and throat infections and who in 1888 had a dangerous bout with pneumonia. Annie would wear herself out, catch cold, keep going if Sarah was not around to scold, and end up seriously ill. From Berwick Sarah would admonish her to slow down and solemnly prescribe, as her father and grandfather had before her, claret with lunch and whiskey before bed. (Annie, herself a physician's daughter, was not averse to prescribing for *her* friends, and once advised Whittier through Sarah to down two tablespoons of rum in milk nightly to ward off neuralgia. Sober Quaker though he was, Whittier obediently choked it down, but had to report that it did him no good whatever.) Some of Sarah's other remedies were innocuous or downright alarming. In 1891 she sent Annie a puzzling toothache remedy, "a little creatur' for your poor aching face" to be administered with the "brown side" next to the tooth.[18] She enthusiastically recommended to friends and family a tonic that contained a dash of strychnine, and she regularly dosed Annie with quinine to cure or prevent colds, blithely increasing the dose if Annie still seemed peaked. For Annie's cough she prescribed "Bryonia," or bryony root, a traditional herbal remedy that can be toxic in large doses, and she once urged on a friend a mixture "with a little cocaine in the bottom of it" as a palliative for cracked thumbs.[19] She treated her mother occasionally, second-guessing the Berwick doctors: "[Mother] seems better tonight than she has at all," she wrote Mary after "venturing a new treatment" in 1882. "We have not come to a rye plaster at all and sister considers she has had luck on the case."[20] Habitually light and self-mocking in this as in most things, she nevertheless took a transparent pride in her skill whenever one of her "cases" happened to improve.

All of this is by way of suggesting, again, the degree to which Mrs. Todd, healer and all-round mother, abode all along in a woman who, outwardly at least, seemed the very opposite of her literary creation: upper class, "delicate," unmarried, self-deprecating, and herself provoking protective feelings in men and women alike. Yet this, like other facets of Jewett's personality, must be sketched with a light hand and above all with saving humor. Jewett-as-mother and Jewett-as-healer dispensed TLC and bromides under the critical eye of Jewett-as-writer, who saw herself no more and no less kindly than she saw one of her own characters, deflating any hint of emotive excess with a flick of irony before it could disturb the symmetry of the persona she created for herself. Her chosen personal metaphor, the daisy, is appropriate not only because it is a common, everyday wildflower (requiring, be it noted, uncommon discernment and close attention to appreciate its qualities), but because it is one of the most obviously symmetrical of blossoms, and the loss of even a single petal spoils the loveliness of the whole.

14

"The Law of Her Nature"

MUCH AS THEY ENJOYED THEIR VARIOUS homes, Sarah and Annie continued to travel often. There were no more trips to Europe in the 1880s, but they took frequent excursions closer to home. Sometimes they visited Whittier at his summer retreat in Holderness, New Hampshire, and at his alternate homes in Danvers, Amesbury, and Newburyport, Massachusetts. In September 1884 they went down to Hartford, Connecticut, to stay with Charles and Susan Warner* and call on the Warners' neighbor Harriet Beecher Stowe. Immediately afterwards, Sarah and Mary took "a scampering journey through Canada,"[1]—probably mostly in Quebec, which held a lasting appeal for Sarah. Earlier that year Sarah and Annie had fled the cold weather as far south as Bethlehem, Pennsylvania, where they visited a Moravian settlement. At least twice in the decade they wintered in St. Augustine, Florida, staying at the luxurious new Ponce de León hotel. In August 1886 Sarah's rheumatism drove her to take the water cure at Richfield Springs, New York, whither Annie accompanied her; and in 1887 and 1888 she sought rest and quiet on tiny Mouse Island, in

---

* Already friends of Annie's, the Warners soon became intimates of Sarah as well. Charles Dudley Warner, editor of *The Hartford Courant,* was a travel writer, essayist, novelist, and co-author with Mark Twain of *The Gilded Age.* His wife, Susan, was an accomplished pianist and a founder of the Hartford Philharmonic Orchestra.

Maine's Boothbay Harbor, the first year with Annie and the second with Alice Longfellow and some other friends. When she was home in Berwick she did not entirely neglect her old haunts, visiting York, Wells, Rye, and the Isles of Shoals from time to time. Many of these trips were taken for health reasons, and St. Augustine, Richfield, and Mouse Island were all sanctuaries to which Sarah returned, alone or with Annie, at least twice in search of cure or prevention of colds and rheumatism.

So, even with the variety of three "permanent" homes, Sarah continued to flit from perch to perch just as she had in her teens. A writer might well falter under the distractions and disruptions of such a life, and Jewett was not one of those unflappable souls who could calmly write reams while the hubbub of daily life went on about their very skirts. When she was in Maine she retired to Uncle William's upper hall or her own room to write, and in Boston she and Annie had separate desks in the library, where by agreement they worked together in silence. But she somehow managed to make a quiet place to work wherever she went, and in the years 1883–90 she published at least sixty periodical sketches and articles, not counting the ones still uncatalogued, such as Contributors' Club pieces and stories for the McClure Syndicate. In that time she also published nine books. Of these, four were collections of stories previously published in magazines. Two, *Betty Leicester* (1890) and *A Marsh Island* (1885), were novels that had first been published in installments. Two others, *A Country Doctor* (1884) and *The Story of the Normans* (1887), were book-length volumes of fresh material.

The Story of the Normans is an anomaly in her career, undertaken at the request of G. P. Putnam's Sons as one of a series of histories for young people. It took her several years: she was researching it at the Boston Public Library as early as 1881, but apparently put it aside. In 1885 she was at work on it again, and she finished it in 1886, pushing herself into illness as she had with *Deephaven*. By the time she finished it, it had become a kind of albatross. As she herself often said, she was no scholar, and she may have agreed to the project during the euphoric period just after *Deephaven* was published, before she understood her own limits. Unable to evaluate her sources and lacking scholarly discipline, she labored conscientiously to marshall such facts as she had and finally produced a lively but historically dubious account, in which she took the opportunity to air her Darwinist views on war ("Wars may appear to delay, but in due time they surely raise whole nations of men to higher levels."[2]) and her belief that the Norman (or gallicized Scandinavian) was racially superior to the Anglo-Saxon and Celt. Both opinions ran counter to her usually liberal slant, and both were based on a mishmash of then-current theory and misinformation. The belief in the superiority of the Germanic peoples was widely in vogue and was promulgated by some of Jewett's favorite authors, among them Matthew Arnold, Charles Kingsley, and Theophilus Parsons. The belief in the cleansing and renewing power of war was based not only on popular Darwinism and the contemporary wave of jingoism in England and America, but on Jewett's personal associations with three "just" and necessary wars fought by her own ancestors and neighbors in the past century. Such conversations as she had with actual war veterans—John Tucker, for example—served rather to glorify the cause than force her to confront the actual horrors of the battlefield. In short, then, *The Story of the Normans* occupies the most obscure corner of the Jewett bookshelf, and the best that can be said for it is that it was not the kind of book that would forever quash its young readers' interest in history.

The three novels all have young women as protagonists, and although only *A Country Doctor* deals with a choice of a specific career, the other two are much concerned with a young woman's decisions about how she will live her life and what her function will be in the world. This is not a frequent theme in Jewett's work as a whole, although it does appear in a few stories that will be discussed separately. There are other aspects the three have in common. All feature a close father-daughter or guardian-ward relationship; and in *Betty Leicester* and *A Country Doctor,* that relationship overshadows all others and is the most important in the girl's life, both affectionally and intellectually. Jewett dedicated *A Country Doctor* to her father, and it seems as if, still grieving for him and trying to live according to his lights, she found comfort in trying to recapture and fix forever both his personality and his crucial influence in her life.

All three novels are populated by sensible country folk, who serve as interpretive choruses or informants to the reader. Often comic in their misunderstanding of city ways (as when Mrs. Owen in *A Marsh Island* indignantly banishes her city boarder's "toadstools" from her kitchen, or when an old woman in *Betty Leicester,* learning that Betty's father is a naturalist, concludes he must belong to some newfangled religious sect), they are never made ridiculous at the expense of their dignity. All three feature the devoted, elderly woman-in-the-kitchen who has served the same family for a generation or two and holds that peculiarly American status of something more than a servant and something less than an aunt. And there are other familiar Jewett figures, especially in *Betty Leicester:* the courtly retired sea captain and the heroic old farm women who live on isolated farms and have done the traditional Maine women's work of nursing, tailoring, berry picking, and rug making to scrape by and in one case send a son through school.

A Marsh Island is the least successful of the three. Published in installments in *The Atlantic* in 1885 and in book form the following year, it was written in response to requests from Whittier and others that she write another long story after the recently published *A Country Doctor.* It took shape in a desultory way, beginning as her works often did with her attraction to a place. Actually there were two places: one was a farm on an island in the marshes of Rowley, Massachusetts (which, if you remember, her Jewett ancestors had founded), seen from a train window on her way to Berwick. The other was the town of Essex, a sleepy old shipbuilding village adjoining Manchester. Lacking a beach and therefore undeveloped as a summer resort, Essex was surrounded by an expanse of salt marsh studded with small islands. Driving through it during her first summer in Manchester, Sarah was captivated by its drowsy charm, imaginatively set the Rowley farm down in the Essex marsh, and began to people it with characters, two of whom (Doris Owen and Dan Lester) were based on patients of her father's. She was not at all sure at first what the characters were going to do, but after a while told Whittier with some surprise that it promised to be "a 'blooming' love story."[3] She soon realized that she was uncomfortable with what she had gotten herself into. "I know I could write a better story without a lover in it!" she lamented to Annie, and like all her similar attempts, this "love" story never warms beyond friendship.[4]

Like *Deephaven, A Marsh Island* sets a city visitor down among rural people and examines the resulting cultural contrast. A young painter named Richard Dale from a rich family happens upon the marsh island farm and persuades the owners to let him board for the summer. Patronizing at first toward the Owen family and casually flirtatious toward their daughter, Doris, he gradually learns to like and respect the parents and almost proposes to the daughter. Like Kate and Helen in *Deephaven,* he is wiser and better by the end of the summer. A spoiled, charming, unambitious but talented artist in the beginning, he is steadied by the experience of knowing the hardworking farm family and ends up beginning to be able to work seriously at his art.

Such as it is, the plot turns on the question of whether the daughter, Doris, will succumb to Dale's big-city charms or prove true to Dan Lester, a local blacksmith she has known since childhood who has never gotten around to proposing marriage. The lack of ardor on everyone's part is, in the end, ludicrous: poor Doris actually feels "dumb before her inevitable fate" when she first thinks Dan is about to propose.* We are constantly aware of an unspoken third possibility for Doris, that of remaining independent and free; in *A Country Doctor,* written the previous year, and in "A White Heron," written about a year later, the author not only makes that alternative explicit but comes down firmly on the side of her young heroine's independence. But the heroine of *A Country Doctor* experiences a definite vocational calling, while the heroine of "A White Heron" is only a child. Less fortunate than either, Doris is an ordinary girl, strong and intelligent but with no definite talent. She and her father are good friends, and there is an implied, might-have-been scenario of Doris remaining on the farm, helping both parents, and eventually inheriting it herself. But Jewett, clearly writing against the grain but determined to write a conventional romance about a "normal" girl, ignores her heroine's half-articulated longing for independence and her identification with the crows, who "were masters of the air, and could fly, while men could not." (p. 776) In the end, after a dangerous trek alone across the marsh at night, Doris sinks exhausted into Dan's arms,

---

* "A Marsh Island," *The Atlantic Monthly* 55 (Jan.–June 1885), pp. 654–55. Subsequent page references are to this serialized version.

which unprecedented moment of feminine helplessness finally provokes him into declaring his love.

In the failed love interest between Doris and Dale there is another alternative lost, that of life in the city and intellectual growth. Part of Doris's attraction for Dale is that she has gone to boarding school and has city manners and city book learning. Yet in the end, country values prevail, and we are not to see Doris as in any way diminished by her future as the wife of a village blacksmith. Unlike her mother, who mourns her own lost opportunities and does not want Doris to "rust out [her life] on the farm" (p. 356), Doris is clearly intended to shine wherever she lives. Of Mrs. Owen, as of Mme Bovary, Jewett repeats the belief she herself had come to in the painful seventies: "It was a great pity she would not be wise enough to love the place where she had been kindly placed." (p. 455)

Jewett's fictional "Sussex" may in fact be a town in which a girl like Doris could be happy, but we are not given any description of the town itself, only of the farm some miles away. Because we are given no idea of the ways in which Doris's life with Dan will be interesting and fulfilling, and because her sudden resolution to marry lacks emotional plausibility, the novel fails even as a potboiler romance. No writing of Jewett's is an utter failure, however, and the descriptions of the marsh and farm life, and the characterizations of the senior Owens and their helper, Tempy, are up to her usual mark.

In *Betty Leicester,* first serialized in 1889 as "A Bit of Color" and enlarged to book length a year later, Jewett has her material more firmly in hand. In this book written in the *Leslie Goldthwaite* tradition as a wholesome novel for teenage girls, we see again the city outsider who comes to a country village, changes it, and in turn is changed. Betty Leicester, a fifteen-year-old girl from one of the town's leading families, has lived abroad, mostly in England, with her father since her mother's death four years earlier. She returns to spend a summer in Tideshead, which in some ways is based on South Berwick as it was in Jewett's childhood. She stays in the ancestral house with her great-aunts while her father, a naturalist, goes on an expedition to Alaska. In the course of her visit, Betty learns to love Tideshead and think of it as home; she, in her turn, as a sophisticated outsider, enlarges the experience and changes the behavior of the village young people. The book can be read as Jewett's affectionate critique, if not precisely of South Berwick, then of towns much like it.

Berwickers by the end of the century, if not earlier, had become somewhat complacent about their town and their way of life and resistant to change. Tideshead, situated like Berwick at the head of the tide, has a similar history and is about as well-off economically, with many people struggling but nobody dirt-poor. Socially it is caught in a time warp. No one has gone to sea for two generations, and people hardly ever stir even as far as Boston. They have forgotten how to be spontaneous, let alone adventurous. As the local doctor tells Betty, "We Tideshead people are terribly afraid of one another, and have to go through just so much before we can take the next step." (p. 201) Tideshead girls fuss a great deal over clothes and make a prodigious amount of work out of any social event. They are astonished when Betty gives a party on the spur of the moment. They jealously enforce class distinctions and cruelly snub the family of a man who has been sent to jail. Jewett represents their provincialism in the characters of Mary Beck and her snobbish, envious, endlessly complaining mother.

Betty, by contrast, is friendly and courteous to everyone, from the men who help her with her luggage on the river packet boat to the children of the jailed man, whom she invites to her party. She confides in old Serena, the countrywoman who has been part of the family for forty years; and she hangs around the stable listening to Jonathan (based on John Tucker), picking up useful wisdom on everything from horses to politics. When she goes with Jonathan and Serena to visit their relatives in the country, she easily and naturally reverses her habitual role with them. They become her host and hostess, and she feels "an unusual spirit of deference and gratitude toward them," while they are "quite conscious of a different relationship toward Betty from that at home." (pp. 144–45) In other words, Betty is perfectly democratic in her manners and respects everyone regardless of their station. Oddly, we are apparently meant to believe she has learned this in class-conscious Britain, whence she has returned more democratic than the Americans she left behind. However this may strain credibility, the point is that Tideshead's loss of contact with the wider world has caused it to shrink and stiffen as compared to the cosmopolitan town it once was. Betty's ability to adapt flexibly to any social situation is seen to have moral implications: the fate of the jailed man's innocent family, and by implication of democracy itself, hinges on the necessity of recognizing the essential equality of all human beings. This does not mean that class distinctions are erased (Betty's late great-grandmother, like Berwick's Elizabeth Cushing, is referred to throughout as "Madame Leicester"), but that they are fluid, defined by the situation of the moment, and always subordinated to membership in the larger human family. Thus the book restates, in simplified terms and without any transcendental overtones, the primary theme of *Deephaven.*

Throughout the story the village young people and Betty learn from each other. In the end the villagers' snobbery has decreased and they are learning to be generally less hidebound, while Betty has come to think of Tideshead as home. Like Doris Owen and Kate Lancaster before her, she decides that God has put her where she is meant to be: "It wasn't the thing one had to do, but the way one learned to do it, that distinguished one's life. Perhaps she could be famous for every-day homely things and have a real genius for something so simple that nobody else had thought of it." (p. 135) In a sense, although the book is dedicated to Annie's and Sarah's friend Mary Greenwood Lodge (who died shortly before it was published), it is a vindication of Mary Jewett's life in Berwick and could well have been dedicated to her.

Betty's relationship with her father is close and exclusive. The mother being conveniently deceased, the book opens with the father and daughter breakfasting tête-à-tête in a Boston hotel. The father, we are told, depends on his daughter to keep his clothes neat and his life in order, and he ritually asks her permission before taking any important step. They look alike and have the same eyes; she is fifteen, he thirty-eight—closer in age than Sarah and her father. When he returns at the end of the book, their public reunion is much more demonstrative than one would expect of New Englanders, and Jewett comments that "they were very fond of each other, these two; but some of their friends agreed with Aunt Barbara, who always said that her nephew was much too young to have the responsibility of so tall a girl as Betty Leicester." (p. 219) As Jewett herself once did, Betty has thought she would like to be her father's ghostwriter or amanuensis, but she has given it up because she has no talent for writing.

The advice Betty's father gives her, an outline for a life of independence and sensitivity to others, clearly echoes Dr. Jewett's own blend of sense and sympathy: "Learn the right way to do things. Do everything that you can for yourself. Try to make yourself fit to live with other people. Try to avoid making other people wait upon you. Remember that every person stands in a different place from every other and so sees life from a different point of view. Remember that nobody likes to be proved in the wrong, and be careful in what manner you say things to people that they do not wish to hear." (pp. 116–17)

There are reminders of Sarah's active girlhood in Betty's fondness for the outdoors (though in truth we never see her do anything more strenuous than walking); and there is a subtle feminist detail in the description of the aunts' best bedroom, decorated with engravings from Élisabeth Vigée-Lebrun and Angelica Kauffmann. One of the best moments of Betty's summer comes when she slips off shoes and stockings and wades to an island in a millpond, where she spends a quiet hour beside a duck's nest, careful not to disturb the bird. Mrs. Beck, the personification of narrow-mindedness, disapproves of girls being allowed to "climb fences and be tomboys," (p. 51) and naturally we side with Betty against the Mrs. Becks of the world. Yet Betty's wade in the millpond is taken furtively, in the sad knowledge that she will never do such a thing again; and Betty's father, who of course speaks for everything that is right and proper and moral for Jewett's young readers, says at the end that "a girl should grow up in a home, and get a girl's best life out of the cares and pleasures of it." (p. 287) So *Betty Leicester* too expresses Jewett's ambivalence toward woman's role, unchanged as she passed forty. We are asked to admire the spirited and achieving women, the Lebruns and Kauffmanns of the world and the fleet-footed Doris Owens, but to expect on behalf of most women the small compass of home and garden, where perhaps they may develop a genius for "every-day homely things."

Written in an entirely different mood, about a woman who escapes the domestic scenario, is the frankly feminist novel *A Country Doctor.* The most autobiographical of her books, it makes no concessions to popular prejudice but is a frankly polemical work in which the argument for vocational equality is presented several times, as in one of those old children's tales where the message is told to the ploughman, the sowers, the old-woman-going-to-market, and so on. Here Jewett seems to turn upside down the values she espouses in *A Marsh Island* and *Betty Leicester,* clearly stating the case for the choice she herself had made, as well as one she might have made. *A Country Doctor* is a kind of fantasy of what might have happened if she had actually followed her father into medicine, and for these few hundred pages she seems to have written only from her own experience, setting aside for a while her imaginative identification with her mother and sisters and the circumscribed female world they represented. The book is interesting too for what it reveals about Jewett's place within the tradition of New England feminism.

The conflict between marriage and profession for a woman doctor had been recently dealt with in two novels by Jewett's friends, both of which must have had some bearing on her decision to write about it herself. *Dr. Breen's Practice* (1881), an unusually flaccid novel by William Dean Howells, is a conventional romance in which the heroine, a homeopathic physician without any real commitment to her profession, retires prettily in favor of matrimony. A much better book with a thoughtful and realistic treatment of the subject is *Doctor Zay* (1882) by Elizabeth Stuart Phelps. The title character, also a homeopathic physician, is a thoroughly dedicated professional with a thriving small-town practice in Maine. She is wooed by a patient, one of those wealthy, aimless young Bostonians who populate the novels of the period. Eventually she succumbs to his suit, with the understanding that she will continue her career. But the practical difficulties ahead—beginning with a lack of reproductive control—are enormous, particularly since Dr. Zay has so exalted a view of marriage that it is clear there will be no room in her life for work. Phelps winks at that dilemma and leaves her heroine in the middle of it; Jewett's book, deliberately or not, clearly presents the alternative choice.[5]

The plot of *A Country Doctor* revolves around an orphan girl, Nan Prince. In the opening scene, Nan's consumptive, alcoholic mother returns by night to her home farm just outside Oldfields. Her melodramatic history, which seems utterly foreign to Jewett's experience, was probably based on an actual incident, the suicide-drowning of a South Berwick woman who had been "wild and astray in her youth" and who was apparently driven to despair by seeing her own sexual transgressions repeated by her grown daughter. Sarah saw the mother's body brought to the town jail and watched the crowd gather outside and the girl emerge from identifying the body, pale and shaken but "trying to be bold" as she made her way through the circle of accusing faces.[6]

In *A Country Doctor* the circumstances are altered and the "sin" of out-of-wedlock pregnancy tidied up for the benefit of popular taste. The mother, who left the farm to work in the Lowell mills, has fallen prey to the charms of a young physician from a wealthy family who (Jewett implies) seduces her but afterwards does the right thing. Both families strongly oppose the marriage, and within a year the husband dies, leaving his wife and baby daughter destitute. Disdaining the offer of his censorious relations to adopt the baby, the mother flees to her home farm, where in her desperation she almost throws herself and the child into the river. But supernatural forces, apparently rising from the family cemetery, cause her to hesitate, and soon she providentially collapses on her mother's doorstep. After lingering a few days she dies, leaving her daughter to her mother's care and imploring the village physician, Dr. Leslie, to watch over her welfare.

Nan lives several years with her grandmother. She is active, strong-willed, and mischievous, given to pranks and "wild as a hawk," according to a neighbor who is the victim of one of them. (p. 60) She hates book learning and confinement and is expelled from school for a summer after luring the other children into truancy in the fields. She is not shy and is "fearlessly friendly with every one," (p. 45) but she does not like other children much, nor they her, and she mostly seeks the company of wild creatures. In short, there is a good deal of Jewett's own solitary childhood self in Nan, as there will be in Sylvia of "A White Heron."

At the same time, Nan has a streak of lawlessness that is missing from the timid, gentle Sylvia and that reminds us of Hawthorne's amoral wood sprite, Pearl. Indeed, the Berwick drowning had brought Hawthorne's tale to Jewett's mind, and she thought at the time it was like having seen *The Scarlet Letter* brought to life. One can imagine that the drowning had evoked comments of "Like mother, like daughter" among the Berwick gossips, and Jewett's own belief that "bad blood" will tell underlies the question, implied throughout the book, of whether Nan's wild streak will lead her to repeat her mother's mistakes as the Berwick daughter did, or will instead be turned to some more creative use. Meanwhile her grandmother, a mild, unimaginative soul much like the grandmother in "A White Heron," is hard put to control her. Eventually the good woman dies, leaving Nan to the care of Dr. Leslie. The girl seems to be about eight or nine.

Long a widower, Dr. Leslie lives alone with a good-hearted, crusty housekeeper, Marilla Thomas. Like Dr. Jewett, he had settled in a country village for family reasons, thinking to move to the city later on, but instead he had stayed and devoted his life to looking after the local people. He is well respected in medical circles and has often been criticized for burying himself in Oldfields, but he himself has never had any regrets. Unlike Dr. Jewett he has gradually withdrawn from professional societies and old friendships, refusing even to teach. He is not active in the town, either, except as a doctor and casual neighbor, but he is universally liked and admired.

Dr. Leslie is most like Dr. Jewett in his scholarly, humanistic cast of mind and his sympathetic insight into human emotions and behavior. In keeping with his respect for individual integrity as well as a certain clinical objectivity, his attitude toward his young ward is one of studied permissiveness. Presumably he sets down certain basic rules of behavior enforced by Marilla and accepted by Nan, who though mischievous and careless is not defiant. Other-wise, believing that children of that age are merely "bundles of inheritances" (p. 102), he waits to see what sort of tendencies will surface. Nan goes to the town school now, and when Leslie sees that she is "pale and drooping" (p. 85, Sarah Orne Jewett's very words about herself at that age), he takes her out for the summer and allows her to drive rounds with him. Under a guidance so unobtrusive as never to provoke rebellion, Nan begins to take an interest in medicine. Following him in and out of patients' houses like "a little dog" (p. 85, another autobiographical echo), she helps him as much as he will allow, and eventually she announces that she wants to become a doctor and share his practice.

Their friend Mrs. Graham, who has undertaken Nan's education in manners and decorum, is shocked when the doctor tells her Nan's intention and wants to know if he doesn't think that "a married life is happiest." But Dr. Leslie, having noticed Nan's complete lack of interest in boys, doesn't think she is the marrying kind, and in the passage quoted earlier says,

> When a man or woman has that sort of self-dependence
> and unnatural self-reliance, it shows itself very early. I be-
> lieve that it is a mistake for such a woman to marry. Nan's
> feeling toward her boy-playmates is exactly the same as to-
> ward the girls she knows. You have only to look at the rest
> of the children together to see the difference; and if I make
> sure by and by, the law of her nature is that she must live
> alone and work alone, I shall help her to keep it instead of
> break it. (p. 137)

As for the social opposition they are both sure to encounter, he is totally indifferent. As he tells Dr. Ferris, who is afraid Nan will "risk her happiness" in following a medical career, "I don't care whether [medicine] is a man's work or a woman's work; if it is hers I'm going to help her the very best way I can." (p. 106)

Nan goes away to boarding school, where she spends several years and is reasonably happy. But this exposure to other girls and their expectations dampens and deflects her ambition. She becomes "a little shy of being found with one of the medical books in her hand, as she tried to fancy herself in sympathy with the conventional world of school and of the every-day ideas of society." (p. 161) But she cannot quite relinquish her hopes of a medical career. Bored by the idea of simply keeping house for the doctor, she is equally repelled by teaching or by the thought of marriage, which seems to "hover like a cloudy barrier" over the future lives of her classmates. (p. 160)

This aimless, drifting period in Nan's life is rather like the similar period in Jewett's late adolescence, when she could not yet believe in herself as a writer and yet desperately needed a focus for her life. Unlike Jewett, Nan does not clutch at religion as a kind of temporary vocation; but like Jewett, she needs a religious justification in order to find the moral courage to choose her own life. She walks one day to the spot where her mother had decided not to commit suicide after all, and there she suddenly resolves to make the fantasy of medicine "a reality." The setting is meant to be important, for just as her life was saved in this place once before for a purpose, so that purpose is now divinely sanctioned and she literally receives a vocation. "God," says the author, "had directed her at last." (p. 166) It is this divine mandate, and the specific talent it confirms, that set her apart most clearly from Doris Owen and Betty Leicester.[7]

Dr. Leslie, who has been quietly anxious over Nan's vacillation, is pleased and relieved. The two of them encounter "much re-proach" in the town, (p. 183) and Nan feels like "a reformer, a radical, and even . . . a political agitator" as she faces her "stormy future." (p. 174) Dr. Leslie shrugs off all opposition and hopes Nan will as well, and in fact Nan's future does not turn out to be particularly stormy. Jewett places her heroine in the most fortunate of environments, where a beloved foster-father provides emotional and financial support and where Nan can gradually establish a practice among people who already know and respect her. Neither in Oldfields nor in medical school, where several of her former schoolmates join her, does she encounter any bruising obstacles. And, three decades after Elizabeth Blackwell gained her M.D., Nan takes heart from remembering "what renown some women physi-cians [have] won." (p. 193)

Her resolution is assailed once more, when during a vacation break from school Nan is reconciled to her father's sister and goes to visit her in Dunport. Here she becomes acquainted with the traditions of the rich, old, respectable Prince family, as embodied in her severely conservative aunt. Anna Prince is one of those sterling, upper-class ladies of the old school who, like Katharine Brandon, often merit Jewett's uncritical admiration; but in this novel the character is an unmarried woman who has become cramped and narrow-minded through living in a small provincial town. Miss Prince has the family's strong will, but she has lacked anything worthy of its exercise and has wasted her abilities on a "comparatively unimportant and commonplace existence." (p. 236) Yet she is lucky compared with another, truly pathetic elderly spinster, Miss Fraley, who has lived all her life with her domineer-ing mother and has never had a moment's independence or a penny to call her own. The worst aspects of spinsterhood without a career are pointedly illustrated in these two, who have been definitely stunted by the circumstances in which they find themselves "kindly placed."

Nan's aunt, scandalized by her choice of profession, deliberately throws her together with an attractive young law student in hopes of subverting her ambition. In spite of Nan's previous indifference to men, she and George Gerry fall in love. She hesitates and falters (for Jewett's depiction of Nan's sudden love for Gerry, while by no means convincing, is at least not absurd); but again she manages to shake herself free and recover her resolve. In a New Testament allusion that would not have been lost on Jewett's readers, she announces to her aunt that "I must be about my business" and hies herself back to medical school. (p. 308) She finishes her education and goes home to share her guardian's practice.

The religious argument for vocational choice set forth so persuasively in *A Country Doctor* was, of course, Jewett's own rationale for her career as a writer. It was well within the feminist tradition, having been first expressed in 1845 by Margaret Fuller, friend and mentor of many of Jewett's own friends. In a sense, Jewett's novel is evidence of how vibrant and far-reaching Fuller's influence was among two generations of Boston women. As Nan believes that she must use the talent God has given her, and as Leslie waits patiently to see what natural abilities will unfold in the growing child, so Fuller had argued in *Woman in the Nineteenth Century* that each soul enters the world with individual gifts that will manifest themselves if unimpeded by prejudice, and that each person has not only the right but the obligation to fulfill her or his potential according to God's plan. As Nan is allowed to develop "as naturally as a plant grows, without being clipped or forced in any direction," and as Jewett herself was encouraged by her father to range freely in all fields of knowledge, so Fuller's fictional Miranda is blessed with a father who shares his own learning with her and respects her as a "living mind."[8] As Nan is described by Leslie as possessing "unnatural self-reliance," so Fuller bases the independence of Miranda, and all free women, on the early development of self-reliance. As Leslie firmly believes "it is a mistake for such a woman to marry," so Miranda is providentially free of all distractions of sexual feeling. And of course Leslie's repeated affirmation that it makes no difference whether medicine is man's work or woman's work as long as it is Nan's work, echoes some of Fuller's most memorable pleas for vocational equality.

Margaret Fuller died the year after Sarah Orne Jewett was born, but in the Boston Jewett knew from childhood Fuller's personal influence was very much alive, as her friends and followers continued to carry her ideals into practice. Perhaps the most visible was Julia Ward Howe, who had attended Fuller's Conversations in the 1840s and gone on to write several books—among them a biography of Fuller—and to become co-founder of the New England Woman Suffrage Association and the New England Women's Club. Thomas Wentworth Higginson, friend of Emily Dickinson, social reformer, champion of women's rights, and himself another of Fuller's biographers, was related to Fuller by marriage and had largely raised her niece and namesake. Another faithful supporter of the women's movement, James Freeman Clarke, had been Fuller's close friend in her youth and had co-edited her *Memoirs*. Lydian Emerson, keen on suffrage in her old age and known to chide daughter Ellen for being lukewarm toward the cause, had attended the Conversations, as had Jewett's old acquaintance Ednah Dow Cheney (who, incidentally, was delivered into the world by Sarah Orne Jewett's father). Jewett's friend Anna Loring Dresel had been a friend of Fuller's as a girl. Louisa May Alcott had grown up with the example of Margaret Fuller before her, while Ellen Hooper Gurney, one of the leaders of the movement to establish Radcliffe College, was the daughter of Fuller's friend Ellen Sturgis Hooper. And it may be more than coincidence that Elizabeth Blackwell's New York pastor and confidant in the 1840s, when she came to her decision to study medicine, was another Fuller friend and *Memoirs* co-editor, William Henry Channing.

It is some measure of how far women had come in forty years that Fuller's views, which provoked controversy and contempt in her own time, could be incorporated into a popular novel without incurring anything worse than mild carping from the critics. Heroism is not required of Nan Prince. In her own words, she is no "reformer," no "radical." She is just an ordinary girl wanting to live a peaceful life in her own town, like many others. For this reason *A Country Doctor* must have helped brace the spirits of many isolated and beleaguered young women. It was possible for Nan and Dr. Leslie to avoid serious ostracism in their small town because of the tremendous changes generated by Fuller and other reformers of the 1840s and 1850s.

But Nan's conviction that she must not marry, Doris Owen's final capitulation to her faint-hearted lover, and Betty Leicester's premature resignation at fifteen to a life of everyday things demonstrate how little progress mainstream, middle-of-the-road feminists, as represented by Jewett and her readers, had made in attempting to resolve the conflict between female sexuality and vocational freedom. Like Jewett herself, Nan Prince is permitted her career by a kind of divine dispensation, and she must be celibate whether she wants to or not. Margaret Fuller in her day had personally found the renunciation of heterosexual love extremely difficult, but had held up as a model for other women the improbably chaste Miranda. Doris and Betty, allowed to marry, must create satisfying lives out of whatever resources come to hand, and presumably Jewett would evade the question of their narrow and confined lives by suggesting that they too were fulfilling God's intention. *A Country Doctor* and its companion novels hold up two continuing, incompatible ideals for women, that of the free spinster and that of the ordinary wife and mother, whose choice is still as constricted as it was in the forties. The dichotomy evident in *Woman in the Nineteenth Century* is expressed in *A Country Doctor* and *A Marsh Island,* whose conflicting views of womanhood might have been created by two different writers.

In one respect Jewett's insight into sexual roles is remarkably clear. Both Richard Dale in *A Marsh Island* and George Gerry in *A Country Doctor* are threatened and chagrined by demonstrations of competence in the women they love (or think they love, or almost love—one is never sure with Jewett). In *A Marsh Island* the scene is comic: Dale, seeing Doris driving a draft team at a good clip, persuades himself that they must be running away with her. In his rush to "rescue" her he falls and hurts his ankle, whereupon she jumps up on one of the "runaway" horses and gallops off to fetch help. In *A Country Doctor,* Gerry is piqued when he watches Nan briskly set a farm boy's dislocated shoulder. "It is in human nature to respect power," Jewett comments. "All his manliness was at stake, and his natural rights would be degraded and lost, if he could not show his power to be greater than her own." (p. 295)

Seldom had a woman novelist described the male need for domi-
nance in quite such plain and unromanticized terms. And indeed
the contest for power was at the heart of the vexed problem of
vocational choice. For, as Margaret Fuller put it, "Each wishes to
be lord in a little world, to be superior at least over one; and he
does not feel strong enough to retain a life-long ascendency over a
strong nature."[9]

Not all feminists shared the vocational conflicts expressed in
A Country Doctor. Christie, the heroine of Louisa May Alcott's *Work,*
takes a series of jobs in order to be financially independent and
escape a stultifying home life. *Work* is an angry book that directly
contradicts Jewett's belief that most rural women should accept the
limitations of their lives as a kind of challenge. But Christie has
no particular vocational direction, and in due course she becomes
a conventional wife and mother, although she is later widowed. For
all her anger, Alcott's book is less subversive than Jewett's, for the
author sees work as a means to an end rather than an end in itself.
Nan Prince's choice is an end in itself, and as such it excludes the
only socially acceptable "end" of a woman's ambition, which of
course was marriage. As long as the last vestiges of puritanism
lingered in America, such a choice would provoke a certain amount
of unease in the woman herself and censure from those around her.

For Jewett personally, her fictional heroine, and Margaret
Fuller, the means of avoiding such unease and censure was the
unanswerable invocation of God's will. In the next two or three
decades, as religion loosened its hold even in New England and
women were able to claim their lives on their own behalf rather
than God's, the argument for equality expressed by Nan and Dr.
Leslie would rapidly become anachronistic. But for New England
women of Jewett's time and place, spiritual daughters and cousins
of Anne Bradstreet, Margaret Fuller, Emily Dickinson, and Harriet
Beecher Stowe, the old theocratic tradition still kept its power both
to liberate and to curse.

15

Calm Seas
and a Following Wind

IN 1873, THE YEAR THE FIRST OF THE
Deephaven sketches appeared in *The Atlantic,* James Osgood published *Among the Isles of Shoals,* by Celia Thaxter. Like "The Shore
House," Thaxter's book took her readers to a small, isolated up-
country community dominated by the sea. She had written it at
the urging of James Fields, Whittier, and Howells, and it was her
first prose book, although she was well known as a poet. Like Annie
and James Fields and Thomas Bailey Aldrich, Thaxter was a better
prose writer than she knew, and *Among the Isles of Shoals* retains, in
spite of the language's tendency to cloy here and there, a unique
place in American nature writing.

Long a friend and literary protégée of Annie's, in the early
1880s Celia joined Sarah's innermost circle of friends as well. Her
life had been picturesque and unusually troubled. Born Celia
Laighton in Portsmouth in 1835, she had spent most of her
childhood on one or another of the Isles of Shoals, rocky outcrop-
pings in the sea a few miles out from Portsmouth harbor. When
she was small her father had been a lighthouse keeper; later her
parents opened a resort hotel on Hog Island, which they renamed
Appledore. There Levi Thaxter, a young Harvard graduate who was
Laighton's business partner and the tutor of Celia and her brothers,

fell in love with the girl when she was thirteen and married her three years later. The marriage was troubled. After a short, idyllic period of living on the island, the couple moved to the mainland and became very poor, Levi being unable to find an occupation that suited him. Celia gave birth to three sons, the eldest emotionally unstable and nearly unmanageable unless Celia was constantly with him. Meanwhile her father died and her mother, whom she adored, became chronically ill. Celia began to divide her year between Appledore and the mainland, keeping her son Karl with her and trying to care for both families. Presently Levi too became ill and began to take long trips to warm climates, further straining the marriage. In the midst of this confusion and anxiety Celia began to write poetry, and soon she was a regular contributor to *The Atlantic* and an immensely popular poet. Her writing supported the family, and in later years she supplemented this income by painting on china.

By the time Sarah moved in with Annie, Celia's most turbulent years were behind her. Her mother had died, and Levi had at last found a vocation as a dramatic reader of Browning's poetry. Their sons were grown and the whole family had a new home in Kittery Point, Maine, not far from South Berwick. But Celia's life was by no means easy. Karl's moodiness was a constant anxiety, and as a result of his quarreling with his brother, he and Celia spent the winters of 1881 and 1882 in a Boston hotel. Levi's health continued to decline, and in 1884 he died.

After Levi's death Celia began to spend each summer in her own cottage on Appledore, taking Karl with her. There, in a parlor crammed with flowers from her remarkably lush and prolific garden, amid pictures and photographs hung frame to frame and a comfortable confusion of wicker furniture, paisley shawls, cushions, and knickknacks, Celia Thaxter established one of New England's more memorable salons. Members of Boston's literary, artistic, and musical worlds, staying at the hotel, would make their way to Celia's parlor to talk or listen to music, while in a corner their hostess quietly worked at her painting. By now she was a stout, silver-haired grandmother with a fine profile, of which she was rather vain. She always dressed in white or gray, with a white fichu over her shoulders and a silver crescent in her hair. She was, in

short, a deliberately composed portrait of herself, just as her parlor—with its two or three vases of flowers on each table, each vase
chosen for its own particular flowers—created an illusion of a life
lived as art, in which no hint intruded of the day she had spent
doing hotel accounts or killing slugs in the garden. No doubt some
people found all this affected, but even they would have to grant
there was a certain gallantry in the way she fought back at the
chaos of her life and created her peace where and how she could.

In the first few years of her friendship with Sarah, Celia was
still grieving for her mother, who had been her best—and for years
almost her only—woman friend. In 1882 she became attracted, or
rather addicted, to spiritualism through the influence of a medium,
Rose Darrah, who claimed she could contact Mrs. Laighton on the
other side. Presently she announced she had talked with James
Fields and Theodore Jewett as well. Susceptible in their own grief,
both Sarah and Annie were temporarily taken in, and both separately consulted an unnamed medium—probably Darrah—before
they sailed for Europe in the spring of 1882. Impressed in spite of
her doubts, Sarah wrote a long letter about it to Whittier, who she
knew would not laugh at her. "I was most suspicious and unbe-
lieving even after what Mrs. Fields told me," she wrote, "and it
really wasn't until after I had gone home [to Berwick] again and
began to talk it over that I quite took in the strangeness of it."
The medium foretold her voyage with Annie (no great feat, since
she had already seen Annie, but Sarah was impressed). She described James Fields "perfectly" and, what was more marvelous to
Sarah,

> told me wonderful things about my father and about his
> death and our relation to each other, and what he said to
> me was amazing. There was a great deal that came from
> him and from Mr. Fields that is the most capital advice,
> the most practical help to me, perfect "sailing orders" you
> know! . . . They said *they* had made all the plans for Mrs.
> Fields and me and helped us carry it out—that we needed
> each other and could help each other. . . . And I was given
> a dear and welcome charge and care over Mrs. Fields which
> I can speak about better than write to you. . . .

As a final persuasion the woman mentioned that Dr. Jewett had found a new friend in the next world, one Bessie Greene, whom Sarah only later placed as a friend of Annie's who had died years earlier. That, to her, was definitive proof that the medium was no sham. All the same, she did not think she would return. She did think she might go to another one someday and compare the two,

> for I still have "an eye out" for tricks of the trade and yet I cant help being ashamed as I write this, for it was all so real and so perfectly sensible and straightforward, and free from silliness.[1]

Throughout the following year all three women's interest remained high, and there was much talk about spiritualism in their letters to one another and to Whittier, who was as curious and open-minded as they. Sarah's interest in Swedenborg deepened, and she reread the books Parsons had given her. All the same, she remained wary. In 1884–85 Mary Greenwood Lodge, who was more suspicious than they were, attended a couple of Darrah's séances with them, the second of which was held in Annie's library. Sarah's dog, Roger, was there too and growled convincingly at a "spirit." This canine testimony notwithstanding, Lodge afterwards pointed out several strong indications of fraud, and after that Sarah and Annie patronized no more mediums. Celia, initially piqued at Lodge's accusations, gradually turned from spiritualism to eastern religion to theosophy, coming to rest at last in a strong, unorthodox form of Christianity. But, like Sarah, she never relinquished her belief in spiritual regeneration, and before she died in 1894 she would say she had seen a vision of her mother at the foot of her bed.

Celia Thaxter's tendency to rapidly fall in and out of love with ideas was one of many traits she shared with Sarah Orne Jewett. Another was an understanding of the natural world that surpassed Jewett's own. A child whose chief playthings are flowers and shells will either come to hate flowers and shells or to appreciate them very much indeed; and while the Thaxter children probably had some conventional playthings, their world was miniature and highly selective, composed of tiny samplings of the larger environment. Other people's commonplaces became their miracles, and on their infrequent trips to Portsmouth they were struck with wonder at the sight of trees and horses. As an adult Celia Thaxter could write about nature's most inconspicuous objects, like rocks and seaweed and grass, with as much sympathy and delight as she felt for obvious exotics like poppies and snowy owls. Her small garden, always brilliant with color, expressed her love for all growing things but also made a kind of statement, like Jewett's, that here a minute symbol of womanly tradition and order made its stand. Like Jewett, too, she felt an immediate link with history, and she had grown up listening to the rough, quirky talk of the island natives and their tales of pirate ghosts. Then, too, her circumscribed childhood, like Jewett's, had left her with a permanent residue of innocence in her personality, a lifelong capacity for being genuinely surprised by experience. And finally, having grown up in a place where time in the usual sense was largely irrelevant, she could not help but embody Jewett's favorite adjective: she was old-fashioned.

The fourth member of this little circle, and one who was the very epitome of old-fashioned, was John Greenleaf Whittier. He too was in Boston during Sarah's first winter there, nursing his sick brother and living in the same hotel as Celia Thaxter. His friendship with the Fieldses went very far back: he had been present at the founding of *The Atlantic Monthly* in 1857 and had dedicated his 1869 book *Among the Hills* to Annie. While he was in Boston he often made his way to Charles Street, coming for breakfast as he had years ago so as to avoid all other visitors except perhaps Holmes. So Jewett began to know face to face the friend she had previously known almost entirely through letters.

As with Thaxter, there were many similarities between them. Whittier's several homes (he had three) were all north of Boston, not far from Sarah's home ground. His mother had been born in Rollinsford, across the bridge from South Berwick, and he knew the countryside almost as intimately as Sarah herself. But he had grown up on a Massachusetts farm, in a simply educated Quaker family where religion did not necessarily preclude belief in supernatural phenomena and where storytelling displaced books as a form of entertainment. Superstitions and folktales were an abiding interest and the stuff of his poetry, and his first book, *Legends of New England,* had been a collection of folklore. From his own childhood he remembered a woman who had had to swear before

a justice of the peace that she was not a witch, and his aunt had
seen a vision of her lover before he died. Like Celia Thaxter, whose
native islands had a rich tradition of tales involving disembodied
spirits, and like Helen and Kate in *Deephaven,* Whittier liked
nothing better than to sit in a dimly lit room and tell ghost stories.
He followed Celia Thaxter's enthusiasm with keen interest for a
while and, like all three women, kept up with the published reports
of the Society for Psychic Research.* But in the end he too was
certain she had been deceived by Darrah and others, telling Annie
that while he "believe[d] there is such a thing as communication
with those who are in another sphere . . . there is also much which
repels and disgusts me."[2]

Sharing Jewett's love of country people and country tales,
Whittier also shared her belief in the moral function of literature.
Although he loved to tell a tale for its own sake, he was above all
a lifelong reformist whose first poem had been published in William Lloyd Garrison's *Free Press.* For many years before the Civil
War he had put not only his pen but his whole person at the service
of the abolitionist cause, speaking at rallies, facing down hostile
crowds, and serving in the Massachusetts legislature. Once the
office of a newspaper he edited was attacked and burned, and he
escaped violence only by disguising himself and mingling with the
mob. His judgment meant a great deal to Jewett, and it was
fortunate for her work that his moral priorities never outweighed
his delight in a good story.

There are more debts to Whittier in Jewett's stories than we
can ever trace. The name of Dr. Leslie in *A Country Doctor* is
probably a nod to Whittier's Amesbury friend Dr. Horace Leslie,
and an article Whittier sent her ("Fish and Men in the Maine
Islands," by W. H. Bishop) helped with background for "The King
of Folly Island" (1886). Jewett named the heroine of that story
after Whittier's niece Phebe and made the story the title piece of
a book dedicated to him. There is also a Phebe in "The Courting
of Sister Wisby" (1887), which was based on one of Whittier's
yarns. "Wisby" is a comic tale of a calculating old woman and an

* Responding to the resurgence of interest in spiritualism, the SPR was
founded in England in 1882 for the purpose of dispassionate investigation of
psychic phenomena. A sister society was founded in America by William James
and others in 1885.

equally shrewd, lazy widower who, in the course of a trial marriage, maneuver to see how much in the way of practical help and material comfort each can wring out of the other. In the end they marry and, in the laconic words of the narrator, Mrs. Goodsoe, "[get] along as well as most folks."[3] The story, with its out-of-wedlock arrangement, is a little more roughhewn than Jewett's usual tales and is probably not one she would have used without suggestion.

Literary aid and model, fellow moralist and spiritualist, country boy and surrogate father, Whittier was many things to Jewett. Above all he was "Thy Friend," an elderly man whose sweet disposition and archaic manners masked a certain moral ferocity, and whose chronic ailments gained him much solicitude from his large flock of women friends. A lifelong bachelor, he was fond of women's company but remained celibate, depending for companionship and domestic comfort on his sister while she lived and later on his niece and cousins. He was plagued by a variety of ailments, including migraines and insomnia, to which in old age were added deafness, rheumatism, failing eyesight, and frequent colds, and he ingenuously exploited the sympathy of his friends by filling his letters with doleful accounts of his sufferings. His chronic self-pity was the subject of some tender mockery in the Jewett-Fields households: "I have had a dear, dismal letter from Thy Friend," Sarah would report to Mary, and forthwith she or Annie would send off a recipe for one of their innocently bacchic remedies.

After Whittier's brother died in 1883 he retreated to his home ground on the North Shore. Sarah and Annie made little pilgrimages to visit him there and at his summer retreat in Holderness, New Hampshire. In 1885 they did their best to tempt him into spending the winter under Annie's roof, and for a while he allowed himself to accept. But then he reneged, pleading fear that his admirers would find him out. There was some truth in this, but another probable reason was his realization that Annie's house was a hospitable one, and that he would be living in the midst of friendly comings and goings and would be obliged, for his hostess's sake, to be politely available. So they saw him only occasionally from then on but wrote frequently, Sarah usually limiting her letters to her months in Berwick so as not to overburden him with correspondence.

Although Sarah made literally dozens of new friends when she

joined Annie (her life in Boston being a constant alternation
between work and friends), none were more important in the early
years than these two. Both Thaxter and Whittier were hugely
popular writers as she was, both brought to the friendship a trove
of rural experience and lore, both were acutely attuned to nature,
and both were committed to an open-minded, unorthodox form of
religion that included spiritualist leanings. All this the three had
in common far more than anything they had in common with
Annie, much as they all loved her. Added to it was a common
characteristic, not exactly of naiveté so much as a kind of willed
innocence: each had grown up protected by some buffer, whether
of Quaker faith, or physical space, or simply in Jewett's case the
sheer decency and intellectual strength of a remarkable parent, that
had preserved untouched the morally virginal quality that distinguished them all. One might be tempted to call them babes in the
wood of the Gilded Age—or the age of the Confidence Man—except that each possessed a degree of courage under adversity that
belied any hint of weakness. But each was as transparent as a child;
there were no murky depths to them, no puzzling twists of mean-
ness or sudden flashes of uncontrolled egotism. What you saw when
you met them, or read when you picked up their books, was more
or less what was actually there all through.

Now that Sarah was spending several months of the year in
Boston, she attended Trinity Church regularly. Annie, whose opinion of Phillips Brooks had been cool when he first came to Boston,
now thought better of him—probably because of his social activism—and sometimes went with her. Perhaps influenced by Brooks's
Low Church theology, Annie's Unitarianism, and Whittier's Quak-
erism, or perhaps because by now she had worked through the
emotional crisis of the seventies, Sarah's religious faith had become
gentler and more easygoing, more like the mellow Episcopal faith
of her early forebears. God's will was less likely now to be the
subject of comment in her letters or anxiety in her daily life. The
transcendentalist strain emerged more clearly now that the pall of
orthodoxy had lifted, and there are passages in her letters that not
only celebrate the beauty and peace of nature (for that she did all
the time), but express a mystical sense of connection with all life.
Walking at night on Academy Hill, for example, she sees

a great grey cloud in the west but all the rest of the sky
was clear and it was very beautiful—When one goes out of
doors and wanders about alone at such a time, how wonderfully one becomes part of nature—like an atom of quick-
silver against a great mass—I hardly keep my separate
consciousness but go on and on until the mood has spent
itself. . . .[4]

Along with this sharpened awareness of the spiritual resonance
of nature she developed a keener, less inhibited delight in the
product of her own pen. She still believed that she was but the
instrument of some Higher Power, but now the thought allowed
her to enjoy her own stories as much as she would those of a
stranger. "When that wrote itself down I couldn't help laughing,"
she chortled over a bit of dialogue in "The Taking of Captain Ball."[5]

As for her belief in the permeability of spiritual boundaries,
like her transcendentalism it was permanently and deeply fixed in
her psyche. Now and then in Berwick she would be seized by the
certainty that Annie was thinking of her or was actually present in
spirit. These suggestions extended to at least one other friend, Sarah
Wyman Whitman, to whom she would write from France in 1892,

I have been thinking of you so much today dear—I wonder
how things are with you—it seems as if something brought
us very near. . . . There seems to be a neutral ground above
the earth and below the sky to which I am often carried
and where today certainly you came and met me. We shall
know better about these things some day.[6]

Such moments were infrequent and should not be taken as evidence
of constant preoccupation with "intimations." They were simply a
part of her normal frame of reference; she habitually lived in a
world that included several spiritual dimensions.

In December 1883 Grandfather Perry completed his ninety-
fifth year, and all the Gilman relations gathered in Exeter to
celebrate along with his fellow townspeople. He celebrated with
the best of them, and the family began to think he might be
indestructible, or at least that he might live to be 100. Around

him were assembled the clan's other sprightly elders, among them
Great-aunt Mary Long, who had still had an uncommonly clear
soprano voice at eighty-three, and who at eighty-eight would
confess to Sarah

> that she could only manage an *alto* now in church, but I do
> believe that she sings to herself sometimes and goes over
> the dear old ballads. . . . She happened to tell me that she
> herself composed the air and accompaniment to that one
> you particularly like. . . . but indeed I should rather hear
> her *play* a song than most people sing it![7]

There too were Great-aunt Mary Bell, Aunt Lucretia Perry, "Young
Doctor" Will Perry, and Great-aunt Helen Gilman, all Grandfather
Perry's white-haired juniors, all of them vigorous in mind and most
in body. They made the middle-aged cousins of Sarah's generation
seem barely out of childhood. Every time Sarah saw them, especially the great-aunts, she must have experienced again the illusion
that within her family, time was magically slowed and that here,
at least, the tide of history flowed sweetly and softly, destroying
nothing.

One memorable guest the tide washed up at the door of
Charles Street that winter was Matthew Arnold, who with his wife,
Frances, was in America to deliver a course of lectures. In the
evenings hostesses and guests would sit around the library fireplace
and listen to Arnold read aloud from "The Scholar Gypsy." Long
a devoted reader of his books, Sarah found her admiration increased
by having met him personally, not least because he comfortably
reinforced her own opinions. Agreeing with his classicism, his
cultural and political conservatism, and his belief in the superiority
of the Germanic peoples, she ranked him with Thackeray, Tennyson, and Tolstoy as "a great man,"[8] although she later modified
that judgment somewhat. The Arnolds returned in 1886, partly to
visit their daughter Lucy, who had married an American, and partly
to profit from yet another lecture tour. Like Dickens before him,
Arnold bought his American success at mortal cost. His exhausting
schedule worsened an existing heart condition, and he died a few
months after his return.

A *Country Doctor* was published a few months after Arnold's visit, and the reviews followed one another throughout the fall. They were mostly condescending or deliberately obtuse. Some reviewers disdained to notice the feminist theme and complained that the book was dull. Some compared it unfavorably to Howells's *Dr. Breen's Practice* and Phelps's *Doctor Zay.* The *Lippincott's* reviewer complained that there were already too many male doctors in the world and that women were "not usually considered scientific or endowed with keen accurate intellectual vision." The *Saturday Review* critic grudgingly approved of Nan Prince's profession, but only because he thought her mother's "hereditary taint" made her unfit for breeding children. Horace Scudder in *The Atlantic,* meaning one supposes to be kind, criticized the unconvincing love scenes but allowed that after all the "womanliness of the work" (meaning the novel, not medicine) was "of a thoroughly healthy sort." Two reviewers were sympathetic to the book's central theme: the anonymous *Spectator* critic noted its "deep, though unobtrusive, religious character," which presumably justified Nan's vocation to him as it did to the author. And William Morton Payne of *The Dial* frankly applauded both theme and treatment, complaining only of the tiresome persistence with which Jewett hammered home her argument.[9] In short, most of the reviews reflected the continued refusal of the public to address the subject of vocational equality on its merits. When *A Marsh Island* was published the following year, critics greeted it with nearly audible sighs of relief: Miss Jewett had gone back to her métier as portrayer of "the poetry of quiet Nature, felt and expressed with equal truth and simplicity."[10]

As usual, Sarah seems to have taken the reviews in stride. Hard at work on *Normans* and *A Marsh Island,* she let her novel take its knocks without comment. She did, however, fire another small feminist shot that year. Among the many stories published in the eighties was "Farmer Finch," which appeared in the January 1885 *Harper's* and therefore probably was written while the reviews of *A Country Doctor* were coming out. The story is about young Polly Finch, who decides to help her father on his farm after his bank fails. Polly's mother urges her to become a teacher, but Polly says she would "rather be a boy, and farm it, than teach any school [I] ever saw." (*A White Heron,* p. 52) Her father is passively disapproving, but the town doctor—not surprisingly—offers emotional and financial support. Polly does become a good farmer, thereby confounding her father and a patronizing former suitor. The townspeople approve in the end because she does not put on airs or become "unwomanly and rough." (p. 81) The doctor points out an ambiguous moral: Polly is one of the people who "look at things as they are, and not as they wish them to be." (p. 83) But Polly, after all, does look at things as she wishes them to be, since she wishes to be a farmer. Equally equivocal, Jewett comments in the end that it is "not very likely" Polly will spend her life as a farmer, since she probably will fall in love with "a much better man" than her former lover. (p. 84) She does, however, leave the final decision to Polly herself.

It was also during 1884–85 that Jewett had her first professional dealings with Samuel J. McClure. Their encounter led to a brief and comical standoff that provoked Sarah to a rare exhibition of temper. Irish-born, charming, self-educated, and erratically brilliant, McClure lived in Boston in 1882–83 as editor of the *The Wheelman.* In 1884 he founded the McClure Syndicate, through which a single story or article could be printed simultaneously in many publications across the country.* Always ready to further young talent, Jewett was one of several New England authors who agreed to send him work. In the spring of 1885 she sent one of her sketches, along with two by Roland Hill, a beginning writer she had taken under her wing.

McClure's manic temperament throve on attempting the impossible, and he was soon running out of money and working himself to exhaustion. For one of these reasons or the other, he did not trouble himself to either return the sketches or pay for them. Some weeks after sending them, Sarah wrote gently requesting a decision; McClure put her off. She wrote again, asking him to return them and offering him a long story. He accepted the story but did not pay for it or return the sketches. Finally she lost her patience and wrote in her crispest Gilman-matriarch voice, rapping the dilatory young publisher into line:

---

* Just how many of Jewett's sketches were published with the McClure Syndicate, as well as the rival syndicate of Bacheller, Johnson and Bacheller, remains to be discovered.

> I must ask you again to send me immediately Mr. Hill's
> sketches. I am very sorry for this delay, it is not business-
> like either on your part or mine. . . . I have waited several
> weeks now, and while I was ready at first to make allow-
> ance for your hurry I cannot help feeling that it is quite
> time the five minutes for sealing them up and addressing
> them to me, should be found—As I have already said
> twice, I will refund the price of the return postage to you
> immediately.[11]

He did return Hill's work, but made her wait another month for
payment for her own and probably got it at a discount. The soul
of moderation herself, Jewett must have been baffled as well as
vexed by so mercurial a personality as McClure's. But she held no
grudge and eventually sent the syndicate more work. She also
published several sketches in *McClure's Magazine* after its founding
in 1893.

Throughout the mid to late eighties Sarah's rheumatism was
unusually severe, continuing to plague her even during the summer. In 1885 she and Carrie spent some time at the Isles of Shoals,
where they undoubtedly joined Celia Thaxter's evening companies.
In August 1886 she and Annie went to a spa at Richfield Springs,
New York, where Sarah endured the standard hydropathic regimen
of baths, wet sheets, rest, and copious draughts of sulphurous water.
June of the following year found them on Mouse Island in Boothbay Harbor, where they found early wildflowers still blooming in
hollows among the hemlocks, and where they would settle every
morning in some grassy clearing at the water's edge and read the
hours away, looking up from time to time to watch the sunlight
glow through the multicolored sails of passing schooners and
yachts.

Sarah loved Mouse Island. She returned to it at least twice that
decade, in company with Alice Longfellow and some other friends.
Its mists and rain seem not to have made her illness worse, possibly
because their effects were offset by the enforced quiet and by her
enjoyment of its woods, harbor, and people. The quiet was not
total, however, for Alice Longfellow was jubilantly healthy and
relentlessly athletic. "To tell the truth," Sarah wrote Annie one day
when the others had gone sailing,

I was glad of the reason of proofs this morning being unable to *continuously* cope with the hardy Alice—She never
gives in except at sailing in the sun, at rowing she *never*
quails—and though I am tough I do sometimes ship my
oars.[12]

When the weather turned foggy Sarah would have been glad to
leave, but was afraid "Al-ices feelings would suffer. She was so
funny going in swimming yesterday—for she carries her head high
and dry and straight up—as if she were simply walking about."[13]
She cannot have found Alice's enthusiasm seriously daunting, for
she returned with her the following year. In normal health Sarah
could almost match Alice stroke for stroke, and when they all went
tobogganing in Jackson, New Hampshire, in 1887, it was Annie
who was lagging behind—Annie who had "never coasted down a
hill in her life, poor little town-y!"[14]

The Jackson trip roughly coincided with Sarah's efforts, as
secretary of the ladies' division of the Longfellow Memorial Committee, to organize an authors' reading in order to establish a
memorial to the poet. It was one of the few public campaigns of
this kind she joined (others included raising a subscription to buy
a house for Walt Whitman and supporting the international copy-
right law), and she did her part efficiently, rounding up within a
few days a good stageful of reluctantly cooperative bards. Among
them were Julia Ward Howe (the only woman), Mark Twain (who
insisted on reading first so he could catch a train), Thomas
Wentworth Higginson (who suggested she not let Holmes choose
the poems he wanted to read because Holmes was such a bad judge
of his own work), and Oliver Wendell Holmes (who undoubtedly
did his own choosing, for how could it be otherwise?). It was
during this period that Sarah came to know Alice Longfellow well.
A trustee of Radcliffe, where one of the buildings is named for her,
Alice Longfellow spent her life in her father's beautiful old Cambridge house, with her married sisters living on either side and her
brother across the street. She remained happily single, maintaining
a lifelong interest in women's education and in native Americans;
in 1900 she and her sisters were made honorary members of the
Ojibwa nation.

Grandfather Perry did not live out his hundred years after all, but died in January 1887 at the age of ninety-eight. The magic circle of elders was breaking up. Sarah spent most of that year in Berwick helping to nurse Uncle William Jewett, and in August, after a long period of increasing disability that he pointedly ignored (planning a seaside jaunt his family knew he would never make, insisting briefly on going to the Rochester Fair until the heat beat him down), he too died. The big house was now vacant, and Mary, Sarah, and their mother stayed in their own place only long enough to renovate the older one, a process that took most of a year. When they had finished they had restored the rooms and furnishings to the airiness and simplicity of the eighteenth century, and any Victoriana that Uncle William had allowed to creep in had been ruthlessly banished. In June 1888, after sending their mother to Exeter to spare her nerves, the sisters completed the move; and shortly afterwards, like players in a game of musical houses, Carrie and Ned Eastman and their son moved into the smaller house. The family compound was again as it had been in their childhoods, and nine-year-old Theodore ("Thider" to his mother, "Stubby" or "Stubbs" to his aunts) was in and out of the kitchen, cadging cookies and tracking up the floor as the sisters themselves had. Mary and her mother moved into two of the sunny, stately upstairs bedrooms, with their tall windows and white-canopied beds, but Sarah took over a small back room with windows on only one side, tucked into its own dim, crooked little hallway and having the door to the backstairs, and thence to the breakfast room and garden, immediately at hand. Markedly less grand than the other rooms, it was also more private and somehow seemed older, almost as if it had been abstracted from another house of earlier and less prosperous times.

In January 1888, a few months before moving, she had had a bad scare when Annie came down with pneumonia. Sarah left the house renovations to Mary and went to oversee the convalescence at Charles Street. A nurse was hired, and Sarah divided her time between bedside watching and reassuring a procession of anxious callers downstairs. Seriously ill, Annie seemed for a while to be about to fulfill Sarah's worst fears, but she slowly rallied, and at the end of February the doctor ordered them south. They chose to go to St. Augustine, Florida, but stopped at Aiken, South Carolina, and at St. Helena, in the Sea Islands, to ease the fatigue of the journey.

At their Aiken lodgings they ran into the distinguished abolitionist Senator George Edmunds of Vermont, who was vacationing there with his family, and the two parties joined forces for a few days. Then, moving on to St. Helena, they stayed with Annie's old friend Laura Towne, a homeopathic physician and educator who, many years earlier, had established a clinic and school on the island for its large population of freed slaves. By 1888 her work was largely done, and the community served as a model for others throughout the islands. Sarah and Annie stayed with Towne at Frogmore, a renovated plantation where she lived with her friend and co-worker Ellen Murray. "The result of her work lay like a map before us," Annie wrote in the elevated style she adopted when she was moved. "Every step spoke to us of the sacrifice and suffering of humanity and of its endurance in the present time."[15]

The summer of 1889 found Sarah spending a few quiet months with her mother while Mary enjoyed a long-postponed tour of Europe. Returning to Boston in October, she found Annie predictably overworked and overtired. Mary Lodge, Annie's old friend and colleague at the Associated Charities, was dying of cancer, and Annie had been struggling to carry both their workloads while helplessly watching her friend's illness progress. "Marigold" died in December, and in February an exhausted Annie was ordered back to Florida by her doctor. There Sarah spent her working hours correcting the proofs of *Betty Leicester,* which was dedicated to Lodge.

The 1880s had slipped by, marked by the deaths of her grandfather and uncle and Lodge, by the publication of nine books, and the gently predictable rhythms of travel and friendship, country and town, illness and health. She was forty years old, but she never mentioned it. It was irrelevant, and perhaps she would never have noticed it at all except for the inevitable signs of aging in Annie. As for the state of the world, she thought against all evidence that private morality was improving. A letter written ten years later to former South Berwick minister Sylvanus Hayward expresses well enough her settled optimism:

It gave me quite a pang when you said that man had taken no steps toward the removal of sin for I cant believe that the real goodness of life and thought have had *no* effect (good sermons for instance!) The world seems to me much better than when I was a child, but perhaps you would say more comfortable and better behaved, not really better?[16]

Hayward's answer, if he had one, is not recorded.

16

"Berwick Dust"

THROUGHOUT THE EIGHTIES AND NINE-
ties, like a leaf in the sleepy river current, South Berwick drifted
gently toward the twentieth century. Elizabeth Cushing died, taking to the grave her memories of the Marquis de Lafayette. Sarah
saw the coffin carried down the box-bordered walk up which she,
as a child, had marched to pay her formal calls. In future years the
house and garden would be demolished to make way for a public
high school, and later yet a fast-food-chain restaurant would occupy
the land next door. But for a while at least Madam Cushing's house
stood fast on its irreproachable character, opposite the Congregational church and within sight of the Jewetts' front gate. Berwick
was content—even soporifically so, as Sarah wryly noted to Annie:

> Every time I come back to Berwick I am so eager to know
> what I can do for it—but the little town is so unconscious
> of possible betterments, and goes on with its cooking stoves
> so comfortably, in spite of Aladdin Cookers that it is like a
> sleeping beauty in its wood—Well—perhaps I am the
> Prince to wake it up but I never know how—[1]

In 1888 she, Mary, and their mother found themselves living
in Grandfather Jewett's house, which for all the time they had spent
inside its walls was not done yielding its secrets. Rummaging
through an old desk one day, Mary found a watch that had belonged

196

to some ancestor or other, nobody knew who, and added it to her existing collection of three ancestral watches plus a modern one. Nearly two decades later, sorting some old linens, she would come upon a small memorandum book containing Orne family records and a few memos in their own grandmother's handwriting, which Mary had never before seen. And Sarah spent one rainy Sunday afternoon, a year or so after they moved in, sitting in the garret reading a collection of "delightful-pathetic old letters of my elders and betters—so that I have felt as if I were living in their world and day."[2]

With the help of a gardener, Mary revitalized the garden, growing lilacs and roses, lilies, fruit trees, and masses of old-fashioned perennials in such profusion that she could give away literally boxfuls and never feel the loss: she once sent Annie Fields so many lilacs that Annie divided the extras among nine friends and institutions. There were frequent exchanges of cuttings with Celia Thaxter, whose garden on Appledore was already famous among her friends. Sarah joined in the weeding and transplanting enthusiastically whenever she felt well enough. Gardens were a strong tradition in the Gilman family; those of Aunts Long and Bell in Exeter have already been mentioned, and Cousin Alice Gilman in Brunswick also had a memorable garden, winning prizes locally for her flowers. They also carried powerful symbolic associations for Sarah, appearing as positive images throughout her fiction. She saw gardens, especially front gardens that greeted the visitor, as an indispensable attribute of a vibrant village society. Mourning their disappearance as a sign that community cohesion and individual self-respect were beginning to crumble, she wrote a strong appeal for their preservation in her 1881 essay "From a Mournful Villager." (*Country By-Ways*, pp. 116–38) A photo of South Berwick's main street in the 1890s, published with another essay ("The Old Town of Berwick," 1894) shows the visual coherence that has been lost despite her efforts: a solid rank of old houses lining the street like family members in a Victorian group portrait, each with its fenced front garden joined to both its neighbors', the whole shaded by elms and maples.

Jewett also saw in gardens a creative medium, one of the few available to countrywomen, as well as a link with nature immediately accessible to the timid, the invalid, and the housebound. And, as Gwen Nagel has pointed out in the central discussion of gardens in Jewett's work,[3] she saw them as a historic link, joining generations not only through gardening lore passed down from mother to daughter but in the living rootstock, as in "The White Rose Road." In her stories they are a place of refuge and comfort, as in "Lady Ferry," and an expression of love—often maternal love, as in "An Only Son."

As part of their duty to church and town, the Jewetts took in delegates to the state missionary meeting and the county ministers' conference. These visitors delighted Sarah, who would on no account absent herself from so rich and original a source for stories. "I can only get a few days [at Manchester] at first," she wrote Annie one summer, "for I find that the County Conference, dear to my heart, is coming on the eleventh, all the country ministers and their wives and delightful delegates who never appear to go anywhere else—nice old country women."[4] Since their father's death the sisters had gradually assumed more and more authority in town, and their name was prominent in the list of sponsors of any worthy civic cause. A word from the family in the matter of noise in the square, gypsy-moth prevention, or any sort of public inconvenience was seriously listened to, and when the church sexton—having fallen into the modern laxity of no longer tolling the bell for funerals—neglected to toll after the death of Ulysses S. Grant, he was quickly shaken into action by Sarah. Both Mary and Sarah belonged to the Maine Historical Association, and in 1901 they established the South Berwick chapter of the Federated Women's Clubs. Over the years Sarah also joined the Audubon Society, the ASPCA, and the Maine Forestry Association, to which she gave Annie a gift membership.

The loss of South Berwick's architectural character, as old houses and gardens were demolished to make way for commercial buildings and newer, cheaper housing, was a continuing cause of anger and sadness. There is no evidence that Sarah and Mary shared the xenophobia of Portsmouth native Thomas Bailey Aldrich, who thought the gates of America should be closed to the flood of new immigrants at the end of the century. The Jewetts' objections to change were rather more complicated. As far as new people were concerned, Sarah shared the sentiments of Kate Lancaster in *Deephaven,* that the influx of newcomers bringing their own kind of Old World traditions was no bad thing for a community. The many sympathetic stories she wrote about Irish and French-Canadian characters, and her manifest affection for the Irish people in her own household and their heritage, are strong testimony to her lack of prejudice against immigrants as such. Nor was she against "progress" *per se,* objecting neither to the railroad (which Aldrich distrusted but which she welcomed as a much-needed convenience) nor to the new stores and mills that brought prosperity to her town. Nor could she be against summer "cottages," since many of her friends owned them. But she hated the architectural muddle that all these things brought with them, and the callous expedience with which ugly new buildings were thrown up overnight with no thought of their relationship to their neighbors, as if a two-hundred-and-fifty-year-old town were nothing but a raw stretch of virgin prairie.

She fretted over the creeping eradication of the town's forests, as old land was sold off and subdivided and as the lumber industry grew ever more desperate to search out the last of the old-growth trees. Sarah was keenly conscious of trees not only as beautiful in themselves but as living beings with a history and individuality of their own; some of them, she said, she regarded as friends.[5] The felling of a single three-hundred-year-old tree to make room for a house or road would goad her into a rage as few other things could, and when she heard that the last stand of old forest in Berwick was about to be cut, she and Mary tried to buy the land, which was owned by the town. But the price must have been too high, for the offer was refused and the trees were lost. The Jewetts were more successful in saving old buildings; they helped toward the restoration of York's historic gaol, and in the late 1890s, when the rundown mansion built in 1785 by Col. Jonathan Hamilton came on the market and the land was in danger of being divided into small lots, Sarah beat the Boston bushes to find a historically sensitive, wealthy friend who would buy the place and restore it. She found Emily Tyson, a Boston widow, who bought the house in 1898 and with her stepdaughter Elise restored it, possibly beyond even Sarah's expectations.

She also took a strong proprietary interest in Berwick Academy, to which she gave most of her philanthropic efforts in the town. Founded in 1791, during the post-Revolutionary period that

was the town's finest hour, the academy was built on land bought—
or at least believed at the time to have been bought—from a
Piscataqua sagamore by the ancestor of one of the founders. As
early as 1797 it had theoretically opened its doors to girls, although
none ventured to enroll until 1828. Its fortunes had risen and fallen
with those of the town: it had had to close its doors for two years
after the War of 1812, and it had been burned down during the
rum rebellion of 1851, to spring up again in a new and grander
building two years later. It had sent many of its sons to be killed
or wounded in the Civil War, including a general who was in the
act of charging Confederate lines at Appomattox when General Lee
surrendered. Since 1868 its doors had been opened to all qualified
Berwick students, the town paying their tuition.

Theodore Jewett and his brothers had gone to the academy, as
had a roster of governors, judges, scholars, and college presidents.
So had the president of the Boston and Maine Railroad. Many of
the Jewetts' friends, including William and Susan Hayes Ward of
The Independent, their aunt, Sophia Elizabeth Hayes Goodwin, historian Dr. John Lord, and the Jewetts' own great-aunt, Elizabeth
Lord Jewett, were both alumni and descendants of the founding
families; and Madam Cushing's nephew and his son both served as
trustees. It was altogether a most gratifyingly prestigious institution, mellow with history and dominating the landscape from its
hill overlooking the river; but it was also Berwick's own village
school, and Sarah's elderly friends could remember when there was
a board partition between the girls' and boys' classrooms with a
gimlet hole for passing notes, and the children left for recess via
planks propped up against the back windows.

Dr. Jewett had served several years on the board of trustees.
His elder daughters, barred from that function, made sure their
opinions were known to friends who were not barred, among them
their brother-in-law, Ned. They served on the library committee,
and Sarah helped select prize books for commencement and judged
the Christmas 1889–90 essays. When the academy magazine, *The
Berwick Scholar,* was founded in 1887, she wrote the lead article,
and it was followed by several more over the years. In 1891 she
and Mary helped organize the school's centennial celebration, Sarah
editing a pamphlet prepared for the occasion and writing an article
for *The Berwick Scholar.* Three years later, in 1894, her friend Sarah

Wyman Whitman designed the interior of an imposing new main building, the Fogg Memorial, which housed the library and several other facilities. For that building Sarah donated, and Whitman designed, a large Civil War memorial window. To coincide with the dedication and to commemorate the intermingled history of the school and the town, Sarah wrote a twenty-four-page article published in the July 1894 issue of *New England Magazine.*

In the article she traces the town's history, from Indian days to the 1890s, focusing on the lives of particular Berwickers. Dense with historical fact but as intimate and informal as a story told to children (as indeed in its many parts it had been, for Sarah and her schoolmates), the essay shows how closely time and place were united in her consciousness, and how the individual fact of "the grandfather who had wintered at Valley Forge" or the captivity of Hetty Goodwin (ancestress of dozens of Goodwins, Hayses, Lords, and Wards, and thus of the academy itself) served to humanize and personalize the past for her.

In spite of growing engagements and attachments in Boston over the years, the time Sarah spent in Berwick did not diminish. She relished village life in a way that puzzled Annie, who politely thought Berwick a bore:

> I am always delighting in reading the old Berwick, pictur-
> esque as it was, under the cover of the new life which
> seems to you so dull and unrewarding in most ways.
> "Where every prospect pleases," etc. ought to be your
> hymn for Berwick, the which I don't suggest unmercifully,
> but rather compassionately, and with a plaintive feeling at
> heart.[6]

She sees this kind of temporal transparency when, for example, a swarm of bees lights in the garden and she tries vainly to entice them into one of the Jewett hives, while

> Carrie's Minnie who is an experienced country person from
> Bantry Bay as we have long known! came out ringing a
> bell as if she were one of those who took the bees in that
> pretty "Georgic of Virgil"—there never was anything sim-
> pler or prettier. We got the *remainder bees* and their pieces of

white new comb into the hive and there they are I suppose
in all the rain—I coveted the big swarm that went away![7]

In the late 1880s she began to enjoy her nephew, Theodore,
who was now old enough to go fishing and rowing with her and
read and discuss some of her favorite books. Theodore was a boy
after his aunt's own heart, an outdoorsy child with a penchant for
raising rabbits and pigeons. He joined Sarah in her rambles about
the fields, and she in turn was not above joining him in a game of
"scouting for Indians":

> You can imagine how we saw feathered heads peering over
> the hills and rode for our lives, and then discovered the
> campfire of these deadly savages and were relieved at discov-
> ering that they were not a war party but had their squaws
> with them and were on their way to the mountains to cut
> tent poles, their own, fastened to their ponies, being worn
> to stubs!! The quiet pastures never knew such works, but
> indeed I can "play" as well as ever I could, and I could be
> dead in earnest with sand piles if occasion offered.[8]

Possibly it was Sarah who made up the ending to their game, which
with another boy might have ended in tomahawks and mayhem.
But it was not out of character for Stubby, who had a peaceable
nature and an enduring interest in northeastern Indians.

In one of her "Berwickish" moods, she took a day off from
writing to sew with Ollie Grant, stitching yards and yards of
box-pleats and listening to her old friend "in the full tide of
successful narration."[9] Another day she went to a charity sewing
bee at Mrs. Burleigh's,* where, she told Annie innocently, she
stitched pillowcases and a sheet and achieved "a good deal of simple
joy."[10] Carrie, who went with her, described the joy to Mary as not
quite so simple, for Sarah afterwards "let out remarks. *Even coming*
across the yard . . . on neighbor land etc. to ease her some what!
but *shameful* clever!"[11]

---

* The widow of Berwick mill owner and U.S. Representative John Burleigh
and an old friend of the senior Jewetts, Matilda Buffum Burleigh was (in Sarah's
words) "a *personaggia*" upon whom she paid a formal call once a year.

In middle age the three sisters were probably better friends than they had ever been in youth. All three had the same zest for small pleasures, the same sense of the absurd, the same curiosity about other people, and the same neighborly but slightly supercilious point of view; in some ways they were like three sides of a single sensibility, though one found herself possessed of an extra dimension that seemed inexplicable and extraneous, to herself more than anyone, as if she had been given a third arm. The voices in their separate letters blend together in a smooth trio, Carrie's having a sharper edge. Thus when Mary went to Europe for the first time, her frankly ingenuous enthusiasm for everything she saw exactly echoed Sarah's of seven years earlier: "Oh a poor crazy having the best time of her life sister, and so full that she is even past babbling, but I must tell you that I am here and can't believe it either."[12]

So well were they attuned to one another's tastes that Sarah in Boston could buy a carpet for Mary's room without consulting her and send it home, or choose a dress fabric in a color she liked to see Mary wear, or dictate peremptorily from Boston the shape of sleeves in Berwick because "sleeves are important!" Mary, for her part, was often Sarah's proxy eyes and ears in Berwick, describing for her a rare walking funeral, or chronicling human frailties in a voice almost indistinguishable from her sister's:

> I do not know when I have ever laughed so hard as at a
> tale Rebecca* just told of that old Aunt Polly Keays of
> Lucys who got queer in her wits and used to go and drive
> home the cows at any hour of the day when the idea struck
> her. Becky said she was all buried in a big cape bonnet, be-
> ing all dried up and as she was apt to do it oftener when
> Lucy had company it was such a mortification to her in her
> younger days. Somehow a vision of those patient mooleys
> coming along with a look of surprise at finding the day so
> short seemed to come over me, and I could seem to see

---

* Rebecca Young, who lived a few doors from the Jewetts, was an old classmate of the sisters from the days of Miss Raynes's school and Berwick Academy and an intimate friend of both Mary and Carrie. She was for many years treasurer of the South Berwick Savings Bank.

them arriving before dinner as Becky says they often did
with the funny little figure shambling along after them.[13]

Carrie too sent occasional vivid snapshots:

Oh Sarah Jewett if *only* you had seen Jane [Carrie's "help"
of the moment] this morning—I don't know when I ever
beheld the size of hoop skirt—and bright blue-striped calico—and her poor legs must have been so cold in the middle of such a tent. I hope she had an ample flannel skirt
but she looked cold.[14]

All three wrote often about John Tucker, who was always an
active member of the household and who became a particular friend
of Theodore's. John's opinion on the state of an aged or ailing horse
was exactly reported to any absent sister, Maine cadences intact:
"John said 'Dam—I'd's lief have [Princess] for a short trip as any
of them. Sh'll winter again.'"[15] John had a wife and children but
was so attached to his horses that he hated to trust them to anyone
else, and his frequently broken resolutions to take a vacation were
a Jewett family joke.

But it must be said that most of the sisters' letters to one
another will not bear extensive quoting, because they are made up
of the fine texture of minutiae that was the stuff of village women's
lives. They touch on each topic as lightly as a bee—from Mr.
Sewall's booming hymn-singing in church, to the shockingly low
yield of the pear trees, to the sight of the "pelters" (the Jewett term
for horses) playing in the pasture, to the sudden, violent dementia
of a neighbor's old mother. All of it gets tossed in at once, in
Carrie's case usually in one long, breathless, scribbled paragraph.
Sarah's letters, of course, are more substantial and more originally
worded and tend to linger longer over a topic, but even Sarah never
dives into heavy subjects but skims over a variety of minor incidents, all of which she finds equally worthy of notice. Politics and
Literature with a capital *L,* those staples of the famous male
correspondents of the last century (William Dean Howells and
Mark Twain, Ralph Waldo Emerson and Thomas Carlyle, Charles
Eliot Norton and just about everybody), are conspicuously absent.
These letters are full of the domestic details that in fact made up

the substance of men's lives too, but were always beneath their notice. The little bits and pieces represent the raw material from which a Sarah Orne Jewett, a George Eliot, or a Mary Wilkins Freeman could reconstruct in fine mosaic the actual pattern of rural lives.

Sarah never tired of rediscovering Berwick. Her youthful discontent once overcome, her love for the village and for the woods and farms around it steadily increased with years. John was her companion on long drives and often their instigator, luring her away from her desk with pointed morning comments about the last of a spell of fine weather or the high surf at Wells. Other times she rode alone on Sheila, picking her way along overgrown, abandoned logging trails and nearly always finding something she had never seen before. On a typical day she rides

> through some woods by a cart path, crossing some wide
> fields and coming out at last on the shore of the river.
> Sheila's hoofs did not make a bit of noise on the turf and
> pine needles, and the birds were all singing—The air was
> so fresh and sweet, and it was so still. I think I shall always
> remember that ride. I scared up a great brown rabbit once
> and it went scurrying off as if I were a dragon and Sheila
> something worse. You dont know how glad I am to get
> back to my own woods and fields, and to the river—[16]

Or she would simply walk over familiar fields, and feel "as if I had seen another country in Europe, Oh a great deal better than that! though I only went wandering over a great tract of pasture—and down along the river."[17]

From these excursions she drew a handful of nonfiction pieces that show more directly than her fiction her love of nature, history, and rural people and the union of the three in her consciousness.[18] In "River Driftwood" (collected in *Country By-Ways,* 1881), she takes a slow, short journey down the river, pointing out favorite landmarks along the way. She ruminates on the river's source, and on all the obscure mountain streams that have joined to form it, and then she drifts slowly past the places that, like the streams, have converged to give it its identity. She points out the Indian fishing grounds, and then reminds us gently of our arrogance in assuming that human history is all there is. Animals and plants lived and died on the river for eons before the first Indians came, though it is "seldom, as yet, that people really care much for anything for its own sake until it is proved to have some connection with humankind." In a transcendentalist mode reminiscent of *Deephaven,* she looks forward to a time of "more truly universal suffrage," when human beings and animals can communicate and each form of life is respected because "its life is from God's life" and each "material shape is the manifestation of a thought, and to each body there is given a spirit." (pp. 4–6) Bodies involve predation and death, which lead her naturally to religion: "Who can say . . . that our death may not be simply a link in a chain? . . . In some way our present state ministers to the higher condition to which we are coming." (p. 7)

Having set the larger context of nonhuman time, she comes to the river's human history, to the gundalows that once plied the river and have not yet quite disappeared, the packet boat that ran in her childhood, and the small packet boat warehouse that leaned crazily over the water for years until, like the old wharves, it rotted away. She imagines John Paul Jones, "a little wasp of a fellow" with his sword point scratching the ground (p. 14), scrambling up the bank in 1777 to recruit a sailor for the *Ranger*—perhaps the one who was in his last years a patient of her father's. She passes Hamilton House, populates its ruined garden and darkened rooms with eighteenth-century gentry, and glances at the young girl who scribbled nonsense verses on its walls in 1802. She points out the smooth green bank where her grandfather once built ships, and passing a reportedly haunted house, tells the story of the spendthrift doctor who once lived there and his two unfortunate wives. One by one, people whose lives have been intertwined with the river's history are called forth and animated, each in his or her proper setting. She ends on a note of regret for the relatively tame and diminished place modern Berwick has become ("It builds cheaper houses, and is more like other places than it used to be" [p. 32]). But the river can only grow deeper with time; it is what bird, beast, flower, Indian, sailor, farmer, and woman in a rowboat have made it. Like Whitman, like Sarah herself, it contains multitudes.

In "An October Ride," published in the same collection, she strikes a similar note. She begins again with the natural world—now her horse, Sheila, with whom she enjoys perfect understanding and mutual respect. Then she takes us to human history, in this case "her farm," an old cellarhole surrounded by forgotten apple trees that will soon be crowded out by the exuberant young pines. She remembers stories of the old woman who lived here, "a thrifty, well-to-do old soul, a famous weaver and spinner." (p. 104) She pictures her sitting on her doorstep at dusk listening to the thrushes tuning up, or making her lonely way to church on Sunday.

A storm comes up, and she shelters in an old house that has been abandoned for a year or two. She has always wanted to see the inside: she explores it all, taking note of the handsome wainscoting and generous hearth, and the recipes for horse-medicines on a cupboard door. She resurrects the comfortable old parson who once lived here, and puts him before his fire with a mug of flip. She builds a fire herself, and fills the house with family and parishioners—children, young couples, ministers soberly arguing theology, a stately and responsible wife. Then the storm stops and she leaves, knowing the roof will soon fall in and the house share the fate of the old woman's farm.

There is no sadness in her nostalgia for these people. Unlike the stereotypical New England writer, she does not mourn for vanished lives or curse the implacable power of nature. The people who lived in these lonely places have either died in the natural course of events or moved on to "find more tractable soil and kindlier neighborhoods." (p. 97) In either case she does not see desolation and ruination taking over. Nature simply "repossesses herself surely of what we boldly claim. . . . God must always be putting again to some use the life that is withdrawn; it must live because it is Life." (p. 102)

Yet her transcendentalism never makes her cold or causes her to withdraw from the "particulars." In "The White Rose Road" (collected in *Strangers and Wayfarers,* 1890), she pays tribute to the persistence of the human spirit, which she finds in the image of the ubiquitous white rose bush that grows in every dooryard, even those with no gardens. She thinks that, like a red rose she knows, it might have come from England with the original settlers, who passed its shoots from woman to woman along the road. She thinks of "the sorrows of these farms and their almost undiverted toil" (p. 263) and passes a place where a young girl, "thin as a grasshopper," is hoeing her own small garden—not a garden of flowers, but one of market crops, to sell for cash. (p. 261) She visits an isolated farm where an old man, crippled by war wounds, sits helpless in his chair all day long as his invalid wife did before him. He has only his two grandchildren, precociously solemn and mature, to look after him. In his patience she sees an Old World reflection, suggesting the accumulated endurance of centuries of hardship: "He might have been a Cumberland dalesman, such were his dignity, and self-possession, and English soberness of manner." (p. 265)

Near the house a brook cascades merrily over some ledges, making a constant music for the old man to listen to. But she thinks the brook, which runs through a marsh higher up, has probably brought illness and grief to the family. Here nature is not benign, nor is the God who creates it merciful in the short run. Nature is simply there, indifferent and often beautiful. The comfort we take from nature (for the essay is set in June, when the fields are lush and the white rose is in bloom) can make our lives bearable; the girl hoeing her vegetables and the old man in his chair both express not only endurance but a kind of toughened grace.

Later she comes to another spring, this one dealing life as the other dealt death. The spring has a romantic story attached to it, that of one of the escaped regicides of Charles I (whose ministers had murdered and persecuted the ancestors of New Englanders). It is said that he escaped to Maine and hid out near the spring for several years, and that some people in York are his descendants. The spring is set in a countryside of burgeoning abundance, where calves and puppies and kittens play in front yards and the air is full of birdsong. In a gesture that recalls the magical properties of many legendary springs, Sarah and John stop to drink "some of the delicious water, which never fails to flow clear and cold under the shade of a great oak." Images of nature feeding body and spirit, and of history and legend nourishing the present, are compounded in this everyday watering place on a country road. Future generations are symbolically invoked: a group of children passes by "in deep conversation," and when Sarah wonders what such "atoms of humanity" could be talking about, John instantly answers, "'Old times.'" (p. 272)

Further on they encounter a group of mourners leaving a funeral and are struck by the figure of the mother of the deceased, a matriarch of

> great age and infirmity. She was like a presence out of the
> last century, tall and still erect, dark-eyed and of striking
> features, and a firm look not modern, but as if her mind
> were still set upon an earlier and simpler scheme of life. An
> air of dominion cloaked her finely. She had long been queen
> of her surroundings and law-giver to her great family.
> (pp. 274–75)

Directly after passing this classically tragic figure they meet the comical grotesque, a neighbor who tells them with ghoulish satisfaction of a man who is dying in that house ("*He* won't last but a day or two") and of another who was struck by lightning that "stove through his hat and run down all over him, and ploughed a spot in the ground." (pp. 275–76) Clearly other funerals are in prospect, and the remaining mourners look at the passers-by "eagerly, as if we too might be carrying news of a fresh disaster." (p. 276) Amused, Jewett refrains from moralizing. She knows that country funerals are sometimes the only entertainment going, and she is not without a certain sympathy for the justified celebration of survivors.

Throughout the essay run images of flowers—not only roses but buttercups, clover, and all manner of June wildflowers, as well as flower gardens fenced with barrel staves against marauding hens. She thinks of a magnificent garden she once knew in Virginia that took years to build and is now, the woman who created it having grown old and moved away, left to be trampled into dust by the tenants' children. She thinks of generations of Maine farm women exchanging cuttings, stealing time from more necessary work to bring their "pleasure-plots" to bloom.

No one she meets is without some affliction. None of them, except the children by the spring, has not been blighted in some way. The narrator, the young woman out for a pleasure drive, realizes the cumulative effect of her day's outing can be disheartening and says as much. But the June day, she adds, is too perfect for sadness. In fact she has been asking us to consider, not ironically, the relationship between the earth's fruition and human pain. In her offhand, casual way she has been talking about the resilient New England spirit that, injured by natural forces, defiantly and even gaily turns those forces around and makes of them a source of renewal.

At the end of the essay Jewett seems to wander into a queer digression, devoting a couple of pages to a polemic against the industrial pollution that has poisoned the fish in the river. In purely literary terms it *is* a digression; but in the context of the necessary historic balance between man and nature, and the yearly cycle that brings back the white rose and makes human life possible and endurable, the spoliation of the river is an act of violence against the whole fabric of life. She begins to be bitter ("Man has done his best to ruin the world he lives in"), but to go on like that would contradict everything she has said before. She pulls herself together and ends on a resolutely upbeat note, believing "that with a little more time we [shall] grow wiser about our fish and other things beside." (p. 278)

There are other Berwick essays, but these are enough to give a sense of how firmly her way of interpreting the world was rooted in her native ground. Like Emily Dickinson or Emerson or Thoreau, she found her own small compass of ground inexhaustibly fruitful, and in its particulars she discovered all the universe she needed.

17

Friends

"THERE IS SOMETHING TRANSFIGURING
in the best of friendship," Sarah once wrote Sara Norton.

> One remembers the story of the transfiguration in the New
> Testament, and sees over and over in life what the great
> shining hours can do, and how one goes down from the
> mountain where they are, into the fret of everyday life
> again, but strong in remembrance. I once heard Mr. Brooks
> preach a great sermon about this.[1]

The first sentence of this passage is often quoted in modern discussions of Jewett and the community of women; the rest is often
left out, as awkward evidence of her adherence to patriarchal
religion. Yet there it is: Jewett was a practicing Christian, and her
use of the magical apparition of the risen Christ to his friends, one
of the central mysteries of Christianity, as a metaphor for the
restorative and vivifying power of friendship is as strong a statement as she could have made about the central place relationships
filled in her life, and by extension in her work. And while most of
those relationships were formed with other women, the depth of
her friendship with Whittier, for one, reminds us that the transfiguring power of friendship certainly was not limited in her own
mind by sex, age, or any other peripheral characteristic. The extraordinary range of sympathy that sustained her emotionally and

that distinguishes her art included both women and men, as well as children, trees, beasts of the field, and even (curiously apropos of her metaphor) the community of the dead; and in that sense the single most descriptive term one can use about her is universality.

Emerging from the nourishing silence of the Maine woods each winter while the leaves still clung to the oaks and the first snows had barely dusted the fields, Sarah plunged happily into the cluttered streets and drawing rooms of Boston as if she had been born to them. Trees might be her dear companions, but their range of conversation was painfully limited, and she had not been in Boston a day before her calendar was filled with luncheons, art exhibitions, club meetings, teas, and various excursions. Presumably she and Annie had some quiet evenings alone, for they continued their readings together, often aloud. Mornings seem to have been largely set aside for work, Annie setting off for Chardon Street while Sarah settled down at her desk in the library. In the evening they sometimes went to the theatre. Dame Ellen Terry was an old friend of Annie's who gave them box seats whenever she played in Boston, and they saw performances by the most famous actors of their generation, including Edwin Booth, Sarah Bernhardt, Helena Mojeska, and Eleonora Duse. The great soprano Adelina Patti came to Boston, as did Paderewski. Every winter Annie and Sarah subscribed to the Boston Symphony Orchestra (though they generally left at intermission), and there were frequent private musicales. Among the distinguished visiting writers who gave public readings was Oscar Wilde, whom Sarah and Mary Lodge could not resist going to see in 1882, "sorely against our principles!"[2]

Annie was at home to her friends every Saturday afternoon, and fifteen or twenty of them were likely to congregate on a typical day. But it was not in salons—not even in Annie's salon, which she enjoyed mightily—that Sarah saw most of her friends, but daily in intimate groups at breakfast, luncheon, tea, or dinner, or at little soirees where Sara Norton might play her cello or Jessie Cochrane, a talented young friend of Annie's from Louisville, play the piano; or at Trinity on a Sunday morning, or simply in little hurried visits of twenty minutes or so, when Sarah would stop on her way to some other engagement to run up the steps of a familiar brownstone, or come in breathless from a round of shopping and calls and find one of her "cronies" waiting for her in Annie's library. These were all cherished friends, for neither Sarah nor Annie wasted her time on people they cared nothing about. Yet so prodigal were these two in their friendships that only a fraction of the chosen can find their way into a biography, and those few must be understood to represent many more.

Among them were old friends of Annie's and James's, many of them authors or the relations of authors. Conspicuously absent were Longfellow and Emerson, who had both died in the spring of 1882, and Hawthorne's widow and children, from whom Annie was estranged; but Alice Longfellow was often at Charles Street, as was Katharine Coolidge, daughter of historian Francis Parkman. James Russell Lowell's daughter Mabel Burnett, who had traveled to Europe in 1869 with the Fieldses, was still close to Annie and became close to Sarah as well, though she lived some distance outside of Boston. Lowell himself returned to Boston from England in 1885 following his wife's death, and began spending his winters there, summering with Mabel. Sarah grew very fond of him in the eighties and especially in 1889–91 when, his health failing and his cocky spirit subdued by grief and illness, he spent his last years in his old home in Cambridge, where Mabel and her family joined him.

Old acquaintances like the Aldriches, the Howellses, the Holmeses, and the Nortons were now doubly cherished, being also friends of Annie's and—most of them—near neighbors. Sarah's bond with the Aldriches became more intimate after Aldrich replaced Howells at *The Atlantic* in 1881. Like Sarah, Aldrich had roots in old Portsmouth, and his 1893 book, *An Old Town by the Sea,* shows a wistful appreciation of the past much like her own. Another of his books, *The Story of a Bad Boy,* attests to the childlike quality they also shared. Sarah's nickname of "the Linnet" was a flattering reference to his poetry, on which he vainly hoped such fame as he achieved would rest. But it was apt enough as a metaphor for the man himself, who with his small stature, blond curly hair parted in the middle, ruddy complexion, nimble movements, and darting wit did have something birdlike about him, though perhaps more of the bantam rooster than the drab little songbird. Unaccountably shy in large groups, he was as unlikely as Whittier to put in an appearance at Annie's Saturdays. But among friends he kept up a steady prattle of inspired foolishness and repartee. Annie was always glad to have him as a dinner guest, for he took all the entertaining on himself and left her nothing to do but enjoy her own party.

As an editor Aldrich had his critics, who accused him of slacking off, taking too many European vacations (he took one almost yearly), and leaving the real work to Horace Scudder, who got no credit for it. He was compared unfavorably to Howells, who always had put in a solid day's work at his desk and had more actively searched for new talent. In his dealings with Jewett, however, Aldrich was conscientious and discerning. Patronizing at first—writing her, for example, "Here is a small proof for Sadie, which I know she will return to me at once like a good girl"[3]—he soon addressed her as an equal, and later still was generous in his praise of her as a writer whose books would far outlive his own. Like Howells, he was firm in rejecting work he did not think was up to her best, and though his firmness did not result in *The Atlantic*'s consistently printing her highest-quality sketches, that was as much a reflection of her uneven output in the eighties as of any editorial softness. He did succeed in capturing some of her finest pieces of the decade, among them "The Dulham Ladies," "The Courting of Sister Wisby," "River Driftwood," and "The White Rose Road."

One friend of Annie and Sarah's who suffered not at all from shyness was Isabella Stewart ("Mrs. Jack") Gardner, a wealthy and high-spirited New Yorker who had married into one of Boston's more staid, old-money families and, for her flirtatious manners and her refusal to fit into the niche assigned her, drawn upon herself a heavy penalty of social frost. Mrs. Jack was not one to be easily tamed by the dowagers of Old Boston, and nothing gave her more pleasure than to put a figurative finger in their collective eye. Old Boston thought it vulgar to flaunt one's wealth or make oneself conspicuous in any way, so Mrs. Jack used her wealth to make herself outrageously conspicuous, flaunting an expensive collection of jewels and showing off her enviable figure in a succession of Worth gowns that were both too daring and too fashionable for Boston. But she also used her money in more constructive ways: at their Beacon Street home she and her husband were just beginning, with the help of Charles Eliot Norton and later his protégé, Bernard Berenson, to build a world-class collection of Renaissance art. Like several of Annie's and Sarah's friends, the Gardners summered in Beverly, so they were near at hand all year.

Manchester· neighbors in summer and Beacon Hill neighbors in winter were Miriam ("Minnie") Pratt and Helen Bell, known familiarly to Sarah and Annie as "the Twins," although in fact they were only sisters. Daughters of the late legendary Boston lawyer Rufus Choate (whom young James Fields used to waylay on the street just to hear him talk), they were good friends of Henry James and, like all his friends, devotees of the word. They exercised it well, being jointly among the most celebrated wits in Boston; like Aldrich or Holmes they automatically guaranteed the success of any party they graced with their presence. *Bons mots* of the Choate sisters were told from household to household in Boston and passed down to the next generation like heirlooms. Mrs. Bell reportedly once remarked of the automobile that it would divide all mankind into two classes, the quick and the dead; and of Henry James's late, nearly impenetrable novel *The Wings of the Dove,* she said that "as it had neither head nor tail the wings were all that was left."[4]

Others welcomed at Charles Street included many women authors and artists. Annie's friendship with the sculptor Anne Whitney dated back to the early years of her marriage. Whitney and her companion, Abby Adeline Manning, lived on Mount Vernon Street and summered in Shelburne, Vermont, where Sarah and Annie stayed with them in 1889. One of the earliest woman sculptors to gain recognition in America, Whitney was a dedicated liberal whose beliefs were reflected in her choice of portrait subjects, among whom were William Lloyd Garrison, Lucy Stone, Harriet Beecher Stowe, and the martyred Haitian leader Toussaint L'Ouverture. In 1875 she won an anonymous competition to design the statue of Charles Sumner now overlooking Harvard Square in Cambridge. The commission was denied her when the judges discovered she was a woman. After much pain and indignation on the part of Whitney and her friends, the statue was finally erected—but not until 1902.

Another very old friend of Annie's was Elizabeth Stuart Phelps, who in 1888 married Herbert Ward, the son of Sarah's friend William Hayes Ward. It was Annie's advocacy that had persuaded

James Fields to publish Phelps's popular 1868 novel, *The Gates Ajar.* The controversy surrounding that spiritualist book and its sequel, *The Gates Beyond,* has obscured the fact that she wrote some fifty-five other books and countless stories, poems, and articles, most of them dealing with issues of social conscience and many of them feminist.

The writer Harriet Prescott Spofford came in occasionally from her home near Newburyport, where Sarah and Annie visited her in 1888. Boston painter Rose (Rosanna Duncan) Lamb, a close friend of both Annie Fields's and Celia Thaxter's, often stayed with Annie when Sarah was in Berwick, as did Jessie Cochrane. Sarah Chauncey Woolsey ("Susan Coolidge") of Newport, author of the children's book *What Katy Did* and its sequels, frequented Charles Street during visits to Boston. Other friends included Helen Hunt Jackson and Katharine P. Wormeley; Jackson's exposé of the government's historic mistreatment of the American Indian, *Century of Dishonor,* had been published in 1881, followed by her widely popular 1884 novel about an Indian heroine, *Ramona.* Wormeley's groundbreaking work with the United States Sanitary Commission had been followed by her founding, in 1879, the Newport Charity Organization, which was organized along lines similar to Boston's Associated Charities. In the 1880s and '90s she was in the process of translating the novels of Balzac in forty volumes.

Annie's old friend Anna Loring Dresel, who had been vice president of the Boston Sanitary Commission during the war and later president of Boston's Vincent Hospital, lived nearby on Beacon Street. Both she and her daughter, Louisa, were distant cousins of Sarah's through the Gilmans, and Louisa ("Loulie"), who was as much Sarah's junior as Sarah was Annie's, became a particular friend of Sarah's. An articulate, imaginative youngster, Loulie painted sporadically in watercolors and studied with local artists whenever she had a chance, but her family traveled abroad almost every year (her father was German), and she was never in one place long enough to concentrate seriously on her art. She looked up to Sarah, brought her small gifts, and wrote her long letters to which, she assured her friend, she expected no reply that was not perfectly convenient. There is a hint in one of her letters that Sarah helped her through a difficult time when she was about twenty, but on the whole Loulie seems to have been far more secure than Sarah had been at that age, and she romped through life like a large and curious puppy. "Loulie," Annie wrote Sarah when the girl reappeared in Boston after one of her absences, "is bigger and more disastrous than ever!"[5] Like Lillian Munger or the Sunday school girls, Loulie was one of a succession of younger women for whom Sarah was a model and older sister; but the Sarah Loulie knew was very different from the one who had consciously set out to morally improve her young pupils in the seventies. Her own youthful anxiety well put to rest, she had little taste left for scrutinizing that of other people.

So the friendship with Loulie was on an entirely equable and comfortable plane. Rather than Sarah pulling the younger woman up to some preconceived level of adulthood, Loulie helped Sarah regain some of the uninhibited fun of adolescence. She was the friend Sarah had longed for years earlier in Berwick, when all her schoolmates had grown up and she had "no one to play with." To Loulie, as well as to Annie, Sarah wrote of borrowing Stubby's sled and coasting down Powderhouse Hill; and it was to Loulie, who more than anyone else would understand, that she wrote appreciatively of George Sand's confession, in a letter to Mme d'Agoult, that she had walked into a river with all her clothes on one day just for the fun of it, and had enjoyed it so much that after she dried off in the sun she did it again. "One feels refreshed oneself," Sarah wrote,

> as one sees how that great woman who was always burdened and excited by her great living and thinking found perfect joy in being a wild creature for a little while, and made herself next of kin to the bushes and the birds.[6]

"A White Heron," the story of a little girl who lives in the woods and makes a painful choice in order to save a rare bird, was told to Loulie long before it was written and in Sarah's mind was specially linked to her young friend.

A particularly close friendship, beginning in the eighties and spanning three decades, was that with Sarah Wyman Whitman. Massachusetts-born but Baltimore-raised, Sarah Whitman had come to Boston in 1866 after her marriage to wool merchant Henry Whitman. The marriage was not a particularly happy one, but Whitman did encourage his wife's art career, allowing her to study after their marriage with Thomas Couture in Paris and later in Boston with William Morris Hunt. By the time Sarah Orne Jewett met her she was well established as a portraitist, but her real interests lay in book and interior design and in stained glass. The leading book designer for Houghton Mifflin in the 1880s and '90s, she designed covers for most of Jewett's books (*Strangers and Wayfarers* is dedicated to her), as well as books by many of Sarah's literary friends. She also designed interiors for Berwick Academy and Radcliffe, as well as the memorial windows Jewett donated to Berwick Academy and Bowdoin College. There are windows by Whitman in Harvard's Memorial Hall, the Trinity Church parish house, the Boston Athenaeum, and Radcliffe College, and there were small Whitman windows in both Annie's house and the Jewett house in Berwick.

But her art, important though it was, reflected only a part of an enormously complex life. A devout Christian, she taught Bible classes at Trinity Church and in Beverly for about three decades; she also taught at Boston's Museum of Fine Arts and served on its permanent committee, and she was a Radcliffe trustee. Like Sarah and Annie she had an immense capacity for friendship, endowing it as Sarah did with a significance that can only be called sacramental. Childless herself, she was drawn especially to young adults, and she had a way of focusing her sympathy on an awkward teenager as if there were nobody more interesting in the world. Samuel Eliot Morison and the younger Holmes both came under her spell, and Morison later remembered her as his dearest friend of the older generation. Unexpectedly shy in some situations, unconsciously bohemian, *exaltée* in manner and language, she attracted a large following but also repelled a smaller number who thought her affected and even cold. She was perhaps the most extreme example in the Jewett-Fields circle of a deeply conflicted woman equally devoted to art, social service, domestic duties, and friendship and determined not to slight any of them; and like another conflicted woman, Celia Thaxter, she was recklessly prodigal with her energy and talent. Her friends wondered where her reserves came from: "How our dear Sarah Whitman," William James remarked after she died, "lived in the sort of railroad station she made of her life—I confess it's a mystery to me."[7]

Whitman was another of Jewett's year-round neighbors, living on Mt. Vernon Street off Charles when she was not in Beverly. Because she saw Jewett so often, their letters are relatively few, but there are enough to show the intensity of feeling between them. Only Annie was dearer to Jewett than Sarah Whitman, and like some of her letters to Annie, some of those to Whitman are truly love letters. Yet this again reminds us of how inadequate is our ability to distinguish among the shades of sexual, nonsexual, and semisexual passion that the nineteenth century accepted as part of the normal spectrum of human emotions. There is no shadow of self-consciousness, and certainly no shade of guilt over any perceived disloyalty to Annie, in such a passage as this:

> This is my love O—as children send a kiss in a letter I
> send one myself to you. And I love you and keep you safe
> in my heart just as if you were the Spring. Which is not
> the flowers or the green leaves or the look of the sky, but
> something warm that has a heart—Something live that
> touches everything dull and makes it begin to bloom. I say
> this and I could not say it if you were here but I wish I
> were with you for all that! Good night dear![8]

This was the emotional tone of the friendship; in its comradely aspect it was about work. Whitman's praise of Jewett's stories was as invariable and indiscriminate as Whittier's, but because of her unusual depth of sympathy she was also able to get at the heart of a Jewett story, the elusive subtext that demands of the reader an intuitive understanding to match the writer's. As Jewett described it in a letter,

> You bring something to the reading of a story that the
> story would go very lame without; but it is those un-
> writable things that the story holds in its heart if it has
> any! that make the true soul of it, and these must be under-
> stood and yet how many a story "goes lame" for lack of

that understanding! In France there is such a "code," such recognitions, such richness of allusions, but here we confuse our scaffoldings with our buildings, and—*SO!*[9]

Jewett's support of Whitman's work was of a different nature, consisting mostly of helping her value her vocation highly enough to make room for it in her life. Whitman had a way of referring to her art as "jobbing," particularly when she was feeling harried— which was most of the time. Jewett would try to set her straight:

> Oh darling dont mind jobbing. I do so long to have you
> keep at your work. I long to have you paint these late
> autumn colors. I never can feel it is right about the job-
> bing—Going to see people married is jobbing *everything* is
> jobbing but just painting. And so I say as cross as *can be*
> with something that hurts in my throat—and I dont think
> I shall ever be so cross again. . . . Good night and I love
> you very much.[10]

Ebullient as Loulie (though twenty-two years older), often weary but above all engaged with all her strength in whatever held her attention at the moment, Sarah Whitman did manage to maintain a more or less steady focus on her art amid details of a cluttered life in which, as Louisa May Alcott had remarked, *"everything else"* somehow got in the way of one's work.

As this partial list of Sarah's friends suggests and as we have said before, the circle of friends at Charles Street always included men. But it is equally true that by far the largest number of friends, and most of her very closest friends, were women. Several of her male friends—including Whittier, Aldrich, Charles Dudley Warner, and "Brother Robert" Collyer, a Unitarian minister who lived in New York but spent at least a week a year with Annie and Sarah—were so close as to be almost family. But it was not unusual for Sarah and Annie to see a dozen friends in a day without any of them being a man. The pattern was that of ordinary upper-middle-class ladies seeking diversion in one another's company; and indeed Sarah would often refer to them all, herself included, in a half-mocking, half-affectionate way as "ladies." "Pinny a great doctor, Ladies!" she would write, as if taking a small bow before the assembled female multitude.[11] Sometimes she would use the term to refer to particular ladies, usually elderly ones like Loulie's maiden aunts the Misses King in Beverly. And in fact all her friends, even the much-talked-about Isabella Gardner, were ladies in the strictest sense. They all, including those who agitated for suffrage or preached in public or founded schools and colleges for women, conformed without question to the current norms set for womanhood, putting family or church before work, dressing in irreproachable fashion with corsets and bustles, and gracefully deferring to the gentlemen when custom required. One could scarcely hope to find a more decorous group anywhere in America.

The circle included quiet, literate women like Sarah's elderly, semi-invalid friend, Susan Burley Cabot, or Mary Lodge's sister, Alice Greenwood Howe, who looked after an invalid husband. Like Sarah's own mother and aunts, they were home-centered and content to be so. Yet most of the women who figured prominently in Sarah's and Annie's life were engaged in some form of absorbing work that made a mark on their society. If one looks at friendships throughout the span of Sarah's life with Annie and includes those friends who lived far outside of Boston, one summons up the names of poets Louise Imogen Guiney, Louise Chandler Moulton, and Edith Thomas; writers Alice Brown, Laura Howe Richards, Mary Noailles Murfree, Octave Thanet, and Kate Douglas Wiggin Riggs; painter and writer Helen Bigelow Merriman; Radcliffe dean Agnes Irwin; W.C.T.U. president Frances Willard; and Baltimore philanthropist Mary Garrett (who founded the Bryn Mawr School, was a major benefactor of Bryn Mawr College and the National American Woman Suffrage Association, and persuaded the Johns Hopkins Medical School to admit women). Add to these the names of friends mentioned earlier in these pages—Celia Thaxter, Julia Ward Howe, Elizabeth Cary Agassiz, Anna Eliot Ticknor, Katharine Loring, and Mary Greenwood Lodge—and one begins to realize that a surprisingly large number of the American "ladies" (setting aside various visiting Europeans) who drank lemonade together in the genteel shade of Annie Fields's piazza would end up a century later listed in the pages of *Notable American Women*. It is also worth noting that many of them lived in "Boston marriages" similar to Sarah's and

Annie's, drawing support and comfort from loving relationships in which neither partner competed with the other, begrudged her success, or assumed a dominant role.*

Many of Sarah's literary friendships, both American and European, were formed when she wrote to thank an author after reading a work she liked. She made a habit of this: "Oh, do let us always *tell* people when we like their work," she wrote Annie. "It does do so much good."[12] Often her correspondents were young women writers who either lived in remote places or were not yet established. She wrote letters of advice and encouragement to young Mary Ellen Chase, still in her teens, and wrote to praise Mary Noailles Murfree ("Charles Egbert Craddock") and Mary Wilkins early in their careers. (Both later wrote works that disappointed her, about which she was tactfully silent.) Alice Brown and Louise Imogen Guiney were writers she wholeheartedly encouraged over a long period, and at one point she used her connections to secure a post at the Boston Public Library for Guiney so that she could leave her grueling postal job.

One would like to have been, as Sarah often said she wanted to be, a fly on the wall to know just what the accomplished women who visited Charles Street and Thunderbolt Hill said when they flocked together. There must have been a certain amount of information exchanged, even apart from the inevitable literary conversation of the writers and the strategy huddles of the social workers. But these women got together for fun, not for professional colloquies. Perhaps the greatest benefit they gained from their friendship was just the sight of one another: the physical evidence that each was not alone, that if she wanted to talk about her work there were listeners who would take her seriously and offer concrete advice, and that she belonged to a group of women for whom accomplishment—most of it involving a high degree of public visibility, creativity, or executive talent—was not an aberration but a normal and enjoyable way of life. In the years when women all over America formed study and discussion clubs (Annie and Sarah founded or belonged to a long succession of them), these friends

---

* Among them were Anne Whitney and Abby Manning; Laura Towne and Ellen Murray; Alice James and Katharine Loring; Louise Imogen Guiney and Alice Brown (who were very close but did not live together); Mary Garrett and M. Carey Thomas; and Sarah Chauncey Woolsey and her sister, Dora.

must have drawn confidence for their own work, as men in men's clubs did, simply from the fact that they formed a critical mass. There was nothing calculated about their collective friendship; they were friends as simply and naturally as if they had been school-mates, and they probably helped one another more than they knew.

Among her friends was one group that did have a direct bearing on Jewett's work, a little flock of artists and writers who summered in the Piscataqua region and shared her antiquarian and pastoral ideals. Antiquarianism was very much in the air in the eighties and nineties. The colonial revival movement had begun in New England even before the 1876 Centennial exhibition had increased Americans' interest in their architectural and artistic heritage, and at Harvard antiquarian interest was sharpened in a generation of students under Charles Eliot Norton and Henry Adams. As Jewett grew older she found her love of old houses and old objects answered and informed by a strong preservationist spirit among her new friends.[13] One of Sarah's pleasures of visiting the Barrell sisters in York, apart from peppermints and genteel gossip, was simply to sit in their parlor, which was a kind of miniature historical museum, with the family coat of arms over the mantel, engravings of various pre-Revolutionary military commanders hung on the walls, and in pride of place a brass urn captured at the siege of Louisburg in 1675. The Barrell sisters were keeping the family treasures for posterity, and posterity enjoys them to this day, for the house is now truly a museum. In 1874, while Sarah was writing *Deephaven,* the Lady Pepperell house where she had encountered the original of Miss Chauncey was rescued from di-lapidation, though it was not fully restored until some years later. In the 1880s restoration fever began to take hold, and in mid-dec-ade Sarah's Boston friends Templeman and Katharine Coolidge bought and rehabilitated the historic Wentworth mansion, just outside of Portsmouth. The following year Sarah and Mary them-selves restored their grandfather's house, and a decade later the Tysons restored Hamilton House with Sarah Whitman's help and Sarah Jewett's energetic approval.

Hand-in-glove with the interest in restoring old buildings came the rise of the aesthetic or Arts and Crafts movement. Inspired by John Ruskin and William Morris in England, it strongly influenced American artisans who exhibited at the 1876 Centennial and at the World's Columbian Exhibition in 1893. Old buckets and pots and teacups became interesting not only because they were old, but because they were the products of individual craftspeople rather than the soulless machine. Fostering creativity on a domestic scale, the movement offered American artisans, especially women, unprecedented recognition and opportunities for new forms of expression. Among Jewett's friends, Sarah Whitman owed a large debt to it. So did Celia Thaxter, whose simple designs of leaves and flowers painted on china were highly prized among her friends, and Harriet Prescott Spofford, whose only nonfiction book was *The Decoration of Furniture.*

The preservationists and the Arts and Crafts enthusiasts both were expressing a widespread reaction to the industrial blight and social disruption of the cities. In France at mid-century the Barbizon school of painting had sprung from a similar impulse. Rejecting both the grandiose academic painting of the salon and the urban milieu that encouraged it, the Barbizon painters retreated to the forest of Fontainebleau, seeking a renewed vision of simplicity and integrity in nature and village life. Among them was Jean-François Millet, who was unique among the Barbizon painters in his preference for figure painting over landscape, and who endowed the ordinary French peasants in his paintings with an undeniably heroic, almost monumental quality.

In the late 1840s a young Boston artist aptly named William Morris Hunt visited Barbizon, met Millet, and became his friend and disciple. Returning to America, Hunt eventually settled in Boston, where in 1868 he became an influential teacher to the rising generation of Boston artists.* William and Henry James both studied with Hunt, as did John LaFarge. So did Sarah Wyman Whitman, Rose Lamb, Helen Bigelow Merriman, and watercolorist Ross Turner, who in turn instructed Celia Thaxter and Louisa Dresel. With the notable exception of LaFarge, most of them continued throughout their careers to paint in the subdued palette of the Barbizon school, resisting the brighter influence of the

---

* Hunt lived in Boston for seventeen years. An intimate friend of Celia and Levi Thaxter's, he died in 1879 by drowning, probably intentionally, while visiting Appledore Island.

Impressionists that captured, for example, Celia Thaxter's friend Childe Hassam.

Sarah and her friends were familiar with Millet's paintings through Quincy Adams Shaw, a son-in-law of Elizabeth Agassiz who owned an extensive collection of the painter's work. They also knew Hunt and his wife, and several of them were Hunt's ex-pupils. An influential teacher—especially among women artists, who in the late 1860s and early '70s had no other studio instruction available—Hunt diffused Millet's influence throughout the Boston artistic and literary community. Evidence of it turns up, for example, in the list of books written by Sarah's friend Helen Merriman, among which is a biography of Millet. But an example much closer to home is in a little privately printed book called *A Week Away From Time.* This was a collection of stories anonymously composed by a group of friends visiting Mary Lodge's summer home on Cape Cod. The mostly amateur authors included Annie Fields, Sarah Whitman, Minnie Pratt, and the young Owen Wister, who was the son of Annie's old friend Fanny Kemble. Sarah Jewett did not contribute to the book but told friends she was "in the secret" and had much to do with it.[14]

Several pages of *A Week Away From Time* are devoted to a description of the local cranberry harvest as viewed by an upper-middle-class pleasure party. The visual description is self-consciously painterly: the "rich crimson berries, with a purple bloom on them . . . cast a warm tinge up through the green"; the bog is "set in a frame of bright foliage," while the shawls and ribbons of the women pickers make "a spot of sympathetic color" here and there. The onlookers are entranced by this vision of happy and productive labor: "Could anything be more picturesque?" one of them cries. "And they are unconscious of making pictures," another answers, "as any of Millet's French peasants."[15]

Sarah herself had already undertaken directly to "make pictures" in the same spirit with her friends Susan Minot Lane (who had studied with Hunt), Emma Lewis Coleman, and C. Alice Baker. Coleman was a photographer and Baker a historian; the three summered at York together. In 1883–86 Jewett and the others collaborated in staging a series of photographs in the Millet style: local models, or sometimes Miss Baker, would dress up in period costume and Coleman would photograph them at everyday rural tasks. Reconstructing historic conditions as accurately as possible, the group also followed Millet in creating images intended to express the beauty and dignity of rural life. The results were obviously staged and entirely lacked the heroic aura of Millet's peasants, but Jewett was pleased with them. A few years later she persuaded Houghton Mifflin to use the photographs as illustrations in an 1893 edition of *Deephaven*.

Jewett's friendships, then, were transfiguring in several ways. First of all, like Berwick they were necessary to her emotional renewal and well-being. She was very lucky in her friends, who in their multitudinous kindness, courtesy, and high-mindedness (for she only saw people who were kind, courteous, and high-minded) formed a sampling of the human community that, if not quite as peaceful as Deephaven or Dunnet Landing, was still remarkably free of quarrels and petty rancor. Almost certainly her own keen sympathies brought out the best in them, and she herself helped generate the magical restorative quality she found in friendship. If she was tired and out of sorts, all she had to do was wait for one of her friends to come and lift her out of it; she rarely had to wait more than an hour or two. Coming as they did from the same narrow stratum of humanity, they daily confirmed her faith in the possibilities of human interdependence. Like Berwick's, their homogeneity may have limited her vision; but as far as it went, that vision was true.

Beyond that, friendships gave her an exhilarating context of women who were living more or less the same kind of life she was, even the married ones. Achievement in the public sphere and personal ambition channeled into some form of human betterment were the normal choices among the women she knew. In this large and diverse group, it was those whose attention was limited to their biological families who were the exceptions.

Third, her friends were a source of information and intellectual growth. This was true even among the less worldly and accomplished, like the housebound, gossipy Susan Burley Cabot, who was a great fan of Gladstone's and once urged a paper of his on Sarah, who glanced at it with a sinking feeling and sent it up to Mary with a plea to get the "*gist of it*" and fill her in.[16] And finally, in their zeal for preservation her friends provided a context for the pastoralism and historical consciousness that was central to her work. Her admiration for Millet was no more than one strand woven into her rich experience of rural life, but her respect for her own Maine people could not help but gain romantic luster from the antiquarian and agrarian enthusiasms she encountered at every turn. Millet's exalted pastoralism provided the backdrop against which Jewett's rural characters occasionally attain truly heroic stature and become, like the Bowdens in their solemn procession to the grove in *The Country of the Pointed Firs,* representatives of a lineage as old as history itself.

10

"A Sound Tap-root"

''To work in silence and with all one's heart, that is the writer's lot," Sarah Orne Jewett once wrote Willa Cather.[1] Yet to read Jewett's letters, or those of Henry James or Edith Wharton, one would think that silence and solitude were experiences almost unknown to them, and that what Jewett calls working with all one's heart amounted to perhaps an hour in bed in the morning, with a writing desk on one's knees and a cup of chocolate at one's side, before the day's engagements began. Nor is it easy to believe, from the evidence of her buoyant spirits and abundant energy, that she ever despaired of her material or emerged from a writing session drained and irritable, as ordinary writers must. Nevertheless her silences were real, and her work demanded enough of her that she typically suffered a reaction of fatigue and depression after she completed a story or a book.

In the years 1879–88 she published five books of collected stories, plus three of the four full-length works discussed earlier and a still-uncounted number of uncollected periodical pieces. The quality of her work over these years varied as she experimented with style and setting. She tried her hand at writing short romances or parables ("A White Heron" and "The Gray Man") that in their strong narrative voice, use of symbol and allegory, and slightly archaic language are reminiscent of Hawthorne.* In her most moralistic vein she wrote a few flat, unconvincing stories like "A Business Man" and "Mère Pochette"—the first about a city entre-preneur, the second about a Quebec grandmother—that are outside her own experience and only serve to emphasize how important to her art were her home landscape and people. But this period also saw the publication of some of her most memorable stories, and in general her country characters really came into their own in the eighties, and the themes and symbolic groupings introduced in *Deephaven* were brought to full maturity.

The single greatest weakness of her work is the moral com-mentary that continued to intrude on all but a handful of the stories. Rarely was she able to adhere to her father's advice and refrain entirely from writing *about* people and events; and the stories in which she does allow her characters to act without comment, such as "The Courting of Sister Wisby" and "The Dul-ham Ladies," are among her finest. Occasional sentimentality is also a flaw, the danger of which she understood but could not always avoid. "The distinction between sentiment and sentimentality is a question of character, and is as deep as one can go in life, and kindness must have a sound tap-root," she once wrote Aldrich.[2] Here she seems to recognize the primary importance of trusting her characters to embody a story, and had she been able consistently to follow her own precept she would have forestalled both the major flaws in her work.

Cavils such as these, however, are small when compared with the overall achievement of the eighties, and it seems hardly fair to carp about characterization when speaking about one of our high practitioners of that art. It is because her most fully realized characters are so whole and vital that we are inclined to criticize when she falls short of the mark. And it is, paradoxically, through

---

* Jewett's supposed debt to Hawthorne was noted by critics throughout her career, somewhat to her annoyance. "I confessed to Mr. [Bliss] Perry that I never was a Hawthorne lover in early life!" she told Charles Miner Thompson in 1904 (Fields, p. 196); and to Anna Dawes in 1877 she complained, "It seems very foolish to say my stories are like Hawthorne's and I wonder why people do." (SOJ to Dawes, LCong, 10/21/77) Both these disclaimers apply to her early career, however, and leave open the question of whether she became more interested in Hawthorne during her early years with Annie.

the vital characters in her least morally explicit stories that Jewett best succeeds as a moralist. The simple statement that "kindness must have a sound tap-root" is, when taken as seriously as she meant it, as full a description as we need of the broad moral purpose of her best work. We can gloss it with an equally uncomplicated statement written to a young reader in 1899:

> The people in books are apt to make us understand "real"
> people better, and to know why they do things, and so we
> learn to have sympathy and patience and enthusiasm for
> those we live with, and can try to help them in what they
> are doing, instead of being half suspicious and finding
> fault.[3]

This, to her mind, is the basic moral function of literature, and in the end all her editorializing is directed to the purpose of extending human sympathy and tolerance.

Another characteristic of her work that ties it firmly, despite its realism, to the Victorian tradition is its optimism. The fact that no Jewett character is ever damaged beyond repair has been a source of criticism of her work almost from the beginning and largely accounts for why, in a century favoring the dark and introspective in literature, most of her books have been allowed to fall out of print. The admiration for Turgenev she expressed late in life is clearly a kind of justification for her own similar point of view:

> There was in him such a love of light, sunshine, and living
> human poetry, such an organic aversion to all that is ugly,
> or coarse, or discordant, that he made himself almost exclu-
> sively the poet of the gentler side of human nature. On the
> fringe of his pictures, or in their background, just for the
> sake of contrast, he will show us the vices, the cruelties,
> even the mire of life. But he cannot stay in these gloomy
> regions, and he hastens back to the realms of the sun and
> the flowers.[4]

But it is also true that the comfortably frugal circumstances of the typical Jewett character were not so different as might be supposed from the experience of most of her neighbors. When

Hamlin Garland, in an 1888 letter, chided her for evading the violence and squalor that he believed haunted the gray shacks and tumbledown farms around her neat New England villages, she answered:

> I listen to all that you say of the dark and troubled side of New England life. Mrs. [Rose Terry] Cooke has felt that and written it, but her Connecticut people are different from those I have known and thought most about. It is a harder fight with nature for the most part, there, and there were not such theologians in the old days here as in that part of New England. Yet the types of humanity are the same varied by the surroundings.[5]

The possibility that "the surroundings" in Jewett's Piscataqua region were different from those in others has generally been overlooked in blanket discussions of New England writers, which usually begin with the assumption that nineteenth-century New England was uniformly distressed economically. In fact, not only was the religious tradition on the Piscataqua gentler than any other in the region, but even at its economic nadir the area was more prosperous than Cooke's Connecticut, Mary Wilkins Freeman's Massachusetts, or Garland's Middle West. Yet the Piscataqua was not immune to hardship, and many of the characters in Jewett's stories, like those in *Deephaven*, suffer grief and deprivation as bitter as any in the works of her less sanguine contemporaries. The loss of sons, lovers, husbands, wives, and children is as common as rain, and the threat of pauperism hovers over several elderly characters, like the seamstress sisters Mary and Martha in the story of that name, or the candy-seller Mrs. Marley and her sister Polly Sharpe in "Miss Sydney's Flowers." Hardly less painful and a good deal more familiar is the fate of old Mrs. Wallis in "A Bit of Shore Life." This bewildered old woman, uprooted from her Maine farmhouse by an overbearing son, sees a lifetime's possessions sold from under her and is about to be set down amid the sterile comforts of the son's city house. Nevertheless, absolute deprivation, not to mention domestic violence and real moral squalor, is almost unknown in Jewett's fiction. Partly no doubt this is because she encountered them so rarely that she could discount them as aberrations, but partly too it is because her worldview is a redemptive one and she inhabited lifelong the friendly universe of Emerson and Swedenborg.

After Jewett's death there was a long period when her works were little read, and if it had not been for Willa Cather's 1925 edition of *Pointed Firs* and F. O. Matthiessen's 1929 biography, they might almost have been forgotten. The patronizing tone that male literary pundits of mid-century assumed toward Sarah Orne Jewett has become a classic illustration of historic male bias in the canon. In 1940 Van Wyck Brooks, after according her craftsmanship the praise that no one ever really denied it, concluded:

> Her vision was certainly limited. It scarcely embraced the
> world of men, and the vigorous, masculine life of towns
> like Gloucester, astir with Yankee enterprise and bustle, lay
> quite outside her province and point of view.[6]

The notion that the physical and emotional lives of half of humanity might be worthy of a writer's attention, or that human experience encompassed something more fundamental than "enterprise and bustle," seems to have been totally beyond his ken. Nevertheless, despite the influence of Brooks and like-minded contemporaries, scholars never wholly neglected Jewett, and three or four decades ago a gradual critical renewal began, led by Richard Cary of Colby College. The rise of the women's movement turned this modest revival into a full renaissance, and with this attention has come a small flurry of new editions of *Pointed Firs, Deephaven,* and selected stories, so that much of her best work is now readily available.

It is not within the scope of this biography to review the recent criticism in detail, but because many readers are not familiar with the scholarly literature, or even with most of the stories themselves, there does need to be some kind of brief summary. In brief, then, the focus on Jewett's work has changed from examining her role as a regionalist or a gently nostalgic voice from a declining culture to recognizing her as an unparalleled portrayer of women and women's lives. Jewett's women are seen as the leaders and sustainers of communities in which the men—most of them retired, elderly sea captains, struggling farmers and fishermen, or spineless young heirs of family fortunes—have been economically marginalized and robbed of significant influence. A number of men have disappeared altogether, lost to the Civil War, the sea, or westward migration; hence the large population of widows and spinsters inhabiting Jewett's farms and villages. Children are rare, as are their young parents, because Jewett liked to write about women in their middle or late years, when they have put domestic ties behind them and achieved their full measure of knowledge and experience. A Jewett countrywoman at sixty, though battered, is just coming into her spiritual prime. She is like the Delft bowl the narrator of "A Bit of Shore Life" discovers in Mrs. Wallis's closet:

> It was badly cracked, and had been mended with putty;
> but the rich, dull color of it was exquisite. One often
> comes across a beautiful old stray bit of china in such a
> place as this, and I imagined it filled with apple-blossoms
> or wild roses. Mrs. Wallis wished to give it to me, she said
> it wasn't good for any thing; and, finding she did not care
> for it, I bought it; and now it is perched high in my room,
> with the cracks discreetly turned to the wall. (*Old Friends
> and New*, p. 245)

Notwithstanding their lack of biological children, these strong Jewett women are all mothers. Members of Mrs. Whitney's larger motherhood, they heal, comfort, and teach everyone within their orbit. They are the emotional mainstays of their weaker men and young folks, and they are the transmitters of the nourishing currents of history and tradition. They usher their neighbors into this world and out of it with patience and skill, and betweentimes they heal their aches with a deftly applied poultice or a stiff herbal brew. Strangely familiar, with their rheumatic knees, their cats, and their knitting, they evoke in many readers a mysterious recognition, a sense of some half-remembered, reassuring presence. In this archetypal maternal image, and in the close affinity of Jewett's wise women with nature and their role as healers and keepers of the gates of birth and death, feminist scholars have detected associations with ancient religions and benevolent witchcraft. In the female friendships throughout Jewett's works they see a mystic bond of compassion and womanly wisdom passed from generation to generation.[7]

Central to feminist analysis of the stories have been the ways in which Jewett's women embody those values of neighboring, nurturing, and nature that were beginning to be threatened by an essentially male, money-oriented urban society. Many of Jewett's stories can be read as a theatre in which the conflict of female/agrarian and male/urban forces is played out, often by a warmhearted resident countrywoman and a coldhearted city man who threatens to disrupt her world. Mrs. Wallis's son, who has made money in the city and returns to forcibly uproot his mother for her own good, is one example; another is the devious Henry Stroud in "A New Parishioner," who returns to his old village, foments dissension, and almost tricks his old sweetheart into becoming his wife, nurse, and financial support. Central to any discussion of this destructive-male/constructive-female dichotomy is the 1886 story "A White Heron," in which Sylvia, a shy child who lives with her grand-mother in the forest, must decide whether or not to betray a rare bird to a visiting hunter for the reward of ten dollars and the hunter's gratitude and friendship. The various aspects of Sylvia's temptation (access to the larger world, sexual initiation, material riches) and her refusal (bonding with nature, loyalty to womanhood and her grandmother, fear of male violence, infantile regression) have generated almost as much discussion as has the entire *Country of the Pointed Firs.*[8] Aside from their merits, the sheer number of analyses of this one story suggests the interpretive richness yielded by Jewett's work under intensive reading, and must finally put to rest the old condescending view of her as a regional writer of pleasant, outdated country tales.

But to acknowledge that the works contain many layers of meaning is not to say that those are the meanings the author intended. Certainly Sarah Orne Jewett would be appalled, not to say horrified, at finding the lofty old pine of "A White Heron" widely interpreted as a phallic symbol. As a biographer I would like to step back from the complexities of modern criticism and limit my discussion as much as possible to what I believe were Jewett's conscious intentions, while stating at the outset that my own reading owes much to recent Jewett scholarship.

The main theme of Jewett's work after *Deephaven* continued to be the spiritual links uniting God, humanity, the natural world, the living and the dead, the past and the present. The typical Jewett plot revolves around the rupture and reconnection of those links as they are expressed in human sympathy: a protagonist is alienated from her or his fellows and then redeemed through an impulse of kindness. Or the protagonist may temporarily put ambition or pride ahead of community, but then has an epiphany of some kind that brings her or him back into harmony with others. The less successful stories are simplistic morality tales, very like her children's stories. More fully imagined but still insistently pedagogic is the early "Miss Sydney's Flowers," in which a rich, solitary old woman is taught to reach out to other people by means of the flowers in her own conservatory. In "The King of Folly Island" the theme is spun out into a long, fully developed story in which a wealthy city man who has allowed himself to drift away from human relationships is brought to a realization of his own failings through the example of another man for whom isolation has become a tragic obsession.

One of Jewett's finest tales about interdependence is "Miss Tempy's Watchers," published in 1888. Two women who scarcely know one another are brought together to watch in the kitchen of a dead friend, who lies in the bedchamber above them. Mrs. Crowe is the wife of a rich farmer, and though kindhearted is apt to be stingy in spite of herself. "It ain't so easy for me to give as it is for some," she confesses in some perplexity, as if she were talking about a physical handicap. (*The King of Folly Island,* p. 213) Her companion, Sarah Ann Binson, is a farmer, the family breadwinner for herself, her widowed sister, and "six unpromising and unwilling nieces and nephews." (p. 210) Her hard life has left her with a rather pinched and frugal look, "a little too sharp-set," to quote her neighbors (p. 209); but her spareness is all on the outside, while Mrs. Crowe's is all on the inside. In the course of reminiscing about their deceased friend Miss Tempy Dent, they exchange confidences they otherwise never would have shared, and through understanding one another's lives and remembering Miss Tempy's they become friends, and Mrs. Crowe's native kindliness expands into what one hopes is permanent bloom. The story is achieved with an impeccable blend of humor and psychological realism, and as readers we spend the night in that country kitchen, nibbling on the funeral cakes to keep up our strength and guiltily nodding off on our hard wooden chairs.

There is nothing fortuitous about the meeting of the two women. Tempy Dent had asked them to be her watchers, and throughout the story her lingering influence is felt, in the loud voice of the brook outside that seems "as if it tried to make the watchers understand something that related to the past," and in the wind that puffs companionably at the window crack. (p. 211) "The watchers could not rid their minds of the feeling that they were being watched themselves," the narrator says, and later on, when they have dozed off despite their best efforts, the narrator wonders if Tempy herself is the only watcher. (p. 212) But this benign manipulation is not, within the framework of Jewett's own belief, Tempy's own: the dead are agents, just as the natural voices of water and wind are agents. The author-narrator herself is an agent. Similarly, Frankfort in "The King of Folly Island," setting out for the islands in the boat of postmaster Jabez Pennell, idly wonders if he was "addressed by fate to some human being who expected him." (p. 6) Human events are helped along by unseen powers, as the writer's imagination is directed by forces beyond her. "Fate," or God, is the best storyteller of all.

Divine plots are sometimes convoluted. In "A Late Supper" Miss Catherine Spring, who is faced with bankruptcy and the loss of her house, goes down the street to borrow a pitcher of cream for unexpected visitors, finds her return blocked by a waiting train, tries to climb across between the cars, and is trapped when the train suddenly starts. Befriended in her distress by two women from the city, she gets off at the next station, returns home, and subsequently is preserved from financial ruin—at least for a while—by the arrival of the two city women as summer boarders. In this early story the narrator buttonholes us at the end to make sure we understand that everyone's life, to quote a sermon title that once caught her eye, is a "Plan of God." (*Old Friends,* p. 113)

Miss Spring's financial disaster is averted not simply because God pities her, but because she herself has generated a chain of kindness in the beginning of the story by offering cake and cream to a pauper child who comes looking for work. The goodwill thus set in motion has its own life, passing from character to character with each adding his or her mite until it comes back to its beginning. Thus by "Plan of God" we are not to understand that Miss Spring's fortune is foreordained, but simply that she has seized an opportunity presented to her and benefited from the results.

Like many of Jewett's stories, this one is deliberately and defiantly commonplace. Miss Spring and village people like her are Jewett's answer both to the studied amorality she had complained of in Flaubert and to the heroic tradition of romantic fiction. "Perhaps her life would seem dull," she writes of one of her old ladies, "and not in the least conspicuous or interesting to most people; but for the dullest life how much machinery is put in motion and how much provision is made, while to its possible success the whole world will minister and be laid under tribute." ("Miss Becky's Pilgrimage," *Country By-Ways,* p. 249) "Dull" is a word she returns to often. Sylvia's is a "dull little life" whose tranquil rhythm in the heart of nature is threatened by the "great wave of human interest" represented by the hunter. (*A White Heron,* p. 15) Andrew of "Andrew's Fortune," capable of silently giving away his inheritance not only once but twice, is drawn to be as dull as possible: "You always felt at once that you could get on just as well without him." (*By-Ways,* p. 43) In "A Landless Farmer" she has pared down one of the great dramatic themes of literature, the story of King Lear, to a pathetic conflict between a helpless old farmer and his two venal daughters. Jerry Jenkins does not rage or go mad; he is simply a sick old man whose relations think he has outlived his usefulness. One can find several like him in any modern nursing home.

The realism of "A Landless Farmer" lies entirely in setting and character. The ending is improbably happy, for God and the author intervene, bringing back the good child, the long-lost son who had been thought dead. Again, the chain of generosity set up by Jenkins's gift to his children is not allowed to be broken. Realism is qualified by moral intention, and as in *Deephaven* the benign influence of the active souls prevails. The Swedenborgian belief in a multilayered universe in which a human being achieves spiritual progression on earth through a series of choices presented by God sits oddly with Jewett's tenderhearted insistence that goodness always finds its immediate reward. She will have it both ways. She insists on free will when it works to the good, as in "The Landscape

Chamber": "God meant us to be free and unconquered by any evil power," the narrator cries to an obsessed old man who thinks he is bound by an ancestral curse. (*King,* p. 113) But she will not leave her characters in despair; God sets hard choices, but He also rescues the deserving through His agents.

The grasping daughters in "A Landless Farmer" are not punished; on the contrary, the elder moves to town and prospers. There she "dress[es] conspicuously," and is "very efficient in the sewing society and the social relations of the parish." Assenting outwardly to Christian doctrines, she "practices very few of them which relate to the well-being and comfort of other people." (*The Mate of the Daylight,* pp. 89–90) The loving son, on the other hand, says he "ain't one to talk religious, but I'm going to look after father." (p. 88) This distinction between the spirit and the letter, between public piety and private charity, is clearly drawn in many of the stories, usually in a comic spirit and often at the expense of ordained ministers. The anticlericalism noted by a recent critic[9] is actually selective, being directed at the worldly, the ambitious, the overfed, and the overlearned, of whom there are many examples. But there are also good ministers, like Miss Becky's late brother and her suitor in "Miss Becky's Pilgrimage." They come in various persuasions, from comfortable Episcopalian to stately Congregationalist, but they are all old-fashioned men who honestly try to live by the gospel.

Supernatural influences abound throughout the stories, and "Miss Tempy's Watchers" is just one of many in which we are surrounded by spirits that protect and instruct. Mrs. Powder of "Law Lane," summoned to attend a neighbor who has fallen from a haymow, instantly knows that the woman is uninjured and sets off in a cheerful frame of mind. She will use that intimation to maneuver the woman into making peace with her estranged son. Miss Peck of "Miss Peck's Promotion," startled at the sound of a carriage, senses it portends "some strange crisis in her life," (*King,* p. 176) while the crooked stick-figure in "A New Parishioner" is a warning to Lydia Dunn that crooked Henry Stroud is up to no good.

The dead are with us as messengers from the past and reminders of the larger whole. Often they are mothers, for as Sherman has pointed out, there is a striking pattern of dead mothers and motherless daughters from *Deephaven* on. In part, of course, this reflects the pervasive nineteenth-century cult of the angel in the house, but it also reminds us of how long and insistent was Jewett's fear of losing her own mother, who did not actually die until Jewett was forty-two. The ideal of the loving mother as a universal model of sympathy and forgiveness literally haunts many of the stories, inspiring the fainthearted. Good characters of both sexes, like son Parker in "A Landless Farmer," take after their mothers and carry on their emotional inheritance.

The most memorable of these departed mothers is the mother of Mrs. Goodsoe in "The Courting of Sister Wisby." Mrs. Goodsoe herself is an herb-woman and all-around healer. Wise, scatter-brained, practical, opinionated, stocked full of miscellaneous lore, and vibrantly linked to the past, she is the spiritual mother of the narrator and probably a whole community besides. But with typical Yankee self-deprecation she herself dismisses her accomplishments as but a poor imitation of her mother's. "Bless your heart," she sighs as she gathers her mulleins, "I don't hold a candle to her; 't is but little I can recall of what she used to say. No, her l'arnin' died with her." (*King,* p. 58) Now, since it is evident to the reader as well as to the narrator that Mrs. Goodsoe's own "l'arnin'" is impressive indeed, the stature of the dead mother assumes awesome proportions, and her influence is evoked in one way or another throughout the story.

"The Courting of Sister Wisby" is perhaps the prime example of Jewett's continuing interest in ESP and spiritualism, which in this story are examined in both a serious and a comic light.[10] Mrs. Goodsoe herself disclaims any gift of extrasensory powers; but her great-grandmother was said to have second sight, and despite her denials it is clear that through that "very understandin'" woman, her mother, (*King,* p. 58) Mrs. Goodsoe not only has come by her herbal lore but has inherited in some mild form the powers attached to it by legend. They manifest themselves in the "temptation" that summons the narrator, Mrs Goodsoe's friend and pupil, across the fields one morning until she finds what she did not know she was seeking, Mrs. Goodsoe's brown cape bonnet bobbing among the junipers.

They begin to gather herbs together, and in the course of their long conversation Mrs. Goodsoe tells two anecdotes that at first glance seem to have nothing to do with each other or with Mrs. Goodsoe herself. The first is about Mrs. Goodsoe's childhood memory of an Irish fiddler, Jim Heron, whose music charmed a bereft mother into shedding lifesaving tears. The woman, Mrs. Foss, had been struck dumb by the loss of her children, so that the neighbors feared for her reason. But Jim Heron came "stealin' right out of the shadows" of the woods one evening and played one haunting tune, and Mrs. Foss climbed into Mrs. Goodsoe's mother's lap (Mrs. Foss being a "little woman") and cried herself to sleep. (p. 66) Here we have a mother comforting a mother, while the voice of the fiddle itself is like "a woman's voice telling somethin' over and over." But equally important is the mysterious gift of Heron the musician, who has come out of the woods to play his single, enchanted tune and who—like Mrs. Goodsoe's own Scotch-Irish grandmother— hails from a spirit-haunted land.

The cluster of associations here—motherhood, music, spiritualism, history, legend, and nature (in Heron's name as well as his association with the forest)—is typical of Jewett's best work and helps explain its elusively evocative quality, particularly as the references accumulate from story to story. One must think of the themes and symbols that are necessarily listed one by one in these pages as being interwoven, as are themes and symbols in *Deephaven,* in a tapestry of some complexity. Jim Heron and Mrs. Goodsoe, for example, are not only both Celtic and possessed of healing powers, they are both artists. Heron's music moves listeners to dancing or tears, and Mrs. Goodsoe is a storyteller whose art, however rambling and ingenuous it seems, is never without its purpose. Both are agents of a liberating, unifying divine force, and both embody the distinction between genuine and sham religion. Heron can set a minister dancing even if he is "all wound up for a funeral prayer,"[11] while Mrs. Goodsoe gets comically exercised on the subject of bad preachers, to the point where her young friend deflects the conversation whenever she senses that subject looming in the distance. Yet Mrs. Goodsoe is a "believer" and tries to "live a Christian life." (p. 62) We are not to take her for some picturesque ancient heathen. She is a behavioral Christian, like Parker in "A Landless Farmer" or any number of other characters whose deeds speak for the state of their souls. Her dislike of pious rhetoric is in direct proportion to her embodiment of Christian values.

The focus of the story now shifts to the false piety and quack spiritualism of Deacon Brimblecom, the subject of Mrs. Goodsoe's second tale. As her tale of Jim Heron and her mother indirectly illustrates her own gifts and spiritual strength, so the tale of Brimblecom's courtship of Lizy Wisby is a caricature of opposite failings: ignorance, laziness, self-importance, and exploitation. Brimblecom's history as she tells it begins with his conversion to spiritualism by a wandering preacher. Convinced he is called by a "spirit bride," he leaves his wife and four children and sets up a rival establishment. But as Mrs. Goodsoe puts it, "by an' by the spirit bride did n't turn out to be much of a housekeeper, an' he had always been used to good livin', so he sneaked home ag'in." (p. 71) He does not enjoy his renewed "good livin'" long, however, for soon his long-suffering wife dies. Providentially seized by yet another "pious fit," he joins the "Christian Baptists" and travels around exhorting, and at a revival meeting he meets Lizy Wisby, a notoriously stingy woman to whom the brethren send Brimble-com to board as a joke. After competing at "expoundin'" for four days, they seem to take to one another, and when the meeting is over they go home to Sister Wisby's to begin a prolonged trial marriage that scandalizes and amuses the whole town. Eventually they really do marry, and during their remaining years together Lizy refines her skill at nagging while Brimblecom takes to drink. The whole tale is a satiric comment on the rewards of looking out for number one and on various sham forms of religion and spiri-tualism, including the wilder varieties of Baptists and the spirit-rappers who had gulled Sarah and Annie only two or three years earlier. The susceptibility of Brimblecom and Wisby to one another and to quick-fix religion is a symptom of their self-absorption and their isolation from the ongoing life outside their own egos.

As Mrs. Goodsoe ends her story we are brought to see once more, by way of contrast, the extent of her own spiritual integra-tion. She begins to talk about her own death, but in the same paragraph and almost the same breath she talks of planting the pits of some peaches she and her friend have just eaten together. Death and life, her own passing and the new life of trees sanctioned by friendship, are all one seamless whole. She says she would like to be buried in an old cemetery in the pasture where she has ranged for many summers. "Seems as if I could see right up through the

turf and tell when the weather was pleasant, and get the goodness
o' the sweet fern." (pp. 79–80) The earth is transparent to her, for
she is already earth and air and Emersonian transparent eyeball;
and the ancestors, be it noted, will be all around her. We are shown
a life that belongs to all levels of existence and will simply be
translated to another plane. The contrast with the comic dishar-
monies of Brimblecom is implicit, and there is no authorial nudge
at the end of this superb story to make the point.

Nature here and throughout the series is an active presence,
at once a symbol for human psychological states and a character in
its own right. The living landscape in "The Landscape Chamber"
is a healthy counterpart to the pinched and thwarted human lives
in the house:

> The very air of the house oppressed me, and I strayed out
> into the beautiful wide fields, and found my spirits rising
> again at once. I turned at last to look back at the group of
> gray buildings in the great level landscape. They were such
> a small excrescence upon the fruitful earth, those roofs
> which covered awful stagnation and hindrance of the proc-
> esses of spiritual life and growth. (*King,* p. 105)

In "A White Heron" nature is a powerful and seductive protagonist. It has claimed Sylvia long before the hunter appears and
literally given her life, so that "it seemed as if she never had been
alive at all before she came to live at the farm." (*A White Heron,*
p. 3) The price of giving one's life to it entirely is acknowledged
to be high, but those fortunates who live balanced between the
natural and human communities, like Mrs. Goodsoe, Mrs. Powder,
Miss Tempy, Eliza Peck, and Lydia Dunn (to name just a few) are
nourished by its influence and in turn can pass it on. Its savage
aspect and meager bounty are recognized but not dwelt upon. In
the universe of the stories the stony Maine earth is "fruitful," and
the sensitivity of a character to natural beauty is inevitably a moral
barometer. "It does seem as if folks might keep the peace when the
Lord's give 'em so pooty a spot to live in," says Lyddy Bangs in
"Law Lane," looking out at the hills from a high blueberry-patch
in midsummer. (*King,* p. 123)

As has been mentioned, gardens are a complex symbol, uniting nature and art, historic tradition and womanly caring. They come in various shapes and sizes. To Lyddy Bangs's friend Mrs. Powder, peacemaker and "whole-souled, hearty woman," the whole of outdoors is a garden: "If I can have a sweet-briar bush and sweet-fern patch and some clumps o' bayberry, you can take all the gardin blooms." (p. 128) Entirely different but equally significant is Miss Cynthia West's garden in "A Bit of Shore Life." Cynthia is a pale, disappointed-looking woman who lives on an isolated farm and defers to her more vigorous older sister. The narrator of the story, a city visitor, is quick to feel sorry for her and draw conclusions about her narrow life. But Cynthia's garden is a riotous cornucopia of blossoms—not Jewett's usual tidy box-bordered affair but an exuberant mélange of strong-colored poppies, larkspur, marigolds, and "old-fashioned sweet, straying things—all growing together in a tangle of which my friend seemed ashamed." (*Old Friends,* p. 264) Celia Thaxter's garden on Appledore was just like this, though "A Bit of Shore Life" precedes it by several years. Both break with the eighteenth-century gardening convention still common in New England, in Thaxter's case because she wanted a cutting-garden and in Cynthia's because all her pent-up affection, creativity, and sexuality have gone into creating this one transient work of art. That her art should be gardening, that the life in the earth responds to her own—that is the prerogative of a Jewett woman. We should not be too quick to imitate the narrator's pity, nor to assume that Cynthia's compensations are inadequate. "There!" she says. "I couldn't live out o' sight o' the woods, I don't believe." (p. 263)

Animals, both wild and domestic, are another link with the larger universe. Like Mrs. Bonny's animals in *Deephaven,* the dog and the cat in the dooryard generally signify a generous soul within. Cats keep Eliza Peck and Mrs. Powder company (Mrs. Powder's is her "darling" and goes blueberrying with her). The narrator of "The Landscape Chamber" rides a "petted" horse that frets itself into a tangle when she leaves it alone by the roadside, much as Jewett's Sheila might have done. The horse is a kind of touchstone for the miserly, unfriendly old man from whom the narrator asks shelter. He is about to refuse when he notices the injured animal; then he softens, and later the narrator comes upon him almost furtively doctoring the bruised foot. His love for horses is a sign of his susceptibility to human affection; it is the means by which the narrator touches his sympathy and is able to win his trust. And later in the story it is another animal, a song sparrow on the windowsill, that calms her fear of the old man and leads to her decision to stay and try to help him and his daughter.

At the same time, Jewett's depiction of animals is rarely sentimental. Although she can lapse into the pathetic fallacy when it comes to trees, she generally has a tough countrywoman's streak when it comes to animals. Abandoned cats in *Deephaven* and "A Bit of Shore Life" are given sympathy only in passing, and woodchucks in the child's story of that name are trapped and beaten to death. Personally she would not have allowed herself to make a pet of the pig that had to be slaughtered in February, and it is doubtful that she herself felt nearly as much antagonism toward the hunter in "A White Heron" as modern urban readers do. Nineteenth-century ornithologists routinely shot birds and stuffed them as specimens. Jewett probably knew one of the most famous, William Brewster, who was a neighbor of the Longfellows and the Lowells. Her own nephew, Theodore, who loved all animals and kept pigeons and rabbits as pets, apparently shot birds as an adolescent, for his Aunt Sarah, watching a flock of flamingos on an 1896 cruise in the Caribbean, regretted that he was not along to shoot one for his collection.[12]

While the layered symbolism and personal moral vision of Jewett's best work are distinctive characteristics, it is her unparalleled portrayal of Maine people and their culture that her readers have always most loved. In fact her moral vision and her regionalism are two sides of the same coin, for Jewett's belief that every person shapes his or her life within a certain God-given arena was expressed in her art through the tradition of Maine stoicism. Here personal and cultural history merge, and her own answer to the problem of living in circumscribed surroundings underlies her sympathetic understanding of the lives of country people. In the up-country code that requires one to make the best of a life of scarcity and solitude, she found an echo of her own early efforts to accept the sleepy village in which she had been "kindly placed." The fact that she was no longer physically limited to Berwick had not changed the permanent sense of liberation she had achieved in embracing it as the place where she was meant to be, and the finding of her vocation as a writer had made that acceptance a liberation in the fullest sense. For Jewett as for her characters, accepting the cards one is dealt is a test of moral courage and understanding.

In Jewett's world one may choose among several kinds of challenge, but one does not weasel out of one's responsibility. To quote a phrase she uses repeatedly, one "stands in one's lot and place." Those who weasel out are—to quote another inimitable Maine expression—"meeching." Deacon Brimblecom is meeching, and therefore "just the kind of man that a hog wouldn't budge for; it takes a masterful man to deal with a hog." (*King,* p. 76) Shifty Henry Stroud, who tries to insinuate himself into Lydia Dunn's life and buy the goodwill of an entire village on phony credit, is definitely meeching. Women who are meeching, meaning women who are always whimpering over imaginary complaints and ailments, are objects of particular scorn by Jewett's strong matrons. "I don't see what folks always want to be complaining for," says Mrs. Beedle in "Andrew's Fortune" of a whining neighbor.

> "She always was just so when she was a girl. Nothin' ever suits her. She ain't had no more troubles to bear than the rest of us, but you never see her that she did n't have a chapter to lay before ye. I've got's much feelin' as the next one, but when folks drives in their spiggits and wants to draw a bucketful o' compassion every day right straight along, there does come times when it seems as if the bar'l was getting low." (*By-Ways,* p. 47)

Meeching people run out on their responsibility to God, themselves, and their community, and because they feel guilty about it they are generally a fairly noisy bunch. To stand in one's lot and place, on the other hand, demands quiet determination that may or may not be noticed by others. Jewett's own father had stood in his lot and place by remaining a country doctor, and many of her strongest characters have achieved a similar renunciation. Eliza Peck of "Miss Peck's Promotion" has sacrificed a schoolteaching career in order to help at home; now "her ambitions were at an end. She would do what good she could among her neighbors, and stand in her lot and place." (*King,* p. 173) Ann Floyd of "Marsh Rosemary," having discovered that her ne'er-do-well husband has deserted her and married another woman, quietly resolves to keep her secret and stand "in her own place" like the sturdy, inconspicuous plant for which the story is named. (*Heron,* p. 123) The increasing option to duck out on life's challenges is one of the chief sins Mrs. Goodsoe holds against the modern world, as symbolized by the railroad. In the old days, she says, people stayed put and developed character by facing their problems: "'T was allowed to be difficult for folks to git about in old times, or to git word across the country, and they stood in their lot an' place, and were n't all just alike, either, same as pine-spills." (*King,* p. 59)

George Quint of Folly Island, who has exiled himself and his family over a petty quarrel with his neighbors, is an example of someone who has run away. "It could not be said that Quint had stood in his lot and place as a brave man should, unless he had left John's Island as the Pilgrim Fathers left England, for conscientious scruples and a necessary freedom." (p. 34) The historic reference tells us of an important distinction that divides the concept of "lot and place" from mere fatalism: one may turn away from present challenges, provided the escape contributes to the greater good.

The silence of those who face up to their responsibilities is a virtue in itself. Following a long tradition in English literature, Jewett's stories derive considerable emotional power from the tension between what is felt and what is said. The code of silent honor, of sacrificing oneself for the sake of someone else or quietly shouldering a burden alone, is as natural to the Jewett character as wearing wool in January. But as all the world knows, the power of passion is magnified by silence. Margaret Fuller felt "all Italy burning beneath the Saxon crust," and Sarah Orne Jewett was well acquainted with the "volcanoes of humanity" smoldering beneath New England reserve.[13] The negative aspect of New England reticence has been explored and exploited by a succession of American writers (some of whom, like Edith Wharton and Eugene O'Neill, were not native New Englanders and saw the phenomenon only from the outside). In Jewett's work silence has various shades of value, and while it is sometimes negative it is more often positive. When the pent-up emotions of Mainers finally break through the ice, they become a powerful impetus in human affairs. Hence the almost magical quality of Mrs. Todd's spare account of her lost lover in *The Country of the Pointed Firs,* and hence the magical quality of Green Island itself, as a place where the danger inherent in such confessions, in letting down one's guard against the unnamed cruelties or malice that can strike the undefended, is in miraculous abeyance.

Reticence can operate in many ways. It can foster the growth of an illusion, as in "A Lost Lover," or it can operate negatively to keep people at a distance, as in "Miss Sydney's Flowers." But usually the reticence of Jewett's characters is a means to preserve one's independence or not to burden others. Examples are almost as numerous as the stories themselves, but one of the best is "A Bit of Shore Life," a long story that, like "Sister Wisby" or "River Driftwood," seems at first to be sprawling and meandering, with no fixed focus. Like theirs, its focus is thematic and must be gradually uncovered. The story concerns a city visitor, the narrator, who is staying in a Maine fishing village for the summer. She is not altogether a city woman, for she has known the area since childhood, but she is sophisticated and educated and evidently has lived a long time away. She is alternately understanding and unconsciously patronizing toward the people she meets, much like Kate and Helen in *Deephaven,* whose story precedes this one by two years.

The narrator befriends Georgie West, a shy, silent twelve-year-old fisherman who has recently lost his mother and who chooses to follow his father's trade rather than go to school. The narrator feels sorry for him ("the brave, fearless steady little soul!" [*Old Friends,* p. 232]) and clearly thinks he must lead a very hard and cheerless life with his father. The father (based on George Hatch of Wells, who was also the original of Danny in *Deephaven*) is an almost wordless solitary like his son. He "took it very hard, losing of his wife," according to a local fisherman, and he refuses to consider marrying one of the "smart, stirring women" who would be glad to look after him and the boy. (p. 231) There is an implied disapproval here and in the narrator's sympathy for Georgie; she clearly sees the father and son as two waifs, deprived of the benefits of womanly care and spending their days in a monotonous and emotionally barren round of silence and hard work.

Later, during an excursion inland with Georgie, the narrator meets Mrs. Wallis, whose furniture is being auctioned off before her eyes. The narrator pities her as well, and then generalizes her pity to all the old women of the countryside, commenting on their "cheerless talk," their "morbid interest in sickness and deaths," and what seem to her to be their endless complaints, disputes, and ancestral feuds. She comments on their lack of merriment and their "odd, rough way of joking," and she wonders rhetorically if all this gloom and heaviness comes about because "their world is so small, and life affords so little amusement and pleasure, and is at best such a dreary round of the dullest housekeeping." (p. 244) She sounds, in short, very like town-bred Annie Fields bemoaning the "narrow round of village life." It is easy to mistake the narrator's voice for Jewett's here, and to assume the passage expresses the author's own impatience with farm life and countrywomen. But the very characteristics the narrator pities are the stuff of Jewett's stories, and we have seen that the word *dull* was one of her favorite challenges to the city reader, and that she consistently tried to show us the real "dramas" that were being enacted within the "dull-looking, quiet homes" of rural New England. ("A Landless Farmer," *Mate,* p. 93)

At the end of their journey Georgie and the narrator come to the house of his aunts Hannah and Cynthia. Hannah is a "master smart woman," a "regular driver," (p. 235) while the younger Cynthia is slight and weak willed. Her main achievement in life seems to be her glorious garden, and at first the narrator pities her a good deal: "I seemed to know all about her life in a flash, and pitied her from the bottom of my heart." But then she is able to step back a bit and see things from Cynthia's point of view: "Yet I suppose she would not have changed places with me for any thing, or with anybody else, for that matter." (p. 257) And Cynthia herself says as much a little later on.

Hard as these people's lives are, it is not for an outsider from the city to presume to wish them otherwise. Georgie's work is his own, passionately chosen (for this is one of Jewett's revisitings of the theme of vocation). His taciturn father is his best friend, and stands looking after him as he sets off inland like an anxious woman watching her man set out to sea. Hannah's life, like Cynthia's, seems wasted, for years earlier she had given up her tailoring trade and a lover to come home and nurse her ailing father. But since her father's death Hannah has been the mainstay of her mother, sister, widowed brother, and nephew, and clearly she has no regrets.

Each of the characters the narrator meets has endured grief and disappointment and has stood fast in his or her lot and place; only the unfortunate Mrs. Wallis has had her life rearranged by a busy intruder.

Reticence is second nature to these people, a means of preserving dignity and self-respect. Among themselves they communicate very well, but seldom with words. Words in any case are often suspect in Jewett's world, the tools of meeching manipulators and canting ministers. Instead, Jewett's country people communicate by deed. The narrator introduces herself to Georgie by silently helping him launch his boat, slightly offending in the process his considerable twelve-year-old machismo. He gives her a surprised glance, "as if he wished to ask me what good I supposed I could do, though I was twice his size." But "he did not say a word to me, nor I to him." (pp. 229–30) When she meets Hannah it is not with a conventional exchange of verbal civilities but by an older ceremony, like two members of different tribes meeting in a forest: the narrator offers Hannah a fish, and Hannah reciprocates by accepting "a little ha'dick" (though not a larger fish, for that would make her too beholden). (p. 235) Andrew West expresses his profound grief for his wife by one laconic sentence that can be taken any way you choose: "I've hed my wife, and I've lost her." (p. 231)

Still waters run very deep in this family, as Hannah later explains. "Ain't he an odd boy?" she says, speaking of Georgie.

> "But he's just like his father and grandfather before him;
> you wouldn't think they had no gratitude nor feelin', but I
> s'pose they have. They used to say my father never'd forgit
> a friend, or forgive an enemy." (p. 236)

She says this with a "shadow of disapproval" on her face, but we find out later that Hannah was devoted to her father and that she was the only sister who could communicate with him. Cynthia, who is talkative and confidential with a city stranger, was terrified of her father and struck dumb in his presence. But Cynthia is weak and dependent, and it is Hannah who is the strong survivor.

Like most Jewett characters Hannah expresses her kindness through actions. Her words are cramped and stingy, but her deeds —especially her culinary deeds—are munificent. The gathering around the table for dinner, tea, and breakfast was the focal point of Jewett's own social and family life, and feasting occurs throughout the stories as an expression of caring for the world at large. Like women everywhere, Jewett's women feed the soul by feeding the body, and Jewett the author and epicure likes nothing better than to regale us with the menu of some sumptuous tea or supper served in a poor country kitchen. So Hannah West, having ritually deprecated in a Mainer's way her house ("It ain't much of a place to ask anybody to") and her supper ("Miss Hannah made many apologies; and said, if I had only set a day, she would have had things as they ought to be"), and having first provided for the creatures as any Jewett woman would (lobster shells for the cat, hay for the horse), sets a groaning board of lobsters, biscuits, honey, hot gingerbread, two kinds of preserves, pie, and tea. (pp. 235, 265)

Throughout the stories the act speaks, while the characters themselves are tongue-tied. Their habitual understatement is an expression of their cultural heritage and the hardships of their lives. Silence is a way of not exhausting the communal "spiggits" of compassion, and to assume one is strong is itself a source of strength. To keep control over one's life and continue one's work are almost as important as life itself, while to lose control, as do Mrs. Wallis, the hapless elderly father in "A Landless Farmer," and the Bray sisters in the 1890 story "The Town Poor," is one of the worst terrors life can hold. At the same time, independence is nothing without recognition of the dependence of everyone on everyone else, and so we have a continual readjustment of the fine balance between reserve and confidence, and between the deed and the word.

As a kind of biographer's postscript to the solemnities of the above discussion, I would like to talk about a story that seems to have nothing whatever to do with God and the Large Questions. Jewett herself underrated it for that reason, preferring "The Gray Man," a sober parable about death as a friend that she wrote at the same time. One of the most tenderly humorous and carefully crafted of all her stories, it is interesting from a biographical point of view because it shows us Jewett's playful wit turned on herself, as she poked fun at some of her own most dearly held beliefs.

"The Dulham Ladies" is about the two aging Dobin sisters,

who live in their childhood home in Dulham. Their late father was a Congregational minister there for many years, and their mother's mother was a member of a distinguished Boston family, the Greenaples. The sisters are acutely conscious of a responsibility to uphold traditional standards of behavior and set an example for the rest of the village. The village, however, is becoming less and less respectful of tradition as newcomers move in. The Misses Dobin are constantly driven to insist on the correct pronunciation of their name: *DO*-bin. The distinction is crucial to their family pride, for the Dobins, like the Jewetts, set great store by their imagined French origins. "The name was originally *D'Aubigne,* we think," Miss Lucinda Dobin explains patiently but vainly to the assembled barbarians of the church sewing-circle. (*Heron,* p. 132) But the barbarians only laugh, and the sisters are "the Miss Dobbinses" to everyone except a few old friends. They feel this slight as if it were

> the sorrows in many a provincial chateau in the Reign of Terror. The ladies looked on with increasing dismay at the retrogression in society. They felt as if they were a feeble garrison, to whose lot it had fallen to repulse a noisy, irreverent mob, an increasing band of marauders who would overthrow all land-marks of the past, all etiquette and social rank. (pp. 132–33)

Realizing that the family ascendency they have always taken for granted is slipping, they decide to take some step to retrieve their authority and thereby stop the shocking erosion of behavioral standards. The step they decide on has the happy promise not only of showing the town that they are as up-to-date as anyone, but also of solving a mortifying problem that neither has had the courage to face. They will buy some frisettes, or false bangs, and at one stroke reassert their connection with the fashionable Boston elite and relieve their secret embarrassment over their thinning hair.

Accordingly, they set off for town on the pretext of Christmas shopping and make their way to the door of the old man who used to keep their father in ministerial wigs. But this trusted acquaintance has gone out of business, and soon they find themselves at the mercy of a modern wigmaker, an obsequious Frenchman who flatters them into buying two heavy, bright chestnut frisettes that he hadn't been able to sell to anyone else. The sisters begin to realize their mistake on the way home as the bangs lose their curl and begin to hang down into their eyes. But though each suffers pangs of doubt on the other's account, they defend their decision even when Hetty, their sensible housekeeper and guardian angel, offers to have the frisettes returned. The story ends as the sisters go off to the sewing-circle, "to be snickered at," as Hetty sighs watching them. "Well, the Dobbin girls they was born, and the Dobbin girls they will remain till they die; but if they ain't innocent Christian babes to those that knows 'em well, mark me down for an idjit myself!" (p. 149)

The germ for the story might be traced to the old patient of Dr. Jewett's who called one day, decked out in velvet bonnet and frisette; and almost certainly the sisters, in their gentleness, unworldliness, and innocent love of tradition are modeled on the Barrell sisters of York. But the amount of mocking self-reference in the story, beginning with the sisters' pretensions to French ancestry, is notable. The Dobins' preoccupation with their highborn relations is perilously close to Sarah's pride in the Gilmans, and the fetish they make of ladylike demeanor is a near-caricature of her own love of antique ceremony. Shopping together, the sisters consult one another's choices and veto the unsuitable, as Sarah and Mary did. Their father, not unlike Grandfather Perry, was a simple farm boy who married above his station and maintained all his life a peasant fondness for Indian pudding. A reference to Great-grandmother Greenaple's taking tea "at Governor Clovenfoot's on Beacon Street in company with an English lord" (p. 125) is, despite its removal in time, very like a tongue-in-cheek reference to the company Sarah and Annie kept in Boston and their own notable Anglophilia. Then too, because the Misses Dobin's parents, like Sarah's elder relations, have lingered "until their children are far past middle age," the sisters remain in a state of miraculously arrested girlhood and "were amazingly slow to suspect that they were not so young as they used to be." (pp. 126, 131) And finally, the elder Miss Dobin parodies the quiet integrity that Jewett valued so highly for herself and her characters: she has tried, she says, to "stand firm in my lot and place." (p. 134)

There is no moralizing at the end, and the sisters are allowed to walk off to their fate with no comment except Hetty's. The narrator's tone is consistently mock-heroic, the elevated language emphasizing the endearing triviality of the plot. A slight but nearly flawless story, "The Dulham Ladies" shows us Jewett thoroughly at home with herself and aware of how easily her own most cherished shibboleths could harden into obsolescence and absurdity.

19

"Their Sky and Their Earth"

WHEN SARAH AND ANNIE WERE IN ENG-
land in 1892 they made the customary pilgrimage to the Brontë
birthplace at Haworth, despite warnings from previous pilgrims
that they would find the church gone, the rectory much changed,
and the village grown into a grimy manufacturing town. In fact
the church was still there, though much altered, and the house at
the top of its narrow hill street

> look[ed] pretty much as it did when that household known
> of the world now, burned their lights of genius like candles
> flashing in a cave, like will o' the wisps of their upland
> country shut up, captives and prisoners in that gloomy old
> stone house. . . . Nothing you ever read about them can
> make you know them until you go there. . . . Never mind
> people who tell you there is nothing to see in the places
> where people lived who interest you! You always find some-
> thing of what made them the souls they were—and at any
> rate you see their sky and their earth.[1]

This is as good a statement as any of what travel meant to
Jewett. It was a chance to immerse herself in place, and through
each place and its natural surroundings to identify with past lives.
The first five years of the nineties brought her a succession of these
experiences of time-within-place, beginning with the European trip

254

(Barbizon and Millet, Yorkshire and her own ancestors) and continuing with more local travels to the Adirondack "wilderness" (what was left of it), Celia Thaxter's little island domain, and finally, her 1895 sojourn in Martinsville, Maine. She went to other places, of course, but these five, all rural and almost unscathed by the hurtling social changes of the nineteenth century, were rich in those associations that had made their present inhabitants "the souls they were."

Another series of events affecting the shape of her inner experience in these years was the loss of several people she loved. She had reached her forties, the time when those in the generation ahead of us whose example and advice we have come to take for granted suddenly begin to disappear from view. It is also the time when one begins to lose one's contemporaries—a possibility in our time, a probability in Jewett's. Depending on circumstances, such losses can leave us feeling not only lonely and mortal but also conscious of our own strong maturity and of the fact that we ourselves have become examples and advisors to those behind us. Such an effect is not always conscious, and perhaps in Jewett's case it was not an effect at all but simply coincidental. Nevertheless, the deaths of several people who were dear to her between 1891 and 1894, far from depressing her or increasing her sense of her own fragility, seem ultimately to have left her stronger physically, emotionally, and artistically.

The first of these was the hardest to bear. In October 1891, a few months after the Academy Centennial, Sarah's mother died. Her illness, which had lasted most of Sarah's lifetime, remains a mystery. Almost certainly not consumption or heart disease, it may have involved the slow deterioration of some other vital organ such as liver or kidneys. Whatever it was, it struck especially hard in the summer of 1890, and though Mrs. Jewett improved afterwards, that was the first of several devastating attacks that finally took her life. Throughout the year Sarah rarely left home. "I have had a very dear quiet time," she wrote Loulie Dresel in October 1890 while Mary was away, "helping my dear mother to keep house and playing that she still could do it all."[2] As their mother's condition steadily worsened, the sisters took turns watching in the sickroom, never leaving her alone. "As for writing," Sarah remarked during one of her mother's brief rallies,

> I keep beginning things, [but] after all I like best to sit by
> the garden window in my mother's room and talk to her
> when she likes it, and look out at the snow and the glisten-
> ing elm twigs. Now that we are not so hurried and anxious
> about the illness my sister and I feel a little dulled and
> tired; it has been a terrible strain and sorrow.[3]

Although in pain much of the time, Mrs. Jewett was heroically patient and uncomplaining, and her daughters responded by jealously keeping her care to themselves, refusing the offers of aunts and great-aunts to come and help. By the time she died they were exhausted, and they could not help but be relieved, not only that their wrenching witness to her suffering was over but that they themselves were freed of the burden of her care.

For Sarah the memory of the long months spent at her mother's side was bittersweet, for through this final illness mother and daughter had achieved the close communion that had always eluded them. The multiple distractions of their lives and the temperamental and intellectual differences that had separated them dropped away, and they discovered an intimacy they had not known since Sarah was an infant. To "find" her mother for so short a time made Sarah's irrecoverable loss both easier and more painful than it would otherwise have been:

> The loss falls . . . heavily in our hearts—perhaps more so
> because all her pain and suffering brought us closer than
> anything else ever did. These last few weeks have been
> most hard to bear but as I look back I find some of the
> dearest and best minutes that my mother and I ever had to-
> gether scattered along the way. I miss her and miss her: it
> seems impossible that she should be gone.[4]

At the same time, the happiness she experienced in their final understanding lingered on, to give deeper emphasis to the maternal theme already central to her fiction. Much of the sense of peace and resolution she now felt would be expressed in future letters of sympathy to friends whose own mothers were dead or dying, like this one to Frances Parkman:

I *know* you are going to feel nearer to your mother now
than you have ever felt before—oh it will be *so* different!
and she will be so much more your mother and your
friend.—The barriers that lie between us and every other
soul, I sometimes think, are meant to be strong else we
should depend too much upon those who *truly* love us here,
but when they are gone, how close how *close* we are and to
our mothers before every one else![5]

Another aspect of this loss, common to everyone but having
particular weight with Jewett, was the realization that with this
surviving parent she had indeed lost the last of her childhood. "I
didn't know," she wrote Mabel Burnett (whose own father had just
died), "what sadness would fall on my heart when I knew that
childhood was strongly and surely living on only while there was
still somebody near whose child I was."[6] It was during the months
of her mother's last illness that she borrowed Stubby's sled to go
coasting and played with him at scouting for Indians in the woods.
One subtle change brought about by her mother's death was that
now she was more likely to address her letters to Charles Street to
"Dearest Annie" rather than to "Fuff" or "Fuffatee," and her signature was more likely to be "Sarah" than "Pinny." But there was no
sharp break in this or any other customary usage, and she by no
means lost hold of the child in herself. It was six years later that
she made her famous remark, "This is my birthday and I am always
nine years old."[7]

As was usual in the Jewett household, the overt expressions of
mourning (except for black-bordered stationery) were soon put
aside, and life was resolutely picked up where death had so rudely
interrupted it. Sarah's grief found indirect expression in renewed
attention to her mother's old friends, from whose old-fashioned
speech and manners she took a kind of comfort. As before, but
possibly more than before, she was attentive to frail, elderly neighbors, calling on widowed invalid Mrs. Paul, who spent her days
confined to a chair by her window, and on her old friend and
dressmaker Olive Grant, who was painfully ill. Elderly friends in
turn were attentive to her, as she wrote to Sarah Whitman:

Yesterday a dear little old woman who rarely leaves her
house came in to see Mary and me. "I know *just* how you
feel dear," she said; "I have been through the same sorrow"—and I could see that it was present yet in her heart
and she almost ninety and missing her mother still.—It
was a most tender and touching little old face—I wish you
could have been here to know the dignity and sweetness of
her visit, dear quaint old lady, mindful of the proprieties;
and one who had seen almost everybody go whom she had
known in youth or middle age even. I wish you could
know some of the village people not the new ones—but
those to whom in their early days Berwick was the round
world itself.[8]

The outside world did not altogether disappear during the
trying months before her mother died. For one thing there was the
Berwick Academy Centennial celebration on July 1, for which both
sisters worked hard all spring in their various organizing and
writing capacities. Luckily their mother was having one of her
respites when the day came, so the whole family could push away
their fears and enjoy the proceedings, of which Sarah was honorary
vice president.

A sobering prelude to the death of Sarah's mother was the
death, on August 12, of James Russell Lowell. One of the giants
of her childhood, and one whose work, like Whittier's, had set a
distinct precedent for her to follow, Lowell had only become real
to her in a human sense since his return to Cambridge in 1889.
She had known him from a distance long before then, through his
daughter, Mabel Burnett, and through his old friendship with
Annie. In the 1880s Lowell had strayed a long way from his native
home and literature, serving as American ambassador to England.
His Anglophilia (he affected a top hat and a dandyish air when he
came home) was one of many tastes he shared with Sarah. In
particular they liked to talk over his affectionate reminiscences of
Whitby, a Yorkshire village not far from Jewett's own ancestral
village where he had spent his English holidays. And he liked to
tease her about country life in "the Deestrict," as he referred to the
District of Maine.

Her last sight of him was in the spring of '91, when during

a flying visit to Annie she drove to Elmwood in search of Mabel and found Lowell alone, in some pain from the cancer that would kill him but sitting peacefully enough on the piazza with a blanket on his knees, reading *The Moonstone.* He was in a mood to talk, and they "had a most beautiful quiet time, and the fringe tree seemed at times to make a third."[9] Sarah had a chance to thank him for a publicity puff he had written at the request of her publishers, in which he likened her to a fine gem cutter (one of those miniaturist metaphors favored by well-meaning male critics) and noted her ability to reproduce New England speech almost without dialect— an observation as generous as it was just, considering Lowell's own heavy use of dialect in *The Biglow Papers.* "How we should talk about dear Mr. Lowell if we were together," Sarah wrote Annie from home after his death:

> Here he is only the "Lowell" of his books, to people, and
> not a single one knows how dear and charming he was and
> how full of helps to ones thoughts and purposes in every
> day life—I wrote Mabel most truly that I was as fond of
> him almost as if I belonged to his household and kindred.
> And I suppose that the last bit of writing for print that he
> may have done was that letter for me.[10]

After Mrs. Jewett died Annie spent a week or more in Berwick, and then she and Sarah left for Boston and a short trip to New York. As was often the case, each regarded the other as rather a frail reed, Sarah having been half-crippled for some months with rheumatism, which affected her eyes and prevented reading, while Annie still seemed depleted from a long attack of "grippe" several months earlier. There had been some talk of Annie's going abroad alone to regain her strength that summer, but to Sarah's relief Annie had decided against it. Now, a family death always being an incentive for such grand escapes, the plan was revived and Mary drawn in. They would all three go; Carrie and Ned could look after family affairs. But now it was Mary who backed out, pleading responsibilities at home, and Sarah was left to choose between going with Annie or staying with her sisters. She delayed and fretted over her decision, and health reasons had to be invoked to allay her own guilt and explain her apparent defection to the

Gilman relations. It was with feelings sore and confused that she boarded the *Werra* in New York on February 27, 1892, and sailed for Italy. Fellow travelers included associate editor of the *Century*, Robert Underwood Johnson, and his wife, Sarah's old friend Mary Garrett, and Charles Scribner.

If she had been superstitious she might have thought in the following weeks that the gods were determined to punish her. The *Werra* rolled and pitched in rough seas, throwing Sarah out of her bunk one night so that she disembarked at Genoa with a black eye. Genoa itself was unseasonably cold, and a day or two after their arrival its blooming roses were blanketed with snow. The party (including Mary Garrett and the Johnsons) lingered only long enough to pay their respects to Mary Cowden-Clarke before hurrying south to Rome and Naples. In Rome Sarah was promptly confined to bed, having come down with tonsillitis. About a week later came an unexpected blow from home: Carrie's husband Ned Eastman, not yet forty-three, had died on March 18 of peritonitis.

Sarah's immediate impulse was to rush home, but Mary urged against it, saying the best way she could help Carrie was to regain her own strength. She added that Carrie was bearing up remarkably well, and Carrie herself wrote a movingly upbeat letter, clearly calculated to demonstrate that she was continuing almost as usual. All the Jewetts, in fact, were once more shaking out their banners in the face of death. Friends came to stay with both sisters, the family lawyer helped Carrie quickly dispose of the store, and twelve-year-old Theodore took his father's place at the table and carved the roast. Mary cast about in her mind for a consoling pleasure for him and lit on the very Mary-like solution of buying him a pony. The little chestnut mare dispensed comfort all around. "You never would grudge the money if you could see how the child has heartened up, and seemed to take new courage, to say nothing of the pleasure of Mr. J. E. Tucker," she wrote Sarah.[11]

Reassured, Sarah stayed on in Rome, where the pleasures of exploring mellow ruins and obscure old churches were enhanced by the company of friends. Half of Boston and a good part of New York seemed to be sojourning in Italy. "Every time we go out we meet friends as if we were stepping across the Common," she wrote.[12] Helen Merriman was there, Alice and George Howe were down the hall in her hotel, and at the entrance to the Sistine Chapel she and Annie literally bumped into Samuel and Olivia Clemens.* The reunions continued in Florence, where they spent a week in April, and in Venice, where Annie's sister Sarah Adams joined them. Venice remained a magical place for Sarah, and they lingered there nearly three weeks, spending every possible moment on the water.

In late May, parting temporarily from the Johnsons and Mary Garrett, Sarah and Annie removed to Aix-en-Provence, where for a month both adhered to a strict regime prescribed by resident doctors. Sarah, whose rheumatism had never been precisely diagnosed, was told she had "rheumatic gout" and that it would probably always be more or less with her. She decided, she said, to "proceed to enjoy myself as a rheumatic gout patient at her best,"[13] and as soon as the doctors released them she and Annie sped off to Paris. There Sarah finally met a woman whom Sarah had known for several years only through her letters: the critic and novelist "Th. Bentzon," in ordinary life Marie Thérèse de Solms Blanc.

At fifty-two Thérèse Blanc was a respected figure in French literary circles, a woman whose work had been thrice honored (*couronnée*) by the Académie Française—though she had not, of course, been invited to join. Thirty-five years earlier, divorced and penniless, she had decided to support herself and her infant son by writing, which she had learned to do with the help of powerful friends, among them George Sand. She was now on the editorial staff of the *Revue des Deux Mondes,* where her lengthy critical essays regularly appeared. She had a longstanding interest in American literature and social customs, and she had translated or written about several American authors, including Thomas Bailey Aldrich, Bret Harte, and Mark Twain. An upper-class French lady to her bones and a liberal-conservative feminist of Jewett's own stripe, she

---

* In 1891 financial reverses and family ill health sent the Clemenses to Europe, where they remained for several years. Sarah saw them at least once more in Italy, but there is no record of their conversation. Sarah once remarked that she liked Mark Twain better every time she saw him, but though they had close mutual friends in the Howellses and Warners, both she and Clemens moved around so much that their meetings were rare.

discovered *A Country Doctor* soon after it was published and wrote a thirty-four-page, largely favorable essay about it for the *Revue*.[14] Sarah wrote to thank her, and the friendship was begun. Later Mme Blanc published a translation of Jewett's sketch "A Little Traveller,"[15] and she helped find a translator for *A Country Doctor,* which was published in France with nine additional stories and her own essay as an introduction. In 1887, in an essay on "Le Naturalisme aux États-Unis" (by which she meant writers about nature), she singled out "A White Heron" for praise and appreciatively mentioned *Deephaven* and *Country By-Ways*.[16] The epistolary friendship, therefore, carried a certain weight of gratitude on Sarah's part, and it was with some unease that she climbed the stairs to Mme Blanc's apartment to meet her old friend for the first time. But the meeting went very well. The formidable French intellectual turned out to be a plump, white-haired person, disarmingly simple and direct in manner. Her literary translations notwithstanding, she was by no means fluent in spoken English; but her attempts to navigate the twists and turns of the language lent it a kind of unintentional poetry and piquancy that soon became, to her listeners, inseparable from the woman herself.

A few days later, having been rejoined by Mary Garrett and the Johnsons, Sarah and Annie were at Barbizon, where Thérèse soon appeared, bringing with her a suitcase full of books. They stayed in a vine-covered stone cottage a stone's throw from the house where Millet had lived. Sarah found images from his paintings everywhere, from the flat brown plain outside the village, to the low church with its pointed tower, to the courtyard outside their own door. Daylight hours were given to walking, while evenings were filled with good talk, in the intervals of which Thérèse read aloud her early letters from George Sand. When they all left a few days later, Sarah and Annie had extracted from her a half promise either to sail home with them in September or follow in the spring.

The rest of the time abroad, from mid-July to late September, was spent in England. There they mostly visited friends, fitting in their sightseeing along the way. Among the highlights of Sarah's stay was another visit with Tennyson, who received her and Annie in his house in Surrey. He recited bits and pieces of his poetry for them and, to Sarah's pleasure, took an interest in a pendant she wore, a crystal set in silver leaves that Sarah Whitman had given her, asking in a teasing way if she found her stories in its depths. His obvious frailty gave his courtesy a kind of anachronistic pathos, and to Sarah he seemed "like a King in captivity, one of the Kings of old, of divine right and sacred seclusions."[17] But like other members of her royal pantheon he was a dying king, and he would be gone by the end of the year.

Among the other friends they saw were Frances Arnold (Matthew Arnold's widow) and her children, and Arnold's niece, Mary Arnold (Mrs Humphry) Ward, the latter meeting the outcome of yet another of Sarah's letters to distant fellow writers. Sneered at in her own time by Virginia Woolf and Arnold Bennett, among others, and since then dismissed as a pompous reactionary, "Mrs Humphry Ward" has labored under the further misfortune of her name, which like that of American composer Mrs. H. H. A. Beach, seems in its very syllables to defy anyone to take its owner seriously. Moreover, Ward was that strange anomaly, a female social reformer who vigorously resisted suffrage. But in her own time Ward's fictional explorations of ethical and religious conflict, particularly her 1888 novel, *Robert Elsmere,* struck an enormously responsive chord in the minds of readers on both sides of the ocean, while the settlement houses and children's hospital she founded in London, like Annie's Associated Charities, set a precedent for other activist women and made a small but significant difference in the lives of the poor. Her novels are not nearly as bad as they have been made out to be, while personally she was as committed to reform as Annie, with the same naive prejudices and the same taste for upper-middle-class comforts. Sarah, sharing them as well, liked her both as a writer and as a person.

Sarah went at least twice to Yorkshire, long associated in her mind both with Lowell and with her own family. In the coastal village of Whitby she visited Lowell's old friend George Du Maurier, longtime cartoonist for *Punch* and lately the author of *Peter Ibbetson,* for which she had written to thank him as she had written Mary Ward. (Serialized in *Harper's* in 1891 and later published in book form, *Peter Ibbetson* is a curious fantasy about a man so obsessed with grief over his lost beloved that he dreams her back to life. It clearly appealed to Sarah's own fascination with the supernatural, the afterlife, and the the power of imagination, and she had gone to the trouble in Paris to search out the Mare d'Auteuil, the small lake in the Bois where much of the story is set.) In nearby Danby she went to see the Rev. John Christopher Atkinson, author of *Forty Years in a Moorland Parish* (1891). In this autobiographical miscellany, laced with anecdotes about the people of Danby, Sarah had been intrigued to find much that was "curiously familiar to a Berwick person in words and ways"—many Berwickers besides the Jewetts being descendants of seventeenth-century Yorkshire dissenters.[18] Not far away was Haworth, where the visitors—despite a gruff reception from the resident vicar, who Sarah suspected was jealous of the Brontës' fame—found in the chill stones and shadowed moors the intimations they were looking for.

Of all her Yorkshire excursions, none gave her more pleasure than her reunion with Annie's old friend Robert Collyer, known affectionately in the Charles Street household as "Brother Robert." (He in turn addressed his hostesses as "Dear Lassies" and Mary Jewett as "Our Mary." A supply of cigars was kept ready for him in Annie's library, and he seems to have been the one person in the world, her own sister included, for whom Mary would drop everything so that she could go visiting.) Tweedy and roughhewn, still a Yorkshire countryman in spite of forty years in America, Collyer had been born in Keighley in 1823 and trained as a blacksmith in nearby Ilkley. Like Dinah in *Adam Bede,* he had become a Methodist lay preacher, educating himself laboriously by night. In 1850 he married and emigrated to America, where eventually he became a Unitarian minister, building large, enthusiastic congregations first in Chicago and later in New York. In 1892 he was asked back to Yorkshire to deliver an honorary address, and there Sarah and Annie met him in August, joining the crowd to hear him preach and later walking the moors with him as he pointed out the landmarks of his boyhood, bringing to life a landscape that, but for accidents of history, might have been Sarah's own.

On September 21, having seen many other places and people, Sarah, Annie, and Mary Garrett sailed home on the *Cephalonia.* Mary Jewett met them in New York, and after a brief stop in Boston Sarah hurried home to Maine, where she spent her third consecutive winter away from Annie. It was a difficult homecoming, with reminders of absence at every turn, though as Sarah wrote Loulie, "we all try hard not to let each other know that we think anything about *that*!"[19] Carrie, for all her whistling in the dark, was still badly shaken by her husband's death and leaned heavily on her sisters for advice and company. Still another loss for Sarah was Whittier, who having survived for many years an assortment of ailments real and imaginary had finally succumbed to one of them about three weeks before Sarah sailed for home. She reacted to all of it by throwing herself into her work, producing by February six new sketches plus several shorter pieces.

In late April 1893, a diversion being needed by everyone, all three sisters and Theodore, Annie, and the two Woolsey sisters went to the World's Columbian Exposition in Chicago. Among the attractions they found there were some that had personal interest: Sarah's own portrait (artist unknown) hanging in the State of Maine building; the Houghton Mifflin building, designed by Sarah Whitman; and a monumental cast of Anne Whitney's *Roma,* depicting the Eternal City as a half-starved old beggar woman. But Sarah's reaction was muted; tired from her winter's work and plagued by spring rheumatism, she probably made the journey more for her family's sake than her own. Over the next few months her pains grew worse, until by late summer she was forced to walk with a cane. The difficulty in focusing her eyes, which rightly or wrongly she associated with her rheumatism, returned as well and forced restrictions in reading and writing. In September she and Mary fled to Richfield Springs, New York, where Sarah took yet another water cure. It helped, but not much. What seems to have finally helped was a return to Annie—which is not to suggest that Sarah's illness was "hysterical," only that boredom and discomfort played their part in magnifying her symptoms. For once she had had more than enough of Berwick, and she rather fretfully blamed her bad health on the closeness of the Berwick house in summer. Altogether she had fought, she wrote Howells in December, "a wicked war of lameness and pain."[20] She had kept on working, preparing a new collection of stories and writing a preface for a new edition of *Deephaven* and at least two new stories, but physically she felt worse than she had since the 1870s. Once in Boston she saw her friend

Ella Dexter, an eye doctor, daily for unspecified but distinctly unpleasant treatments, and she must have wondered what would happen if her eyes failed altogether.*

In November Thérèse Blanc appeared, having come to keep her promise and to examine for herself, as a feminist and a writer, the condition of women in the United States. She did so with scholarly thoroughness, sweeping back and forth across the country as far west as Chicago and as far south as New Orleans, visiting in every major city settlement houses, schools, colleges, prisons, and other social institutions run and staffed by women, most of them middle-class volunteers. During her periodic visits to Boston she stayed at Charles Street, where Annie's ready-made network of friends gave her as broad a sampling of female social activism as she would find anywhere in the country. She sat in on one of the weekly conferences at the Associated Charities, and Alice Longfellow showed her around Radcliffe, painter Sarah Choate Sears took her to the women's prison at Sherborn, Pauline Agassiz Shaw gave her a tour of a public kindergarten,† Katharine Coolidge told her more than she wanted to know about Christian Science, and Julia Ward Howe drank tea with her at Annie's and preached to her from the pulpit of the Church of the Disciples. (Delighted with Howe, Thérèse described her in terms she could just as well have used of herself: "L'étude et la réflexion lui ont laissé une spontanéité toute juvénile, assaisonée d'un grain de malice. Il serait difficile d'avoir plus d'esprit."‡[21]) The resulting report, published first as an article and later expanded into a book,[22] paints a more hopeful

---

* Like rheumatoid arthritis and the common cold, eye diseases were treated inadequately and could cause temporary or permanent disablement. Victims Sarah would have known included Francis Parkman, Rudyard Kipling, Harriet Beecher Stowe (who had once been blind for months), young Mark deWolfe Howe, and Henry Wadsworth Longfellow, whose wife's reference in her letters to the "dosings and blisterings" he underwent set one's teeth on edge. See Fanny Appleton Longfellow, *Mrs. Longfellow*, p. 96.

† Daughter of biologist Louis Agassiz, stepdaughter of Radcliffe president Elizabeth Cary Agassiz, wife of Millet collector Quincy Adams Shaw, and mother of Civil War hero Robert Gould Shaw, Pauline Shaw followed Elizabeth Peabody in the development of American kindergartens and was the first to introduce them into public schools.

‡ "Study and reflection have not robbed her of a childlike spontaneity, seasoned with a grain of malice. It would be difficult to have more wit."

picture of American female activism and social institutions than the grim conditions of 1893 warranted, but it is by no means uncritical. Mme Blanc was amused, for example, by the sexual naiveté of American women, who insisted that their men were as virginal as themselves, and she deplored the puritan tendency of social workers (among whom Annie Fields was a prime example) to ruthlessly exclude the undeserving poor from their largesse. On the whole, though, she described American women and democracy in the friendly spirit of Tocqueville, and her writings remain a valuable index to the ways American women found to assert their growing independence.

Sarah gave Thérèse a glimpse of New England village life by carrying her and Annie off to Berwick for Thanksgiving, where her voluble presence helped greatly to keep the family from "being silent at table and thinking too much of missed faces."[23] It was a constant revelation to see one's own country through her eyes: to share, for example, her pleasure when she had the first sleighride of her life, or sat in her first rocking chair or discovered her first public library. Returning to Charles Street, Sarah worked with her every morning, "translating" two articles she wrote for American magazines, which really meant listening to Thérèse read them aloud in her garbled English and writing them down again in corrected form. In the next few years Sarah would similarly edit and place with editors two or three more articles, receiving for each the fifty dollars Thérèse insisted on paying her. Thérèse's linguistic drolleries ("I leave you all with *horror*," she once said in her exaggerated French-English, when she only meant she was sorry to go)[24] emphasized the quaint disparity between her disciplined mind and her expansive personality and made her seem, in this setting of Anglophile Boston, a visitor not only from another culture but even, like Tennyson, from another era. She seemed to fill the whole house while she was there, and Sarah liked to look out the window and watch her launch herself down Charles Street in full Paris regalia of purple bonnet and brocade cloak, the cloak billowing out behind like the sails of some antique French galleon.

After Thérèse left for the West and South in late December, Sarah spent a fortnight with her elderly friend Susan Burley Cabot, in what had come to be a regular twice-yearly visit. The wealthy widow of a former sea captain and mayor of Salem, Mrs. Cabot was widely read and seems to have been related, in the Boston way, to much of the population of Back Bay and of Beverly, where she spent her summers. She was a sociable woman with a voracious appetite for gossip, and consequently her semi-invalidism imposed on her a severe hardship of solitude. Her semiannual summons to Sarah, at once imperious and pathetic, was never refused no matter how inconvenient, and she would send her carriage at an appointed time to make sure of her prize. Sarah would sometimes inwardly rebel, for writing was difficult at Mrs. Cabot's, with her hostess likely to appear in her room in the midst of a morning's work, wrapped in a voluminous shawl and starved for a great "dish of talk." On the other hand, it was a relief to Sarah herself to rest from the hurly-burly at Annie's, and her affection for Mrs. Cabot was genuine, as was her own taste for uninhibited gossip. The invariable evening whist game, however, was a test of true friendship she feared she would someday fail.

In April Thérèse returned briefly to Boston, and there was another flurr of translating and sightseeing before she sailed on the 27th. Di ing her absence Sarah and Mary had labored hard at the Fogg Memorial project at Berwick Academy, both of them heading the design committee and Sarah writing her historical paper and serving as intermediary between the trustees and Sarah Whitman, who was designing the library interior and Sarah Jewett's Civil War memorial window. The dedication took place on June 30, 1894, and Sarah's friend Charles Dudley Warner came up from Hartford to address the gathering.

A few weeks earlier another project had been finished with substantial help from Sarah: Celia Thaxter's book *An Island Garden* was published in April 1894. In the decade since her husband's death, Celia had given every spare moment to cultivating her small garden on Appledore, fighting the multiple onslaughts of pests and climate with the zeal of a warrior in a holy cause. Armed only with the primitive weapons of the time, she defeated or aided nature (the ambiguity, like that in "A White Heron," also belongs to the time) with a determination just short of fanaticism. She battled her archenemy the slug, for example, by encircling each plant or grouping with lime or salt each evening, and then—because both lime and salt can poison plants—scraping it all up again at dawn. As a result of such attentions the thin soil, normally the habitat of wild roses and poison ivy, produced the luxuriant masses of flowers that have been recorded for us in the paintings of Thaxter's friend Childe Hassam.[25]

In the late 1880s, as the garden reached its peak and Celia herself finally achieved some stability and contentment in her life, she began to suffer attacks of nausea and acute abdominal pain. The usual futile panaceas were prescribed; one doctor put her on champagne, which for a while made of her "a new creature quite."[26] But the attacks grew worse, and to be near her brothers and second son, John, she and Karl began to spend winters in Portsmouth. There, over the winter of 1892–93, amid a window-clutter of boxes of seedlings straining toward the light, she began to write a book that would somehow combine everything she felt about her garden with everything she had learned. Sarah often drove over from Berwick to see her, and Celia talked about her struggle with the manuscript, which had taken on a will of its own like some sprawling and overfed vine. Sarah read it through at least twice, suggested changes and cutting, and finally helped with the copying when Celia felt too sick to do it herself. Published with decorative wash drawings by Hassam and a cover designed by Sarah Whitman, *An Island Garden* is a minor classic in its genre and betrays none of the exhaustion and near despair it caused its author in the writing.

By then Celia was on Appledore, where in July all three Jewett sisters, young Theodore, Childe Hassam, and one or two other old friends were asked to join her. Celia seemed to feel well, and they sailed and climbed all "over those picturesque and dream-making islands," as Sarah wrote later,

> with [Celia] for Homer of her little Troy, as I have not
> done for many and many a year before. Rose Lamb was
> there too and when I think of it I see either a fringe of bay-
> berry against the sky from the shady side of a ledge, or else
> my eyes blink with the light on the water.[27]

It was a summing-up and a more or less conscious leave-taking. Celia died on August 27. Sarah, who was spending a fortnight alone in Richfield Springs, could not reach Appledore in time and

so missed the funeral put together by friends, with Celia lying on
a bed of bay leaves in her parlor while, as Mary wrote,

> presently the people came straying in just as if they were
> going to hear music, and [William] Mason played a little
> thing of Dvoraks and then the Pinafore Sunset, and [James]
> De Normandie read a few selections and one of her poems
> that is in the Island Garden about the "handfull of earth,"
> and we all said the Lords Prayer after he had said a few
> words of affection about her.[28]

Then her brothers and friends carried the bier to the top of the
hill, lowered it into the grave, and tossed flowers on top of it, until
the place simply looked like a sunken garden.

Meanwhile Sarah spent the day alone in her room mourning
a friend with whom she had been "more neighbours and compa-
triots than [with] most people."[29] No one had come closer to
sharing her feeling for the ways the New England landscape shaped
its people, whether over centuries or—as in Celia's own case—over
a single lifetime; and probably no one so nearly understood her
sense of the spiritual immanence in nature. Over the next two years
she edited selections of Celia's poems and children's stories for
Houghton Mifflin, while Annie Fields and Rose Lamb prepared a
selection of letters—discreetly cut and rearranged, after the fashion
of the times.

Unlike her stay in 1893, Sarah's 1894 stay at Richfield Springs
was not for treatment but for prevention. In fact she enjoyed robust
health that year; even her eyes had improved, which makes one
wonder if her eye trouble wasn't rheumatism after all, as she
thought it was. In September, freed from the tiresome routine of
the spa, she left it with the relief of a child let out of school and
headed for the Adirondacks, where she and Annie spent a week
with Mary Garrett in the gentrified wilderness of Raquette Lake.

Thirty-six years earlier Emerson, Lowell, and several other
Saturday Club members had camped on these lakes, cutting their
firewood with "the first axe" (as Emerson liked to think) "these
echoes ever heard."[30] Now, like Newport or Beverly or Northeast
Harbor, the region had become a resort for the very rich. The trees
still grew thick and tall; Sarah measured one at fifteen feet around

John Greenleaf Whittier
(Peabody Essex Museum, Salem, Massachusetts)

William Dean Howells
(Picture Collection, The Branch Libraries, New York Public Library)

Annie Adams Fields, by John Singer Sargent
(*Boston Athenaeum*)

"In the Garden" (Celia Thaxter), by Childe Hassam
(National Museum of American Art, Smithsonian Institution)

Sarah Orne Jewett in the cap and gown she wore at Bowdoin, 1901 (photo 1903)
(Elise Tyson Vaughan; courtesy Society for the Preservation of New England Antiquities)

Sarah Orne Jewett in her bedroom, South Berwick
(Houghton Library, Harvard University)

Sarah Wyman Whitman, by Helen Bigelow Merriman
(Schlesinger Library, Radcliffe College)

Sarah Orne Jewett and Emily Tyson, 1905
*(Elise Tyson Vaughan; courtesy Society for the Preservation
of New England Antiquities)*

Hamilton House, 1904
*(Elise Tyson Vaughan; courtesy Society for the Preservation
of New England Antiquities)*

four feet from the ground. But some had been cut down to build huge hunting lodges where, with the help of large staffs and local guides, seasonal visitors from New York played at being Natty Bumppo. Sarah visited one of these "camps" and marveled at its thirty-foot main hall, which with its long table, scoured wooden benches, huge stone fireplace, and rough walls festooned with traps and pelts made her think of roistering Vikings. There a chef imported from the city fed the ladies a rustic meal of soup, trout, haunch of venison, vegetables, and an "eminent dessert of little cream cakes heaped up about with whipped cream and bedecked with snips of candied fruit."[31]

Sarah and her friends stayed in a small house, probably a satellite of one of the larger ones, sleeping outdoors in cocoons of blankets beside a fire and waking to the call of loons—and no doubt to the clouds of mosquitoes that Emerson had vainly hoped would "[protect] . . . this superb solitude from the tourists."[32] Days were spent in canoes exploring, with the help of two guides, their own lake and several neighboring ones; and though the men did the paddling and portaging, the trails between lakes were long and rough, and with their long skirts and thin boots the women had enough to do simply to carry themselves from place to place. Wildlife was abundant and was regarded by everyone as both exotica and game; Sarah told her sisters with evident delight of one party of campers who "can hear bears growl over there Carrie, and *are now after one* with cubs."[33] The height of her own adventuring was jacking deer at night from a canoe, going as Emerson had

> In the boat's bows, a silent night-hunter
> Stealing with paddle to the feeding-grounds
> Of the red deer, to aim at a square mist.

Their own deer, after a snort of surprise, bounded away unhurt. Sarah was mildly sorry on the guide's account, but what she had come for, after all, was to be out on the lake by moonlight, watching the paddle stir the silvered water and startling the creatures in their wild privacy—a pleasure she, like Emerson before her, found totally compatible with a taste for venison.

If Sarah's nephew, Theodore, had not been deeply immersed in his studies at Berwick Academy, Sarah and Annie certainly would have taken him along. Sarah *had* taken him in August on a brief trip to see the Merrimans and their son, Roger, in the White Mountains, where the whole party had camped and fished at Sabbaday Brook Falls. Then it had been Sarah's schedule that cut the expedition short; now it was Stubby, just turned fifteen and already with an eye on Harvard, who could not afford to leave his books. In the two years since his father's death he and his aunts had naturally grown closer, as Carrie had turned to her sisters for support and they had tried to help fill the role of the missing parent. Sarah was part mother, part sister, and part comrade, and because she was so much in Berwick from 1890 to '94 she and Stubby had more time together than they ever had had before. One of the old stereotypes that still linger about Jewett is that of the childless old maid whose knowledge of ordinary people has been stunted by her being deprived of the experience of motherhood. Although she was never drawn to babies, she enjoyed older children and they enjoyed her, partly because she never talked or wrote down to them. Helen Howe, daughter of Mark deWolfe Howe, has written of going to visit Sarah and Annie at Charles Street after the turn of the century, when Helen was four, Sarah fifty-odd, and Annie close to seventy, and finding the ceiling of the drawing room bright with floating balloons.[34]

As Theodore grew into his teens he would visit Aunt Sarah and "Aunt Annie" once or twice a year to see the magnificent Fourth-of-July bonfire on Manchester harbor or have Sarah supervise the making of the year's school clothes. On his account she worked up a liking for football, and she often took him to such Boston entertainments as Keith's vaudeville show or a Hasty Pudding play at Harvard. They were almost equally fond of soda fountains, and both were keen sailors. When the cat killed two of Stubby's pet pigeons, Sarah quickly bought him two more in Boston and sent them home with instructions to tighten the coop. In short, she was closely involved in raising a boy, and when young Joel Smith snitches Mrs. Powder's nightcap from the ironing board in "Law Lane" (1887) and dances around the kitchen with it on his head, we can guess at a likely nearby source in Stubby, then eight years old.

Of course, Aunt Sarah was also one of three women microarranging his life, and the effect of this triple solicitude was undeniably smothering. When Theodore suddenly shot up in his early teens and grew thin and weedy, all three sisters worried over his "spindling," and probably the contents of some noxious bottle or other were added to his daily menu. At one point Carrie sought and received permission for him to study at home rather than at school for part of the day, for fear he was overtaxing his strength. With no close male friend except the faithful John Tucker and the Exeter uncles, Stubby matured into a suspiciously unobjectionable young man, much like his aunts in manner and adept at paying courtesy calls and charming elderly ladies. He never seems to have given anyone any trouble whatever. Uniformly pleased and proud, Sarah watched his serene progress through the academy, Harvard, and medical school, and the only cause for disappointment he ever gave her was that, unlike Roger Merriman, he did not manage to study at Oxford. He does not seem ever to have courted a girl, and like his aunts he never married.

A few weeks after Sarah and Annie left the Adirondacks they took a trip to Hartford, where they stayed at Nook Farm with the Warners and had a last pathetic glimpse of Harriet Beecher Stowe, who at eighty-three had slipped, like Emerson before her, into her own private inner world. She would slip away from that in turn in less than two years. Holmes too had died, in October 1894. They were the last of the great personalities whom Jewett had admired and followed from childhood, and with their going and that of Lowell, Whittier, and Tennyson, the literary and moral landscape shifted as if a familiar range of hills had sunk into the ground. Sarah grieved for them separately and for those other moral giants Phillips Brooks and James Freeman Clarke, but never directly commented on the collective emptiness they left behind. Having no models left she had become a model herself, sending autographs and dispensing literary advice and criticism to anyone who asked. Her own admiration was transferred to younger writers: to Kipling, whom she met two or three times while he lived in Vermont and of whom she remarked that she "felt like the old woman when she first saw the sea and thanked the Lord there was enough of something!";[35] to Stevenson, whose works she owned in a rare edition and to whose stylistic grace, especially in the essays, she paid the respect due one master from another; and to many lesser writers like Mary Arnold Ward, Mary Noailles Murfree, and George Washington Cable. If she allowed herself to recognize a flattening of the literary horizon it was only indirectly, in the form of uncharacteristic doubts about the durability of her own talent. She, whose stories had always tumbled into her consciousness like apples into a barrel, began to wonder early in 1895 if she had anything left to say.

In part this was the result of physical depletion, for in December 1894 she came down with bronchitis that later developed into pneumonia. It was not until March that she began to think about writing again, and by then she had fallen far behind in filling her commitments to publishers. As she struggled to catch up, laboring at a potboiler for the Bacheller syndicate,[36] she found herself refusing two offers that normally would have tempted her. One was a request for "a little novel" from the English publishers Smith and Elder, which "quite cheered me up," as she wrote Annie, "just as I was having a time of thinking that I had said over twice everything I had to say."[37] The other was a request to write a biography of an American woman, possibly Mercy Warren or Abigail Adams, for a series published by Scribner's Sons. She pleaded illness and pressure of work to both, and it is bemusing to realize that if she had accepted either assignment or given in to her self-doubt there probably would have been no *Country of the Pointed Firs*.

The genesis of that book began when, in late August of 1895, Sarah joined Mary Garrett again, this time in Penobscot Bay, where Mary had rented a house on the island of Islesboro. Sarah spent only two or three days there, but she loved the place, "all among the 'pointed firs,'" with its little coves and views across the bay of the Camden Hills.[38] She spent her time sailing at dawn with a local master, circling the island behind two neat trotters, and learning to ride a bicycle. Then Annie arrived by steamer, and after taking leave of Mary and paying a call on the Aldriches at their new summer place in Tenant's Harbor, they went to Martinsville, near Port Clyde. There, with Annie's cook and housekeeper Margaret and Cassie, they settled into a little rented house called The Anchorage, to stay a whole month and "sit like *hopper toads* . . . speaking from time to time and dwelling in the sun among the goldenrod."[39]

Martinsville was a small hamlet, unnoticed by the fashionable or even the moderately prosperous, where the hum of fat bees gorging themselves on goldenrod and clover was the loudest sound to disturb an afternoon nap. Sarah had brought proofs and a bit of writing along and set up shop at her bedroom window, where she could look down a lane between stone walls and catch a glimpse of schooners at rest in the bay.* Beside the lane was a potato field, "where the figures of J. F. Millet work all day against a very un-French background of the pointed firs that belong to Maine like the grey ledges they are rooted in."[40] She and Annie soon met all their neighbors, there being only four families: the Dwyers, who brought them their mail and kept them supplied with fish and lobsters; two families of Clarkes, one of whom sold them fresh-killed ducks; and their nearest neighbors, the Bachelders, to whom they turned for borrowed odds and ends and all conversational "particulars." That was the village, except for two empty houses. "*Sister Carrie* would like the neighborhood dreadfully," Sarah wrote Mary, "in that there is not much going on. I keep expecting something to happen and it doesn't! But 'peace has settled down on this Law Lane' so far as I know though perhaps the two Mis' Clarkes don't speak for all we know."[41] In fact, Cassie brought home a tale of how the Dwyers and the Clarkes had quarreled over a patch of cranberries and very possibly did *not* speak, "or if they do it is but to revile!! Cassie was so funny; you know she doesn't have much to say usually—but this seemed like the celebrated difference of the Montagues and the Capulets and we heard all about it as far as it has gone. I don't dare to so much as look at a cranberry for fear of enemies."[42]

But it was Mrs. Rosilla Bachelder who held this fractious little community together. She had a husband and at least one son; but

---

* The misconception that Jewett rented the Martinsville schoolhouse to write in was revived fifty years ago in a newspaper interview with a Bachelder descendant. (Alice Frost Lord, "Port Clyde Claims Setting in Which Sarah Orne Jewett Wrote Famous Maine Story, 'Country of the Pointed Firs,'" *Lewiston Journal,* magazine section, 2/6/43) But Jewett explicitly described her bedroom workspace in a letter to Louisa Dresel, and it is very unlikely she wrote any of the *Pointed Firs* sketches while she was still in Martinsville. She did once think of renting a schoolhouse in South Berwick to work in, purely for the atmosphere, but nothing came of it.

she herself, a woman who was *"the full of a door* and wears a blue dress,"[43] was the center of the place, the person to whom

> everybody goes . . . for everything. When A.F. stepped for
> the cinnamon "a lady" had come to get Mrs. Bachelder to
> help her with a dress and it was a cutting out on a table.
> You will have words about the garden with her Mary. She
> has got all her window ledges full of things in cups and tin
> cans so that none of them look as if they could be opened.[44]

Sarah and Annie called on her daily and were disappointed if they found she had gone to Tenant's Harbor to the funeral of an uncle who had "died very sudden with a heart complaint,"[45] or that she was "gone back up o' Rockland to a Soldiers reunion."[46] Welcoming and sociable, she sent them little gifts of sweetpeas and fresh-picked blackberries, and if she was home she was always ready to sit down and have a good talk. Sarah felt "much drawn to her,"[47] and one cool afternoon, following the example of her own narrator in "The Courting of Sister Wisby," she went "trailing out in the sun in search of The Cape bunnit":

> I found it soon down among the golden rod and asters and
> I picked cranberries a long time ever so many little pailsful
> and my back got {tanned} a light brown in the hot sun.
> She had an old hooked rug to put under our knees and
> room was made for me to have the end of it and then we
> picked clean as we went a strip right across the patch to
> the stone wall. It is an extra year for cranberries.[48]

Toward the end of the month Mary came down from Berwick and joined them, so that she too had a chance to meet the "Cape bunnit" and perhaps pick her own share of cranberries. When they finally left, the five women had memories to talk over in Boston or Berwick, as if September had given them a summer's stored warmth to see them through the winter. And no doubt they carried it away in some more tangible form, for it is hard to see how Mis' Bachelder would have let them go off without at least one jar of cranberry preserves.

20

The Country of the Pointed Firs

T H E   C O U N T R Y   O F   T H E   P O I N T E D   F I R S
was serialized in four issues of *The Atlantic* in 1896 and appeared
in book form before the end of the year. Jewett wrote the sketches
rapidly, beginning soon after her return from Martinsville. She
returned to the area once in the summer of 1896, just before
writing the two additional chapters that would round out the
whole. (The two were "Along Shore" and "The Backward View."
She also combined two serialized chapters into one, making a total
of twenty in the finished work.) "How little I thought of the
Pointed Firs being eminent and turning into a book of parts when
I began!" she wrote Mary before she left. "I want to keep my work
in mind, and though it is only jobbing I must do the best I can
with it."[1] Probably what she meant by "jobbing" was the two extra
chapters, and not the whole book. But it is clear that she took the
writing of *Pointed Firs* much more lightly than she did many of
her lesser works, and later she would be surprised at the volume
of praise that greeted it.

Unlike *Deephaven,* this work needed no revision. Not a word
of the existing chapters was altered between serial and book publication, and not a word of the finished work could be wished
unwritten. Its themes and symbols are fugal in the typical Jewett

style, mingling and resonating from chapter to chapter.* Given her cavalier attitude toward the book, we must suspect that there was ultimately more art in it than she knew. Several waves of criticism have washed over American literature since it was published almost a century ago, but *The Country of the Pointed Firs* has held its own place and remains as much loved and as much read as another offbeat classic, *Walden.* Like that book too it has continued to provoke new interpretations, depending on the generation and experience of its readers.[2]

Like *Deephaven,* "A Bit of Shore Life," and "The Courting of Sister Wisby," *The Country of the Pointed Firs* is about a city woman—in this case the narrator—who spends a summer in a small rural community and finds herself changed by it. She has visited Dunnet Landing briefly before during a sailing cruise, and now she comes back, looking for a quiet place to work (she is a writer) and for some other quality that is hard to put in words: "quaintness," and a "mixture of remoteness, and childish certainty of being the centre of civilization." Like most summer people she expects to be lulled by the tranquillity of a place removed from time, and to be amused by antiquated manners and customs. But she is also a "lover" of the village, a middle-aged woman seasoned enough to appreciate the "gayety and determined floweriness" of its small gardens, and to see a certain wariness in the sharp-gabled houses, with their high windows that watch over sea and land like "knowing eyes." Dunnet Landing may be quaint, but since it belongs to the Maine coast it is not idyllic. Its gardens are made to bloom through will and hard work, and its windows are not only high but small-paned, so that the breaking of one pane by hurricane or nor'easter leaves the remainder strong. The visitor's curiosity as well as admiration are piqued, and she expects her love to deepen with time: "The process of falling in love at first sight is as final as it is swift in such a case, but the growth of true friendship may be a lifelong affair." (p. 2; all page references are to the 1896 edition.)

She stays with Almira Todd, widow and herbalist. Like Rosilla

---

* *The Country of the Pointed Firs* as published in 1896 had twenty chapters. In later editions three additional stories—"A Dunnet Shepherdess," "William's Wedding," and "The Queen's Twin"—were incorporated into the text. (See Chapter 21.) In the present chapter I discuss the book in its original form.

Bachelder, Mrs. Todd is the full of a door, and her heavy step as she moves about her herb garden in the morning fills her boarder's room with the scent of crushed thyme. In keeping with Jewett's belief that a person's house is the outer shell of her personality, Mrs. Todd's house seems at first glance to be private and reserved, being sited endways to the road and half-hidden behind its bushy green garden. But there is a steady stream of foot traffic up and down the walk, as Mrs. Todd's clients come to buy remedies for their ailments or a swig of her famous spruce beer. Mrs. Todd herself can be crusty and off-putting, and her innermost feelings are kept well hidden from general view; but she is also affectionate and sensible, a general arbiter and counselor in the village. From the first she calls the narrator "dear" or "darlin'," which is all the name we ever know her by.

The writer sets up a workplace in her room and tries to give her mornings to writing. But July is Mrs. Todd's season for harvesting wild herbs, and whenever she is out ranging the fields, the job of answering the knocks at the door and dispensing remedies falls to the guest. The more she does of this the better she becomes at it, until her hostess is moved to tell her that with practice she could be "very able in the business." (p. 9) But her own work suffers, so she decides to hire the vacant schoolhouse and work there every morning.

Even there she cannot escape the pull of the village. Mrs. Todd appears, ostensibly to gather tansy but evidently curious to see just what a writer does with all that solitude. A woman the narrator has come to know dies, and she watches the walking funeral from her schoolhouse and is sorry not to be a part of it. Captain Littlepage, a retired sea captain whose wits are a little turned, labors up the hill to see her and talks away the better part of the morning. Presently she repents of abandoning Mrs. Todd entirely in the busy season and makes excuses to stay home now and then so that business can go on. And gradually she becomes so involved in the life of the village and her growing friendship with Mrs. Todd that her work disappears, if not from her life at least from her narrative. By the end of the summer she begins each day in sleepy Dunnet Landing feeling "hurried and full of pleasant engagements" (p. 208), much like Sarah Orne Jewett waking up on a winter morning in Charles Street.

The community is larger than the village, including scattered farms for miles around; the gathering for the funeral is large, and at the end of a day's fishing a hundred sails can be seen making for shore. The narrator meets many people, but as in *Deephaven* we learn about only a representative few. Several of these—Captain Littlepage, Joanna Todd, Santin Bowden, and Elijah Tilley—have been pushed by some painful event in their lives into the closed round of a private obsession, from which they barely notice the ordinary comings and goings of their fellow human beings. At the other extreme is Mrs. Todd's eighty-six-year-old mother, Mrs. Blackett, who despite living on an island and visiting the mainland only rarely is "always the queen" (p. 161), not only of her own extended family but of the whole countryside. Sprightly in the literal sense of being spiritually animated, Mrs. Blackett seems as openhearted and uncomplicated as a child, and indeed she is compared to a child several times in the text. She is one to whom aging has been a disemburdening, not only of old griefs but of the petty irritations that clog the sensibilities of the middle-aged. Her island, where nothing superfluous exists, is a symbol of the simplicity of her spirit; but there is nothing simple about her mind, which while hardly profound seems quite shrewd enough to deal with such of the world's business as she encounters. Like her daughter, "she's seen all the trouble folks can see, without it's her last sickness; an' she's got a word of courage for everybody. Life ain't spoiled her a mite." (p. 46)

People ask for Mrs. Blackett when they are dying. She seems to be far more in demand than the minister, whose presence at a deathbed, we discover, would be not only futile but depressing. Mrs. Todd, on the other hand, is the person people ask for when they are still in hope of healing in this world. Earthy and heavy-bodied, attuned to the natural cycles of life and death, Mrs. Todd too has seen her share of trouble, having lost both lover and husband years earlier. The narrator guesses early on that

> it may not have been only the common ails of humanity
> with which she tried to cope; it seemed sometimes as if
> love and hate and jealousy and adverse winds at sea might
> also find their proper remedies among the curious wild-
> looking plants in Mrs. Todd's garden. (p. 5)

There are repeated allusions in the text to a primeval or mythical quality in Mrs. Todd, recalling legendary archetypes of female power and sorrow. She is compared to a sibyl, a caryatid, the grieving Antigone. Even more than Mrs. Goodsoe, Mrs. Todd is linked to images of the mysterious and the occult. But the goddess co-exists in the same body with the aging, overweight Maine widow, and to make too much of her "magical" powers is to distance her from the mortal sufferings that are the true source of her ability to heal. Sometimes the narrator's references to the precedents of myth and history are playful, implying (as in "The Dulham Ladies" or "Wisby") an ironic contrast between the heights of literature and the plain reality of Yankee lives. At these moments she sees Mrs. Todd as the heir of sadly diminished powers:

> There were some strange and pungent odors that roused a
> dim sense and remembrance of something in the forgotten
> past. Some of these might once have belonged to sacred
> and mystic rites, and have had some occult knowledge
> handed with them down the centuries; but now they per-
> tained only to humble compounds brewed at intervals with
> molasses or vinegar and spirits in a small caldron on Mrs.
> Todd's kitchen stove. (p. 4)

When the narrator returns in the afternoon from her working day at the schoolhouse, she "usually [meets] the flavor, not of the herb garden, but of Mrs. Todd's hot supper." (p. 13)

But there are times when the images are not comic—when Mrs. Todd truly seems, to the narrator's literary eye, to expand before her eyes into the avatar of some ancient and titanic being. Such a moment is invariably tied to an emotional epiphany, a leap of sympathy not only between the two women but between them and the larger human family. And because the images are all ancient, they serve to remind us of the temporal kinship of that family, and of the fact that sympathy and forgiveness are as much a part of its endlessly repeated cycles as loss and decay. As in *Deephaven,* the visitor's sojourn in the village and her growing friendship with Mrs. Todd are marked by her deepening under-standing of each individual's responsibility to the others, and of the fact that living human beings are only one part of the cosmic whole. When people are unable to fulfill their part, when their empathic abilities are blocked by ignorance, egotism, or madness, then the social order is threatened, nature is alienated, and the lives of the dead have been lived to no purpose, since their lessons are inaccessible to the present. In the microcosmic community of Dunnet Landing, this kind of disintegration is prevented largely through the example and advice of Mrs. Todd and her mother, Mrs. Blackett, who between them gather in the stragglers—those who have broken away and are adrift in isolation. Mothers of the whole countryside, they heal the rifts between people and, as the narrator says of Mrs. Blackett, "keep the balance true." (p. 73)

The narrator is a kind of disciple, but unlike Helen and Kate, she is no ingenue. A mature woman, she must demonstrate to Mrs. Todd the extent of her own existing knowledge and understanding in order to prove herself worthy of the older woman's love and confidence. In effect, she passes a series of small tests. First of all there is her offer to interrupt her own work so as to free Mrs. Todd for hers, and the skill with which she takes over as substitute comforter and healer. "I have never had nobody I could so trust," Mrs. Todd confesses, and from this time on, the narrator says, "a deeper intimacy seemed to begin." One night the older woman tells the younger "all that lay deepest in her heart," the story of her early lover, who "come of a high family" and married someone else. She still loves him and mourns his loss, and it has taken all her new trust in her friend for her to overcome her native reserve and disclose her pain. At this moment the narrator has one of those transforming visions when the past is superimposed upon the present, and Mrs. Todd, with her tale of star-crossed love in a Maine village, seems to transcend time and place and become an embodiment of ancient and prophetic female wisdom:

> She stood in the centre of a braided rug, and its rings of
> black and gray seemed to circle about her feet in the dim
> light. Her height and massiveness in the low room gave her
> the look of a huge sibyl, while the strange fragrance of the
> mysterious herb blew in from the little garden. (pp. 8–10)

Another step in the narrator's friendship with Mrs. Todd involves Captain Littlepage, a desiccated little old man who spends most of his days sitting behind a closed window watching his neighbors pass by. The narrator has asked Mrs. Todd about him before, but that lady has only shaken her head, seeming to "class him with her other secrets." (p. 17) After the funeral Littlepage pays a call on the narrator in her schoolroom and tells her a fantastic tale of a place he heard of once from another sea captain, a town far to the north, "a kind of waiting-place between this world an' the next" where the silent, gray inhabitants are hardly distinguishable from the surrounding fog. (p. 39) The tale has seized the old captain's imagination, and he tells it to his captive listener in a kind of frenzy, like a latter-day Ancient Mariner.* The narrator hears him out politely and afterwards helps him down the hill, holding his arm (for he is frail and lame). Mrs. Todd comes out to meet her wearing "an anxious expression":

> "I see you sleevin' the old gentleman down the hill," she suggested.

> "Yes, I've had a very interesting afternoon with him," I answered, and her face brightened. (p. 44)

Clearly Mrs. Todd has been afraid that the city woman would laugh at her old friend Littlepage or be annoyed by the interruption. But the visitor has treated him with gentleness and respect, and once more Mrs. Todd's trust is strengthened and the narrator has her reward. As they stand on the shore the older woman points out Green Island, where her mother lives, and promises to take her friend out for a visit. At that moment a shaft of sunlight breaks through the clouds overhead and the illuminated island shines out like a paradisiacal vision, "a sudden revelation of the world beyond this which some believe to be so near"—and therefore the direct opposite of the ghastly limbo of Littlepage's tale. (p. 45) Mrs. Todd herself, poised on a rock looking out to sea, seems "grand and

---

* There are several parallels between Coleridge's poem and Littlepage's tale, among them the image of the living dead, the almost physical compulsion to tell the tale, the land of ice and snow, the mysterious current that guides the ship, and the narrator's blindness to the natural world. But the Mariner learns to bless God and all living things and thus is periodically freed from his curse, while Littlepage, unable to care for anything except his visions, remains imprisoned by them.

architectural, like a *caryatide*." Again, an image of ancient female power is linked to a manifestation of sympathy, not only between the landlady and her boarder but between both of them and the demented old man. When they go home Mrs. Todd fetches the narrator a mug of spruce beer flavored with camomile and another, more mysterious herb. "I don't give that to everybody," she says, and the narrator is briefly reminded of spells and incantations. But all that happens (which, in a sense, is everything) is that they plan their excursion to Green Island.

Mrs. Blackett has lived on Green Island with her son, William, since her daughter's marriage forty-odd years earlier. They live alone but not in isolation, since the old lady is tied to the mainland by friendship, kinship, and periodic calls for her nursing skill. William transports her back and forth but is painfully shy and avoids people as much as possible. With Mrs. Blackett, the narrator is instantly at ease: "You felt as if Mrs. Blackett were an old and dear friend before you let go her cordial hand." (p. 56) Mother and daughter banter back and forth, implicitly drawing the newcomer into the circle of their affection. But William has seen the stranger from a distance and makes himself scarce. She finally manages to meet him when, having dug some potatoes in the garden for Mrs. Blackett, she lifts the heavy basket and finds the shy man at her side offering to help her carry it. So, through one of those silent, benign gestures typical of Jewett characters, they too become friends, and a few minutes later they go off for a walk together.

Later, after dinner, Mrs. Todd announces that she is going to gather herbs and gives the narrator a choice of going with her or staying in the house. The narrator would rather stay, but she goes with Mrs. Todd so that Mrs. Blackett can have a nap. It is at this point—following the narrator's kindness to the old lady and the winning of William's trust—that she is admitted further into Mrs. Todd's confidence.

They climb to a lonely clearing above a steep cliff, where the waves crash against the rocks below. In the grass around their feet grow spikes of pale-blue pennyroyal, and Mrs. Todd picks a bunch, presses it between her hands to bring out the fragrance, and offers it to her friend to smell. "Don't it do you good?" she asks. "There, dear, I never showed nobody else but mother where to find this place; 't is kind of sainted to me." (pp. 76–77) This is where she

and her husband, Nathan, used to come courting, she says; his ship
went down within sight of it. But a sharper grief than simple loss
has tormented her all these years, for although she liked Nathan
Todd she never really loved him, and even while they sat there
together she would always be thinking of "the other one." If her
husband had lived, she believes, he would have found out; and so
her sorrow at his death was mixed with guilty relief. But because
her remorse has been transformed into forgiveness of other people's
secret failures, it has been a bitter herb that "does her good." For
the third time, the narrator sees in her an image transcending time
and place:

> She might have been Antigone alone on the Theban plain.
> It is not often given in a noisy world to come to places of
> great grief and silence. An absolute, archaic grief possessed
> this country-woman; she seemed like a renewal of some his-
> toric soul, with her sorrows and the remoteness of a daily
> life busied with rustic simplicities and the scents of
> primeaval herbs. (pp. 77–78)

The fourth step into Mrs. Todd's confidence comes along when
her old friend Mrs. Fosdick comes for an extended visit. The three
women spend their evenings together, Mrs. Fosdick and Mrs. Todd
reminiscing while the younger woman mostly listens and observes.
One night Mrs. Todd makes a passing reference to a place called
Shell-heap Island, but she quickly changes the subject. Curious,
the narrator maneuvers the conversation back to it, and Mrs.
Fosdick tells her something of the island's history—of the Indians
who once camped there and the legends surrounding them, and of
the island's "beautiful spring o' water." (p. 100) Mrs. Todd confirms
all this but again tries to change the subject. Mrs. Fosdick is not
done with Shell-heap Island, though, and she plows right into the
topic Mrs. Todd wants most to avoid: "I was talking o' poor Joanna
the other day," she says, explaining that Joanna Todd, a cousin of
Mrs. Todd's husband's, was "a sort of nun or hermit person" who
"lived out there for years all alone on Shell-heap Island." Mrs.
Todd's discomfort grows worse with every word. "I never want to
hear Joanna laughed about," she warns. "Nor I," Mrs. Fosdick
replies. (pp. 102–3)

Reassured, Mrs. Todd joins in telling the story. Jilted by the man she loved, Joanna fled to Shell-heap Island, where her father had built a cabin years earlier, and there she spent the rest of her life alone. Her brother and friends left provisions for her on the shore, but she refused to see anyone. One day, though, the minister, Mr. Dimmick, decided that the time had come for him to go out to the island and help her "consider her spiritual state." (p. 111) Inept at sailing and nervous about his reception, he invited the young Mrs. Todd along to manage the boat and smooth the way. Joanna received them politely, and the minister exhorted and scolded and talked about the voice of God in the whirlwind, and when Joanna had listened long enough so that the minister could decently feel he had done his duty she sent him out to see the Indian shell-heap as if he were a little boy. The male intruder thus disposed of, the two women hugged one another and Mrs. Todd begged Joanna to come and live with her or her mother. But Joanna replied that she had "committed the unpardonable sin"—in her anger at her lover's betrayal she had had "wicked" thoughts toward God—and she couldn't expect ever to be forgiven. (p. 120)

So, Mrs. Todd continues, Joanna stayed there doing penance over twenty years, until she died there. Her friends faithfully continued to leave gifts, and now and then she would consent to see one or two of the "old folks," among them Mrs. Blackett, who tended her on her deathbed. Her funeral on the island drew people from twenty miles around, some of them curious but most "real respectful, same's if she'd always stayed ashore and held her friends." (pp. 124–25) Joanna had rejected the community, in other words, but the community had never rejected her.

Joanna is another of Mrs. Todd's spiritual waifs, self-maimed and self-imprisoned like Littlepage but even more pitiable because she loved and missed the human companionship she denied herself. The narrator hears her story sympathetically, and soon afterwards she gets her sailing companion, Captain Bowden, to land her on Shell-heap Island. She follows the path to the traces of Joanna's cabin and garden and stops to drink at the spring. And she reflects that each of us carries inside us some "place remote and islanded, and given to endless regret or secret happiness; we are each the uncompanioned hermit and recluse of an hour or a day; we understand our fellows of the cell to whatever age of history they may belong." (p. 132) So she joins hands metaphorically not only with Joanna but with Mrs. Todd, who also carries her island of endless regret, and with poor deluded Littlepage and with the unseen people on a passing boat whose voices and laughter she can hear from where she stands, as Joanna herself must have heard and been cheered by voices years before.

It is immediately after this passage, as another counterpart to a sympathetic impulse, that Mrs. Todd invites the narrator to the Bowden family reunion. She does so with wonderfully comic Yankee indirectness, by way of grumpy silences and oblique hints that are meant to be contradicted; but her guest knows her well enough by now to counter with the right questions, and soon the two of them, with Mrs. Blackett, set off for the annual celebration. The reunion is the emotional center of the book. The culmination of the narrator's acceptance by the community and by Mrs. Todd (whose honorary kin she now becomes), it is also the symbol of her membership in the larger human family. Jewett, speaking through the narrator, compares it to those rituals through which people have always affirmed their sense of union and mutual responsibility. Like Decoration Day, which always moved her strongly when it was celebrated in Berwick by its thinning ranks of elderly veterans; or the Old Home Weeks that brought New England's scattered children and grandchildren back every year; or the Exeter Academy reunions of her youth, in which her Gilman relations played a prominent part; or the Berwick Academy celebrations of 1891 and 1894—like all these, the Bowden family reunion reconnects people with each other and allows them formally to acknowledge their interdependence. Such an event taps emotional depths in New Englanders that are otherwise buried under layers of workaday silence:

> Such is the hidden fire of enthusiasm in the New England
> nature that, once given an outlet, it shines forth with al-
> most volcanic light and heat. In quiet neighborhoods such
> inward force does not waste itself upon those petty excite-
> ments of every day that belong to cities, but when, at long
> intervals, the altars to patriotism, to friendship, to the ties
> of kindred, are reared in our familiar fields, then the fires
> glow, the flames come up as if from the inexhaustible burn-

ing heart of the earth; the primal fires break through the
granite dust in which our souls are set. Each heart is warm
and every face shines with the ancient light. Such a day as
this has transfiguring powers, and easily makes friends of
those who have been cold-hearted, and gives to those who
are dumb their chance to speak, and lends some beauty to
the plainest fact. (pp. 156–57)

Its significance is as old as human history:

We were no more a New England family celebrating its
own existence and simple progress; we carried the tokens
and inheritance of all such households from which this had
descended, and were only the latest of our line. (p. 163)

It is not by chance that Jewett has Mrs. Todd remark, as their
wagon approaches the Bowden farm, that "when you call upon the
Bowdens you may expect most families to rise up between the
Landing and the far end of the Back Cove." (p. 157) The ancestors
are symbolically present in the honor done them by the occasion.
The narrator imagines the more recent ones (of six or seven centuries earlier) seated "in the great hall of some old French house in
the Middle Ages"—Mrs. Todd, in accordance with Jewett's own
Francophile prejudices, having claimed descent from "very high
folks in France." (pp. 167, 173) But the inheritance is far more
ancient, reaching back through the classical age ("We might have
been a company of ancient Greeks. . . ." [p. 163]) to the far more
remote past recalled by Mrs. Todd's shadow aura, when the very
grass and trees seemed infused with spiritual power and there was
no schism between humanity and nature. For a few hours, at least,
the Bowdens "[possess] the instincts of a far, forgotten childhood."
(p. 163)

     That afternoon the narrator meets another of the local eccen-
trics, Santin Bowden. He is a "straight, soldierly little figure of a
man," (p. 162) who is busying himself with organizing the milling
hordes of Bowdens into neat processional ranks. Mrs. Caplin, foil
to Mrs. Todd in this conversation as Mrs. Fosdick was in the earlier
one, answers the narrator's question about him with criticism.
Santin Bowden is the self-appointed marshal of this and all other

large public gatherings, and though he is efficient enough at his job, Mrs. Caplin says, he "stim'lates"—that is, he drinks. (p. 165) Mrs. Todd instantly springs to his defense, not by contradiction but, Yankee-like, by feigning not to have heard an offensive remark. "No," she says, in a pointed non sequitur, "Santin never was in the war," although he had a passion for military strategy and could have been a great general. Turned down by the army for health reasons, he has had to settle for life as a shoemaker, and marshaling at public celebrations is his only chance to do what he was obviously born for. Like Joanna and Littlepage, he is not to be belittled for something he can't help: "Strange folks has got to have strange ways for what I see." (p. 168)

Santin is one of many men at the reunion, for this is not one of those stereotyped, dwindling New England families in which the males have all died off or left for California. Women have a prominent place: they cooked the feast, Mrs. Blackett is its queen, and the Bowden farmhouse sits in its field like a "motherly brown hen" waiting for its flock to come home. (p. 159) They do indeed have more vitality than the men, and they do represent redemptive power. But—also because this is a Jewett book—no one in *Pointed Firs* is deliberately excluded or put below anyone else. The motherly farmhouse is the birthplace of Mrs. Blackett's father and of "five generations of sailors and farmers and soldiers." Men greet Mrs. Todd's wagon and lead away the horses, and it is a man who lifts Mrs. Blackett down and "kiss[es] her with hearty affection." (p. 161) During the afternoon Mrs. Todd promises her mother to invite her old friend Captain Littlepage to dinner the next day, and Mrs. Blackett's last comment on the reunion is about the singing of the final hymn: "There was such a plenty o' men's voices; where I sat it did sound beautiful." (p. 183)

The serial form of *Pointed Firs* broke off at this point. Jewett put her three women in their wagon and left them there, safely trundling their way home, without further comment. The subject of the first of the added chapters, Elijah Tilley, had been sitting patiently in his own corner of her memory for a decade of more, since she first met his original on the beach at Wells. In 1888 she had written about him to Annie Fields and Louisa Dresel, describing his grief and his knitting and his perpetual references to his "poor dear." By then he was already an old acquaintance, one of several fishermen she visited whenever she went to the shore.[3] Loulie had urged her then to put him in a story, but it took her until 1896 to find the right one.

The chapter opens with the narrator walking along the shore, watching the erratic course of a distant lobster smack. By now she is so much a native that she recognizes the boat by a patch on its sail, but it is an old fisherman who suddenly appears at her side who explains the reason for its odd behavior: the boy at the helm has fallen asleep, and the dark object they see landing in the water as they watch is that same boy being waked up by the captain. So the narrator makes the acquaintance of Elijah Tilley, a man almost as elusive as William Blackett.

Tilley is one of four "large old men at the Landing, who were the survivors of an earlier and more vigorous generation." (p. 186) Together they form a single unit, watching one another's boats come in and out, tending one another's traps, helping the other fishermen clean fish or sliver porgies for bait, meeting each boat as it returns and carrying it, two on a side, safely ashore. As with Mrs. Todd, there is something primal and enduring about them, a subverbal connection to nature and the past. They are beyond, or above, the need for words: "You would as soon have expected to hear small talk in a company of elephants as to hear old Mr. Bowden or Elijah Tilley and their two mates waste breath upon any form of trivial gossip." If they spoke at all "you felt almost as if a landmark pine should suddenly address you in regard to the weather, or a lofty-minded old camel make a remark as you stood respectfully near him under the circus tent." (p. 187) The narrator's friend Captain Bowden, the nephew of one of them, tells her, "They was always just as you see 'em now since the memory of man." (p. 188)

But the narrator's acquaintance with Elijah Tilley allows her to see beyond this archetypal exterior to a solitary old man, very much caught in time, and to discover, beneath his habitual silence, an unexpected torrent of words. Invited to call on him, she expects to find a dim bachelor lair, but instead sees a neat yellow-and-white house, as trim in its isolated field above the beach as any in the village. It is just as neat inside, its clean, sunny kitchen bearing witness to the care of some unseen housekeeper. As Tilley begins to talk she learns that the housekeeper is the man himself, or rather the man animated by the memory of his departed wife. "Poor dear" (the only name he gives her) has been gone eight years, and her husband's grief has taken the form of keeping the house exactly as she kept it. "None on 'em thought I was goin' to get along alone, no way," he says, "but I wa'n't goin' to have my house turned upsi' down an' all changed about; no, not to please nobody. I was the only one knew just how she liked to have things set, poor dear, an' I said I was goin' to make shift, and I have made shift." (p. 194) Through taking up his wife's work he has learned to see things through her eyes: he now understands, for example, how worried she must have been as she waited alone by her window when he thoughtlessly stayed out too late at sea. But his wider understanding is no use to himself or anyone else because he is caught in the round of his own self-pity. "Yes ma'am, I'm one that has seen trouble," he says, echoing earlier references to both Mrs. Todd and Mrs. Blackett. But while the two women have imaginatively turned their own "trouble" into empathic understanding of the suffering of others, Tilley has turned his inward. Like Littlepage, Joanna, and Santin Bowden, he is trapped by an obsession, but unlike them he is also one of those emotional panhandlers whose appetite for sympathy is inexhaustible. Perhaps for this reason, he is the only one of the town eccentrics whose plight leaves Mrs. Todd unmoved. "'Lijah's worthy enough," she allows. "I do esteem 'Lijah, but he's a ploddin' man." (p. 206) The narrator, however, reaches beyond her tutor in this case and becomes Elijah's friend. His is the last face she sees when she leaves at the end of the summer, when he favors her with a "solemn nod" by way of good-bye. (p. 212)

The chapter on her departure, "The Backward View," is as good a measure as any of how far Jewett has traveled as a writer since *Deephaven.* In the early book Helen and Kate indulge in fantasies of return, and on its imagined effect on themselves many years hence—such thoughts as were appropriate to the late adolescence of both characters and author. In *Pointed Firs* the focus is rather on separation unsoftened by promises of return, and on the renewed sorrow and loneliness of Mrs. Todd, which the narrator has unwittingly increased. On the morning of parting Mrs. Todd has stomped about the house in silence, speaking gruffly when she has to speak at all. Finally she leaves on a pretext, waving away her friend's attempt to say good-bye. But she has left behind speaking gifts: a supper packed in a basket she knew the narrator liked; a sprig of bay (tacit recognition of the writer's calling); a bunch of southernwood;* and a coral pin Nathan Todd had given his wife and she in turn had tried to give Joanna, who for self-denial's sake refused it. The pin has many associations: kinship (Joanna was a Bowden cousin, and the narrator has come "near to feeling like a true Bowden" [p. 180]); grief and exile; Nathan's love for his wife and hers for the younger women.

As the narrator leaves Dunnet Landing, all its magical, larger-than-life qualities disappear like Cinderella's coach at midnight. Green Island, which she first saw shining like revelation, is now "small and darkly wooded," just one island among many. (p. 211) From the deck of her steamer she watches the village merge with "the other towns that looked as if they were crumbled on the furzy-green stoniness of the shore," (p. 213) until even they are lost in the anonymous dark line of the coast. The magic is gone, and the narrator's last sight of Mrs. Todd is of a small figure crossing an open pasture, "mateless and appealing," vulnerable in her ordinary humanity but still "strangely self-possessed and mysterious," for no representative of humanity is altogether ordinary. (p. 211)

While several sources for *Deephaven* are easily traced, most of the sources of *The Country of the Pointed Firs* come from underground. Elijah Tilley comes directly from Dan Butland of Wells, Mrs. Todd less directly from Rosilla Bachelder of Martinsville. There is the familiar figure of the village doctor, humorous and discerning as always; and in the larger sense, of course, the entire book is pervaded with Dr. Jewett's genial humanism and his gift for healing. Overt references to Swedenborgian or Christian beliefs have been subsumed; Jewett at forty-seven had no need to appeal to external authorities to define her convictions. The moralism is self-evident, the mysticism implied in references to time and nature. The dead, too, are absent as personalities, except for Mrs.

---

* A member of the artemisia family with silvery leaves and a fresh lemony scent; "aromatic, astringent, bitter and tonic." (Meyer, p. 69)

Tilley, whose memory—unlike that of other benign ghosts in earlier stories—cannot influence the living in any positive way. But the influence of the collective dead is present throughout.

The interchangeable mother-daughter aspect of the relationship between Mrs. Todd and Mrs. Blackett, wherein each is sometimes the "child" and sometimes the "mother," mirrors the same flexibility between Jewett and Annie Fields, or for that matter between Jewett and any of her women friends. "There, mother, what a girl you be!" Mrs. Todd says, (p. 140) while Mrs. Blackett in turn clearly feels a maternal pride in her daughter's accomplishments. Having grown up taking care of an invalid mother, thinking of herself sometimes as a healer and sometimes as an invalid herself, sometimes as the strong and famous author and sometimes as Mary's cherished and rather pampered younger sister, Jewett had experienced more consciously than most people a double need to be both responsible and playful, protected and protective. Her ability to preserve her childhood self was clearly important to her sense of well-being and probably to her creativity as well; but in her ability to heal and advise, and in her friends' general perception of her as a calm and sympathetic counselor, she was a mother to everyone around her—as were Annie, Sarah Whitman, and Celia Thaxter, to give just three other examples. This double aspect of maturity in her friends was not necessarily limited to women; her own father was shy or mischievous at times, and nothing in the character of Holmes, Aldrich, and Robert Collyer endeared them more to Sarah than their antic streak and their pointed refusal to assume at all times the stance of the all-wise and stoically superior American male. Clearly the repeated emphasis she gives this duality in *Pointed Firs* reflects the importance she felt it deserved in human relationships as a whole. But as always, she expressed it as she knew it best, through womanhood.

Taking another biographical view of the maternal theme, we can guess that the character of Mrs. Blackett and the place of Green Island owe something to Celia Thaxter, her mother Eliza Laighton, and the Isles of Shoals. Celia's death was fresh in Jewett's mind while she wrote *Pointed Firs*. In fact, she was probably reading the proofs for Thaxter's *Stories and Poems for Children* at Martinsville in 1895, and she edited the *Poems* directly afterwards. Celia had led Sarah over the islands and relived her childhood shortly before she

died, and her enhanced memories may have been the beginning of
the charmed quality of Green Island. Jewett may never have met
Mrs. Laighton, who died in 1877, but she knew a great deal about
Celia's devotion to her mother, which was so strong as to cause a
serious strain in her marriage. It was Celia's lingering grief over
her mother's death that lured her into spiritualism in the early
eighties; and it is very likely Celia's claim to have seen a vision of
her mother before her own death that appears, transmuted into
fiction, in Jewett's story "The Foreigner" (1900). Mrs. Laighton
seems to have been a remarkably strong, capable, and warmhearted
woman—strong enough to follow her husband to a tiny island in
the Atlantic and raise three children there, capable enough to
co-manage a resort hotel with several hundred guests. Physically
she was heavy, and in later years confined to a chair; but Mrs.
Blackett's qualities of generalized maternal affection and common
sense have less to do with Mrs. Laighton herself than with Celia's
idealized image of her. To this we should add, of course, Jewett's
idealized memory of her own mother, whose loss was still keenly
felt. Mrs. Todd's remark that "you never get over bein' a child
long's you have a mother to go to" (p. 55) echos Jewett's own
letters.

Perhaps because of a too-close association with the images of
Caroline Jewett and Eliza Laighton, Mrs. Blackett never quite
seems to be solid flesh and blood. Her daughter, on the other hand,
has enough flesh for both of them, her ample girth corresponding
to the liberal compass of her tolerance. But her tolerance is not
unlimited; she has her share of normal human failings, and there
are some people she simply can't abide. Only mildly irritated by
Elijah Tilley's maunderings, she is sharply critical of Captain Littlepage's narrow-minded, carping housekeeper, Mari' Harris, who
makes the old man's life miserable by trying to make him recant
his fantastic stories. Mari' might have the grace to humor him,
fumes Mrs. Todd, "an' let him think he had his own way, 'stead o'
arguing everything down to the bare bone." Later she confesses her
groundless dislike for a cousin of her husband's, whom she has tried
to avoid at every family function for four decades. "There she goes
now," she says. "Do let's pray her by! . . . I hate her just the same
as I always did; but she's got on a real pretty dress." (p. 171) In
short, Mrs. Todd's faults of temper are sufficient to make her a

credible fictional character. Her mother says "Live and let live," (p. 169) which is all very well; but Mrs. Blackett will return to her island, where she has one foot in heaven already, while Mrs. Todd has to live down the road from the likes of Mari' Harris.

Her endearing crankiness recalls a theme familiar from earlier Jewett stories, the tension between silence and words. Like her predecessors, Mrs. Todd distrusts words as a vehicle for emotional expression; hence her silence (which has as much anger in it as sadness) when her friend is about to leave her. Her endless teasing of her brother, William, masks her love for him, as his silence does his "very deep affections." (pp. 64–65) Her contempt for Elijah Tilley is partly based on his verbalizing—and thus trivializing—his sorrow, while she has quietly borne her own for years. When expressing an opinion she is as voluble as anyone, but the nearer a subject is to her heart the more tongue-tied she becomes.

For Elijah Tilley words have become a kind of wall that keep him immured within his grief. They have been even more danger-ous for Captain Littlepage, upsetting his reason altogether. "He's been a great reader all his seafarin' days," Mrs. Todd says. "Some thinks he overdid, and affected his head." (p. 44) Littlepage's favorite author is Milton, that most literary and rarefied of poets. As for Shakespeare, he "copied life, but you have to put up with a great deal of low talk." (p. 21) Littlepage himself has become a "little page" in the sense that he lives entirely in a world of fantasy. As has often been observed, the window of his house is symbolic of the inner barrier that separates him from reality, as if he himself were one of the living dead in his tale.

Joanna Todd too has been unhinged by words, in her case the words of Calvinist sermons. The minister who tries to persuade her out of her delusion is no better off, being so in love with the sound of his own words that he is, to quote Mrs. Todd, "very numb in his feelin's." (p. 110) Mrs. Todd, in a careful distinction between the Bible and Calvinist dogma, wishes he had had sense enough to "lay his hand on [the Bible] an' read somethin' kind an' fatherly [to Joanna] 'stead of accusin' her" (p. 119), but because he is so lacking in the Spirit he is no father to his flock and the Bible itself is literally a closed book to him. All four—Tilley, Littlepage, Joanna, and the minister—have been seduced by the power of language to create a private world more orderly than the messy,

unpredictable world of human relationships. As a writer taking
refuge in her schoolhouse, the narrator too may be in danger of
retreating from the substance and challenge of reality, and it is that
very substantial person Mrs. Todd who shepherds her back again.
In this sense the book can be read as the story of the induction of
a writer, or any too-literary person, into the actual human drama
on which all literature is based. This was the way Jewett herself
lived, alternating periods of solitary work with engagement in
village life and the company of friends.

The opposition of the word to experience reminds us that
Jewett's universe is still, almost twenty years after *Deephaven,* very
close to that of Emerson. The role of nature in *Pointed Firs* remains
essentially transcendentalist, wild creatures and plants being both
embodiments and messengers of a universal anima. Birds in particular serve as a kind of ironic commentary on the limited per-
ceptions of human beings. During the walking funeral, the song
sparrows "sang and sang, as if with joyous knowledge of immor-
tality, and contempt for those who could so pettily concern themselves with death." (p. 18) Early in Littlepage's monologue a
swallow flies into the schoolhouse for a minute, beats its wings
against the window, and then "escape[s] into the open air," as if to
show the man the way to freedom; but he, already locked into his
vision of "one of the greatest discoveries that man has ever made,"
takes "no notice whatever." (p. 25) A few minutes later the narrator
hears the song of a "golden robin" and the sound of a wave on the
beach—the robin a "joyful and eager" counterpart to the old man's
diatribe against modern times, the wave a warning that the tide is
about to turn, as Littlepage's mind retreats into fantasy. (p. 30)

For William Blackett, who like Sylvia in "A White Heron" is
one of nature's children and who, like her, is "afraid of folks," nature
becomes—as it is for her—an intermediary between himself and
another human being. He shows the narrator the sights on the
island that have most meaning to him: a great wasps' nest and
some fishhawks' nests in a bit of swamp. He gives her a few sprigs
of linnaea, whose delicate, fragrant, pink nodding flowers pass for
speech in his spare vocabulary. And in the tale of Joanna Todd, one
of Joanna's tame sparrows lights on her coffin while the Reverend
Mr. Dimmick preaches his dreary funeral sermon and sings a
sermon of its own, and Mrs. Todd "wa'n't the only one thought

the poor little bird done the best of the two." (p. 125) When the narrator makes her pilgrimage to the island twenty-seven years later, she finds the sparrows there still tame, enduring witness that Joanna's loss of human companions still left her access to nature and—in spite of her despair—God. The island's spring, at which the narrator drinks and which provided Joanna's water, has the same multiple connotations as the spring in "The White Rose Road": the revivifying power of nature; the traditionally magical properties of springs; and the continuing inheritance of the past—for this spring, like Old York's, is rich with associations from "old times."

As can be inferred from all this, Jewett treats formal religion roughly in *The Country of the Pointed Firs.* Mr. Dimmick is rather like Deacon Brimblecom in "The Courting of Sister Wisby," a man of much noise and little light. But Mrs. Todd goes to meeting and sings hymns in her herb garden, William asks a blessing over supper, and Joanna keeps her Bible, though she is unable to get much good out of it. The religious base of this as of earlier works is basically Protestant Christian, emphasizing human forgiveness, direct communion with the Deity, and the elevation of the Spirit over the Letter. Despite the allusions to ancient female powers, Mrs. Todd's gifts as healer and peacemaker are more Episcopal than pagan. Yet there is no doubt that this is, as Josephine Donovan and others have pointed out, a feminized religion, centered on the Mother rather than the Father. It is Mrs. Todd, and particularly Mrs. Blackett, who are the real spiritual leaders of Dunnet Landing—a fact acknowledged by the Bowdens when they ask Mrs. Blackett to join the ministers in leading the reunion procession.

A reader familiar with Jewett's signature themes will recognize them like old friends throughout the book. There are instances of spiritual communication, as when a signal sent "from the heart on the shore to the heart on the sea" tells Mrs. Todd her mother has seen her. (p. 55) There is a hint, too, that Mrs. Todd really does influence nature beyond the usual, when she twitches the sheet of a drooping sail and is immediately rewarded with "a fresh gust." (p. 55) Yet none of these is truly outside the natural, and most instances of sharpened perception are just that: intuitions developed over long experience of living.

Another familiar Jewett image, the garden, is as always an outward expression of inner character. There are two, Mrs. Todd's and Mrs. Blackett's. Mrs. Todd's is busy and responsible, being entirely given over to herbs except for a few token flowers crowded up against the house wall. "Oh, what a poor, plain garden!" her mother laments. "Hardly a flower in it except for your bush o' balm." (p. 140) Mrs. Blackett's own garden is all untidy frivolity, "a mass of gay flowers and greenery" that straggles off into grass and wild mallows and shelters a pair of half-grown chickens. (p. 60)

Social ceremony, always in Jewett's works the expression of communal solidarity and goodwill, is represented in the reunion feast, the supper on Green Island, the ritual teas that William and Mrs. Blackett enjoy alone together, and Joanna Todd's "beautiful, quiet manners." (p. 116) It is expressed too in a series of parlors or best rooms, of which Mrs. Blackett's is representative. On Green Island, Mrs. Blackett shows her company in through the never-used front door and they spend some ceremonial minutes in the parlor, as a gesture of welcome and respect to the newcomer. Then they go into the kitchen, where the usual business of life goes on. But this parlor is not an emotionally sterile room, for Mrs. Todd was married here; it is, rather, a special room for "serious occasions." The narrator reflects that

> it was indeed a tribute to Society to find a room set apart
> for her behests out there on so apparently neighborless and
> remote an island. Afternoon visits and evening festivals
> must be few in such a bleak situation at certain seasons of
> the year, but Mrs. Blackett was of those who do not live to
> themselves, and who have long since passed the line that di-
> vides mere self-concern from a valued share in whatever
> Society can give and take. (p. 63)

Finally, there is the theme of lot and place. In this work more than others, the role of God, or Providence, in determining human events is questioned, but the question is always asked from the point of view of the narrator or another character. Mrs. Todd is disappointed that her brother never "made something o' himself, bein' a man an' so like mother." But she adds, "I think it is well to see any one so happy an' makin' the most of life just as it falls to hand." (p. 75) The narrator in turn raises a similar question about Mrs. Todd, whose social gifts begin to shine amid the "proper surroundings" of the reunion; from there she goes to musing in a general way on

> the waste of human ability in this world, as a botanist won-
> ders at the wastefulness of nature, the thousand seeds that
> die, the unused provision of every sort. . . . More than one
> face among the Bowdens showed that only opportunity and
> stimulus were lacking,—a narrow set of circumstances had
> caged a fine able character and held it captive. (p. 174)

This somehow calls to mind an image of the gigantic shades of Darwin and Swedenborg confronting one another head to head; but it is, after all, only the narrator trying to justify God's ways to man in the light of her own education. As for her musings about Mrs. Todd, they are balanced by comments by Mrs. Blackett. While the city visitor wants to transplant Mrs. Todd to the city, to Mrs. Blackett Dunnet Landing is metropolis enough:

> "I always think Providence was kind to plot an' have
> [Almiry's] husband leave her a good house where she really
> belonged. She'd been very restless if she'd had to continue
> here on Green Island. You wanted more scope, didn't you,
> Almiry, an' to live in a large place where more things
> grew?" (pp. 81–82)

So in the end, as in "A Bit of Shore Life," where the narrator's view of Cynthia's plight is formed by her own urban experience, the judgment that another person's life is wasted is limited by our own values. Mrs. Todd's judgment is limited as regards William, the narrator's as regards Mrs. Todd. Mrs. Blackett, who can see farther than anyone, contradicts them both. The implication, as in *Deephaven,* is that there is a higher purpose now and justice here-after; but here it is assumed rather than spoken.

The role of Mrs. Blackett is the least equivocal of all. Her physical distance from the mainland simply emphasizes the reach of her sympathy and the degree to which she, far more than her daughter, mimics on a human scale an all-encompassing, divine love. She has, the narrator says, "that final, that highest gift of heaven, a perfect self-forgetfulness." (p. 73) In terms of the book's primary theme of interdependence and community, she is the center uniting all the disparate lives around her, including outcasts like Littlepage and Joanna who cannot respond to anyone else. She had been set in that lonely place, the narrator decides, "to keep the balance true"; in terms of the continuing moral purpose of Jewett's work, the same can be said of *The Country of the Pointed Firs.*

21

At Home and Abroad

THE WRITING OF *THE COUNTRY OF THE Pointed Firs* went along so smoothly that Jewett, having completed two of the four *Atlantic* installments in about three months, was free to go on a Caribbean cruise with Annie, the Aldriches, and their friend Henry Pierce on Pierce's steam yacht *Hermione.* They sailed from Georgia in January 1896, intending to touch at Palm Beach and the northern islands and then turn south to the Windwards, but persistent high seas kept them in northern ports. For weeks the *Hermione* scurried from island to island, each short voyage an ordeal for everyone aboard, even the captain. Finally word of a yellow-fever quarantine put an end to the cruise, and by early March Sarah and Annie were back in their old quarters in St. Augustine.

Disappointing though the trip was in some ways, it did have its good moments. Sarah spent long, sleepy days on deck in one flower-rimmed port or another, reading the letters of Mme de Sévigné or listening to Annie read aloud from Stevenson's letters from Valaima. Sights of extraordinary beauty lodged in her memory: a school of flying fish leaping from the water in silver arcs and landing on deck (to be eaten for dinner the next day); a flock of flamingos on the tiny island of Inagua, moving like blown flames across their own reflections on the wet sand.

Although Sarah suffered less from seasickness than the others, by the time the *Hermione* reached Florida she had lost nearly ten pounds and was tired from lack of sleep. She immediately set to

301

work on *Pointed Firs,* but she caught the "grippe" in New York on the way home and was still feeling shaky as she wrote the story of Joanna and Shell-heap Island. Much of the summer was spent recuperating and visiting around, and she finished her installments, made a quick cruise to Penobscot Bay on the *Hermione* to refresh her memory for the book, and with Annie traveled to Hartford to attend the funeral of Harriet Beecher Stowe, who had finally died after a long and sad mental deterioration. In August Sarah and Sarah Whitman went to Ashfield, Massachusetts, to attend Charles Eliot Norton's annual "Ashfield dinner," a fund-raising event begun years earlier by Norton and his friend George William Curtis on behalf of the local academy.* The dinners were always held in the town hall, where the townspeople and an assortment of New England professors and writers paid a dollar apiece to eat at long tables and be regaled by some well-known speaker enlisted from among Norton's distinguished friends. The invitation to speak, entailing as it did the leaving of one's own comfortable summer retreat, was never welcome but seems to have been rarely refused. Sarah went to several of the dinners and always enjoyed them—no doubt partly because, being a woman, she never had to worry that her turn was next.

In the fall she lured Annie to Berwick for a week, baiting her hook with a week's driving tour to visit the Shaker community at Canterbury, New Hampshire. Sarah and Mary had a longstanding friendship with some of the Shakers from Alfred, Maine, who often called in as they went from town to town selling their handcrafted wares. She found a few old acquaintances at Canterbury too, and was "deeply touched at heart to find the old sisters knew my stories ever so long ago, and were getting up a little excitement about my being there. . . . Such days are almost too much pleasure for my heart to bear—the pathos, the joy of those faces, the innocent gayety of their dull lives."[1] She saw in the Shaker communities the American counterpart of old European convents, and while she had no sympathy with the restrictive side of monasticism, she loved the order and serenity of cloistered lives. Her correspondents in these later years of her life included two Catholic nuns, Sister St.

---

* One of the last surviving members of Brook Farm, Curtis had edited *Harper's Weekly* for nearly thirty years until his death in 1892.

André of Quebec and Sister L. Theresia of St. Augustine, whose faith she treated so gently that one of them asked her to recruit novices, while the other offered Masses for Sarah's own conversion, in the patient belief that all it needed was a little extra tug from Heaven. The Shakers did not try to draw her in, but they did ask her to send them any wandering souls she thought would be content with them. Like Howells, who had sympathetically portrayed a Shaker village in *The Undiscovered Country*, Sarah admired the Shakers' spiritual integrity, self-sufficiency, and discipline, their quaint courtesy and the perseverance that had preserved their tradition for two centuries. In her remark about the "innocent gayety of their dull lives" one sees, of course, her sympathy for all obscure lives honestly lived—in a word, for her own characters.

Yet no one should suppose that the only correspondence her characters found in the "real" world was in these cloistered villages. Readers wrote to her all the time telling her how much her characters and settings corresponded to people and places they knew, or to themselves. Not surprisingly, the most appreciative were the people from her parents' and grandparents' time, the generation to which, she once said, "I really belong—I who was brought up with grandfathers and grand uncles and aunts for my best playmates."[2] In her stories they recognized, albeit with the sentimental nostalgia of the elderly, a vanishing company in which they had once been completely at home. Sally Kaign, an old Quaker lady from New Jersey, is representative:

> Thy wonderful gift of understanding lonely lives, especially
> those of elderly women, is so unusual. There is such a win-
> ning cheery tone in describing the narrow limitations of
> some of our lives, and yet they never seem hopelessly ridicu-
> lous, as when *others* attempt to describe them. . . . How
> often after a tiresome day, I have sat down and read one of
> thy spicy little stories, and felt so comforted and cheered,
> with my heart filled with a loving pity for those whose
> limitations were greater and harder than my own.[3]

"Thee knows," the same woman wrote in another letter, "I am one of thy old women, *which one* I hardly know."[4] Another woman found a special appeal in the stories for *younger* women: "There is no poverty of soul in any outward poverty of what you write—but . . . such women as yours take their place as *real souls* in the world, and are of infinite encouragement to other women, either in just such or wholly different surroundings—It is the New England *faith* that I deeply thank you for."[5] Such letters remind us that women have always read Jewett's work with a start of recognition, as if coming across themselves in print, although until a few years ago those reactions were seldom publicly heard.

Late in 1896 *The Country of the Pointed Firs* appeared in bookstores, greeted by Jewett's usual favorable reviews, although —also as usual—some were qualified by the adjectives reserved for "feminine" art: "She may, like Virgil's shepherd, sing a slender song," said the *Critic* reviewer, "but her vocalization is beyond reproach and almost beyond praise." More robust was the reviewer in *The Spectator,* who wrote that her characters "are given with a graphic touch that makes them live. There is not a jarring word in *The Country of the Pointed Firs.*"[6] William James sent an appreciative letter halfway through the serial publication, and Kipling wrote "to convey some small instalment of our great delight"—our purring satisfaction in that perfect little tale:

> It's immense—it is the very life. It's out and away the love-
> liest thing of yours I've ever read. . . . So many of the peo-
> ple of lesser sympathy have missed the lovely New England
> landscape; and the genuine breadth of heart and fun that
> underlies the New England nature. I maintain (and will
> maintain with outcries if necessary) that that is the reallest
> New England book ever given us.[7]

He added in a P.S., "I don't believe even *you* know how good that book is." He was right. Pleased though she was by all the acclamation, Jewett still did not recognize her own best work when she saw it. Just as she valued the sentimental sketch "Decoration Day" above her other late stories, so she would tell an interviewer five years after the publication of *Pointed Firs* that she thought her best work was *A Marsh Island,* while her personal favorite was *A Country Doctor.*[8]

With the coming of winter the inevitable respiratory complaints descended on Charles Street. Sarah struggled with rheumatism and a series of colds, while Annie's illness settled in her chest. A warmer climate was suggested, and on the strength of a friend's recommendation they traveled to Hot Springs, Virginia, in February. They found it cold enough—snowy, in fact—but they settled in nevertheless and waited for spring, which presently arrived in the form of flowers and deep red mud. As usual, simply being away from the pressures of work and society worked a kind of cure on Annie, while Sarah daily underwent a regimen that included ten minutes under a forceful overhead stream of water (an improvement over being hosed down, as she was at Aix), followed by fifteen minutes of resting wrapped in blankets, followed by "rubbing" by a Danish masseuse. Eager to be released, she set her mind on working and asked Mary to see about renting an abandoned schoolhouse to which she had taken a fancy. As the end of March drew near, she and Annie looked forward to a reunion in Baltimore with Thérèse Blanc, who was sailing to America with her friend Ferdinand Brunetière (editor of the *Revue des Deux Mondes*) and his wife. When Mary mentioned in passing in one of her letters that both Carrie and Theodore were ailing, Sarah responded with suggestions for bottled remedies and sisterly cautions about change of air.

But either Mary had been deliberately minimizing Carrie's illness or no one had realized just how serious it was. According to John Frost's biography, Carrie became acutely ill during a visit to Exeter and returned to South Berwick, where she underwent surgery for an abdominal abscess.[9] Sarah was urgently summoned home and arrived on March 29, leaving Annie behind. Three days later, on the evening of April 1, Carrie died.

This third family death in seven years left sixteen-year-old Theodore totally orphaned and was as much of an unexpected shock as the death of his father. Carrie had been plagued by digestive upsets for years, but no one had ever thought she was at risk. In January she had come to Boston to consult Sarah's eye doctor and visit Theodore, who was now attending the Noble and Greenough School in that city. She had enjoyed her usual rounds of shopping and seeing old friends, and Sarah had taken her for a long drive in Mrs. Cabot's big carriage. She was the most ebullient of the sisters, and the silence she left behind was full of echoes. Mary chose not to rent the house next door to strangers, and it remained empty.

"It is important to get over the feeling that something of me died and not the living brightness and affectionateness of my sister," Sarah wrote several months later,[10] and it was at least partly to accomplish that end that Thérèse, whose presence had comforted the grieving family once before, came to Berwick in May. "The French guest is always more delightful than ever," Sarah told Sarah Whitman,

> and thanks to her help I have got pretty well through with the dullness, the hopeless anxiety and even the heavy indifference which comes after a great shock—At first one is half conscious of a great [stimulation] and uplifting and it is when that is done and over that the hard pull comes. I shall long look back to these dear rainy days and to the comfort of looking up at so dear a face—And the stories! They begin in just the right moment: "Madame-de-Beau- laincourt has-told me once—" "A friend-of mine who was-a Russian—" "In the country of Madame Delzant which is the country of les Guerins-Maurice and Eugenie—" and so they begin and go on! "Les Rohans sont toujours."[11]

Thérèse stayed in Maine about three weeks. She was there on Decoration Day, whose annual parade of aging veterans, many of them laboring like John Tucker under the pain of old wounds, had increasingly brought Sarah to understand the devastation of the war she had barely noticed in childhood. Thérèse had been enough moved by Sarah's story "Decoration Day" to translate it for the *Revue des Deux Mondes* in 1894, but she had missed the day itself on her earlier visit. Now she joined her friends in observing this ritual of historic pathos, in a country that many Europeans (though not Thérèse) believed was without a sense of history. Immediately afterwards they went to Boston to witness the dedication of the Saint-Gaudens monument to Col. Robert Gould Shaw and his black regiment.* There they watched another parade, featuring the

---

* Young Shaw, grandson of Louis and Elizabeth Agassiz, had commanded the 54th Massachusetts, the only black Union regiment allowed into combat. Displaying great courage in the assault on Fort Wagner, South Carolina, almost half of the men were killed, along with Shaw and most of the officers. The victorious Confederates had buried them all in one grave, thinking to dishonor Shaw by burying him with his "niggers."

grizzled survivors of the 54th, and afterwards there were speeches by local dignitaries and Booker T. Washington, "le *lion,*" according to Thérèse, "de cette journée."[12]

A little later in Thérèse's visit they took an overnight trip to Boston to attend the Harvard and Radcliffe commencements. The ambivalence of Thérèse's feminism, representative not only of herself but of Sarah and Annie and even the dean and president of Radcliffe, is revealed in her published comments about a Radcliffe woman who had fulfilled all the requirements for a Ph.D. but was, of course, denied it. She was given a special award instead. "Puissent nos doctoresses de l'avenir ressembler à miss Kate Peterson, si parfaitement féminine dans sa souriante acceptation d'une différence injuste au fond," Thérèse wrote.[13] The injustice is important, but even more important is to accept it with feminine grace.

There was one other bit of Americana Thérèse especially wanted to see: a Shaker village. Years earlier a friend of hers, an English-born Frenchwoman, had decided to renounce the world and had spent several years as a Shaker sister in Mt. Lebanon, New York. Later she had returned to Europe and joined a Catholic order, and she had often talked to Thérèse about her American experience. Sarah wrote to her friend Elder Henry Green in Alfred, Maine, and gained permission to bring her friend to stay overnight and (an unusual concession) witness a Sunday service. They planned to travel by carriage and see the countryside, but a powerful storm struck the New England coast, flooding roads and washing away bridges, and they were forced to change their plans. They went by train on June 15 and were met by Elder Green and driven to the tranquil hillside community, where they were greeted with sober hospitality. After dinner Sarah entertained the sisters with an account of her Caribbean cruise, and then she and Thérèse were taken to a small, airy guest room, where they hung their clothes on pegs, lay down on two narrow beds, and fell asleep to the metronomic chant of a whippoorwill.

Thérèse also spent some days with Annie in Manchester, but she seems to have stayed mostly with Sarah, who was home alone while Mary went visiting. Together they explored old woods roads behind the Jewetts' sturdy team, the horses patiently nosing the boughs aside while the wheels rolled soundlessly over the grassy track. Now and then Sarah would jump down and remove some obstacle with a strong and practiced hand ("une main adroite et forte").[14] "I have given [Thérèse] some sweet fern and some bayberry and some young checkerberry leaves," Sarah reported to a friend, "and so now she knows New England"[15]; indeed in Thérèse's recitation of the names of New England plants one can almost hear Sarah's prompting voice, and behind it the faint echo of Sarah's own father, teaching her the same names forty years earlier: starflower, bobolink, mocking bird, white pine, Quaker lady, and—yes—checkerberry. But it was typical of Thérèse's way of scrambling the language that she remembered bayberry as "waxberry," and that, having been told the history of Witchtrot Road (named for a seventeenth-century man arrested for sorcery who craftily led his captors astray by that route), she recalled it as "Witchman's Trot."[16]

In the streets of South Berwick itself Thérèse discerned an air of prosperity, the mills along the river adding rather than detracting from the picturesque. Her continental eye, used to making class distinctions at a glance, found no familiar clues: the houses all appeared to be bourgeois, as did the men who worked in the mills, while working women wore "des toilettes des dames." The town, she decided, was mostly inhabited by comfortably fixed workers, "des artisans enrichis."[17] As for the members of "good society," the elderly spinsters and sea captains of Miss Jewett's stories, they had almost entirely disappeared.

After Thérèse left them, Sarah, Mary, and Theodore traveled to Quebec; Thérèse herself had hoped to join them but apparently was prevented. Afterwards Sarah stayed with Mary through the summer and fall, visiting Annie from time to time and making shopping forays into Boston to buy curtains and furniture for Theodore, who entered Harvard in September. When she finally arrived at Charles Street for the winter, she found Annie suffering yet another of her bronchial infections. They passed the time during her convalescence planning their third trip to Europe. Sarah prepared herself by hiring a French tutor and by exercising at a gymnasium to limber up her rheumatic joints, but as in 1892 she was of two minds about the whole project. Again she was leaving Mary behind after a family death, and this time Mary was utterly alone. She set about persuading her sister to follow in the summer and bring Theodore with her. Mary hesitated, for America and

Spain were on the brink of war and she was afraid of bombardment at sea. Eventually she consented to go, but not until after Sarah had sailed.

This was a very long trip, lasting from spring into autumn. Most of it was spent in France, where they toured Provence, Brittany, and the Loire Valley as well as spending a few days in Paris and most of June at Thérèse's country house. Bracketing the French sojourn were several weeks spent in England, three at the beginning and about five at the end.

As before, many of the best moments had little to do with official sights. In Provence they visited the poet Frédéric Mistral and his wife at their house near St. Rémy. A leader of the movement to revive the ancient Provençal language and culture, Mistral was known to literary Americans thanks largely to the efforts of Sarah's onetime friend Harriet Waters Preston, who had translated his *Mireio.* The men of southern Provence are the cowboys of France, priding themselves on the white horses and black cattle that have been bred for centuries in the Camargue; and so it was not surprising that Mistral felt a kind of kinship with the American West and had made the trip to Paris to see Buffalo Bill's Wild West show not long before. He had brought back two small dogs abandoned by the troupe, one of which he called "Bouffe" in honor of its erstwhile master. "You see," said the moustachioed poet, tilting his black hat to one side, "I look like him." The visitors politely agreed, though he also must have reminded them of a kindly *bandito.*[18]

At La Ferté, Thérèse's country house near Paris, Sarah found leisure to take in the details of a small corner of a foreign country, as Thérèse herself had in Maine. The countryside was not very different from her own: gently rolling, forested hillsides dotted with fields; a sleepy river; birdsong and church bells. But underneath the resemblances the differences were immense: in a tiny church in the village of Jouarre-sur-Marne, hidden among its ordinary and much-mended windows, she discovered an intact bit of very old stained glass depicting King David with his harp. "I almost cry as I think of it," she wrote to an unidentified friend. ". . . I am sure that you would say that it [is] as exquisite as it can be in colour and feeling and the sense it gives of great rapture in music. . . . I cannot forget it."[19] Color and feeling and a sense of

the musician's creative rapture—all were part of her strong emotional response; but perhaps also the privilege of discovering it for
herself as if it were some personal message left by Time, and the
realization that the sunlight had lit up King David's robes and
golden harp for five or six hundred years, ever since he had been
set there by some forgotten, anonymous human hand.

In England they all went almost immediately to Yorkshire in
order to join Robert Collyer, who had asked them to meet him in
Ilkley as they had in 1892. Widowed and in his mid-seventies,
Collyer had become the last of Sarah's and Annie's grand old men,
succeeding Whittier and Holmes as a particular kind of male
presence in their lives—elderly, solitary, vulnerable, and witty, part
father and part brother, someone who seemed to need female
attention and did not object to a little pampering. Physically
Collyer was made of tougher mettle than Whittier, priding himself
(as much as was pardonable in a man of the cloth) on his robust
health. But like Whittier he was tenderhearted and emotionally
susceptible—so much so that he never had succeeded in reading
The Scarlet Letter all the way through because he found it unbearably
tragic. Now, as in 1892, he had come to Yorkshire to preach in
one of the villages that claimed to have a part in his life; he would
also be honored by a school he had once briefly attended. Sarah
and Annie timed their arrival in England so as to see him again
on his native ground.

They spent the remaining weeks ranging widely over the
country. Sometimes the four of them stayed together and sometimes they split up, Mary and Theodore sightseeing while Annie
and Sarah visited literary friends. Many of those were now into the
second generation, the children and relations of the departed great:
the Hallam Tennysons, Charles Kingsley's daughter, Rose; Dickens's sister-in-law, Georgina Hogarth; Mrs. Gaskell's daughters.
They spent a day at Mary Arnold Ward's country house and saw
the Kiplings at Rottingdean, and in London Annie paid a call on
John Singer Sargent. Early in September, not long before they left,
they spent a day with Henry James.

Annie's friendship with James went back to the days when she
had encouraged her husband to publish his early stories in *The
Atlantic.* Although not so wholehearted an admirer of his work in

later years and not above laughing at it (Wagner's operas and James's novels were standard targets for jokes in Annie's circle), she still thought him a major writer and would stand up for him if the jibes got too pointed. Sarah knew him slightly, being better friends with his brother William.

Since the death of his parents, James had had even less reason than before to visit Massachusetts, a place he always wanted to leave as soon as he got there in any case; and so American friends who wanted to see him had to journey to Rye. There Sarah and Annie arrived one morning, having seen Mary and Theodore off on a sightseeing junket. The visit was ceremonious and—reading between the lines of Annie's diary—a little reminiscent of two elderly ladies in one of Sarah's stories calling on the new minister. James appears to have been a trifle flustered, perhaps seeing too much of Boston embodied in his lady visitors; while the visitors, like the narrator in *Pointed Firs* calling on Elijah Tilley, seem to have been a little surprised not to discover the dining-room floor littered with bones. "Everything was of the severest plainness but in the best taste," Annie noted, and she was amused to see James jump up in the midst of their conversation and disappear into the kitchen like any careful housewife to check on the progress of lunch. Presently the conversation turned to Sarah's stories, James praising them all but saying how much he particularly admired *The Country of the Pointed Firs.* He asked if Sarah really had visited such a village and such an island as she described. No, she said, not precisely.* "And Mrs. Dennet," James went on, "how admirable she is." One can imagine the slight pause that followed this remark, but Sarah kept a straight face and according to Annie she and James "were very much at home together" from then on.[20] After lunch James, perhaps somewhat at a loss for entertainment, decided to take his guests to Hastings, a nearby seaside resort where he thought they would enjoy the view. They all went by train—James, his secretary, Sarah, Annie, and James's small black-and-tan dog.

* She added, puzzlingly, that the book was chiefly written before she visited the locality itself, implying that it was written before she went to Martinsville. I believe she was being deliberately evasive here, as she was when similarly questioned about *Deephaven.* In general she disliked having specific sources identified for her characters and settings.

A public ordinance required that the dog wear a muzzle, but James apparently hated the muzzle for the dog's sake and took it off at every opportunity, eventually losing it altogether. So their drive along the Hastings esplanade partly became a search for a shop that sold muzzles, which probably amused the guests more than a view that was, after all, "decidedly unromantic." The afternoon ended with tea and cakes—James claiming, like a little boy, to have eaten ten cakes in order to tease the waitress—and they all parted at the station.

Despite the little awkwardnesses on both sides, James's admiration for Sarah's work, and for Sarah and Annie together, was genuinely felt. His later remark about their friendship, "their reach together was of the firmest and easiest," is often quoted,[21] and after Sarah's death he would volunteer to write an introduction to her letters, although bad health finally prevented his doing so. The basis for their understanding one another, both of them belonging as much to the Old World as to the New and both wary on some level of untold barbarisms to come, was established during this visit to Rye, and afterwards they exchanged letters occasionally for as long as Sarah lived.

By the time the maples reddened in Maine the Jewetts were home. As was often the case, this journey taken ostensibly for health and rest had thoroughly exhausted Sarah. She spent much of the winter of 1898–99 laid up with rheumatism and flu, passing the time by helping prepare a catalogue for Berwick Academy. Late in June, still unable to write, she went off to Mouse Island alone, Annie for some reason being unable to join her. There she spent long mornings in the woods, sometimes reading and sometimes stalking a mother partridge with newly hatched chicks—minute, brown-striped creatures that scampered through the underbrush like so many animated fuzzy walnuts. On clear days she went sailing with a sun-browned captain who could have stepped straight out of one of her own stories, and except for missing Annie and regretting certain deficiencies in the inn's cooking, she began to feel well. She tried to remedy the latter problem by buying Uneeda biscuits and candy to nibble on, but trading at the island store was not easy, since the proprietor preferred painting his boat to keeping his store and was, in any case, curiously lacking in entrepreneurial spirit:

[I] casually inquired if he didn't keep candy as it seemed to
be a moment for sassafras and peppermint sticks. He said
that he did, but he didn't *seem to want to open the box*—it
spoiled so when it was open!! I thought he little knew
what a customer was in his easy grasp. . . . I came away
and left the wooden box of selections intact and tried to
console myself by thinking that all it held were cinnamon
colored chocolates with rose stuffings.[22]

Perhaps he was saving his stock for the tourists, who soon arrived
in force, scaring Sarah off to Manchester and the partridges to
deeper cover.

Throughout these years Sarah kept up her regular visits to
Susan Burley Cabot, spending a week at her Boston house in
January and a week at Beverly in July. Nothing less than a family
death or a trip to Europe was allowed to break this commitment.
Now in her mid-seventies, Mrs. Cabot was troubled by chronic
gastric complaints that now could no doubt be easily diagnosed
and cured but then were treated with bed rest and doses of nux
vomica. She was nevertheless an irrepressibly cheerful and energetic
soul, though a less-than-ideal hostess for a writer with deadlines to
meet. "There were trottings in, so affectionate, to see how I was
getting on," Sarah wrote from Beverly one year. "I am not sure that
I shall get much done in this visit, Mary, but every little helps."[23]
But there were compensations. Few people Sarah knew had developed the art of gossip to such uninhibited perfection as Mrs. Cabot.
Frequently ordered to bed, she would sit propped up against a
mound of pillows, her face angelically framed in a ruffled nightcap,
and pass in review

a series of subjects . . . from Mrs. Gardner to Marianne
Brimmer, which pretty well included all this range of the
North Shore. . . . She was uncommon funny giving great
flounders and little smart kicks in bed by way of proper emphasis—. . . All thoughts of literature and politics were set
aside, and when we speak of Mrs. Tyson and the stone wall
we are always heart to heart as you may say, but the deeper
confidences of the Brimmer drains which "caused malaria"
to the Montagues and so travels [*sic*] to the Capulets (whose

drains they were) were reached this night Mary, and Marianne Brimmer *little* knows that she is now in ruins according to the best of my belief—Oh do tear up this foolish
letter![24]

The Mrs. Tyson who was the subject of "heart to heart"
confidences in Beverly that year was probably the same Mrs. Tyson
who would soon help the Jewett sisters achieve a significant small
victory in South Berwick. In "River Driftwood" Sarah had written
of Hamilton House, one of the most beautiful of South Berwick's
remaining eighteenth-century houses and certainly the most dramatically placed, set on a point in the Salmon Falls River with its
face toward Portsmouth and its broad lawns sweeping down to the
water. Built just after the Revolution by Col. Jonathan Hamilton,
the square mansion with its four tall chimneys stood next to the
site of Grandfather Jewett's shipyard; and it had a small link to
the family history in Charlotte Hamilton, widow of Jonathan, who
had later married Gov. John Gilman of Exeter. (She was the woman
who, in family stories, always insisted on lighting and extinguish-
ing her stoves on the same calendar date.) But personal interest
aside, the house on the river was full of distinguished ghosts and
was a kind of symbolic gatekeeper for the town. When it came on
the market in 1895 and the Jewett sisters heard that a developer
wanted to tear it down and break its land into house lots, Sarah
launched a personal crusade to rescue it.

It was not unusual for her to try to interest her city friends
in buying or renting some vacant old farmhouse that she thought
needed adopting, like a stray dog. But none had meant anywhere
near as much to her as this house, in whose rooms she had roamed
and daydreamed since childhood. Word went out along the avenues
of Back Bay and the lanes of Beacon Hill, and no doubt as far south
as New York, Hartford, and Baltimore, that Miss Jewett was
looking for a summer neighbor. She was helped in her search by
the fact that the preservationist spirit was now at its height. Rich
Americans were in love with old things, and if they couldn't
physically import large chunks of the Old World like Isabella
Stewart Gardner, who was building a Venetian *palazzo* in Boston,
they built sprawling gothic mansions complete with turrets, gar-
goyles, and priests' holes.

The call was not answered immediately, but luckily the developers held off and in 1898 Emily Tyson, a wealthy Boston widow, flew into Sarah's friendly net. Hamilton House was rundown and unpainted, its lawns and gardens chewed to the ground by sheep; but with the help of Sarah Whitman, among others, Mrs. Tyson set about restoring her house as the Jewetts had theirs, with a combination of historic fidelity and Arts and Crafts inventiveness. By the summer of 1899 she was able to move in, along with her stepdaughter, Elise. For Sarah and Mary their arrival brought a small social renaissance to South Berwick, as friends from Boston came to see both families and circulated freely between the houses. And they had the satisfaction of having saved the house—even though that was the year they lost the last of the town's old-growth forests.

At the end of 1899 Sarah published her eighteenth book, *The Queen's Twin and Other Stories.* Two stories in the collection, the title story and "A Dunnet Shepherdess," brought the *Pointed Firs* narrator back for a reunion with Mrs. Todd. A third Dunnet Landing story, "William's Wedding," was set aside for some reason and was not published until 1910. A fourth, "The Foreigner," was written sometime during the fall and winter of 1899 and published the following year. Clearly her readers were not willing to let Mrs. Todd disappear, "mateless and appealing," into the woods, and Sarah was willing to oblige them. As was mentioned earlier, two or three of the stories have been incorporated in later editions of *The Country of the Pointed Firs,* but although they always have pleased readers, they are longer than the original chapters and upset the formal balance and thematic flow. They are best read separately, as the afterthoughts they were.*

By now Sarah's royalties had made her rich by some standards, although she was, if anything, less interested in money than she ever had been. She invested most of her income and left herself an

---

* "A Dunnet Shepherdess" and "William's Wedding" were included in the 1910 Houghton Mifflin edition; Willa Cather included these and "The Queen's Twin" in her 1925 edition. In *The World of Dunnet Landing,* edited by David Bonnell Green (1962), the original form of *The Country of the Pointed Firs* is restored, and the three stories are printed separately along with "The Foreigner," which had not been printed since its original appearance in the August 1900 *Atlantic.*

allowance in the bank, the amount of which she never could keep track of. There were frequent appeals to Mary to "ask Becca" (Rebecca Young, treasurer of the South Berwick Savings Bank) just how much she had, and at one point she noticed with some surprise that money seemed to be piling up and proposed to Mary that they reinvest only part of it and have the rest "to play with."[25] They played like the ladies they were, never making a big splash. In the nineties they spent modest amounts on travel and on the house, updating the plumbing and changing the exterior color from brown to white. They bought the occasional new horse, and Sarah splurged on a fur-lined cloak, justifying it partly no doubt on grounds of health. Christmas gifts to one another and to friends remained the knickknacks they had always been—a framed photo, a china bowl. Money remained an exterior concern; if she had lost most of it she probably would not have lived very differently, except for privately skimping on the cream and worrying over the future like Miss Jaffrey in "A Village Shop" or Miss Spring in "A Late Supper."

Some of it always went for good works. Sarah seems to have briefly served as secretary of the Associated Charities,[26] and of course she must have given money regularly to Annie's cause. Berwick Academy, too, would have received donations over and above her various volunteer efforts, and now and then she bought a supply of goods from the Shakers to be donated to church fairs. But the number and extent of her charities is unknown, for never did a Yankee family more scrupulously observe the biblical injunction to let not the right hand know what the left hand was doing. Only occasionally does a reference surface in the letters, as in a query from Sarah to Mary about whether they might do something discreetly through Uncle John for an elderly Exeter woman. In 1898 Mary offered Carrie's vacant house to a pair of old friends whose income had been suddenly reduced, and once or twice the Jewetts or Annie arranged for Irish women working for them to return to Ireland, either for a visit or to retire. As Jewett's characters behaved so did she, hewing to the line of individual responsibility, each person taking care of her neighbor at the waning edge of a century in which most people had always known exactly who their neighbors were.

Of other kinds of good works, specifically the help she gave other writers, there is abundant proof. First among these is the work she put into the American publications of Thérèse Blanc, not only "translating" them but helping to find publishers, reading proof and trying (unsuccessfully) to defend Thérèse's sprawling text against editorial cuts. She shepherded three essays through publication in 1896, and in 1899 read and passed on to Scudder an entire book, Thérèse's *Causeries de morale pratique* (although expressing reservations with which Scudder, after he read it, agreed). Another example is her tutoring in 1899–1900 of Celia Thaxter's son, John, who sent several of his stories to Sarah for criticism. She wrote him several long, detailed letters, including specific suggestions on plot and character; she recommended likely editors, following up at least once with a word in the editorial ear over after-dinner coffee. Thaxter never published much, but it was not for lack of effort on the part of his mother's old friend.

One writer in whom she took a keen interest was the Boston poet Louise Imogen Guiney. The only child of Irish immigrant parents, Guiney had been orphaned at sixteen when her brilliant father—who had been successively a machinist, lawyer, brigadier general, and politician—died suddenly, leaving his wife and daughter with next to nothing. Louise left her convent school and began writing, gaining recognition as a coming young poet on both sides of the Atlantic but earning very little. She kept at it doggedly, supporting herself and her mother as best she could and continuing to educate herself until she became a first-rate literary scholar. In the mid-nineties she was working as postmistress in a Boston suburb—a drudging, physically demanding job that exposed her daily to insults from anti-Irish, anti-Catholic bigots. Sarah and Annie, along with Dr. Holmes and T. W. Higginson, were among the many writers whose encouragement helped her keep going.

In 1896 Sarah tried to wangle a cataloguing job for Guiney at the Boston Public Library, possibly through her early mentor Judge Mellen Chamberlain, who had been the library's director from 1878 to 1890.[27] The attempt fell through, apparently because Chamberlain was not personally involved and because neither Sarah nor Louise understood when they went for an interview that the library bureaucracy required a formal, written application. Three years later, Sarah's influence having grown a little heavier (she served on the library's examining committee in 1900–1901), she finally succeeded in landing the job for her friend. Guiney worked there at least over that winter, in a position that asked humiliatingly little of her as a scholar but at least offered her a quiet place to work and a desk of her own. But by now, at thirty-eight, she was totally worn out. She moved to England and stopped writing poetry, although she continued to publish anthologies and biographical studies.

In February 1900, after a working winter spent mostly in Maine, Sarah set off with Annie and Mary Garrett on what would be her final trip to Europe. They went to Italy, Greece, and Constantinople, taking a quick look at Paris and Thérèse before returning home in early June. This was very much Annie's kind of trip, a revisiting of the classical settings of her poetry. By nature urban and literary, she was intellectually more at home in the hills of Greece than in those of her native New England. Sarah enjoyed tagging along and on at least one occasion—among the marbles in the museum at Athens—experienced another intense epiphany, half-aesthetic and half-temporal, like the one that overcame her as she contemplated the image of King David in the church at Jouarre. But there seem to have been none of those friendly encounters with farmers, eccentrics, and children, and none of those sojourns with writers comfortably at home in their own landscape that had enlivened earlier trips.

In June of the following year Bowdoin College awarded Sarah Orne Jewett an honorary Doctor of Letters degree. The fact that she was the daughter of a distinguished alumnus had something to do with the school's decision, and she was introduced to the assembled scholars as "the only daughter of the college" in a tacit reference to her father.[28] All the same, her honorary degree was the first ever awarded to a woman by an American male college, and she took a frank pleasure in it as she did in all good things that came along. Like her own Nan Prince, she had achieved recognition simply by going her own way and doing what she liked to do.

22

"The Queen's Twin" and Other Citizens of the World

IN THE SHORT STORIES OF THE 1890S (and I include here some that were written earlier but published in collected form in 1890), Jewett continued to focus on the sympathetic ties binding people to one another and to the rest of creation. In general, the subject matter and settings are more varied in this decade. She wrote several stories about Irish immigrants, which she hoped to collect into a volume called *Transplanted Shamrocks*. There were two about the negative effects of industrialization ("The Failure of David Berry" and "The Gray Mills of Farley") and two dealing with the effects on the southern gentry of the Civil War ("The Mistress of Sydenham Plantation" and "A War Debt"). All of these stories took her far outside her own experience and suffer from an excess of moral solemnity, although her impeccable ear for Irish speech gives them some lively moments. She is at her best when she stays among her old women, who in this decade grow older still and often live on stonier ground and lonelier hillsides than their predecessors. All the more credit to them, then, for standing firmly in their lot and place and cherishing the spirit over the letter, as they almost all do.

Two who waver are Mrs. Flagg and Miss Cynthia Pickett, the main characters in "The Guests of Mrs. Timms." This is a comedy of manners, a study of the nuances of class and strategies of social climbing as they are played out against the background of New England village democracy. It is also a contrast between behavioral Christianity and the pretensions of secular churchgoing. As the story opens, Mrs. Flagg, a wealthy woman who is much respected in Woodville, has decided to enhance her status by visiting Mrs. Timms of Baxter, who as a captain's widow enjoys an even higher rank. Mrs. Flagg knows Mrs. Timms only slightly, but in the course of a county church conference Mrs. Timms has dropped a casual invitation to Mrs. Flagg and her friend Cynthia Pickett to come and see her some day that week, and Mrs. Flagg is determined to take her up on it. She has decided that Wednesday would be the day most convenient for Mrs. Timms, who will have done her washing and ironing by then. Miss Pickett, a timid woman whose social standing is well below Mrs. Flagg's, has doubts about the whole enterprise and wonders if they are not presuming too far. But she allows herself to be persuaded, partly because she hasn't the courage to contradict her friend, and partly because she too has her ambitions and the very fact of making the journey to Baxter with Mrs. Flagg is a privilege too great to be resisted. The two set off in early morning with high hopes for a good dinner and (on Mrs. Flagg's part) a possible invitation to stay overnight.

On the coach to Baxter their traveling companion is a stranger on her way to visit Mrs. Beckett, who lives about halfway between the two towns. She too was invited at a church conference, but it was some time ago and she has clearly brought enough luggage for a long visit. Moreover, she is a Free-Will Baptist and not a member of the orthodox (Congregationalist) church. On all these accounts the two Woodville women feel themselves to be on a higher plane, and they watch with frank enjoyment as their companion descends from the coach and is met by her bewildered hostess, who frankly announces that she remembers neither the guest nor the invitation. They want to stay and watch the inevitable rebuff played out, but the coach moves on.

Reaching Baxter late in the morning, they pace up the pleasant main street and rap confidently on the door of Mrs. Timms's big house. Mrs. Timms is a long time coming, but eventually she welcomes them with a smile, though in the flurry of greetings "nobody stopped to think . . . what kind of a smile it was." (*The*

Life of Nancy, p. 231) She invites them into the shuttered parlor, deftly kicking the cat into the more comfortable sitting room as she goes by and closing the door behind it. She shows them to chairs; she hopes they are going to stay in town awhile and says how glad she is that they came to see her *first;* she discusses the minister and congregation and other topics of general interest, and offers her visitors cake and wine (though as far as they can see in the darkened room there is no sign of either one). In short, she "said everything that she should have said, except to invite her visitors to walk upstairs and take off their bonnets." (p. 234)

The ladies from Woodville refuse refreshment, gather the shreds of their pride about them, and take their leave. By now very hungry, they make their way to the door of Nancy Fell, an old acquaintance—and a woman of even less means and rank than Cynthia Pickett—who receives them with pleased surprise and serves them a good dinner. On the way home the coach stops again at Mrs. Beckett's, but only long enough for her to ask the driver to bring her guest's other trunk, since she will be making a good long visit. Mrs. Flagg is suddenly approving; she decides to renew her lapsed acquaintance with Mrs. Beckett, who seems "a friendly sort of woman." "I think myself," she adds, "gen'rally speakin', 't is just as well to let anybody know you're comin'." "Them seemed to be Mis' Cap'n Timms's views," Miss Pickett mutters, but so low that Mrs. Flagg doesn't hear. (p. 243)

Told thus in outline, the thrust of the story is clear and hardly needs the insertion of a biblical quotation, "Better is a dinner of herbs where love is," (p. 239) to remind us of the contrast between empty word and bountiful deed. The mastery of its telling lies in the minute, nimble accommodations the characters make to shifting social circumstances, adjusting not only their expectations but their values according to what the moment brings. Mrs. Flagg's moral agility is obviously born of long practice. She is able to piously lecture Miss Pickett on the ethics of hospitality ("'T ain't what you give folks to eat so much as 't is makin' 'em feel welcome," p. 221) and a short while later entertain herself with visions of chicken pies, hints for which she had taken the precaution of dropping in the ear of Mrs. Timms. She packs overnight essentials in a big handbag but conceals them from Miss Pickett for fear that two handbags would appear obvious. She rejects Miss Pickett's

suggestion that they visit Nancy Fell when she sees no benefit to
herself, but later agrees when she perceives the promise of a meal.
She enjoys watching Mrs. Beckett's discomfiture at the sight of her
visitor, but later on is quite ready to go and call on her. Mrs. Flagg
is the quintessential courtier, one who will declare yon cloud very
like a whale or very like a camel or what you will, all the while
preserving a miraculously unshaken faith in her own rectitude. "I
can forgive a person," she remarks ominously as they leave Mrs.
Timms's door, ". . . but when I'm done with 'em, I'm done."
(p. 237) It is not in the power of Mrs. Timms, exalted though she
may be, to insult such a personage as Mrs. Flagg.

Cynthia Pickett, on the other hand, is always on slippery
ground. If Mrs. Flagg is changeable out of opportunism, Miss
Pickett is changeable out of weakness. Harboring reasonable doubts
about the genuineness of Mrs. Timms's invitation, she easily allows
herself to be half-bullied and half-persuaded by her stronger friend,
in part because she too has something to gain. She joins in laughing
at Mrs. Beckett's unwanted surprise and saves up the scene to tell
Mrs. Timms. Gentler and poorer than Mrs. Flagg, she is herself an
opportunist, and though her final remark suggests that she has
returned from her journey a little stronger than before, she still has
not the courage to speak out.

All three main characters are active church members, and the
biblical text is a comment on how little effect religion has on these
women, who are nevertheless quick to distinguish themselves from
someone of another "persuasion." The dinner at Nancy Fell's is one
of Jewett's communion feasts, replacing the denied cake and wine.
It is also a ritual of democracy, elevating the poor women while it
implicitly humbles the rich one—even if she herself is oblivious of
that fact.

The same themes are expressed in many other stories, among
them "The Town Poor," which also opens with two women of
disparate rank making a journey together. Like Mrs. Flagg and
Mrs. Timms, Mrs. Trimble is a wealthy woman of some influence
in town, while her companion, Rebecca Wright, is a spinster of
less means and status. Both are active church members, and they
are returning from witnessing the installation of a new minister
when they stop to call on the Bray sisters, who had been "bid off"
several months earlier.

The practice of auctioning off the indigent—that is, sending them to board with the lowest bidder—was evidently followed in South Berwick concurrently with the practice of maintaining a poor farm where they could all be housed under one roof. Jewett defended both systems to her friend Fanny Morse, who was outraged at the fate of the sisters in "The Town Poor." "I am afraid," she wrote,

> that there is nothing exaggerated about the Story of the
> Town Poor! but that system is far better, to my way of
> thinking than the one that prevails in New Hampshire,
> . . . [where] they gave up town farms and have county
> "farms." In Strafford county nearest us, there has been a mis-
> erable state of things—twice there have been dreadful fires
> in the buildings. . . . All these investigations and disclo-
> sures have made a slightly better state of things—but you
> put your finger on the cure when you wish for women visi-
> tors and inspectors, especially in country neighbourhoods.[1]

In other words, she felt that abuses were likely to occur on county-run farms, as opposed to either town farms or the bidding-off system, because they were out of sight of the former neighbors of the inmates. She would have liked to see the casework methods of the Associated Charities applied to the care of the poor, but she was not ready to accept the idea of the town supporting them in their own homes. Just why some of the poor were auctioned off and others sent to the poor farm is not clear. Perhaps it was a matter of the farm having only a limited number of beds. At any rate, Jewett was reluctant even after writing "The Town Poor" to admit that the auction system positively invited the kind of abuse documented in the story.

Mrs. Trimble and Miss Wright find the frail, elderly Bray sisters living in a chilly attic room in the house of a neglectful, shiftless farmer and his meeching wife. Pathetically glad to see visitors, the sisters have been housebound all winter for lack of "good stout shoes an' rubbers." (*Strangers and Wayfarers,* p. 52) No one from their church has come to see them, not even the minister. As for Mrs. Trimble and Miss Wright—one was laid up with pleurisy and the other was visiting relations when the sisters were bid off, and neither has thought to visit them at this out-of-the-way farm. Both are shocked and shamed at the sight of the sisters, who were schoolmates of one of them. The sisters themselves have forgotten their troubles in their pleasure at having company and serve up a spare Jewett feast of crackers, cold tea, a bit of cheese, and hoarded preserves. The New Testament allusion is explicit: Ann Bray, with her back to the window, stands at the head of the table "in a kind of aureole," and Mrs. Trimble, watching her, "thought of the text about two or three being gathered together, and was half afraid." (p. 56)

Like "The Guests of Mrs. Timms," this story revolves around the contrast between the word and the deed. On their way home, the visitors scold themselves for their negligence and plan their own kinds of action. Mrs. Trimble plans to raise enough money (partly from the town, partly from neighbors, and partly from her own income) to restore the Bray sisters' dispersed possessions and support them in their own home. Miss Wright is going to try to persuade the doctor to reset Ann Bray's lame arm and improve her sister's failing sight so that they can hook rugs or braid straw as they used to. And she threatens to "preach next Sunday, 'stead of the minister, an' I'll make the sparks fly." (p. 53)

The blame for the Bray sisters' plight is spread around among church, neighbors, and town government, but the largest share lies with men and male institutions. It falls especially on the sisters' late father, Deacon Bray, a brimstone Christian who donated so much money for new church pews that he had none to leave his daughters, and on the indifferent minister and selectmen. In a larger sense, it lies with the tendency of government (male, of course) to remove the poor from the sight of their neighbors: "What's everybody's business is nobody's business," Miss Wright complains (p. 53) in what might be a gloss on Jewett's letter. It is up to women to humanize the system and, like Mrs. Blackett, Mrs. Todd, and Nancy Fell, restore to religion the basic impulse of the larger motherhood. In other Jewett stories this impulse, as regards the poor, is still intact: Ma'am Stover in "By the Morning Boat" is an invalid pauper completely dependent on her neighbors, though she has lost none of her old authority in their eyes and holds "firm sway over the customs and opinions of her acquaintance." (*Strangers,* p. 209) Mrs. Price in "The Coon Dog" frankly lives by begging from her friends, and they think none the worse of her for that. "'T ain't much for a well-off neighborhood like this to support that old chirpin' cricket," one of them says. (*The Queen's Twin,* p. 173) When government takes over this responsibility it is women who must keep it honest. "I wish to my heart 't was to-morrow mornin' a'ready, an' I a-startin' for the selec' *men,*" says Mrs. Trimble with italics that are all her own. (p. 59)

While "The Town Poor" is mainly about the interdependence of the human community, it is also about the integrity of the individual, and about the problem of preserving that integrity as one ages. As is true in the earlier stories, this New England vision of community depends on the ability of each member to shoulder as much responsibility as possible, lest the "spiggits" of compassion run dry and the collective strength be exhausted. The elderly Bray sisters have worked as long as they could and have consented to lose their home because "they felt 't would come easier for all than for a few to help 'em." (p. 40) The horror of their plight lies not in their poverty but in their loss of both work and home, which to a Jewett character is a serious loss of identity. The home and the objects within it are the tangible history of a life, particularly of a woman's life; they are links with the past, and often they are all the evidence a woman has of her passage on earth. The Bray sisters have been set adrift, and their friends make a point of restoring not only their house but some remnants of their possessions and their work.

In "The Flight of Betsey Lane" Jewett presents a very different view of poverty, but with a similar emphasis on communal ties and the tension between dependence and independence. Here the setting is the town poor farm, an institution housing fewer than twenty (of whom seven are children), where everyone is part of a "strange family related only through its disasters." (*A Native of Winby,* p. 197) Except for the mother of the children, a widow who bitterly resents being there, the inmates are elderly townspeople who have worked as long as they could before being taken over by infirmity. Their idyllic little community is mysteriously free of the drunken, the violent, and the willfully unemployed. Several residents are seasonal, living at the farm only in winter and flitting from relative to relative all summer. There is no stigma attached to their pauperism, and the farm seems to serve much the same purpose as Social Security does today. The inmates belong to a class hierarchy mirroring that of the town, and Betsey Lane—having been housekeeper to the family of a widowed general—is near the top of it.

Betsey has come to the farm voluntarily, having "sensibly decided it was easier for the whole town to support her than for a part of it." (p. 181) It is Betsey's right to decide, and to retain some control over her life, upon which the story turns. When one of the general's daughters visits her and gives her a gift of money to spend as she chooses, she does just that. She has always had a hankering to travel and see the world, and while the money will not take her very far, it will pay her way to the 1876 Centennial Exhibition in Philadelphia. There she finds a sampling of all the places she has always wanted to see, and she comes home with stories enough to keep her fellow paupers entertained for months to come.

Betsey flees in secret, mystifying and alarming her friends. She has not told them about the money partly out of pique at being teased about her visitor, but partly because "she knew that everybody would offer advice or even commands about the spending or saving of it; and she brooked no interference." (p. 204) Among those who would offer advice would be the town selectmen, who might decide that she had no right to the money at all. Betsey's choice to flee is an act of defiance and a statement that, having worked hard all her life, she is her own person; and even during her flight she barters woman's work—sewing on buttons—to the male crew of a freight train in exchange for a ride. Her class pride is inextricably linked with her pride in her work and her independence, and when her rich visitor asks her if there is anything she needs, Betsey Lane asks for a looking glass.

The theme of autonomy achieved through work, then, as a counterpart to sympathy and mutual dependence, continues strong in the stories of the nineties. We meet a succession of elderly women farmers, most of them having been widowed early and raised their children alone. Among them are Mercy Bascom of "Fair Day," Mrs. Peet of "Going to Shrewsbury," Mrs. Tobin of "A Winter Courtship," Abby Hender of "A Native of Winby," and Abby Martin of "The Queen's Twin." Mrs. Trimble is a successful businesswoman, Esther Hight of "A Dunnet Shepherdess" has devised a better way of raising sheep, and little Katy Hilton of "The Hiltons' Holiday" is a "a real little farmer," even though her father wants her to be a teacher. (*Nancy,* p. 99) The comedy of "The Passing of Sister Barsett" hinges partly on the indignation of professional nurse Sarah Ellen Dow, whose place at her old patient's bedside has been usurped by invading relatives. She is feeling positively ill herself from the shock of it: "If I could ha' done as I wanted to I should be feelin' well enough, but to be set aside an' ordered about, where I'd taken the lead in sickness so much, an' knew how to deal with Sister Barsett so well!" (*Winby,* p. 149) It is not to be supported, and it takes all the diplomatic skill of her friend Mrs. Crane, plus deep cups of tea and generous helpings of hot shortcake and citron-melon preserves, to restore her temper.

Very few of the main characters in the late stories are young, or even middle-aged. Jewett's old people tended to age ahead of her, and vigorous octogenarians like Mrs. Blackett, Lavinia Dow, and the crippled, dictatorial Thankful Hight of "A Dunnet Shepherdess" maintain their place beside their gray-haired juniors, like Jewett's own great-aunts still presiding over four generations of Gilmans. Sometimes a valedictory theme emerges, a kind of stocktaking before death. "A Native of Winby," in which a renowned U.S. senator revisits his old village and sweetheart, is one of Jewett's less successful stories on this theme. Much better is "Fair Day," in which Mercy Bascom, a widow whose son and daughter-in-law have persuaded her to lease out her farm and live with them, steals back home one day when everyone else has gone to the fair. Like Betsey Lane, Mercy is a strong woman who undertakes her journey in secret, defying male authority and achieving a new level of self-understanding and peace of mind. She lost her drunken husband at twenty-eight and raised her children herself, he having "left but slight proofs of having ever existed at all, except in the stern lines and premature aging of his wife's face." (*Strangers,* p. 118) Now seventy-three, having lost both work and home, she is literally being coddled to death by her son and his wife, who leave her nothing to do but a little cooking and sewing.

Mercy cuts briskly across country to her old farm ("Runnin' away just like a young-one, that's what I be" [p. 127]). She finds the house empty, drinks from her own clear well, gathers some spice-apples, and eventually finds the key and half-guiltily, half-

triumphantly roams around inside, retrieving bit by bit pieces of
her own life that the house gives back to her: "It was like some
shell-fish finding its own old shell again and settling comfortably
into the convolutions. . . . She was not curious about the Browns'
worldly goods; indeed, she was nearly unconscious of anything but
the comfort of going up and down the short flight of stairs and
looking out of her own windows with nobody to watch." (pp. 133–
34) She recognizes a unity and achievement in her days that she
could not see when she was too busy living them. She also realizes
that she must regain some share of work and home: "The ground's
too rich for me over there to Tobias's," she thinks. "I don't want
things too easy, for my part. I feel most as young as ever I did,
and I ain't agoin' to play helpless, not for nobody." (p. 130) She
decides to come back to the farm, stay with the Browns, and help
out for a while. (Her welcome is assumed; in Jewett's world of
hardscrabble farming, live-in help is always needed.) Not to have
the ground too rich, to retain the old challenge of maintaining
one's lot and place, is necessary to survival; otherwise one's appointed task on earth is done and one might as well pack up and
leave. Mercy Bascom has settled her accounts and has even decided
to patch up a forty-year-old quarrel; but she has not prepared for
death so much as regained her strength for living.

While Betsey Lane achieves rejuvenation through travel real
and imaginary and Mercy Bascom achieves it through partly re-
gaining home and work, several other elderly characters achieve it
through courtship and marriage. The subject of matrimony, which
Jewett had portrayed sourly or coldly in earlier works like *A
Country Doctor, A Marsh Island,* and "The Courting of Sister Wisby,"
is seen more positively now that sexual identity and the loss of
autonomy and vocation are no longer issues for Jewett personally.
Courtship in the earlier works had often been a contest for power:
would Sister Wisby rule Deacon Brimblecom or the other way
around; would George Gerry rob Nan Prince of her vocation by
subjugating her in marriage; would Ann Floyd remake her feckless
younger suitor into an industrious husband. To some extent that
contest still goes on, but now the balance of power is in the hands
of women and is always benign. In "The Taking of Captain Ball,"
the old captain, though he is not technically married in the end,
is maneuvered into a pseudo-matrimonial partnership by a wily

middle-aged housekeeper who is also his niece. In "All My Sad Captains," a widow plays her three suitors off against one another, finally marrying Captain Witherspoon and dismissing the other two as swiftly and painlessly as any experienced courtesan. Husbands in this land of strong old women are not so much married as adopted: "Boys is boys, ain't they?" says Mrs. Stevens in "A Second Spring." "Men is boys," her sister-in-law replies. (*Nancy,* pp. 170–71) "They're nothin' but a pack o' child'n together," Mrs. Hilton reflects as she watches her husband and daughters drive off to town. (*Nancy,* p. 111) This is not necessarily an insult, for childlikeness is associated with gentleness and imagination. But obviously it reflects Jewett's sense of the power of womanhood. Feeling as Jewett herself felt toward her elderly male friends and toward her own grandfather in his later years, her women characters regard men neither as bedfellows nor as breadwinners but rather as large, amiable creatures blundering through the world, who "always want motherin' and somebody to come to." (*Nancy,* p. 171)

Since Jewett's elderly men rather enjoy the attention of their strong women (the women being as amiable as themselves), power is not an issue in these courtship stories. Nor, in general, is sex, though Fanny Tobin and Jefferson Briley of "A Winter Courtship" find that sharing the same buffalo robe on a cold day warms up the feelings considerable. Marriage is an alliance against loneliness; it is also an economic partnership, an implicit defense against the kind of displacement and threat to identity suffered by the Bray sisters. Thus Mrs. Tobin brings her farm to the marriage and Mr. Briley brings his savings and his earning power as a mail driver. Their courtship is conducted on two levels, one a coy exchange of compliments and the other a sober consideration of the practical advantages of joining forces. Habitually distrustful of words, they conduct their wooing in a creaky parody of the mating rituals of the young, and when Briley finally tires of the game and blurts out his honest opinion ("You know you covet me same's I do you"), Mrs. Tobin is only briefly offended and after a few minutes returns in kind: "I do' know's I should do better." (*Strangers,* pp. 14–15) Hardly less bluntspoken is Israel Haydon, finally driven to propose to his housekeeper by the prospect of losing her. "I never was a great talker," he explains, and then goes on to baldly outline the financial rewards of becoming his wife. (*Nancy,* p. 191) The housekeeper is of a romantic turn of mind and consents out of honest affection, but it is not until after they are married that she discovers the affection is returned.

In fact, none of these elderly unions, so bleakly contracted with their talk of money and land, is without its living current of emotion running underneath the crust of New England silence. Like the journeys of Betsey Lane and Mercy Bascom, they represent a rupture of hardened old boundaries, an expansion of the self to a larger sphere, and a reconnection to other lives. And like the journeys they are a source of physical rejuvenation and well-being. Maria Haydon's neighbors remark on her "fresher color and eager enjoyment of the comfort and dignity of the situation," (*Nancy,* p. 193) while Fanny Tobin's triumph at winning Jefferson Briley makes her feel "but twenty-five years of age." (*Strangers,* p. 16)

Another example of the revivifying effect of elderly courtship is the pair of stories about William Blackett and Esther Hight. Written after *The Country of the Pointed Firs,* "A Dunnet Shepherdess" and "William's Wedding" bring the narrator back to Dunnet Landing, where she becomes privy to William's long and patient wooing of Esther and eventually, during a second return, sees them achieve their long-postponed marriage. Esther and her mother live on a remote farm, on high, poor land that has defeated the neighboring farmers one by one. As silent and shy as William and like him belonging more to the natural world than the human one, Esther receives her suitor's annual visits for decades as both advance beyond middle age, she bound to her mother by ties of duty, he to his by ties of love. Finally old Mrs. Hight dies, and the sexogenarian lovers go off to live with Mrs. Blackett. "They were going to be young again now," the narrator observes (*The World of Dunnet Landing,* p. 338), and indeed they have regained their youth at every meeting through the years, like stiff old apple trees reminded into bloom. An afternoon in Esther's company makes William look "almost bold, and oddly like a happy young man rather than an ancient boy," while Esther with her "young blue eyes" in her lined face "might have been Jeanne d'Arc returned to her sheep." (pp. 245, 248)

The marriages in these late stories are hardly distinguishable from friendship, based as they are on affection lit by only the mildest of sexual afterglows. Jewett's persistent references to Esther

Hight's saintliness, which mar and finally spoil an otherwise promising story, dampen any suggestion of sex and finally make us see the couple as two incongruously gray-haired innocents, going home hand in hand to Mother Blackett. The transformation wrought on them, and on the Haydons, Fanny Tobin, and Jefferson Briley, is similar to the "transfiguring effect of friendship" that Jewett experienced in her own relationships with other women, except that it is milder. It lacks the intensity that characterizes, for example, the love between Kate and Helen in *Deephaven* or between the *Pointed Firs* narrator and Mrs. Todd. Heterosexuality in the old was as bewildering to Jewett as it was in the young, and she must have been relieved that the conventions of her time allowed her to escape depicting it except in an oblique and generally comic light. What her elderly lovers find with one another is a union that is transfiguring in the sense of two lives completing and changing one another, but it is a union that promises rest, not change. For Jewett's ideal of passionate friendship, the kind that can powerfully influence the course of a life, we must turn to her stories about women.

The 1897 story "Martha's Lady" is often cited as the best example of Jewett's portrayal of a transfiguring friendship. A clumsy young maid from the country, Martha, is permanently transformed by a brief acquaintance with a young city woman, Helen Vernon, who spends a few weeks one summer visiting Martha's mistress. Helen is the most vivid and thoroughly alive person Martha has ever seen, and she is kind to the girl, helps her learn her job, and shields her from the consequences of her mistakes. Martha falls in love with Helen, who is unconscious of the effect she creates. Although the two do not meet again until they are in their sixties, Martha lives her life according to what she imagines Helen would expect her to be, "trying to please the ideal, that is to say, the perfect friend." Outwardly she is one of Jewett's dull country people ("Nobody's life could seem duller to those who could not understand"), but privately her life is full of drama, since "she was capable of the happiness of holding fast to a great sentiment, the ineffable satisfaction of trying to please one whom she truly loved." (*The Queen's Twin*, p. 153)

Like friendship, marriage, and vocation, the power of the imagination is a means of extending the self beyond the limits of habit and external circumstance. Betsey Lane's imagination has taken her on many other journeys before she finally goes to the Centennial, so that although she enjoys the exhibition she is not astonished by it. "It is only unimaginative persons who can be really astonished. The imagination can always outrun the possible and actual sights and sounds of the world; and this plain old body from Byfleet rarely found anything rich and splendid enough to surprise her." (*Winby*, pp. 207–8) This does not detract from her delight but rather concentrates her attention. She sees everything, unlike "the indifferent, stupid crowd that drifted along, with eyes fixed at the same level, and seeing even on that level, nothing for fifty feet at a time." (p. 209) Martha of "Martha's Lady" keeps the imagined image of her beloved before her for forty years, while the Hiltons of "The Hiltons' Holiday" magnify an outing to a neighboring town into an experience that leaves the Hilton girls seeming "older and taller" at the end of the day. (*Nancy*, p. 125) Given meager material to work on, these New England minds make the best of what they have and transcend the conditions that hem them in.

The power of imagination is the central theme of "The Queen's Twin," one of the four Dunnet Landing stories Jewett wrote after *The Country of the Pointed Firs*. Mrs. Todd's old friend Abby Martin lives alone on a remote hill farm, having lost her husband early and raised her children by herself. She kept her spirits up during those difficult years by a fantasy born of a curious coincidence: she had been born on the same day and hour as Queen Victoria, and unknowingly had married a man named Albert and named her first two children Victoria and Edward. After she found out, she waited to name her other children (she had only two more) until she knew what the Queen had named hers. And over the years her relationship to the Queen has become a governing ideal in her life, just as Helen Vernon's image is to Martha. "I sometimes seem to have her all my own, as if we'd lived right together," she says. "I've often walked out into the woods alone and told her what my troubles was, and it always seemed as if she told me 't was all right an' we must have patience." (*The Queen's Twin*, p. 31) She confesses to having once carried her fantasy so far as to prepare all day for a visit from the Queen, making the beds up with her best sheets and blankets and preparing a special feast. As evening came on, the fantasy faded and she became depressed, but a foolish old cousin happened by, and Abby astonished her by giving her a splendid meal. "'T was childish of me to go and get supper," she says. But Mrs. Todd, having lost father, lover, and husband, answers, "I guess you wa'n't the first one who's got supper that way, Abby," and nothing more is said. (pp. 34–35)

Even Mrs. Todd has to admit that Abby "might be called a little peculiar," (p. 13) but her obsession extends her reach rather than constricting it, and so she is not to be classed with Captain Littlepage or the other self-imprisoned eccentrics at Dunnet Landing. In centering her life around a remote and impossible ideal, she has not left family and friends any poorer. Like Betsey Lane she is a citizen of the world, and like Martha she has overcome a dreary environment by constructing a larger one around it and comfortably inhabiting both.

Abby Martin's imagination is her consolation and her bridge to the rest of the world. The imagination of Mrs. Tolland in "The Foreigner" is both consolation and curse, allowing her to connect with far places but isolating her from the people around her. In this fine late story Jewett portrays more frankly than she has before the petty conventionality of a New England village and the cruelty with which country people can punish nonconformity. Mrs. Tolland's story is told by Mrs. Todd during one of the return visits of the narrator of *Pointed Firs*. Its events happened decades earlier, when Mrs. Todd was a young wife. Four Dunnet Landing sea captains, one of them Mrs. Todd's father, rescue a young French widow from harassment by a group of drunken men in Jamaica and bring her home to Maine, and one of them marries her. The village women are suspicious of the stranger, and while her husband is away voyaging she commits some social blunders (correcting the musical ineptness of some of the women, dancing in the vestry during a church social) that harden the general antagonism and leave her totally isolated. Only Mrs. Blackett, and Mrs. Todd at Mrs. Blackett's urging, befriend her.

The villagers' distrust of the foreigner is really a distrust of imagination and creativity. She sings and plays the guitar, she dances, she is skillful at embroidery and is an accomplished cook. She understands the curative properties of plants and is suspected of working charms. Worst of all, she is a Catholic and walks out

of meeting the only time she attends (out of unbearable homesick-
ness, Mrs. Todd believes). Like Jim Heron's fiddle in "The Courting
of Sister Wisby," Mrs. Tolland evokes traditional associations of art,
healing, and the supernatural, and the villagers' response is that of
Puritan to witch.[2]

Captain Tolland is lost at sea, and Mrs. Todd and her uncle
are delegated to tell his wife. It is evening, and as they approach
the house they find the best room lighted up and decorated with
garlands. The young Frenchwoman, wearing a gold chain, is playing her guitar and singing. She greets her visitors gaily and tells
them it is her fête day (which they do not understand). "An' there
she was, poor creatur'," Mrs. Todd remembers, "makin' believe have
a party all alone in her best room." (*Dunnet Landing,* p. 272) When
they tell her their news she collapses with a stroke, and she hovers
near death for a few days with Mrs. Todd watching her. At one
point a shadowy apparition appears in the doorway for an instant,
and both women see it. Mrs. Tolland recognizes it as her mother.
She dies a few minutes later, but not before receiving Mrs. Todd's
assurance that she saw the figure too.

The symbolic and structural complexity of "The Courting of
Sister Wisby" are recalled in this story, which most critics agree is
one of Jewett's strongest. What is most important in the context
of this discussion is the all-encompassing reach of Mrs. Tolland's
imagination, which is capable of extracting from its spare surroundings all the ordinary joys the villagers reject and can create its own
company, reach across the ocean and across time, and even bridge
the void between the living and the dead. The ghost of the mother
is not illusory, since Mrs. Todd sees it too; but it appears only to
minds that have the sympathetic and imaginative capacity to see
it. Thus it is visible not only to the daughter, who is drawn to the
mother by love, but to her friend, who also loves the girl and whose
mind is also wide-ranging and free. Physically imprisoned by the
village, the foreigner is a citizen not only of this world but of the
universe, and it is the villagers who are real prisoners, shut inside
their barren religion and encrusted prejudice like Captain Littlepage behind his window.

Jewett's main preoccupation as a writer, then, remains the
theme of transcendence explored in *Deephaven.* But except for "The
Foreigner," these stories are less complex than those written before

The Country of the Pointed Firs. The mystical intensity of the earlier years, with its suggestion of the active personal influence of the dead and the immanent presence of the Deity in nature and human affairs, recedes somewhat as the writer focuses less on her characters' relationship to God and more on their relationship to one another. Open references to fate and the supernatural are fewer, while the number of Christian references increases, in the form of biblical verses scattered throughout the stories and the use of obvious Christian symbols, some of them gratuitous and poorly integrated, like the scarecrow-cross in "The Flight of Betsey Lane" or the lamb Esther carries in "William's Wedding."

The meeching are as absurd as ever. Sister Barsett of "The Passing of Sister Barsett" is a meecher of real distinction: "She has been the first to have all the new diseases that's visited this region. I know she had the spinal mergeetis months before there was any other case about." (*Winby,* p. 144) Her neighbors are hard put to find anything good to say about her, even when they think she is dead. Most of the other elderly people in these stories do not talk about the need to stand in their lot and place, since they have already done so. Indeed, the only open use of the term is distorted, when Israel Haydon refuses all help after his wife dies and insists that he must "stand in my lot and place" alone. Here New England courage is a mask for pure stubbornness, and God's will is used as an excuse to withdraw: "The impossibility of forming new habits of life . . . made a wall about his very thoughts." (*Nancy,* pp. 165, 167) But like other immured characters, Israel eventually breaks free.

Nature remains both an immanent power and an embracing presence. It encloses "The Hiltons' Holiday" in scenes of evening tranquillity, the landscape merging into the character of gentle John Hilton, "a creature of the shady woods and brown earth, instead of the noisy town." (*Nancy,* p. 97) His daughter Katy is like him, and like Sylvia of "A White Heron" and William Blackett: "shy with new folks," a child who will "stand an' hark to a bird the whole forenoon." (pp. 100–101) Topham Corners, the town they visit, is a harmless and indeed necessary element in Katy's education. But increasingly in the late stories the noisy town and its alienating, exploitive image become an explicit threat, and the symbolic hunter of "A White Heron," who was only a thoughtless and kindly young man who went away again, becomes an actively evil character like Ferris of "A Neighbor's Landmark." Ferris is a timber dealer who, as Jewett says in words that have a contemporary resonance,

> always stripped land to the bare skin; if the very huckle-
> berry bushes and ferns had been worth anything to him, he
> would have taken those, insisting upon all or nothing, and,
> regardless of the rights of forestry, he left nothing to grow;
> no sapling-oak or pine stood where his hand had been.
> (*Nancy,* p. 254)

The two giant pines threatened with destruction in this story are representative of the very fabric of the human, natural, and supernatural order, as well as the collective memory that maintains that order. In her anger Jewett comes close to endowing them—as she has endowed other trees she has known—with a sentience they neither need nor deserve:

> The great pines could remember all the Packers, if they
> could remember anything; they were like some huge ar-
> chaic creatures whose thoughts were slow and dim. . . . It
> must have been that the great live things felt their responsi-
> bility as landmarks and sentinels.

A link between man and nature and a physical embodiment of the past, they are also (as a reference to the biblical verse forbidding the removal of landmarks suggests) a symbol of the relationship between man and God. Continuity and unity in one, "they stood and grew in their places, while a worldful of people lived and died, and again and again new worldfuls were born and passed away, and still these landmark pines lived their long lives, and were green and vigorous yet." (pp. 256–57) They are saved, but only just; and to a modern reader the Victorian melodrama of the timing seems not entirely far-fetched.

"A Neighbor's Landmark" is not one of the better stories of this decade, though its very lack of subtlety makes it an easy example. It would be nice to be able to point to a steady progression in quality over the years as Jewett marched along from

Deephaven through *The Country of the Pointed Firs,* but in fact the quality of her work remained uneven. Sentimentality remained her most besetting sin, as she still felt obliged, even in her better stories, to remind her readers what they ought to feel. She has most difficulty with stories in which she has evidently decided to extend her range, or with stories written around a particular setting. As has been said, a crumbling New England farmhouse would generate characters in her head of itself; and she seems to have tried to summon up this genie from a variety of places she casually passed through: Beaufort and the Sea Islands, which she and Annie had visited in 1888; St. Augustine; Ireland. One story ("A War Debt") was written about Virginia before she visited it and is probably based on John Tucker's war memories. All of the stories written this way are failures, the southern ones showing in addition a strong, off-putting identification with dispossessed slaveholders.

No doubt her friends and readers praised them all. One of the most significant factors in Jewett's lack of growth as a writer must be the adulation of her friends and the dearth of intelligent criticism she received. As a beginning writer she had had Howells and Scudder to help her move in the right direction; but as a mature writer she either had grown beyond the range of their criticism or never thought to ask for it. The modest expectations of the periodical reader therefore became her own, and her father's early advice to tell things as they really are never was helped by the later reinforcement it needed. When she reached beyond herself and produced *The Country of the Pointed Firs* or a story on the level of "The Foreigner" or "The Queen's Twin," she was not able to analyze the work and see where its strengths lay—or indeed to recognize that it had unusual strengths at all. It is too bad, for she had early shown a capacity to absorb criticism easily and learn from it.

Still, the 1890s saw the emergence of a sturdy dozen or more stories that have seized the imagination of several generations of readers, despite the efforts of literary naysayers, and that with their forerunners illuminate the themes and symbolism of *The Country of the Pointed Firs.* After the criticism of the last two decades, it is no longer possible to describe them merely as quaint depictions of rural folk whose way of life has become extinct. Nor is it possible to see them as disparate and accidental. Thematically Jewett's stories form a coherent whole, expressing concerns about spiritual alienation, social fragmentation, commercial exploitation, and the failure of the national memory that not only are still relevant but are increasingly so. In works from *Deephaven* on, she recalls us to a sense of community: not only the obvious kind of neighbor-helping-neighbor community but the larger family that includes all living things, as well the forebears who have shaped our society and the children who will inherit it. And her characterizations of strong women, old women, strong old women are unique in American literature. "Thee knows I am one of thy old women," wrote fortunate Sally Kaign. Many of us are not yet, but hope to be.

23

The Tory Lover

I T W A S I N 1 8 9 9 T H A T J E W E T T E X -
pressed to her former minister her faith that not only was the world
growing more comfortable but that people were, on the whole,
better than they had been in earlier years. Yet she fumed over the
greedy developers, the get-rich-quick artists, the growing hordes
of the poor, and the sorry procession of corrupt governments in
Washington—all of which contributed to a widening sense of
malaise, a loss of communal cohesion on a national scale, and a
general cultural amnesia that had long distressed contemporaries
like Charles Eliot Norton and Henry Adams. It was this malaise,
at least in part, that fed the growing interest in historic restoration,
the taste for expatriate living or at least long sojourns abroad, the
nostalgic allusions in American architecture, and a spate of historical novels, of which *The Tory Lover* was one.

This novel, which takes place mainly in South Berwick and
England, is set in an earlier period than Jewett had depicted in her
other stories and is about the bloody and painful processes by which
a new country had defined its identity. Thirty-five years earlier she
had seen that identity reaffirmed at the cost of yet more pain and
blood, and as the century ended she may have felt that America's
sense of itself was again slipping away. She loved the new comforts
and innovations the nineteenth century had brought—among them
Boston's new subway and the telephone, now augmenting the daily
exchange of letters between Boston and Berwick. Best of all was

that enchanting new toy the automobile, which horse-loving Sarah welcomed without any intimation of what it meant for thousands of gentle beasts and quiet roads. Yet even her serene and optimistic spirit was affected, as stories like "A Neighbor's Landmark" and "The Failure of David Berry" attest, by the darkening of the national mood.

As we have seen, Jewett lived very much from day to day and was never given to weighty ponderings, and she was not one to knit the evidence of the time into some sort of fabric of seamless gloom. Her life was as near the ideal of comfort and fulfillment as chronic disease would allow, and added to the advantages of wealth and fame was the comforting encirclement of friends, most of them wealthy and famous too, who insulated her from many unpleasant realities. But she had the experience of Annie's work and the daily frustrations her friend brought home to remind her of the fragility of the social structure built by the generation of her great-grand-parents. In the years when she wrote *Deephaven,* her work had sprung as much from pure affection for the disappearing elders as from any presentiment of what their disappearance meant to the larger society. In later work, especially *The Country of the Pointed Firs,* there is a more urgent and poignant sense of loss. Mrs. Todd and the Bowdens, containing ages in themselves, represent the basic values and collective memory of the society. "Pay attention to them," the subtext of the book tells us, "and once you have recognized them do not let them go."

The Tory Lover was serialized in *The Atlantic* in 1900–1901 and soon afterwards published in book form. In this novel Jewett returns to the disappearing elders—to those, in fact, who disap-peared even before her time but whose stories were kept alive by children and grandchildren and by the buildings and objects they left behind. The book is first of all a homage to her own village and its part in the War of Independence. But by focusing on the point at which each American had to decide not to be English, and by portraying sympathetically the attachment to England and showing the process by which the ties of family and allegiance had to be unraveled or torn, she was also emphasizing a connection between old and new that has nothing to do with politics. There is no magic in *The Tory Lover,* no transcendental intimations and no hints of ghosts or primeval deities. God is mentioned only as an object of perfunctory worship. It is a conventional historical novel with the usual amount of skullduggery and hairbreadth escapes. But it is not a radical departure for Jewett because, like earlier works, it is about reconciliation and continuity.

The book has always disappointed critics, and not without reason, for its main characters never really come to life. Modern scholars have tended to dismiss it as a potboiler hastily tossed off at the twin suggestions of Houghton Mifflin and Charles Dudley Warner.* But there is evidence in the letters that Jewett had been working on the novel for several years, and that elements of its theme had been developing even earlier. In a larger sense, she had been preparing to write it all her life.

The story is about a young upper-class man, Roger Wallingford, who despite lingering Tory sympathies volunteers to serve as lieutenant aboard John Paul Jones's *Ranger* in 1777. His reasons are not entirely clear, but in the beginning, anyway, they have much to do with his love for the staunchly patriotic Mary Hamilton. In the course of the voyage he and Paul Jones become friends and Roger becomes fully committed to the American cause, but through the treachery of a villainous crew member he is captured during the *Ranger*'s 1778 raid on the English port of Whitehaven. He is sent to the infamous Mill Prison at Plymouth. Mary Hamilton and his mother travel to England to try to obtain his release, but meanwhile he escapes and hides on the moors. Through various means too complicated to relate here, he and Mary are finally reunited and return to America.

The novel is historically accurate in many respects, especially in the personality of John Paul Jones and the career of the *Ranger* from the time she left Portsmouth in November 1777 through the Whitehaven raid. The names of many of the crew members reflect those Paul Jones recruited from Berwick, Portsmouth, and surrounding communities, and the mutinous first mate is based on a historical figure of the same name. But Jewett felt free to take liberties with other aspects of her story. There was a Lieutenant Wallingford on board the *Ranger*, for example, but he was Samuel

---

* Cary, for example, says, "Scudder seems to have prompted her to act on Charles Dudley Warner's suggestion that she write an historical novel about John Paul Jones's activities in Maine." All Jewett herself said about Warner's role is that he gave her the "final push." (Cary, *Letters*, pp. 92 n., 95)

Richard Wallingford from Portsmouth, not Roger from Rollinsford. Mary Hamilton was Jonathan Hamilton's first wife, not his
sister, and Hamilton House, where the novel begins, had not yet
been built in 1777.*

In her choice of setting and characters in these opening scenes
we can see Jewett's use of local landmarks and names that had held
personal significance for her since childhood. The first was Hamilton House, which she loved only a little less than her own birthplace. Not only was it beautiful with the kind of serene, classical
beauty she associated with the Constitution and the philosophical
basis of democracy, but it belonged to the river and looked out
toward Europe, representing those multiple associations of order
and harmony between peoples, and between man and nature, that
she always held dear. Similarly, most of the men she introduces in
the opening scenes were founders of Berwick Academy, and one of
them (Tilly Haggens) also lived in Jewett's own house. In order to
assemble them for her scene she had to award Parson John
Thompson his Berwick pulpit six years before he actually left his
previous one. Founded in 1791, Berwick Academy is not mentioned in the book, nor is there any reason why it should be; but
by bringing these men together to support the Revolution, and
especially by bringing in Thompson, who was the primary founder
of the Academy, Jewett seems to be privately acknowledging the
crucial relationship between education and the young republic—a
relationship that was expressed not only in her own town but in
many others that established academies at the end of the eighteenth
century.

Other people and places whose stories she had known all her
life are scattered through the novel. We have seen that her great-
great-aunt Charlotte Gilman had once been married to Jonathan
Hamilton, and Sarah's diary soon after her eighteenth birthday
recorded the day her father brought home a portrait of that gentleman, "the great man of Berwick . . . a hundred years ago—more
I guess," she noted with a fine disregard for arithmetic.[1] She
thought then that a century was "a *tre* mendous while," but its

---

* Jewett may not have known that Hamilton House was built after the
Revolution. In her 1881 essay "River Driftwood" she envisioned John Paul Jones
visiting it in 1777, prefiguring the scene in the novel. The essay, of course, was
intended to be historically correct.

span seemed to decrease steadily as she grew older and discovered more reminders of people who had lived before her: the writing on the window of Hamilton house, scratched by a bored youngster in 1802; the story of the abduction of Hetty Goodwin by Indians, as told by Mrs. Jewett's close friend Sophia Goodwin; Sarah's friends the Barrell sisters, who lived in the house of their Tory great-grandfather surrounded by mementos of the 1745 siege of Louisbourg. History nestled comfortably among the papers in the library secretary, where her grandfather's records of Lafayette's visit lay, or in the attic among letters written during the War of 1812. During her childhood her grandfather's wharves rotted away within sight of Hamilton House, and in an old burying-ground at the Wallingford house (birthplace of her childhood friend Madam Cushing), she copied the inscriptions on the graves of Roger Plaisted and his sons, killed during an Indian raid in 1675. Near them was the grave of Elizabeth Wiatt, who died in 1713 at the age of eighteen, "a very beautiful and accomplished girl, according to some old lady who told father about her."[2] Jewett did Elizabeth the favor of resurrecting her, young and beautiful and sixty-four years out of her time, in Chapter IV of *The Tory Lover*. Roger Plaisted is remembered in the first name of her novel's hero.

Except for *A Country Doctor, The Tory Lover* is the most autobiographical of all Jewett's books, but unlike the earlier novel it is not autobiographical in the sense of rehearsing an individual life. Rather it is a kind of reference list of people and places that had helped her locate herself in the world and formed her characteristically personal sense of history. To borrow a phrase she once used to Willa Cather, they had all teased her mind over years, waiting for their time to be written.* Many of them had appeared in the Berwick essays, beginning in 1881 with "River Driftwood." Through them and others like them she had gained that consciousness of the past as a living and informing presence that underlies nearly everything she wrote. The past in *The Tory Lover* is only a century old, while the past evoked in *The Country of the Pointed Firs* is far more ancient; but they are links in the same human chain.

* "The thing that teases the mind over and over for years and at last gets itself put down rightly on paper—whether little or great, it belongs to Literature." Willa Cather, preface to *The Country of the Pointed Firs and Other Stories*.

Three historical figures that had long fascinated Jewett are sources for major characters in *The Tory Lover*. The first is John Sullivan, the original of the "Master Sullivan" whose letters Mary Hamilton carries to England. The real John Sullivan, like the character in the book, was descended from an aristocratic Irish family who had been exiled to France for their Jacobite sympathies. Young John left France for America around 1723, married an Irish peasant woman, and began his new life in York, Maine, probably as an indentured servant. After a few years he moved to Berwick, where—as in the novel—he became a legendary schoolmaster. Two of his sons, both mentioned in *The Tory Lover*, contributed largely to his adopted country—one as a general, the other as a jurist and historian, and both as governors of New Hampshire. Henry Dearborn, a relation of Jewett's great-grandfather, had served with Gen. John Sullivan at Valley Forge, and she had long been fascinated by the romantic history of the Sullivans and had wanted to write their story in some substantial way.[3] She had mentioned them in "The Old Town of Berwick" in 1894, but that had not given her scope enough. The romance of their origins (complete with ruined castles, the names of which she knew), the marriage of aristocratic rank and hardy peasant, the rise of the American sons from schoolmasters' children to national leaders, and the modesty and scholarship of the old man all appealed to her sense of the national mythology.

A second character that had long teased her imagination was Benjamin Thompson, Count Rumford. He too was distantly connected to her own family. His daughter—Sarah, Countess of Rumford—finished her days in Concord, New Hampshire, and Sarah Orne Jewett grew up hearing stories about her from Aunt Lucretia Perry, who was her cousin. Countess Rumford in old age was almost as eccentric as Lady Ferry or Miss Chauncey and may have contributed to both characters. But the life of her father, the Count, was a historical novel in itself. Born into a Massachusetts farming family in 1753, Thompson was a mathematical and scientific prodigy who opened his own academy in Concord, New Hampshire, at the age of seventeen. During the next few years he closed his school, married a wealthy widow, and became very friendly with New Hampshire's Tory governor and his circle. When hostilities broke out with England his loyalties were questioned, and though he offered his services to the patriots, his house was mobbed and he was forced to flee to England, leaving behind his wife (from whom he was now separated) and their infant daughter. He enlisted in the British army and after the war served brilliantly in various military and civil capacities under both the King of England and the Elector of Bavaria. He turned his hand to almost anything, from military strategy to the abolition of pauperism, but his most lasting accomplishments were scientific, and he eventually founded the Royal Institution in London. He was knighted by George the Third and was made a count of the Holy Roman Empire by the Elector. He chose the title Count Rumford, after the original name of Concord. Forgiven by Americans, who elected him to the Academy of Arts and Sciences, he always planned to return to New England but never quite managed to do so.

Like the Sullivans, the Thompsons interested Jewett over a period of years, probably from the mid-1880s. In 1890 she apparently wrote a paper on the Countess that has since been lost,[4] and she intended to write about the Count as well, but other projects intervened. Her notes about him express her regret that his talents were lost to his country, and also a sympathy for those who, like him, wavered and ended up on the other side:

> His fellow New Englanders could not then believe in the honest opinions of those who sided with the mother country. It is only of late years that we have begun to understand the deep sorrow which that great war made in many a loyal conservative heart whose every instinct flew toward patience and delay and the interference and pacification of statesmanship rather than the provocation of such a bloody quarrel.[5]

Count Rumford's political ambivalence—-though not his brilliant and erratic personality—finally found fictional expression in the character of Roger Wallingford. Clearly Jewett means us to understand, through Roger's vacillation, the anxiety of honestly perplexed English subjects who were slow to disengage old loyalties and who hoped the quarrel could be smoothed over. Jewett claimed Tories among her own forebears, and the Barrell sisters' great-grandfather in York was stripped of his various offices and at one point threatened with mob violence. He appealed to Judge Benjamin Chadbourne, one of Madam Wallingford's rescuers in *The Tory Lover,* to prevent it, and Chadbourne apparently did.

The third major character, that of John Paul Jones, had the longest gestation. Jewett heard about him in childhood from an elderly patient of her father's who actually had served on the *Ranger.* Years later "the peppery little Captain . . . a little wasp of a fellow, with a temper like a blaze of . . . gunpowder" appeared in "River Driftwood," where she imagined him visiting the Hamiltons and Wallingfords. In 1894–95 she began seriously preparing to write about him, consulting "nice dusty books" in the Boston Athenaeum[6] and traveling to New York in December 1895 to read one of his ship's logs. "My mind is running so on the Paul Jones story that I hate to do anything else in the world but write it," she wrote afterwards to Mary,[7] but her Caribbean cruise and illness prevented her beginning the novel for some time. She wrote a "good piece of it" around 1897,[8] then put it aside again until, encouraged by the publication of two other novels set in the Revolutionary period,* she finally finished it in 1900.

John Paul Jones was a Scottish gardener's son who ran away to sea as a boy and, after a brilliant but tempestuous career in the infant American navy, died in obscurity in France in 1792. Widely recognized now as a crucially important figure in naval history, he was slighted and patronized by the American government while he lived and never received adequate acknowledgment of his services. Samuel Eliot Morison's modern biography confirms his small physical stature, charming manners, dandyism, irascibility (he once kicked a lieutenant of the *Ranger* downstairs), and susceptibility to women. Jewett's portrait of him was anticipated in Churchill's *Richard Carvel* (1899), but Churchill makes him a half-comic figure who speaks braw Scots and is absurdly obsessed with clothes. Jewett's depiction of the man is more romanticized but brings out the essential weaknesses of hypersensitivity and ill temper. Generous to a fault, Jones paid his surly crew out of his own pocket when the government withheld funds (only to have his draft dishonored); later he was instrumental in obtaining the exchange of 288 Americans held by the English at the Mill and Fortin prisons.

* *Hugh Wynne: Free Quaker* (1896) by S. Weir Mitchell and *Richard Carvel* (1899) by American novelist Winston Churchill.

Like the Sullivans and Count Rumford, Paul Jones was a real-life swashbuckler, a historical character who easily matched anything a novelist's fantasy could conjure up. Like the Sullivans he was a Celt with a grudge against England, and like both the Sullivans and Benjamin Thompson he was an example of the new, self-created American, someone who rose from poverty to brilliant achievement through sheer native talent and who reconciled in himself wide polarities of class, being both farmer and gentleman. Jewett may have been drawn to all of them by their very contradictions, which mirrored the contradictions of nationality, class, and allegiance that had to be resolved in the making of the new American identity. All these men, like Roger Wallingford, belong as much to the Old World as to the New, and their lives were a study in the process of becoming an American. (Even Thompson, estranged from his country, had been formed by it and never renounced it.) Herself strongly drawn to England and conscious of an English legacy both cultural and physical, she tried to dramatize in her novel not only the necessary rupture between England and America but the ties that survived the rupture and that gradually would strengthen and be healed.

While the political divisions in the novel are represented by men, the overriding theme of unity between people is represented by women. The two main female characters, Mary Hamilton and Roger's mother, Madam Wallingford, are strongly committed to their respective sides but put aside their political opinions in their concern for Roger and one another. They maintain their convictions, each respecting those of the other, and in their peacemaking journey from New World to Old they represent the joining of the present to the past and the shared traditions that will survive the war.

Written by the conscious will rather than from the deeper sources that gave her *The Country of the Pointed Firs*, *The Tory Lover* meant more to Jewett precisely *because* she had put it together as an assemblage of personal associations. She was completely oblivious to its flaws. Although some scenes work well, the main characters except for Paul Jones are stiff and the plot seems contrived even by the standards of the genre. Jewett received many positive letters about it, but gentle complaints came in from her friends, the best known being that of Henry James. It was almost impossible, he said, for a modern writer to "*think* a man, a woman—or rather fifty—whose own thinking was intensely otherwise conditioned [than your own]. You have to simplify back by an amazing tour de force—and even then it's all humbug." He begged her to "go back to the dear country of the Pointed Firs, *come* back to the palpable present *intimate* that throbs, responsive, and that wants, misses, needs you, God knows, and that suffers woefully in your absence."⁹ Jewett accepted the criticism with her customary grace. "I am not so much disappointed by your not caring for the Tory Lover, as if I had not known that other very kind readers did not care for it either," she wrote to one friend. "I cannot believe that so much of my heart was put into it without some life staying there—I could not have died until I got it done!"¹⁰ The valedictory note is a little startling, but it is clear that, whatever its faults in the eyes of the world, its author saw *The Tory Lover* as a completion and a summing-up.

24

Last Years

ON SEPTEMBER 3, 1902, THE SWAMP maples around the river marshes in South Berwick were beginning to flare into color, one here and one there, scarlet torches above the black water. Along the roadsides purple asters and yellow goldenrod rioted discreetly, while the bracken ferns, beginning to fade and dry, filled the woods with their spicy fragrance. It was Sarah's fifty-third birthday and the beginning of her favorite time of year, and she took her sister, Rebecca Young, and another friend for a drive.

They were descending a hill when the horse slipped on a loose stone and stumbled. The carriage lurched, and both Sarah and Rebecca were thrown out. Rebecca was only bruised, but Sarah suffered a concussion and some damage to the neck, perhaps a fractured vertebra, that was never clearly diagnosed.

The immediate effects of pain and dizziness kept her in bed for weeks. Annie came to stay until she seemed to be improving and then went home. A few weeks later, at a Boston Symphony performance on October 24, Annie suddenly pitched forward in her seat, falling onto Isabella Stewart Gardner, who was sitting ahead of her. It was up to Mrs. Gardner, who went home with Annie and spent the night, to write to Sarah and tell her that Annie had been overtired after a busy day (she was entertaining the British feminist Isabel [Lady Henry] Somerset) and had fainted. All she needed was rest and quiet, and Sarah was not to worry. In fact

Annie, apparently overwrought with anxiety over Sarah, had had a mild stroke.

Annie's condition was not serious, but all the same it was nearly three months before she ventured downstairs. The worst of this period for each friend was her worry over the other, and Theodore (who was now a medical student) began spending nights at Charles Street and helping Annie's nurses so that he could carry firsthand reports to Sarah on weekends. Gradually they both improved. By Thanksgiving Sarah felt well enough to eat dinner with the family, and in April 1903 she was able to go to Boston and Manchester for a visit.

As more time went by, however, it became clear that she had been hurt more severely than had been thought. In October 1903, more than a year after the accident, she wrote the novelist and neurologist S. Weir Mitchell that she was staying in bed, feeling "verry 'Dumpy' and confused or creeping out into the old garden with a stick—walking zig-zag and swaying about."[1] Her doctors spoke of Time: "You know how tiresome such cases can be to *doctor and patient,*" she confided in her doctor-to-doctor voice.* To nonmedical friends she was less candid, trying to put the best face on her condition; but she continued to suffer from stabbing pains in her head and neck, memory loss, dizziness, and inability to concentrate for nearly four years after the accident. There were periods when she could not read and was reduced to sewing and crocheting. She managed to write letters, but serious writing was out of the question. Train rides or any kind of jolting brought on pain, so that she always had to pay for her trips to and from Boston.

In December 1903 Annie went abroad for four months, probably on doctors' advice. Sarah stayed alone at Charles Street for a while and rather enjoyed being sole mistress of the domain, but then she went to stay with Susan Cabot, who wanted to take care

---

* Mitchell was the author of *Hugh Wynne: Free Quaker,* a historical novel whose publication had encouraged Jewett to write *The Tory Lover.* A paradoxical figure from a feminist point of view, he counted many distinguished women among his friends, among them Dean Agnes Irwin of Radcliffe, but disapproved of higher education for women. He invented the infamous rest cure inflicted on Charlotte Perkins Gilman and Virginia Woolf, among others; Howells's daughter Winifred died under his misguided care. But he was ahead of his time in acknowledging that physical illness could be psychogenic.

of her. The combination of that old friend's solicitude and evening whist parties proved too much for her, and Mary rescued her on a pretext in March. The sisters went straight to Baltimore, where Sarah underwent treatments at Johns Hopkins under the famous neurologist Dr. William Osler. They seem to have helped very little, and that summer she was packed off to the Merrimans' in New Hampshire for a rest cure, while Annie—who had collapsed with the flu on her return—remained in Manchester. A few weeks later Mary Jewett, driving in South Berwick, was thrown from a carriage in an accident weirdly similar to Sarah's two years earlier, though luckily she was only bruised. Altogether 1904 was a thoroughly wretched year, with very little to recommend it. And in June Sarah Whitman died.

Although she had been suffering from heart disease for some time, Whitman's death was a severe shock to her friends. "She leaves a dreadful vacuum in Boston," said William James, who was one of her pallbearers. "All of Boston—I mean the few whom we know—had gone out" to the funeral at Trinity Church.[2] The day before the funeral she lay in state in her Mount Vernon Street house like a figure in a pre-Raphaelite painting, robed in white with long, straight folds, surrounded by candles in high sconces, her hands crossed on her heart, with lilies at her head and feet and white Canterbury bells above her. People brought their children and knelt as if to a saint—which to some she almost was. It was a scene Whitman herself would have appreciated, but Sarah had to rely on friends' descriptions, being too ill to go.

No one except Annie and Mary was dearer to Sarah than Sarah Whitman. No one was more unreservedly affectionate and generous, nor—in spite of all the conflicting demands she placed on herself—was any other creative person Sarah knew more dedicated to her craft. It was immediately after Whitman died that Sarah was ordered to New Hampshire, where she and a nurse took over the Merrimans' summer house for several weeks while their hosts traveled. It is impossible to guess how much this loss, which followed hard on Annie's spring illness, aggravated Sarah's illness that summer, but something besides her physical condition seems to have severely shaken her and brought her close to emotional breakdown. Like any rest-cure patient, she was forbidden to read or write (though her new nurse, Miss O'Bryan, won her immediate

trust by producing a smuggled copy of Alice Meynell's poems).
Helen Merriman, reporting on her condition in August, advised
Mary not to "go over the past, or her health, in any way, nor discuss
plans—and *most* particularly I would avoid telling her of any small
events of daily life that have only a temporary significance. Large
simple quiet things are best for her, and but few of those. If she
can be kept from too much activity and from spending too much
sympathy, I am sure she will accumulate strength and gain faster
and faster."[3] Later Sarah herself confessed to Annie that "some of
the trees I *hated* last summer—I used to feel as if they were coming
at me! but at last I went out in the dusk by myself before I came
away and got over that!"[4] If Sarah Orne Jewett had been brought
to the point of hating trees she must have been in a perilous state;
but like her early diary confession of rage, this is a fugitive reference
and otherwise her letters show only her rational, normal self.

It was not until the summer of 1906 that she regained "some
sense of pleasure in life," though she still felt "like a dissected map
with a few pieces gone."[5] She was still unfit for writing, though
she jotted down notes and bits of dialogue on scraps of paper as
she always had. One task for which she did feel well enough was
writing a preface for a volume of Sarah Whitman's letters that was
published in 1907. The actual selection of letters apparently was
done by someone else, a Miss Foster, who edited them so heavily
as to deprive them of almost all life. But even in their enervated
state they do suggest, as Sarah writes in her preface, "the high
pressure at which she lived. Yet no one ever found her too occupied
to listen to the call of friendship, for to her its master word was
service." She approvingly quotes one of Whitman's friends who,
hearing a complaint that her art suffered from her devotion to
friendship and worthy causes, answered, "Ah, but she has made the
choice between living for Art's sake and living for Love's sake, and
we must not quarrel with that."[6] Clearly Jewett, who herself had
been able to lead a life perfectly balanced between art and love,
agreed that Whitman had sacrificed wisely for a higher good. The
obituary in a Boston paper was insultingly dismissive: "She was
one of the women on whom we have been accustomed to rely for
counsel and cooperation when anything artistic of a public or
semi-public nature has been undertaken here. And she was always
helpful."[7]

By the time the Whitman letters were published, Sarah was fairly well recovered and had even resumed some pleasure driving, though she preferred winter sleighing to bumping over summer roads. She took some short sailing cruises with friends, revisiting the pointed firs country and finding relief in the smooth motion of the boat. Whitman's death was only one of a number of losses the decade brought, two of the worst being those of Thérèse Blanc and Susan Burley Cabot, both in 1907. Thérèse had been ailing for some time and her death was not unexpected. Mrs. Cabot had sprung up from her deathbed with cap-ribbons flying so many times that it seemed incredible that her old enemy had finally wrestled her to the ground. She left Sarah a generous legacy and her hereditary membership in Boston's venerable private library, the Boston Athenaeum.

Other old friendships deepened, among them that with Julia Ward Howe. Howe and Annie Fields had had their differences decades earlier, when Howe had written a rather too candid review of one of Annie's poems. But advancing age, along with a certain sense of growing alliance as guardians of the past, increasingly brought them together. Doughty and puckish as ever, though rather deaf and not always able to summon the voice for yet another dinner-party rendition of "The Battle Hymn of the Republic," Mrs. Howe published her *Reminiscences* at the age of eighty-one and still was much called upon to lecture, particularly at the chapters of the Federated Women's Clubs that she had helped found. She had become a kind of national monument, a visible symbol like Queen Victoria (whom she somewhat resembled) of the country's history. Wryly she put up with the infirmities of age, accepting the cane Sarah sent for her eighty-third birthday in the lighthearted spirit in which it was given and parading it "daily in the sight of the Boston Public."[8] Flanked by one or another of her daughters, she visited South Berwick several times from 1895 on at the Jewetts' request, lecturing at local Women's Clubs and afterwards delightedly touring the village shops with Sarah, yielding as easily as her guide to the temptations of pins and flower-bordered handkerchiefs. She always accepted these invitations happily but had trouble remembering what she had lectured on the year before and would appeal to her hostesses' memories: Would they like "Women in the Greek Drama" or "Patriotism in Literature"? Or

perhaps "A Century Since Emerson's Birth"? Activist and interna-
tionalist to the last, she took up the causes of persecuted Armenians, Russians, and Greeks, and 4,000 Armenians honored her at
a Boston rally in 1904.

In 1904–05 Henry James hove into view, homesick at last for
America. He came to dinner or tea at Charles Street several times
during his flittings through Boston, and Sarah took her aching head
to hear him lecture at Harvard and enjoyed almost all of it, despite
feeling afterwards as if she had been through the wars. Confined
to Maine during one of his visits, she missed a dinner party at
Annie's during which James, in a curious lapse that must have
reminded Sarah of their day at Hastings, slipped Sarah's presentation copy of deWolfe Howe's *Boston: The Place and the People* into
his pocket and afterwards took it home to England. In an apologetic letter, he explained that Sarah herself had lent it to him and
that it must have "tumbled recklessly into my luggage."⁹ Sarah, of
course, could not possibly have lent it to him and was amused that
when he came to Berwick some weeks after the party (the book
still in his possession) he "never dared to confess."

His afternoon at Berwick was one of the few bright spots in
that otherwise dismal and pain-plagued summer. He was staying
with Howells, who now spent his summers at Kittery, and a trolley
line newly installed between the towns made an afternoon call very
easy. Sarah wanted Howells to come as well, but knowing that
company brought on headache he delicately refused, saying it was
"wisest and best to let you have James quite to yourself."¹⁰ Neither
Jewett nor James left any record of their conversation, though it
is safe to assume it included an earnest defense of *The Tory Lover*
on her side and some gracious capitulation on his. At any rate, she
had one of her "beautiful times" with her new-old friend, who like
Howells was struck by the simplicity and dignity of the old house
and by how perfectly and almost inevitably it expressed the inner
form of its occupant, as if she herself had imagined it into being.

As her health improved, Sarah continued to help other writers.
In 1907 she tried to place a series of essays by the British writer
Violet Paget (Vernon Lee) but could not find an editor willing to
take them. A protégée of Thérèse Blanc, Paget lived near Florence
and had met Sarah and Annie during one of their trips abroad.
Annie had also encountered her in 1904. Sarah had admired her

work since the late 1880s, but was particularly moved to help her now because of shared grief over the death of Thérèse.

Her friendship with another younger writer, although it lasted only a year, had a permanent impact not only on the writer but on American literature. Willa Cather met Sarah Orne Jewett and Annie Fields in the spring of 1908 while she was in Boston on a research assignment for *McClure's*. At thirty-six Cather was still painfully uncertain of herself as a writer. She had published one volume each of verses and short stories but had spent all her working life as a teacher and journalist. For the past two years she had been an investigative reporter, researcher, ghostwriter, office manager, and general dogsbody for Samuel McClure, who drove her as mercilessly as he drove himself and all his people. Exhausted, Cather wanted to break away and write full time but doubted she had enough talent to justify the financial risk.

In some ways her dilemma matched that of her friend Louise Imogen Guiney, whom Jewett had tried to help several years earlier. For Guiney Jewett's help had been too little and too late; she was already burned out as a poet. Cather must have known of Jewett's efforts for her friend, and she also knew of Jewett's interest in her own work. In 1905 a *McClure's* colleague had sent Jewett a copy of Cather's book of stories, *The Troll Garden.* In a letter that Cather must have seen, Jewett commented that she was disappointed by their pessimistic strain; ever the moralist, she wished that so promising a writer had chosen to show "the hopeful, *constructive* yes—even the pleasant side of unpleasant things and disappointed lives!" But she praised the writing, especially singling out "The Sculptor's Funeral," which she had read "again—and again." She thought she and Cather "should have much to say if we could talk together."[11]

Apparently they did. Cather's initial call at Charles Street was quickly followed by others, and later by a summer visit to Manchester and one to South Berwick in the fall. She was strongly drawn to both older women, and Sharon O'Brien has characterized their relationship with her as maternal in contrasting and complementary ways, each answering to a separate aspect of the daughter in Cather.[12] Annie was the medium by which the young westerner could place herself within the context of a revered, and mostly male, literary tradition. The fact that Annie, as a woman, had the power to give access to that tradition gave Cather, as spiritual daughter, the power to belong to it. But beyond that, Annie had created at Charles Street a place where one did not so much hear about the past as experience it. Her house was not a place where the past lay quiescent, to be picked up, admired, and put down again; rather it was a place where the past "lay in wait for one at all the corners," and where its embodiment at age seventy-two was still a beautiful and vibrant woman. It was "a sanctuary from the noisy push of the present,"[13] but there was nothing forced or fearful about its exclusiveness. The present belonged to Annie too— though brushed and combed and with its fingernails well cleaned.

But O'Brien points out that Cather was also a little afraid of Annie's sterner aspect, the side that she once remarked could "do police duty."[14] She seems to have reined herself in in Annie's presence, and she once confessed to her friend Elizabeth Sargent that she took no pleasure in writing letters to Annie, never knowing when she would commit some unforeseen blunder.

Jewett, on the other hand, was all gentleness and encouragement. Cather describes her as Jewett often described her own mother and grandmother, as "a lady, in the old high sense,"[15] and her letters to Jewett were addressed Dear Lady and signed simply and confidingly with her first name, as the young Jewett used to sign her letters to Theophilus Parsons. Like Annie Fields, Jewett also represented access to tradition, but her tradition was primarily rural, American, and female. Although Jewett herself identified strongly with England as well as Maine, Cather saw her as most people did, as a native plant, belonging to the place where she had grown up as Cather herself never had. The serene old house in Berwick, with its wide center hallway leading straight from formal front walk to shaded rear garden, and with sunlight spilling over its polished floors, was a place to which Cather returned several times after Jewett died, so intimately did its peacefulness belong to the woman whose life it had helped to shape. Jewett's literary environment too was native, not only because her art was drawn from her own people and landscape but because the spiritual affinities expressed in her work and the self-created, affirmative stance of her characters were natural flowerings of the climate of Emerson and Margaret Fuller. And finally Jewett belonged to a succession of women writers, mostly New Englanders, that went back through Harriet Beecher Stowe and Rose Terry Cooke to colonial poet Anne Bradstreet—who, according to some accounts, was yet another of Jewett's illustrious ancestors. Through Jewett's sponsorship Cather was able to authenticate herself and claim her own traditions, so that she could write from who she was rather than who she thought she ought to be.

In her partnership with Annie, Jewett offered authentication of another sort. Always drawn to women emotionally and sexually, Cather when she met Jewett was about to make a decision to live with her friend and *McClure's* colleague Edith Lewis. It is not clear whether she had ever encountered a "Boston marriage" before she met Jewett and Fields; given how common they were among "notable women" it seems unlikely she had not. But possibly she had never seen one that so perfectly enhanced the lives and careers of both friends. The public attitude toward lesbian relationships, or toward those that appeared to be lesbian, was beginning to harden at the turn of the century, and a partnership that had been accepted as perfectly innocent and appropriate in Jewett's youth might now be questioned and censured. Conscious of her sexuality as Jewett never had been, unwilling to suppress it and half-defiant, half-guilty about its orientation, Cather found in the Charles Street household a model of living that was obviously fulfilling while remaining above the possibility of scandal.

After their first meeting Jewett and Cather corresponded often, and though some letters have been lost, enough remain to show how frankly Cather confided in Jewett and how Jewett's advice influenced both her decision to write full time and the direction her work later took. The December *McClure's* contained Cather's story "On the Gull's Road," about which she was characteristically apologetic, fearing it was too sentimental. On the contrary, Jewett wrote,

> You have drawn your two figures of the wife and her hus-
> band with unerring touches and wonderful tenderness for
> her. It makes me the more sure that you are far on your
> road toward a fine and long story of very high class.

She added the often-quoted advice to avoid writing from a man's point of view, echoing suggestions Fields or Howells had sent Jewett herself years earlier: "You could almost have done [the male character] as yourself—a woman could love her in that same protecting way—a woman could even care enough to wish to take her away from such a life, by some means or other."[16] But this was not advice that Cather as a writer, working in a later era and far more expressive sexually than Jewett, could afford to follow in her work. It did lend direct support to the choice she made in her life. And indirectly it encouraged her to create the strong woman character, the woman protecting, rescuing, acting rather than acted upon.

A fortnight later, apparently without waiting for Cather to reply, Jewett wrote again, a long letter full of suggestions that Cather later cited as crucial to her development. It began with Jewett's most immediate concern, the dissipation of Cather's creativity. It was not just the nature of the job that concerned her; it was the nature of the employer. Jewett knew Sam McClure well enough to understand the peculiar danger he posed to Cather's talent. Charming, manipulative, and utterly at the mercy of his own demons, McClure was capable of permanently destroying Cather's fragile self-confidence and diverting all her energy to his own ends. Jewett could not say this directly, since Cather regarded McClure as a friend, but she approached it in a characteristically tactful way:

> I do think that it is impossible for you to work so hard and
> yet have your gifts mature as they should—when one's
> first working power has spent itself nothing ever brings it
> back just the same, and I do wish in my heart that the
> force of this very year could have gone into three or four
> stories.[17]

She went on to offer specific literary advice, but always implicitly based on the rest and silence that could only come from leaving *McClure's*: "You must find a quiet place near the best companions (not those who admire and wonder at everything one does, but those who know the good things with delight!)." She asked Cather to draw on her own native material:

I want you to be surer of your backgrounds,—you have
your Nebraska life,—a child's Virginia, and now an intimate knowledge of what we are pleased to call the "Bohemia" of newspaper and magazine-office life. These are
uncommon equipment, but you don't see them yet quite
enough from the outside,—you stand right in the middle
of each of them when you write, without having the standpoint of the looker-on who takes them each in their relations to letters, to the world. . . . You must find your own
quiet centre of life, and write from that to the world that
holds offices, and all society, all Bohemia; the city, the country—in short, you must write to the human heart. . . . And
to write and work on this level, we must live on it—we
must at least recognize it and defer to it at every step.

Finally she returned to the crucial need for independence:

To work in silence and with all one's heart, that is the
writer's lot; he is the only artist who must be a solitary,
and yet needs the widest outlook upon the world. . . . You
need to have time to yourself and time to read and add to
your recognitions.[18]

The letter provoked a long, anguished reply from Cather that
cannot be quoted here because of restrictions on the publication of
her letters. She wrote of her exhaustion and despondency, of feeling
like a trapeze artist forced to leap from bar to bar and never sure
when she will miss. She didn't think she had grown as a writer
since *The Troll Garden,* and she wondered if McClure was right
when he said all she was good for was the job he gave her to do.
The fact that she didn't see how self-serving this pronouncement
was shows how deeply the job and the destructive magnetism of
the man had undermined her faith in herself.

Whatever reassurance Jewett sent in return has been lost, but
eventually her advice had its effect. Over two years later, in 1911,
Cather finally mustered courage enough to leave *McClure's.* By then
Jewett had died, and Cather's friend Elizabeth Sargent thought that
the sight of Jewett's letter, published that year in the volume edited
by Annie Fields, finally moved her to act. The advice to find her

own center and believe in her own material found its first full expression in *O Pioneers!* (1913), dedicated to Sarah Orne Jewett. Here Cather wrote about the people and landscape she knew best and, dropping the Jamesian persona she had assumed in earlier works, told her story in a voice as simple and direct as Jewett's in *The Country of the Pointed Firs.* In the character of Alexandra Bergson, "a tall, strong girl [who] walked rapidly and resolutely, as if she knew exactly where she was going and what she was going to do next,"[19] and in Alexandra's close bond with her father, her farming skill, and her dislike of housekeeping and all pent-up women's work, we can detect traces of Nan Prince, Katy Hilton, Polly Finch, and even Jewett's more domesticated young farmers, going back to Doris Owen of *A Marsh Island.* And in fact Cather had discussed the characters and story with Jewett in 1908, for they had been working in her mind that early.

In two other respects Cather carried on Jewett's legacy. One was her profound conservatism, a distrust of all things mechanistic and commercial that deepened as she grew older into a passionate dislike of her own time. Jewett's Emersonian faith in universal order and her personal connection to eighteenth-century colonial ideals were not available to Cather, whose spiritual discomfort finally led her (as Jewett had been led, but much earlier and for different reasons) into the Episcopal church and possibly into Catholicism. The character of the avaricious, exploitive man (it is always a man) that had begun harmlessly in "A White Heron" and sharpened in "A Neighbor's Landmark" becomes in novels like *A Lost Lady* a powerful and malicious antagonist. Cather's pastoralism is more defiant than Jewett's, less based on a mystical identification with nature than on hatred of urban capitalism.

The second expression of the legacy was a public tribute. In 1925, when Cather had won a Pulitzer Prize for *One of Ours* and Jewett was out of favor with a war-weary and tough-minded public, Cather edited a new selection of Jewett's works for Houghton Mifflin. In a preface that has become a classic of Jewett criticism, Cather acknowledged her debt to the older writer and tried, more successfully than most, to analyze her enduring appeal. Although she ranked Jewett with Hawthorne and Mark Twain, in some ways she underestimated her friend, missing the themes of transcendentalism and historical and social cohesion and seeing the stories essentially as superior local-color chronicles of "fisher-folk and seaside villages; with juniper pastures and lonely farms, neat gray country houses and delightful, well-seasoned old men and women." She incorporated three of the Dunnet Landing sequels into *The Country of the Pointed Firs,* throwing the novel's delicate pacing and thematic unity out of balance.

But her discussion of Jewett as a stylist is written from the standpoint of a friend who understood how inseparable the art of this particular writer was from the personality of the woman. She heard the sound of Jewett's voice in the stories as if Jewett herself were reading them:

> [A great story] must leave in the mind of the sensitive
> reader an intangible residuum of pleasure; a cadence, a qual-
> ity of voice that is exclusively the writer's own, individual,
> unique.

She remarks on Jewett's impeccable ear for the language of her own corner of America, language that cannot be taught or learned but is "made in the hard school of experience. . . . Such an idiom makes the finest language any writer can have; and we can never get it with a notebook. . . . It is a gift from heart to heart." Her description of Jewett's relation to her characters applies equally to Jewett's relations with living people: "spirited, gay, tactful, noble in its essence and a little arch in its expression." And she understood, having experienced it herself, that the sympathetic imagination that was expressed in Jewett's gift for friendship was not measurably different from that expressed in her art. The best writer, Cather says, "fades away into the land and people of his heart, he dies of love only to be born again."

It was as a friend as well as a perceptive critic that Cather understood how deeply personal was Jewett's art, the best of it springing from experience so perfectly integrated into life that she was unaware of creating it herself and could exclaim to Annie, *"Who does it?* For I grow more and more sure that I don't!" This seamless merging of the artist and the art gave the work an inevitability that Cather likened to a sleek yacht under full sail, or to "living things caught in the open, with light and freedom and air-spaces around them."[20]

By January 1909 Sarah felt well enough to accept an invitation to read aloud at Simmons College. It was an untypical engagement, for she had always refused to give public readings, saying she had neither the voice nor the aptitude. But perhaps she reversed herself out of frustration at not being able to write, and out of goodwill toward a women's college. Afterwards she lingered and talked to some of the students from Maine.

Two months later, on March 9, she suffered a stroke at Charles Street. Paralyzed on one side but lucid and cheerful, she lay there for several weeks under the care of two nurses, while Annie, afraid of overexciting her, hovered outside her door and paid only fleeting visits. Willa Cather came up from New York the day after Sarah was stricken, stayed with Annie an hour, and left. Mary came down from Berwick to stay and Theodore, now a physician at Massachusetts General Hospital, was in and out daily. On April 21 Sarah was moved by special railroad car and ambulance to South Berwick, where she was put in the big front guest room where Annie usually slept. Drifting in and out of sleep, she was able to tease her night nurse, a young Maine girl barely out of school, and would send her out on drives with John Lyon* and afterwards ask her for a list of the wildflowers she had seen. She wrote short notes to Annie, the distorted handwriting and strange misspellings clearly indicative of her illness but the playful voice still clearly her own. Annie was not fooled, and on the bottom of one—in which Sarah wrote hopefully of coming to stay at the Parker House in Boston, which had an elevator—she later wrote, "My courage and hope ended with this note."[21] A few weeks later, on June 23, Sarah died.

As she intended, she left the lilacs green and all the chairs in their places. Annie lived six more years, surrounded by friends who closed ranks and made sure she was rarely alone. Mary lived until 1930, invalided by rheumatism but still the *grande dame* of South Berwick, dispensing pound cake to neighborhood children and watching the square from her window like Mrs. Graham of *A Country Doctor* or Miss Jaffrey of "A Village Shop." She left the house to Theodore, who barely survived her, and he in turn left it to the Society for the Preservation of New England Antiquities.

* John Tucker's replacement; Tucker had died in 1902.

They still maintain it in somewhat diminished but recognizable splendor, along with Hamilton House and the home of "the Barr'll Girls" in York. The town is much changed, its elms and front gardens demolished; but the river still flows beside it, drowsy and full of secrets.

Notes

There are small numbers of Sarah Orne Jewett's letters in libraries and archives across the country, but the major collections are at Houghton Library, Harvard University; The Society for the Preservation of New England Antiquities; and Colby College. The letters to Anna Dawes are at the Library of Congress; those to Lillian Munger are at the University of Virginia.

The estimated dates on undated letters and diaries are usually my own and often disagree with those of Annie Fields, whose memory for dates was erratic. Exceptions are the undated SPNEA letters, most of which were reliably dated by Mary Rice Jewett.

For convenience's sake the following abbreviations have been used in the Notes:

AF: Annie Fields
BPL: Boston Public Library
CJE: Caroline Jewett Eastman
Colby: Colby College
ConnHist: Connecticut Historical Society
EsIns: Peabody Essex Museum
Fields: *Letters of Sarah Orne Jewett* (ed. Annie Fields)
Hayes: Rutherford B. Hayes Presidential Center

HL: Houghton Library, Harvard University
LCong: Library of Congress
MHS: Massachusetts Historical Society
MRJ: Mary Rice Jewett
Schlesinger: Schlesinger Library, Radcliffe College
SOJ: Sarah Orne Jewett
SPNEA: Society for the Preservation of New England Antiquities

USC: University of Southern   UNH: University of New
    California   Hampshire
UVa: University of Virginia

Full citations of libraries mentioned above, and of others whose names
are self-explanatory in the Notes, will be found in the Acknowledgments.

PROLOGUE

1. SOJ to AF, Wednesday night (1891), HL. In the published letters
Annie Fields included this passage with others dated December 4, 1889
(Fields, p. 50), but a reference in a January 1891 letter from Louisa Dresel
confirms the later date. (Louisa Loring Dresel to SOJ, Feb. 5, 1891, UVa)
This is just one of many instances where Fields misdated a letter from
memory.

2. Alfred Kazin, *A Writer's Tradition: Landscapes in Literature* (New York:
Knopf, 1988), pp. 134–38.

CHAPTER 1. BEGINNINGS

1. Abbott, *History of Maine,* p. 164
2. SOJ, "The Old Town of Berwick," p. 589
3. SOJ, "Looking Back," p. 4
4. SOJ, "Looking Back," p. 6
5. "River Driftwood," *Country By-Ways,* p. 19
6. Ms. diary (anon.), 1782, HL
7. Dudley, p. 12
8. Dudley, p. 17
9. SOJ to AF, Thursday night (1882), HL
10. SOJ, "Recollections of Dr. William Perry of Exeter," typescript, HL

CHAPTER 2. EARLY YEARS

1. SOJ, "Dr. Theodore Herman Jewett," typescript, HL
2. William Dean Howells to SOJ, Sept. 15, 1903, HL
3. "Lady Ferry," *Old Friends,* p. 188
4. "From a Mournful Villager," *Country By-Ways,* p. 135
5. "From a Mournful Villager," *Country By-Ways,* pp. 137–38
6. "From a Mournful Villager," *Country By-Ways,* p. 138
7. "Looking Back," p. 6
8. "Looking Back," p. 6; *Country Doctor,* p. 85
9. SOJ to Emma Claflin Ellis, Oct. 2 (1888), Hayes. There are several
variations on this in the letters and writings.

CHAPTER 3. FATHER AND MOTHER

1. SOJ, "Dr. Theodore Herman Jewett," typescript, HL
2. Cyrus Hamlin to SOJ, Sept. 23, 1878, HL
3. SOJ, "Dr. Theodore Herman Jewett," typescript, HL
4. Dr. J. E. Tyler to Dr. John Lord, Sept. 1866, as quoted in SOJ, diary (1871–1879), HL
5. *Country Doctor,* p. 112
6. SOJ, "Dr. Theodore Herman Jewett," typescript, HL
7. MRJ to CJE, July 18 (1889), HL
8. SOJ to MRJ, Thursday morning, SPNEA
9. Sherman, *Sarah Orne Jewett,* p. 53

CHAPTER 4. GIRLHOOD

1. "From a Mournful Villager," *Country By-Ways,* p. 133
2. *The Independent,* Feb. 19, 1874, pp. 13–14
3. SOJ to MRJ, Tuesday morning, SPNEA
4. Perry, p. 59
5. SOJ to MRJ (1899), SPNEA
6. SOJ to AF (Sunday), HL
7. SOJ to AF (Friday afternoon), HL
8. Perry, pp. 24–26, 37

CHAPTER 5. "NEITHER MARRYING NOR GIVING IN MARRIAGE"

1. SOJ to Mrs. Henry (Ida) Higginson, June 22, 1877, Colby
2. In *Disorderly Conduct: Visions of Gender in Victorian America.* (New York: Oxford, 1985), pp. 53–76. First published in *Signs: Journal of Women in Culture and Society,* vol. I, no. 1 (1975).
3. Diary 1869, Sept. 15, 1869, HL. Subsequent quotations are from this diary until otherwise indicated.
4. Diary 1867–68, Sept. 29, 1867, HL
5. Diary 1867–68, HL
6. Extract book 1866–67, Aug. 19, 1866, HL
7. Extract book 1866–67, HL
8. Diary 1869, Jan. 25, 1869, HL
9. Diary 1867–68, Sept. 29, 1867, HL. Subsequent quotations are from this diary until otherwise indicated.
10. Diary 1869, HL. Subsequent quotations are from this diary until otherwise indicated.
11. *Country Doctor,* p. 137
12. Diary 1869, HL
13. Smith-Rosenberg, "The Female World," pp. 58–59

14. See Donovan, "The Unpublished Love Poems of Sarah Orne Jewett," in Nagel, pp. 107–117.

15. Beam, p. 89

Chapter 6. Finding Her Way

1. "The Editors" to SOJ, Aug. 1, 1868, HL
2. William Dean Howells to SOJ, Feb. 6, 1871, HL
3. William Dean Howells to SOJ, Mar. 11, 1871, Colby
4. William Dean Howells to SOJ, May 21, 1875, HL
5. Horace Elisha Scudder to SOJ, July 24, 1870, HL
6. SOJ to Horace Elisha Scudder, July 13, 1873, Colby
7. Diary 1869, Aug. 18, 1869, HL
8. Diary 1871–79, Sept. 3, 1873, HL
9. SOJ to Henry Mills Alden, Feb. 19, 1880, Colby
10. SOJ to Horace Elisha Scudder, July 13, 1873, Colby
11. SOJ to Horace Elisha Scudder, July 13, 1873, Colby
12. SOJ to Theophilus Parsons, Oct. 25, 1874, Colby
13. SOJ to Lillian Munger, Aug. 9, 1880, UVa

Chapter 7. "Be Good Sweet Maid"

1. SOJ to Anna Dawes, July 26, 1876, LCong
2. SOJ to Anna Dawes, Oct. 8, 1876, LCong
3. SOJ to Anna Dawes, July 25, 1877, LCong
4. SOJ to Anna Dawes, Sept. 10, 1877, LCong
5. Diary 1871–79, June 17, 1872, HL
6. Diary, 1871–79, Sept. 3, 1873, and Aug. 14, 1874, HL
7. Diary 1871–79, June 17, 1872, HL
8. Diary 1871–79, May 24, 1871, HL
9. Diary 1871–79 (Jan. 1872), HL
10. Kate de C. Birckhead to SOJ, Apr. 17, 1870, HL
11. Diary 1871–79 (May 1873), HL
12. SOJ to Theophilus Parsons, Apr. 26, 1874, Colby
13. SOJ to Theophilus Parsons, Aug. 24, 1876, Colby
14. Theophilus Parsons to SOJ, Sept. 18, 1873, HL
15. SOJ to Anna Dawes, May 10, 1877, LCong
16. SOJ to AF (1885), HL
17. Theophilus Parsons to SOJ, Sept. 18, 1873, HL
18. SOJ to Lillian Munger, Oct. 31, 1878, UVa
19. Louis A. Renza, *"A White Heron" and the Question of Minor Literature* (Madison: University of Wisconsin Press, 1984). This does not exclude Renza's suggestion that Jewett's role of minor writer may have been a conscious or unconscious strategem to avoid being judged in terms of the traditional male literary canon.
20. SOJ to Theophilus Parsons, June 4, 18—, Colby
21. SOJ to Theophilus Parsons, Nov. 14, 1872, Colby

22. SOJ to Theophilus Parsons, Oct. 25, 1876, Colby
23. SOJ to Theophilus Parsons, Sept. 27, 1874, Colby
24. SOJ to AF (1884), Fields, pp. 21–22

CHAPTER 8. *DEEPHAVEN*

1. SOJ to Horace Elisha Scudder, July 1, 1873, Colby
2. William Dean Howells to SOJ, Nov. 11, 1876, HL
3. SOJ to AF, 1892, Fields, p. 90
4. SOJ to Theophilus Parsons, Apr. 24, 1877, Colby
5. SOJ to AF, Jan. 29, 1889, HL
6. SOJ to AF (1891?), HL
7. Donovan, "Sarah Orne Jewett's Critical Theory," in Nagel, p. 216
8. SOJ to Miss Elizabeth Porter Gould, Dec. 31, 1902, BPL
9. Donovan, "Unpublished Love Poems," in Nagel, p. 115
10. SOJ to Anna Dawes, July 7, 1878, LCong
11. SOJ to Anna Dawes, Oct. 8, 1876, LCong
12. SOJ to Theophilus Parsons, Jan. 7, 1877, Colby
13. SOJ to Charles Gilman, May 14, 1878, Bowdoin
14. SOJ to Louisa Loring Dresel, Mar. 4, 1891, Colby
15. Dudley, p. 24
16. SOJ to Anna Dawes, May 29, 1876, LCong
17. Parsons, *Outlines of the Religion and Philosophy of Swedenborg,* p. 91
18. Ammons, "Jewett's Witches," in Nagel, pp. 165–84
19. Among the discussions are Sherman's essay "Victorians and the Matriarchal Mythology" and her book *Sarah Orne Jewett: A New England Persephone,* both on the mother-daughter theme in Jewett's work; Donovan, "A Woman's Vision," on spiritually transfiguring forms of friendship; Johns, "'Mateless and Appealing,'" on spinsterhood and community; and Ammons, "Jewett's Witches," on female bonding and the passing of a spiritual legacy between generations.
20. SOJ to Theophilus Parsons, Aug. 24, 1876, Colby
21. Vella; Smith in Nagel, p. 69; Folsom in Nagel, pp. 76–89

CHAPTER 9. BEYOND THE VILLAGE

1. SOJ to Lucretia Fisk Perry, Jan. 28, 1872, Colby
2. SOJ to Jackie, Nov. 12, 1873, Dartmouth
3. SOJ to William Dean Howells, Oct. 17, 1871, HL
4. SOJ to Sara Norton, Apr. 13, 1875, HL
5. Albright, p. 322
6. SOJ to Charles Eliot Norton, Christmas, HL
7. SOJ to Harriet Waters Preston, fragmentary draft (1877), HL
8. SOJ to Emma Claflin Ellis, Feb. 6, 1878, Hayes
9. John Greenleaf Whittier to SOJ, July 24, 1877, HL
10. "We have known [Sarah Orne Jewett] for several years because her native land is the neighborhood of Portsmouth, New Hampshire. . . ." AF

to unidentified friends, Feb. 20, 1882, Annie Fields papers, Schlesinger. A presentation copy of James Fields's *Verses* is inscribed "For my Berwick neighbour up the river," signed at Portsmouth in 1879.

11. SOJ to Anna Dawes, Oct. 8, 1876, LCong
12. Ellen Mason to SOJ, Mar. 2 (1880), HL

CHAPTER 10. KEEPING HER BALANCE

1. SOJ to Anna Dawes, Oct. 21, 1877, LCong
2. SOJ to Anna Dawes, July 25, 1876, LCong
3. SOJ to Harriet Waters Preston, May 23, 1877, HL
4. SOJ to Miss Baker, June 20, 1878, UVa
5. SOJ to Theophilus Parsons, Sept. 9, 1874, Colby
6. SOJ to Anna Dawes, Sept. 10, 1877, LCong
7. SOJ to Anna Dawes, May 14, 1878, LCong
8. SOJ to Anna Dawes, Sept. 10, 1877, LCong
9. Diary 1871–79, Feb. 24, 1879, HL
10. Diary 1871–79, n.d. and Feb. 24, 1879, HL
11. Diary 1871–79 (1879?), HL
12. SOJ to Lillian Munger, Aug. 9, 1880, UVa
13. SOJ to AF, Nov. 23, 1880, Pierpont Morgan Library

CHAPTER 11. ANNIE

1. Henry James, "Mr. and Mrs. James T. Fields"; Willa Cather, *Not Under Forty,* pp. 52–75; Harriet Prescott Spofford, *A Little Book of Friends,* pp. 1–20
2. CJE to MRJ, Friday night, SPNEA
3. Cather, *Not Under Forty,* p. 67
4. Cather, *Not Under Forty,* p. 57
5. James, "Fields," p. 29
6. Gollin, p. 30
7. Judith Roman, *Annie Adams Fields,* p. 41
8. AF, diary (Sept. 26, 1872), MHS
9. AF, diary (Sept. 17, 1876) MHS
10. Gollin, p. 34
11. AF, diary (May 1872), MHS
12. Celia Thaxter to AF, Oct. 23, 1881, BPL

CHAPTER 12. EUROPE

1. SOJ to AF, Feb. 16 (1882), HL
2. SOJ to AF (Mar. 1882), HL
3. Fields, p. 21
4. SOJ to MRJ, June 3 (1882), HL
5. SOJ to MRJ (Mar. 4, 1882), SPNEA
6. SOJ to MRJ, June 8 (1882), HL

7. SOJ to MRJ, June 3 (1882) and June 8 (1882), HL
8. SOJ to MRJ, June 8 (1882), HL
9. SOJ to Caroline Perry Jewett, June 12 (1882), HL
10. SOJ to MRJ, June 15 (1882), HL
11. SOJ to MRJ, June 15 (1882), HL
12. SOJ to MRJ (June 18, 1882), HL
13. SOJ to MRJ, June 16, 1882, HL
14. SOJ to MRJ, July 2, 1882, HL
15. SOJ to MRJ, July 20, 1882, HL
16. SOJ to MRJ, Sept. 29 (1882), HL

CHAPTER 13. SARAH AND ANNIE

1. James, "Fields," p. 24
2. James, "Fields," p. 30
3. SOJ to MRJ, Wednesday 6 o'clock, SPNEA
4. SOJ to MRJ (June 27, 1897), SPNEA
5. SOJ to AF (March 1882), HL
6. AF to John Greenleaf Whittier, June 20, 1887, EsIns
7. Judith Roman, "A Closer Look," in Nagel, p. 127
8. SOJ to John Greenleaf Whittier, April 28 (1883), EsIns
9. SOJ to John Greenleaf Whittier, May 5 (1882), EsIns
10. SOJ to John Greenleaf Whittier (summer 1883), EsIns
11. SOJ to AF, Monday morning, HL
12. SOJ to AF, Wednesday night, HL; words supplied where ms. torn
13. SOJ to AF, Monday night (1884), HL
14. SOJ to MRJ, Wednesday (1899?), SPNEA. Scudder's *James Russell Lowell: A Biography* was published in 1901.
15. Celia Thaxter to AF, Sept. 18, 1882, BPL
16. AF to John Greenleaf Whittier, Jan. 22, 1883, EsIns
17. SOJ to AF, Tuesday (spring 1882), HL
18. SOJ to AF, Sept. 16, 1891, HL
19. SOJ to MRJ (Dec. 8, 1893?), SPNEA
20. SOJ to MRJ, Mar. 14, 1882, SPNEA

CHAPTER 14. "THE LAW OF HER NATURE"

1. SOJ to Rose Terry Cooke, September (1884), ConnHist
2. *Normans,* p. 256
3. SOJ to John Greenleaf Whittier, Aug. 7, 1884, EsIns
4. SOJ to AF, Thursday 5 o'clock (1884), HL
5. For useful discussions of the three novels see Masteller, "The Women Doctors," in Nagel, pp. 135–47; and Michael Sartisky, Afterword to Phelps, *Doctor Zay,* pp. 259–321.
6. SOJ to AF, Monday afternoon, HL
7. For an earlier discussion of the theme of the religious "calling" as it appears in *A Country Doctor,* see Snow, "'That One Talent.'

8. Fuller, *Woman,* p. 38

9. Fuller, *Woman,* p. 43

CHAPTER 15. CALM SEAS AND A FOLLOWING WIND

1. SOJ to John Greenleaf Whittier, Apr. 4 (1882), EsIns

2. John Greenleaf Whittier to AF, Dec. 1, 1884, Pickard, p. 491

3. *The King of Folly Island,* p. 79

4. SOJ to AF, Monday night, HL

5. SOJ to John Greenleaf Whittier, Sept. 21 (1889), HL

6. SOJ to Sarah Wyman Whitman, June 12 (1892), HL

7. SOJ to Mrs. (Lucia) Alexander, Dec. 4, 1892, HL

8. "What a great man he is! That holds the truth of the matter if anything does." SOJ to AF, Thursday night (1884), Fields, p. 22

9. Nagel and Nagel, pp. 8–11

10. Nagel and Nagel, p. 12

11. SOJ to Samuel J. McClure, Aug. 10 (1885), UVa

12. SOJ to AF, Saturday (1888), HL

13. SOJ to AF, Friday morning (1888), HL

14. SOJ to John Greenleaf Whittier, Mar. 4 (1887), HL

15. AF to Anna Loring Dresel, June 18, 1888, Schlesinger

16. SOJ to Rev. Sylvanus Hayward, Nov. 4, 1899, Colby

CHAPTER 16. "BERWICK DUST"

1. SOJ to AF, n.d., HL

2. SOJ to AF, Monday morning (1889?), HL

3. Nagel, "'This prim corner'"

4. SOJ to AF, n.d., Fields, p. 68

5. See especially "A Winter Drive," in *Country By-Ways,* pp. 163–85.

6. SOJ to AF, n.d., Fields, p. 33

7. SOJ to AF, Monday morning (summer 1891), HL

8. SOJ to Louisa Loring Dresel, Nov. 10, 1890, Colby

9. SOJ to AF, n.d. (October), Fields, p. 37

10. SOJ to AF, Saturday morning (July 6, 1895), SPNEA

11. CJE to MRJ (July 6, 1895), SPNEA

12. MRJ to SOJ, Friday (1889), HL

13. MRJ to SOJ, Mar. 5, 1898, HL

14. CJE to MRJ and SOJ, Tuesday (Sept. 26, 1893), SPNEA

15. CJE to MRJ and SOJ, Tuesday (Sept. 26, 1893), SPNEA

16. SOJ to AF, n.d., HL

17. SOJ to AF, Wednesday (1883), HL

18. In a 1979 essay, Mary C. Kraus discussed Jewett's conception of time as a "moving point in eternity," approaching the subject from a philosophical and theological base and drawing examples from "River Driftwood" and other Berwick essays. Although my chapter was written independently, the general thrust of the following pages is close to Kraus's argument that

Jewett's view of time was essentially cosmic, and that she saw any given moment of the present as containing both chronological time and eternity. The difference between us, I think, is that I believe Jewett's sense of time was more personal than cerebral, being based mostly on a powerful empathic identification with nature and other people, especially with her own ancestors. Kraus, "Sarah Orne Jewett and Temporal Continuity."

CHAPTER 17. FRIENDS

1. SOJ to (Sara Norton), Sept. 3 (1897), Fields, p. 126
2. SOJ to Mary Claflin Ellis, Jan. 31, 1882, Hayes
3. Thomas Bailey Aldrich to SOJ (1882), HL
4. AF, diary, Jan. 4?, 1905, MHS
5. AF to SOJ, Friday, HL
6. SOJ to Louisa Loring Dresel, Aug. 12, 1890, Colby
7. William James, *Selected Letters,* p. 225
8. SOJ to Sarah Wyman Whitman (1888?), HL
9. SOJ to Sarah Wyman Whitman, Tuesday morning (Sept. 28, 1897), HL
10. SOJ to Sarah Wyman Whitman, Nov. 3, 1895, HL
11. SOJ to AF, Sunday afternoon, HL
12. SOJ to AF, n.d., Fields, p. 11
13. I am indebted to the editors and contributors of the exhibition catalog *"A Noble and Dignified Stream": The Piscataqua Region in the Colonial Revival, 1860–1890* (Old York Historical Society, 1992) for information and insights concerning Sarah Orne Jewett's relationship to the colonial revival and the aesthetic movement.
14. SOJ to Francis Rives Lassiter, May 27, 1887, Duke
15. (Lodge), *Week,* pp. 133–36
16. SOJ to MRJ (Apr. 18, 1895), SPNEA

CHAPTER 18. "A SOUND TAP-ROOT"

1. SOJ to Willa Cather, Dec. 13 (1908), Fields, p. 250
2. SOJ to Thomas Bailey Aldrich, n.d., Fields, p. 79
3. SOJ to Mary E. Mulholland, Jan. 23, 1899, Colby
4. SOJ to Charles Miner Thompson, Oct. 12, 1904, Fields, pp. 195–96
5. SOJ to Hamlin Garland, Oct. 24, 1888, UCal
6. Brooks, *New England: Indian Summer,* pp. 347–48
7. I have in mind primarily the works by Ammons, Sherman, and Donovan listed in my bibliography, but the number of essays on aspects of female bonding and female community in Jewett's work is extensive and continues to increase yearly.
8. Examples include Renza, *"A White Heron"*; Pool, "The Child in Sarah Orne Jewett"; Pratt, "Women and Nature"; Ammons, "The Shape of Violence"; Held, "Heart to Heart"; Hovet, "America's 'Lonely Country Child'"; and Smith, "The Language of Transcendence."
9. Margaret Roman, *Sarah Orne Jewett,* pp. 74–75

10. My own understanding of this story was helped by Ammons's discussion of Mrs. Goodsoe as white witch in "Jewett's Witches."

11. *King,* p. 64. This phrase recalls some lines by Robert Burns, to whose poems and essays Jewett returned with renewed pleasure in the eighties: "The minister kiss'd the fiddler's wife/An' could na preach for thinkin' o't" ("My Love She's But a Lassie Yet").

12. SOJ to MRJ, Jan. 25, 1896, SPNEA

13. *A Country Doctor,* p. 100

CHAPTER 19. "THEIR SKY AND THEIR EARTH" (1890–1895)

1. SOJ to Sarah Wyman Whitman, July 30 (1892), HL

2. SOJ to Louisa Loring Dresel, Nov. 10, 1890, Colby

3. SOJ to Louisa Loring Dresel, Jan. 20 (1891), UNH

4. SOJ to Louisa Loring Dresel, Oct. 28 (1891), Colby

5. SOJ to Frances P. Parkman, Wednesday afternoon, HL

6. SOJ to Mabel Lowell Burnett, Oct. 28 (1891), HL

7. SOJ to (Sara Norton), Sept. 3 (1897), Fields, p. 125. The year can be determined by a reference to her first reading of *The Life and Letters of Benjamin Jowett,* published in 1897.

8. SOJ to Sarah Wyman Whitman, Thursday (1891), HL

9. SOJ to Mabel Lowell Burnett, Saturday morning (June 1891), HL

10. SOJ to AF, Wednesday night (1891), HL

11. MRJ to SOJ, Apr. 11 (1892), HL

12. SOJ to Sarah Chauncey Woolsey, Apr. 2, 1892, Johns Hopkins

13. SOJ to Sarah Wyman Whitman, July 8, 1892, HL

14. Bentzon (Mme Blanc),"Le Roman de la femme-médicin," pp. 598–632

15. *Magasin Pittoresque,* Sept. 30 and Oct. 15, 1885

16. Bentzon (Mme Blanc), "Le Naturalisme aux États-Unis," pp. 428–51

17. SOJ to AF, Friday noon (Oct. 1892), HL

18. SOJ to AF (1891), HL

19. SOJ to Louisa Loring Dresel, Friday morning (Oct. 7, 1892), Colby

20. SOJ to William Dean Howells, Dec. 1 (1893), HL

21. Bentzon (Mme Blanc), "Condition," p. 103

22. Bentzon (Mme Blanc), "Condition"; *Les Américaines*

23. SOJ to William Dean Howells, Dec. 1 (1893), HL

24. SOJ to MRJ, Thursday morning (1897), SPNEA

25. See David Park Curry, *Childe Hassam: An Island Garden Revisited* (The Denver Art Museum and W. W. Norton, 1990).

26. Celia Thaxter to Adaline Hepworth, Apr. 8, 1890, Celia Thaxter, *Letters,* p. 174

27. SOJ to Sarah Wyman Whitman, July 17, 1894, HL

28. MRJ to SOJ, Aug. 29, 1894, HL

29. SOJ to Sarah Wyman Whitman, Aug. 29, 1894, HL
30. "The Adirondacks." Emerson's journal description of sending one of the party up a giant pine to reach an osprey's nest, and of Lowell's wish to shoot the bird, curiously anticipates Sylvia's experience in "A White Heron," although the journal was not yet published when Jewett wrote her story. See Emerson, *Journals,* pp. 159–60.
31. SOJ to MRJ and CJE, Wednesday morning (Sept. 19?, 1894), SPNEA
32. Emerson, *Journals,* p. 161
33. SOJ to MRJ and CJE, Tuesday morning (Sept. 20?, 1894), SPNEA
34. Helen Howe, *Gentle Americans,* p. 74
35. SOJ to MRJ, Sunday night (Dec. 9, 1894), SPNEA
36. A swashbuckling tale set in England, "A Dark Night" was serialized by Bacheller, Johnson & Bacheller in spring 1895.
37. SOJ to AF, Friday (March 1895), HL
38. SOJ to MRJ (Aug. 29, 1895), SPNEA
39. SOJ to MRJ and CJE, Sunday morning (Sept. 8, 1895), SPNEA
40. SOJ to Sarah Wyman Whitman, Sept. 8, 1895, HL
41. SOJ to MRJ, Sept. 2 (1895), SPNEA
42. SOJ to MRJ and CJE, Tuesday morning, Sept. 3, 1895, SPNEA
43. SOJ to MRJ, Monday, Sept. 2 (1895), SPNEA
44. SOJ to MRJ and CJE, Sunday morning (Sept. 8, 1895), SPNEA
45. SOJ to MRJ and CJE, Sunday morning (Sept. 8, 1895), SPNEA
46. SOJ to MRJ and CJE, Tuesday morning, Sept. 3, 1895, SPNEA
47. SOJ to MRJ, Monday, Sept. 2 (1895), SPNEA
48. SOJ to MRJ, Wednesday (Sept. 11, 1895?), SPNEA

CHAPTER 20. *THE COUNTRY OF THE POINTED FIRS*

1. SOJ to MRJ, Sunday afternoon (Aug. 1896), SPNEA
2. Feminist scholars in particular have discussed *Pointed Firs* not only as Jewett's finest work but as their primary example of the theme of female bonding. Marjorie Pryse and Sarah Way Sherman both see in the friendship between the narrator and Mrs. Todd a paradigm of the quest of each woman, as daughter, to be reunited and identified with the mother. (Pryse, Introduction; Sherman, "Victorians" and *Sarah Orne Jewett*) Elizabeth Ammons sees in this and other works an illustration of Jewett's belief in a telepathic female psychic energy that bonds women together in a kind of "occult sisterhood." (Ammons, "Witches," p. 168) Josephine Donovan too discerns an overriding theme of extrasensory and intuitive female bonding, in which the herbalist-healer is "a kind of beneficent witch," and community is sustained by strong, maternal women in a kind of "matriarchal religion." (Donovan, "A Woman's Vision," p. 367)

All these interpretations, as well as that by Marcia McClintock Folsom (Folsom, "'Tact'"), recognize the primary importance of empathic imagination in Jewett's work. But as with earlier works, I believe the feminist view of

The Country of the Pointed Firs excludes too much, violating the larger theme of universal harmony and interdependence.

3. SOJ to AF, Sunday afternoon (June 1888); SOJ to Louisa Loring Dresel, June 10, 1888, HL

CHAPTER 21. AT HOME AND ABROAD

1. SOJ to —? (1897), Fields, p. 134
2. SOJ to Sarah Wyman Whitman, Tuesday morning (June 19, 1897), HL
3. Sally A. Kaign to SOJ, Feb. 10, 1896, HL
4. Sally A. Kaign to SOJ, Nov. 29, 1897, HL
5. Natalie (Rice) Clark to SOJ (Feb. 1900), HL
6. Nagel and Nagel, pp. 32–33
7. Rudyard Kipling to SOJ (January 1897), HL
8. *Daily Kennebec Journal,* Aug. 31, 1901
9. Frost, pp. 125–26
10. SOJ to Grace Norton (January 1898), HL
11. SOJ to Sarah Wyman Whitman, June 18 (1897), HL
12. Bentzon (Mme Blanc), "Dans la Nouvelle-Angleterre," p. 550. Page references for the next four paragraphs apply to this essay.
13. p. 532
14. p. 574
15. SOJ to Harriett Prescott Spofford, June 9, 1897, Colby
16. p. 573
17. p. 545
18. AF, diary, "Today in Provence" (1898), MHS
19. SOJ to —, June 10 (1898), HL
20. AF, diary, Monday, Sept. 12 (1898), MHS
21. James, "Fields," p. 30
22. SOJ to MRJ, Friday night (June 30, 1899), SPNEA
23. SOJ to MRJ (Aug. 1897), SPNEA
24. SOJ to MRJ, Thursday night (Aug. 5, 1897), SPNEA
25. SOJ to MRJ, Sunday afternoon (Feb. 19, 1899), SPNEA
26. She refers to attending an 1899 meeting as the "poor unworthy secretary," though possibly she was just filling in. SOJ to MRJ, Wednesday night (Mar. 22, 1899), SPNEA
27. The 1896 date is speculative, taken from a letter dated in another hand. What is certain is that this first attempt failed.
28. *Somersworth Free Press,* undated clipping (June 1901)

CHAPTER 22. "THE QUEEN'S TWIN" AND OTHER CITIZENS OF THE WORLD

1. SOJ to Frances Rollins Morse, Feb. 13, 1895, HL
2. See Ammons, "Jewett's Witches," pp. 178–80

Chapter 23. *The Tory Lover*

1. Diary 1867–68, Sept. 29, 1867, HL
2. Diary 1869, n.d., HL
3. Jewett's notes on the Sullivans are at Houghton Library.
4. "I . . . got my paper on 'Sarah, Countess of Rumford' off my mind. . . ." SOJ to Louisa Loring Dresel, Nov. 28 (1890), Colby
5. Notes on Count Rumford, n.d., HL
6. SOJ to MRJ, Friday morning (fall 1895), SPNEA
7. SOJ to MRJ (December 1895), SPNEA
8. SOJ to Lucy Keays Hayward, June 12, 1901, Colby
9. Henry James to SOJ, Oct. 5, 1901, HL
10. SOJ to George Woodberry, Jan. 6, 1904, HL

Chapter 24. Last Years

1. SOJ to S. Weir Mitchell, Oct. 27 (1903), HL
2. William James to Henry James, June 28, 1904, *Letters,* p. 207
3. Helen Bigelow Merriman to MRJ, Aug. 13, 1904, SPNEA
4. SOJ to AF, Monday eve. (1905), HL
5. SOJ to Sara Norton, Aug. 5 (1906), Fields, p. 218
6. Whitman, *Letters,* v–vii
7. Unidentified clipping enclosed in Helen Bigelow Merriman to MRJ, July 3, 1904, HL
8. Julia Ward Howe to SOJ, May 31, 1902, HL
9. Henry James to SOJ, as quoted in SOJ to Mark Anthony deWolfe Howe, Sunday night (1905), HL
10. William Dean Howells to SOJ, June 16, 1905, HL
11. SOJ to Witter Bynner, May 3, 1905, HL
12. O'Brien, pp. 314–32
13. Cather, *Not Under Forty,* p. 61
14. Cather, *Not Under Forty,* p. 58
15. Cather, *Not Under Forty,* p. 85
16. SOJ to Willa Cather, Nov. 27, 1908, Fields, pp. 246–47
17. SOJ to Willa Cather, Dec. 13, 1908, Fields, p. 247
18. SOJ to Willa Cather, Dec. 13, 1908, Fields, pp. 247–50
19. Cather, *O Pioneers!,* Chapter 1
20. Cather, Preface to *The Country of the Pointed Firs and Other Stories* (Boston: Houghton Mifflin, 1925)
21. SOJ to AF, Thursday (May) 20 (1909), HL

Bibliography

BOOKS BY SARAH ORNE JEWETT

Deephaven. James R. Osgood, 1877

Play Days. Houghton, Osgood, 1878

Old Friends and New. Houghton, Osgood, 1879

Country By-Ways. Houghton Mifflin, 1881

A Country Doctor. Houghton Mifflin, 1884

The Mate of the Daylight, and Friends Ashore. Houghton Mifflin, 1884

A Marsh Island. Houghton Mifflin, 1885

A White Heron and Other Stories. Houghton Mifflin, 1886

The Story of the Normans, Told Chiefly in Relation to Their Conquest of England. G. P. Putnam's Sons, 1887

The King of Folly Island and Other People. Houghton Mifflin, 1888

Tales of New England. Houghton Mifflin, 1890

Betty Leicester: A Story for Girls. Houghton Mifflin, 1890

Strangers and Wayfarers. Houghton Mifflin, 1890

A Native of Winby and Other Tales. Houghton Mifflin, 1893

Betty Leicester's English Christmas: A New Chapter of An Old Story. Privately printed for the Bryn Mawr School, 1894

The Life of Nancy. Houghton Mifflin, 1895

The Country of the Pointed Firs. Houghton Mifflin, 1896

The Queen's Twin and Other Stories, Houghton Mifflin, 1899

The Tory Lover. Houghton Mifflin, 1901

An Empty Purse: A Christmas Story. Privately printed, 1905

BIBLIOGRAPHY

Abbott, John S. *The History of Maine.* Revised by Edward H. Elwell. Augusta, Me.: Brown Thurston, 1892.

———. *The Life and Adventures of Rear-Admiral John Paul Jones, Commonly Called Paul Jones.* New York: Dodd, Mead, 1874.

Albright, Raymond W. *Focus on Infinity: A Life of Phillips Brooks.* New York: Macmillan, 1961.

Aldrich, Lilian Woodman. *Crowding Memories.* Boston: Houghton Mifflin, 1920.

Aldrich, Thomas Bailey. *An Old Town by the Sea.* Boston: Houghton Mifflin, 1893.

Ammons, Elizabeth. "Jewett's Witches." In Gwen L. Nagel, ed., *Critical Essays on Sarah Orne Jewett,* pp. 165–84. Boston: G. K. Hall, 1984.

———. "The Shape of Violence in Jewett's 'A White Heron.'" *Colby Library Quarterly* 22, no. 1 (Mar. 1986), pp. 6–16.

Ballou, Ellen. *The Building of the House: Houghton Mifflin's Formative Years.* Boston: Houghton Mifflin, 1970.

Baring-Gould, S. *Vicar of Morwenstow: A Life of Robert Stephen Hawker, M.A.* New York: Thomas Whittaker, 1883.

Beam, Lura. *A Maine Hamlet.* New York: Wilfred Funk, 1957.

Bell, Charles Henry. *History of the Town of Exeter, New Hampshire.* Boston: J. E. Farwell, 1888.

Bentzon, Th. (Mme Blanc). *Choses et gens d'Amerique.* Paris: Calmann Levy, 1898.

———. "Condition de la femme aux États-Unis." *Revue des Deux Mondes* 25 (Sept. 1, 1894), pp. 94–131.

———. "Dans la Nouvelle-Angleterre." *Revue des Deux Mondes* 150 (Dec. 1, 1898), pp. 542–82.

———. "Le Naturalisme aux États-Unis." *Revue des Deux Mondes* 83 (Sept. 15, 1887), pp. 428–51.

———. "Le Roman de la femme-médicin." *Revue des Deux Mondes* 67 (Feb. 1, 1895), pp. 598–632.

———. *Les Américaines chez elles.* Paris: Calmann Levy, 1896.

Berthoff, Warner. "The Art of Jewett's Pointed Firs." In Richard Cary, ed., *Appreciation of Sarah Orne Jewett,* pp. 144–61. Waterville, Me.: Colby College Press, 1973.

Bishop, Ferman. "The Sense of the Past in Sarah Orne Jewett." In Richard Cary, ed., *Appreciation of Sarah Orne Jewett,* pp. 135–43. Waterville, Me.: Colby College Press, 1973.

Bishop, W. H. "Fish and Men in the Maine Islands." *Harper's Magazine* 61, no. 363 (Aug. 1880), pp. 336–52.

Bowditch, Mrs. Ernest. "The Jewett Library." *Colby Library Quarterly* 5, no. 12 (Dec. 1961), pp. 357–65.

Brooks, Van Wyck. *New England: Indian Summer (1865–1915).* New York: E. P. Dutton, 1940.

Buchan, A. M. "'Our Dear Sarah': An Essay on Sarah Orne Jewett." In Richard Cary, ed., *Appreciation of Sarah Orne Jewett,* pp. 85–111. Waterville, Me.: Colby College Press, 1973.

Carson, Richard G. "Nature and the Circles of Initiation in *The Country of the Pointed Firs.*" *Colby Library Quarterly* 21, no. 3 (Sept. 1985), pp. 154–60.

Cary, Richard, ed. *Appreciation of Sarah Orne Jewett.* Waterville, Me.: Colby College Press, 1973.

———. "Jewett on Writing Short Stories." *Colby Library Quarterly* 6, no. 10 (June 1964), pp. 425–40.

———. "Jewett to Dresel: 33 Letters." *Colby Library Quarterly* 11, no. 1 (Mar. 1975), pp. 13–49.

———. "The Literary Rubrics of Sarah Orne Jewett." In Gwen L. Nagel, ed., *Critical Essays on Sarah Orne Jewett,* pp. 198–211. Boston: G. K. Hall, 1984.

———. "Miss Jewett and Madame Blanc." *Colby Library Quarterly* 7, no. 11 (Sept. 1967), pp. 467–87.

———. *Sarah Orne Jewett.* New York: Twayne, 1962.

———. "Some Bibliographical Ghosts of Sarah Orne Jewett." *Colby Library Quarterly* 8, no. 3 (Sept. 1968), pp. 139–45.

Cather, Willa. *Not Under Forty.* New York: Knopf, 1936.

———. Preface to *The Best Short Stories of Sarah Orne Jewett.* 2 vols. Boston: Houghton Mifflin, 1925.

Chapman, Edward M. "The New England of Sarah Orne Jewett." In Richard Cary, ed., *Appreciation of Sarah Orne Jewett,* pp. 52–63. Waterville, Me.: Colby College Press, 1973.

Chapman, John Jay. *Memories and Milestones.* New York: Moffart, Yard, 1915.

Crumpacker, Laurie. "The Art of the Healer: Women in the Fiction of Sarah Orne Jewett." *Colby Library Quarterly* 19, no. 3 (Sept. 1983), pp. 155–66.

Donahue, Marie. "At Home with a York Harbor Tory." *Down East,* October 1981, pp. 39–41.

———. "The Hayes/Lord Legacy." *Berwick Academy Today,* Winter 1991, pp. 14–16.

———. *The Old Academy on the Hill: A Bicentennial History, 1791–1991.* Camden, Me.: Picton Press, 1992.

———. "Sarah Orne Jewett's 'Dear Old House and Home.'" *Down East* 24, no. 1 (Aug. 1977), pp. 62–67.

Donovan, Josephine. "Nan Prince and the Golden Apples." *Colby Library Quarterly* 22, no. 1 (Mar. 1986), pp. 17–27.

———. *New England Local Color Literature; A Woman's Tradition.* New York: Continuum, 1988.

———. *Sarah Orne Jewett.* New York: Ungar, 1980.

———. "Sarah Orne Jewett's Critical Theory: Notes toward a Feminine Literary Mode." In Gwen L. Nagel, ed., *Critical Essays on Sarah Orne Jewett,* pp. 212–25. Boston: G. K. Hall, 1984.

———. "The Unpublished Love Poems of Sarah Orne Jewett." In Gwen L. Nagel, ed., *Critical Essays on Sarah Orne Jewett,* pp. 107–17. Boston: G. K. Hall, 1984.

———. "A Woman's Vision of Transcendence: A New Interpretation of the Works of Sarah Orne Jewett." *Massachusetts Review* 21, no. 2 (Summer 1980), pp. 365–80.

Dover, New Hampshire: Its History and Industries. Compiled by A. E. G. Nye. Dover, N.H.: Geo. J. Foster & Co., 1898.

Dudley, Frances Perry. *The Mid-Century in Exeter.* Exeter, N.H.: News-Letter Press, 1943.

Eakin, John Paul. "Sarah Orne Jewett and the Meaning of Country Life." In Richard Cary, ed., *Appreciation of Sarah Orne Jewett,* pp. 203–22. Waterville, Me.: Colby College Press, 1973.

Emerson, Ralph Waldo. *Journals* (1856–1863). Edited by Waldo Emerson and Waldo Emerson Forbes. Boston: Houghton Mifflin, 1913.

Faderman, Lillian. *Surpassing the Love of Men: Romantic Friendship and Love*

Between Women from the Renaissance to the Present. New York: Morrow, 1981.

Fields, Annie. *How to Help the Poor.* Boston: Houghton Mifflin, 1887.

————. *Whittier: Notes of his Life and of his Friendships.* New York: Harper, 1892.

(————). *James T. Fields: Biographical Notes and Personal Sketches.* Boston: Houghton Mifflin, 1881.

Fike, Francis. "An Interpretation of *Pointed Firs.*" In Richard Cary, ed., *Appreciation of Sarah Orne Jewett,* pp. 170–80. Waterville, Me.: Colby College Press, 1973.

Folsom, Marcia McClintock. "'Tact is a Kind of Mind-Reading': Empathic Style in Sarah Orne Jewett's *The Country of the Pointed Firs.*" In Gwen L. Nagel, ed., *Critical Essays on Sarah Orne Jewett,* pp. 76–89. Boston: G. K. Hall, 1984.

Frost, John Eldridge. *Sarah Orne Jewett.* Kittery Point, Me.: The Gundalow Club, 1960.

Fuller, Margaret. *Woman in the Nineteenth Century.* New York: Norton, 1971.

Garnett, Edward. "Miss Sarah Orne Jewett's Tales." In Richard Cary, ed., *Appreciation of Sarah Orne Jewett,* pp. 21–25. Waterville, Me.: Colby College Press, 1973.

Gaskell, Elizabeth. *Cranford.* Edited by Elizabeth Porges Watson. Oxford: Oxford University Press, 1972.

Gollin, Rita. "Annie Adams Fields." *Legacy* 4, no. 1 (Spring 1987), pp. 27–33.

Grattan, C. Hartley. "Sarah Orne Jewett." In Richard Cary, ed., *Appreciation of Sarah Orne Jewett,* pp. 81–84. Waterville, Me.: Colby College Press, 1973.

Griffin, Sarah L., and Murphy, Kevin D., eds. *"A Noble and Dignified Stream": The Piscataqua Region in the Colonial Revival, 1860–1930.* Old York Historical Society, 1992.

Griffith, Kelley, Jr. "Sylvia as Hero in Sarah Orne Jewett's 'A White Heron.'" *Colby Library Quarterly* 21, no. 1 (Mar. 1985), pp. 22–27.

Held, George. "Heart to Heart with Nature: Ways of Looking at 'A White Heron.'" In Gwen L. Nagel, ed., *Critical Essays on Sarah Orne Jewett,* pp. 58–68. Boston: G. K. Hall, 1984.

Hobbs, Glenda. "Pure and Passionate: Female Friendship in Sarah Orne

Jewett's 'Martha's Lady.'" In Gwen L. Nagel, ed., *Critical Essays on Sarah Orne Jewett,* pp. 99–107. Boston: G. K. Hall, 1984.

Hoppin, Martha J. "Women Artists in Boston, 1870–1900: The Pupils of William Morris Hunt." *American Art Journal* 13, no. 1 (Winter 1981), pp. 17–46.

Hovet, Theodore R. "America's 'Lonely Country Child': The Theme of Separation in Sarah Orne Jewett's 'A White Heron.'" *Colby Library Quarterly* 14, no. 3 (Sept. 1978), pp. 166–71.

Howe, Helen. *The Gentle Americans.* New York: Harper & Row, 1965.

Howe, M. A. deWolfe. *Memories of a Hostess: A Chronicle of Eminent Friendships, Drawn Chiefly from the Diaries of Mrs. James T. Fields.* Boston: Atlantic Monthly Press, 1922.

Howells, William Dean. *Dr. Breen's Practice.* Boston: James R. Osgood, 1881.

———. *Literary Friends and Acquaintance.* New York: Harper & Bros., 1900; Greenwood Press, 1970.

———. *The Rise of Silas Lapham.* New York: Harper & Bros., 1884.

James, Henry. "Mr. and Mrs. James T. Fields." *Atlantic Monthly* 116 (July 1915), pp. 21–31.

James, William. *Selected Letters.* Edited by Elizabeth Hardwick. Boston: David R. Godine, 1980.

Jewett, Sarah Orne. "The Centennial Celebration." *The Berwick Scholar* 4 (March 1891).

———. *Letters.* Edited by Richard Cary. Waterville, Me.: Colby College Press, 1956.

———. *Letters.* Edited by Annie Fields. Boston: Houghton Mifflin, 1911.

———. "Looking Back on Girlhood." *Youth's Companion* 65, no. 5–6 (January 7, 1892).

———. "My School Days." *The Berwick Scholar* I (October 1887).

———. "The Old Town of Berwick." *New England Magazine* (New Series) 10, no. 5 (July 1894), 585–609.

———. *The Uncollected Stories of Sarah Orne Jewett.* Edited by Richard Cary. Waterville, Me.: Colby College Press, 1971.

———. *The World of Dunnet Landing.* Edited by David Bonnell Green. Lincoln: University of Nebraska Press, 1962.

Johns, Barbara A. "'Mateless and Appealing': Growing into Spinsterhood in Sarah Orne Jewett." In Gwen L. Nagel, ed., *Critical Essays on Sarah Orne Jewett,* pp. 147–65. Boston: G. K. Hall, 1984.

Johnson, Robert Underwood. *Remembered Yesterdays.* Boston: Little, Brown, 1923.

Kelley, Mary. *Private Woman, Public Stage: Literary Domesticity in Nineteenth-Century America.* New York: Oxford University Press, 1984.

Kraus, Mary C. "Sarah Orne Jewett and Temporal Continuity." *Colby Library Quarterly* 15, no. 3 (Sept. 1979), pp. 157–74.

Laighton, Oscar. *Ninety Years at the Isles of Shoals.* Boston: Beacon Press, 1930.

Leary, Lewis. *John Greenleaf Whittier.* New York: Twayne, 1961.

(Lodge, Mary Greenwood, ed.) *A Week Away From Time.* Boston: Roberts Bros., 1887.

Longfellow, Fanny Appleton. *Mrs. Longfellow: Selected Letters and Journals of Fanny Appleton Longfellow.* Edited by Edward Wagenknecht. New York: Longmans, Green, 1956.

Lynn, Kenneth S. *William Dean Howells: An American Life.* New York: Harcourt Brace Jovanovich, 1970.

Magowen, Robin. "The Outer Island Sequence in *Pointed Firs.*" *Colby Library Quarterly* 6, no. 10 (June 1964), pp. 418–24.

———. "Pastoral and the Art of the Landscape in *The Country of the Pointed Firs.*" In Richard Cary, ed., *Appreciation of Sarah Orne Jewett,* pp. 187–95. Waterville, Me.: Colby College Press, 1973.

Martin, Theodora Penny. *The Sound of Their Own Voices: Women's Study Clubs 1860–1910.* Boston: Beacon Press, 1987.

Masteller, Jean Carwile. "The Women Doctors of Howells, Phelps, and Jewett: The Conflict of Marriage and Career." In Gwen L. Nagel, ed., *Critical Essays on Sarah Orne Jewett,* pp. 135–47. Boston: G. K. Hall, 1984.

Matthiessen, Francis Otto. *Sarah Orne Jewett.* Boston: Houghton Mifflin, 1929.

Mawer, Randall R. "Setting as Symbol in Jewett's *A Marsh Island.*" *Colby Library Quarterly* 12, no. 2 (June 1976), pp. 83–90.

May, Ralph. *Early Portsmouth History.* Boston: Goodspeed, 1926.

Mayer, Charles W. "'The Only Rose': A Central Jewett Story." *Colby Library Quarterly* 17, no. 1 (Mar. 1981), pp. 26–33.

Meyer, Joseph E. *The Herbalist.* Revised ed. Glenwood, Ill.: Meyerbooks, 1960.

Mobley, Marilyn E. "Rituals of Flight and Return: The Ironic Journeys of Sarah Orne Jewett's Female Characters." *Colby Library Quarterly* 22, no. 1 (Mar. 1986), pp. 36–42.

Morison, Samuel Eliot. *John Paul Jones: A Sailor's Biography.* Boston: Northeastern University Press, 1985.

Nagel, Gwen L., ed. *Critical Essays on Sarah Orne Jewett.* Boston: G. K. Hall, 1984.

———. "'This prim corner of land where she was queen': Sarah Orne Jewett's New England Gardens." *Colby Library Quarterly* 22, no. 1 (Mar. 1986), pp. 43–62.

Nagel, Gwen L., and James Nagel. *Sarah Orne Jewett: A Reference Guide.* Boston: G. K. Hall, 1978.

Nail, Rebecca Wall. "'Where Every Prospect Pleases': Sarah Orne Jewett, South Berwick, and the Importance of Place." In Gwen L. Nagel, ed., *Critical Essays on Sarah Orne Jewett,* pp. 185–98. Boston: G. K. Hall, 1984.

Norton, Charles Eliot. *Letters.* Edited by Sara Norton and M. A. deWolfe Howe. Vol. I. Boston: Houghton Mifflin, 1913.

O'Brien, Sharon. *Willa Cather: The Emerging Voice.* New York: Oxford University Press, 1986.

Parsons, Theophilus. *Outlines of the Religion and Philosophy of Swedenborg.* Boston: Roberts Bros., 1876.

Perry, William Gilman. "Exeter in 1830"; and Bell, Charles H. "Exeter in 1776." (Pamphlet containing two essays.) Hampton, N.H.: Peter E. Randall, 1972.

Phelps (Ward), Elizabeth Stuart. *Doctor Zay.* With Afterword by Michael Sartisky. New York: The Feminist Press, 1987. (Originally published 1882.)

Piacentino, Edward J. "Local Color and Beyond: The Artistic Dimension of Sarah Orne Jewett's 'The Foreigner.'" *Colby Library Quarterly* 21, no. 2 (June 1985), pp. 92–98.

Pickard, John B., ed. *Memorabilia of John Greenleaf Whittier.* Hartford: The Emerson Society, 1968.

Pollard, John A. *John Greenleaf Whittier: Friend of Man.* Boston: Houghton Mifflin, 1949.

Pool, Eugene Hillhouse. "The Child in Sarah Orne Jewett." In Richard Cary, ed., *Appreciation of Sarah Orne Jewett,* pp. 223–28. Waterville, Me.: Colby College Press, 1973.

Pratt, Annis. "Women and Nature in Modern Fiction." *Contemporary Literature* 13, no. 4 (Autumn 1972), pp. 476–90.

Pryse, Marjorie. Introduction to Sarah Orne Jewett, *The Country of the Pointed Firs and Other Stories,* pp. v–xix. New York: W. W. Norton, 1982.

———. "Women 'at Sea': Feminist Realism in Sarah Orne Jewett's 'The Foreigner.'" In Gwen L. Nagel, ed., *Critical Essays on Sarah Orne Jewett,* pp. 89–98. Boston: G. K. Hall, 1984.

Reid, John Phillip. *Chief Justice: The Judicial World of Charles Doe.* Cambridge: Harvard University Press, 1967.

Renza, Louis A. *"A White Heron" and the Question of Minor Literature.* Madison: University of Wisconsin Press, 1984.

Rhode, Robert D. "Sarah Orne Jewett and 'The Palpable Present Intimate.'" In Richard Cary, ed., *Appreciation of Sarah Orne Jewett,* pp. 229–37. Waterville, Me.: Colby College Press, 1973.

Ricker, Jennie de R. "South Berwick, Me.: Pages from the Past." Pamphlet. Publisher and date not given.

Roman, Judith. *Annie Adams Fields: The Spirit of Charles Street.* Bloomington: Indiana University Press, 1990.

———. "A Closer Look at the Jewett-Fields Relationship." In Gwen L. Nagel, ed., *Critical Essays on Sarah Orne Jewett,* pp. 119–34. Boston: G. K. Hall, 1984.

Roman, Margaret. *Sarah Orne Jewett: Reconstructing Gender.* Tuscaloosa: University of Alabama Press, 1992.

Romines, Ann. "In *Deephaven*: Skirmishes Near the Swamp." In Gwen L. Nagel, ed., *Critical Essays on Sarah Orne Jewett,* pp. 43–57. Boston: G. K. Hall, 1984.

Rowe, William Hutchinson. *The Maritime History of Maine: Three Centuries of Shipbuilding and Seafaring.* New York: Norton, 1948.

Rutledge, Lyman V. *The Isles of Shoals in Lore and Legend.* Barre, Mass.: Barre Publishers, 1965.

Sherman, Sarah Way. *Sarah Orne Jewett: A New England Persephone.* Hanover, N.H.: University Press of New England, 1989.

———. "Victorians and the Matriarchal Mythology: A Source for Mrs. Todd." *Colby Library Quarterly* 22, no. 1 (Mar. 1986), pp. 63–74.

Short, Clarice. "Studies in Gentleness." In Richard Cary, ed., *Appreciation of Sarah Orne Jewett,* pp. 128–34. Waterville, Me.: Colby College Press, 1973.

Smith, Gayle L. "The Language of Transcendence in Sarah Orne Jewett's 'A White Heron.'" In Gwen L. Nagel, ed., *Critical Essays on Sarah Orne Jewett,* pp. 69–76. Boston: G. K. Hall, 1984

Smith-Rosenberg, Carroll. "The Female World of Love and Ritual: Relations Between Women in Nineteenth-Century America." In Smith-Rosenberg, *Disorderly Conduct: Visions of Gender in Victorian America,* pp. 53–76. New York: Oxford University Press, 1985.

Snow, Malinda. "'That One Talent': The Vocation as Theme in Sarah Orne Jewett's *A Country Doctor.*" *Colby Library Quarterly* 16, no. 3 (Sept. 1980), pp. 138–47.

Spofford, Harriet Prescott. *A Little Book of Friends.* Boston: Little, Brown, 1916.

Stearns, Frank Preston. *Sketches from Concord and Appledore.* New York: Putnam's, 1895.

Stouck, David. "*The Country of the Pointed Firs*: A Pastoral of Innocence." In Richard Cary, ed., *Appreciation of Sarah Orne Jewett,* pp. 249–54. Waterville, Me.: Colby College Press, 1973.

Stowe, Harriet Beecher. *Oldtown Folks.* Boston: James R. Osgood, 1869.

———. *The Pearl of Orr's Island.* Boston: Ticknor & Fields, 1866.

Tharpe, Louise Hall. *Mrs. Jack: A Biography of Isabella Stewart Gardner.* Boston: Little, Brown, 1965.

Thaxter, Celia. *Among the Isles of Shoals.* Boston: James R. Osgood, 1877.

———. *Letters of Celia Thaxter, edited by her friends A.F. and R.L.* Boston: Houghton Mifflin, 1895.

Thaxter, Rosamond. *The Life and Letters of Celia Thaxter.* Francestown, N.H.: Marshall Jones, 1963

Thompson, Charles Miner. "The Art of Miss Jewett." *Atlantic Monthly* 94 (October 1904), pp. 485–97.

Thorp, Margaret Ferrand. *Sarah Orne Jewett.* Pamphlets on American Writers, no. 61. University of Minnesota Press, 1966.

Toth, Susan Allen. "The Value of Age in the Fiction of Sarah Orne Jewett." In Richard Cary, ed., *Appreciation of Sarah Orne Jewett,* pp. 255–63. Waterville, Me.: Colby College Press, 1973.

Tryon, Warren W. *Parnassus Corner: A Life of James T. Fields, Publisher to the Victorians.* Boston: Houghton Mifflin, 1963.

Tutwiler, Julia R. "Two New England Writers—In Relation to Their Art and to Each Other." In Richard Cary, ed., *Appreciation of Sarah*

Orne Jewett, pp. 26–31. Waterville, Me.: Colby College Press,
1973.

Vella, Michael W. "Sarah Orne Jewett: A Reading of *The Country of the
Pointed Firs.*" *Emerson Society Quarterly* 19 (1973), pp. 275–82.

Voelker, Paul C. "*The Country of the Pointed Firs*: A Novel by Sarah Orne
Jewett." In Richard Cary, ed., *Appreciation of Sarah Orne Jewett*
pp. 138–48. Waterville, Me.: Colby College Press, 1973.

Waggoner, Hyatt H. "The *Unity* of *The Country of the Pointed Firs.*" In
Richard Cary, ed., *Appreciation of Sarah Orne Jewett,* pp. 162–69.
Waterville, Me.: Colby College Press, 1973.

Weber, Carl J. "New England Through French Eyes Fifty Years Ago."
New England Quarterly 20, no. 3 (Sept. 1947), pp. 385–95.

Weber, Clara Carter, and Carl J. Weber. *A Bibliography of the Published
Writings of Sarah Orne Jewett.* Waterville, Me.: Colby College Press,
1949.

Westbrook, Perry D. *Acres of Flint: Sarah Orne Jewett and Her Contemporaries.*
Metuchen, N.J.: Scarecrow Press, 1981.

———. *The New England Town in Fact and Fiction.* East Brunswick, N.J.:
Associated University Presses, 1982.

Whitman, Sarah Wyman. *Letters.* Cambridge, Mass.: Riverside Press,
1907.

Whitney, Adeline Dutton Train. *A Summer in Leslie Goldthwaite's Life.*
Boston: Ticknor & Fields, 1867.

Whittier, John Greenleaf. *Letters.* Edited by John B. Pickard. Vol. 3.
Cambridge, Mass.: Belknap Press, 1975.

Wilson, Forrest. *Crusader in Crinolines: The Life of Harriet Beecher Stowe.*
Philadelphia: Lippincott, 1941.

Wood, Ann Douglas. "The Literature of Impoverishment: The Women
Local Colorists in America 1865–1914." *Women's Studies* 1, no. 1
(1972), pp. 3–46.

Woodress, James. *Willa Cather; A Literary Life.* Lincoln: University of
Nebraska Press, 1987.

Zagarell, Sandra A. "Narrative of Community: The Identification of a
Genre." *Signs* 13, no. 31 (Spring 1988), pp. 498–527.

Index

ABOUT THE AUTHOR

Paula Blanchard is the author of two highly acclaimed biographies: *Margaret Fuller: From Transcendentalism to Revolution* and *The Life of Emily Carr,* which was a selection of the Canadian Book of the Month Club and won the University of British Columbia's Award for Canadian Biography. She lives in Lexington, Massachusetts, and has spent much of her life near the coastal New England world of the "pointed firs."